So What?

THE Writer's Argument, with Readings

Second Edition

Kurt Schick

Laura Schubert

both of
James Madison University

New York Oxford
Oxford University Press

Oxford University Press is a department of the University of Oxford.
It furthers the University's objective of excellence in research, scholarship, and education by publishing worldwide. Oxford is a registered trade mark of Oxford University Press in the UK and certain other countries.

Published in the United States of America by Oxford University Press
198 Madison Avenue, New York, NY 10016, United States of America.

For titles covered by Section 112 of the US Higher Education Opportunity Act, please visit www.oup.com/us/he for the latest information about pricing and alternate formats.

Library of Congress Cataloging-in-Publication Data

Names: Schick, Kurt, 1964- author. | Schubert, Laura, author.
Title: So what? with readings : the writer's argument / Kurt Schick, Laura Schubert both of James Madison University.
Description: New York : Oxford University Press, [2017] | Includes index.
Identifiers: LCCN 2016016810 | ISBN 9780190209131
Subjects: LCSH: English language--Rhetoric--Study and teaching. | Report writing--Study and teaching (Higher)
Classification: LCC PE1404 .S3373 2017 | DDC 808/.0071/1--dc23 LC record available at https://lccn.loc.gov/2016016810

9 8 7 6 5 4 3 2

Printed by LSC Communications, United States of America

contents

preface

ACADEMIC WRITING confounds many college students—not because they lack sophistication, but because of the natural expertise that they already possess. Decades of real-world language use have taught them that authentic writing involves a genuine audience, purpose, and context—all of which school writing seems to lack.

So What? The Writer's Argument approaches college reading, writing, and argument as scholarly activities and treats students as apprentice scholars. *So What?* gives writing a real audience, purpose, and context by teaching apprentice scholars authentic styles, organizing structures, and persuasive moves that they can use in writing classes and beyond. This book introduces students to many of the thought processes, motivations, and strategies that scholars use to answer questions, to solve problems, and to defend their ideas.

To the Instructor

Professors, employers, and politicians agree that college students should learn to write well, but not everyone agrees how or why. Should writing classes prepare students to write in their majors? Should we teach writing skills for the workplace, or for citizenship? Should we focus on the processes of writing or critical thinking, or on various types and technologies of writing? Which approach will have the greatest impact?

Learning how to write arguments accomplishes many of these outcomes at once. By blending communication with problem solving, argumentation prepares students to use language and thinking so they can participate effectively in their academic, civic, and professional communities. As writing scholar David Fleming explains, arguing teaches a process of "reasoning with others."

Still, teaching argument doesn't magically solve a challenge that writing teachers and students inevitably face: motivation. What kinds of authentic arguments can students make while in school? How can they discover something interesting to argue about when academic writing often seems like regurgitating the words and thoughts of others? Too often, students cannot imagine significant reasons for writing other than for a grade and some blurry sense of audience and purpose. Left without reasons to care about their writing, students (and their readers) are often left wondering, *so what?* Students and faculty need an approach that teaches argument as useful and meaningful.

The Scholarly Apprentice Model

Our solution is not to separate academic writing from the "real" world but to teach it as an authentic activity. We invite students to participate in scholarly argument, to apprentice alongside their scholarly mentors (professors) who use writing to understand the world and engage others. Our apprentice model elevates students by treating them as colleagues. Redefining students as scholarly apprentices invites them to become active citizens of the scholarly community from which they often feel disconnected or even alienated.

This book seeks to open students' eyes to the notion of the academy—a place where scholars debate, create, and communicate knowledge. *So What?* treats students as apprentices with less experience and knowledge but with equal potential to contribute to the vibrant conversations that characterize higher education. Given the opportunity to create knowledge—for themselves and sometimes for others—students are more likely to make what they're doing matter.

The apprentice-scholar framework in *So What?* gives students a meaningful way to view academic writing, one that they can use to understand the technical moves of argumentation. Rather than defining argument only as persuasion, designed primarily to change people's minds, we teach students how to use argumentation to create knowledge, promote understanding, and bridge differences—the way experienced scholars do. Scholarly argument seeks to enlighten, to open new areas of discussion, and to advance society, not primarily to convert or persuade.

In addition to motivating students and legitimizing their work as apprentices, by training them to think like scholars, *So What?* teaches students habits of mind that will benefit them personally and professionally. While we champion the vision of the classical liberal arts, we also recognize students' and society's desire for practical education that prepares graduates to transition quickly and smoothly into the workforce and civic life. Rather than focusing on specific genres or technical knowledge, we believe the most transferable skills that students can learn through argument are scholarly habits of mind that writing teachers can model and teach.

Transferability

Recent studies indicate that introductory writing classes may not bring as many long-term benefits as we once imagined. Students do not automatically "transfer" what they learn into their major studies ("near" transfer), and they don't always apply the skills and understanding to new contexts outside of school ("far" transfer).

To improve transfer, we must imagine learning outcomes that can be woven through the curriculum—skills, habits, and knowledge that will be relevant in many different situations. Recently, organizations of writing teachers and professors (the Council of Writing Program Administrators, the National Council of Teachers of English, and the National Writing Project) developed an inventory of "intellectual and practical" habits of mind that "will support students' success in a variety of fields and disciplines" (http://wpacouncil.org/framework). *So What?* reinforces these habits through each chapter:

- **Engagement**—"a sense of investment and involvement in learning." We introduce scholarly argument as a means of engagement and the writing process as an investment worth students' time and effort. We present argument as a tool to discover, communicate, and revise what we know, think, and believe.
- **Curiosity**—"the desire to know more about the world." We encourage students to follow an inquiry-based writing process, inspired by questions, careful reading, and analysis. Apprentice scholars learn how to discover compelling questions and problems and situate their arguments within scholarly conversations.
- **Creativity**—"the ability to use novel approaches for generating, investigating, and representing ideas." Our chapter on creating a compelling thesis explains that behind every relevant, significant, and original thesis is a compelling, challenging, and controversial question or problem awaiting a creative response. Descriptions of stylistic choices throughout the book encourage students to approach writing creatively.
- **Openness**—"the willingness to consider new ways of being and thinking in the world." Our chapter on supporting arguments helps students effectively choose and evaluate evidence and other sources. Arguing in conversation with sources helps students understand the value of enlarging their perspectives.
- **Metacognition**—"the ability to reflect on one's own thinking as well as on the individual and cultural processes used to structure knowledge." A chapter on organization and development shows students how to structure arguments to meet their audience's needs, and another chapter on finding faults provides practice in scrutinizing reasoning. Many of the exercises throughout the book stimulate students' metacognitive thinking skills.
- **Persistence**—"the ability to sustain interest in and attention to short- and long-term projects." Several of the chapters encourage students to investigate issues exhaustively and to defer conclusions until weighing all evidence and assumptions. Practicing scholarly

argument as case building helps students see knowledge building as an iterative process.
- **Responsibility**—"the ability to take ownership of one's actions and understand the consequences of those actions for oneself and others." A chapter on using sources models how to design arguments by responsibly borrowing and building on the words and thoughts of others. Responsibility can also be developed by collaborating with others, as writers often do in a classroom that focuses on argument.
- **Flexibility**—"the ability to adapt to situations, expectations, or demands." The introductory chapters on rhetoric and scholarly processes—along with our attention to style throughout the book—maintain students' focus on the craft of writing, developing a tool kit of options that can be adapted for various audiences, purposes, genres, and contexts.

Contents

We have arranged the book's contents in the order that makes most sense to us and to our reviewers. However, writing and research processes are neither neat nor linear, so you may find it useful to assign chapters in whatever sequence works best for your class. *So What?* begins by explaining how a scholarly apprenticeship can build skills, knowledge, and habits that students can use throughout college and in their personal and professional lives. Chapters 2 and 3 focus on college-level literacy, guiding students toward a more sophisticated, adaptive process of reading, writing, and using sources. Chapters 4 and 5 teach students how arguments work and how to analyze them effectively. From Chapter 6 onward, we explain how to create and develop arguments for various purposes and audiences, explaining how to support, organize, and troubleshoot arguments. The final chapter—along with exercises throughout the book—focuses on developing a more flexible, deliberate writing style. Appendices provide techniques for peer review and collaboration, along with common layouts for various argument genres.

Our approach to argumentation continues the classical and modern rhetorical tradition, owing heavily to Aristotle, Cicero, and Stephen Toulmin. Although we do introduce some fundamentals of rhetoric (stasis questions, appeals, fallacies, genre, and style), we do not overwhelm students with unnecessary technical jargon or theory. We also do not attempt to introduce every scholarly style or genre, or even specific disciplinary research techniques; rather, we attempt to teach students how to learn these things for themselves by providing them with heuristics and tools that help them think like writers and scholars.

We have attempted to write in a style that would be straightforward and engaging. In doing so, we risk oversimplifying complex theories and practices of argument that scholars have been developing and debating for the past 2,000 years. As a selection and interpretation of that tradition, the book is itself a kind of argument. We anticipate that both students and instructors will find points of clarification and points of disagreement with our work. Indeed, we hope that readers will use the book to generate discussion, debate, and inspiration for further investigation.

Features

- CHAPTER CHECKLISTS present the key topics included in each chapter.
- CONSIDER THIS activities embedded in each chapter provide opportunities for students to reflect on the book's content and style and on their own writing. These exercises maintain a focus on the craft of writing throughout the book.
- TRY THIS exercises allow students to practice or investigate what they learn immediately via short exercises that can be used in class or as homework.

- WHAT'S NEXT features conclude each chapter with activities and assignments that help students transfer and apply what they've learned into other classes and beyond school.

In addition:

- APPENDICES at the end of the book provide quick guides for peer review and collaboration, and for organizing arguments. Students can refer to these guides to complement their writing and reading process.

Readings

In addition to providing a selection of interesting material for students to read, this edition is designed to facilitate discussions about writing. Five themed sections on compelling and timely topics demonstrate how writers engage with subjects in thought-provoking and diverse ways. Readings include a variety of genres, such as scholarly articles, student essays, magazine articles, opinion pieces, interviews, narratives, and blogs. We have also included an annotated reading (Friedersdorf) and a sample rhetorical analysis with peer review commentary (Appendix C). These readings can model different argument techniques and stylistic moves that students can identify, discuss, analyze, and emulate. Questions for analysis and suggestions for writing assignments help students learn, apply, and practice concepts and techniques described in the book.

To the Student

Many new college students either think that they already know how to write well (because teachers told them so and they believed it) or they cannot write well (because teachers told them so and they believed it). Both perspectives contradict the idea that writers can always improve their craft. Probably the most important factor for learning to write, or do most anything else, is to embrace a "growth mindset"—a belief that practice pays off. After all, none of us were born knowing how to speak or walk or drive a car, either. **Thinking that your writing ability is "fixed" or biologically predetermined nearly guarantees that you won't improve.**

Most students who saw themselves as "good writers" before college eventually discover that whatever formulas they mastered previously cannot guarantee their success in college or beyond. For example, knowing how to write research reports or five-paragraph themes with correct grammar and citations will not necessarily enable you to perform the following tasks:

- For your environmental science class: Write a public policy recommendation on hydraulic fracturing ("fracking") for natural gas based on current laws, economic factors, and scientific research.
- For your boss: Write a memo justifying why your team cannot complete a project on time in accordance with your client's contract.
- For your local planning commission: Write a letter requesting a zoning exception so you can build an addition to your house that violates existing code.

Each of these tasks would require you to adapt your message for a different audience, purpose, topic, and type of writing. The good news is that you can learn to be a more adaptable writer by studying and practicing the kind of arguments that scholars use to discover, improve, and communicate ideas.

Similarly, learning more about argument can help if you've struggled with writing in the past. The most important challenges of writing in college or in the workplace are not grammar and punctuation (although those are also important for many readers). Good writing is not just pretty words and sentences but carefully crafted ideas. **The**

most difficult part of producing good writing is finding something significant and compelling to write about.

So What? will teach you how to invent and present significant, compelling arguments. The core lessons will teach you how to discover controversies or public problems to argue about, plus patterns of organizing and supporting arguments that address those controversies. Mastering these techniques will help you find something substantial to write about in almost any situation.

Creating arguments to solve problems that matter to others is a powerful and valued skill in college and in the workplace. Why not seize the opportunity to learn these essential habits of mind now? Your professors, through years of study and practice, have mastered the arts of argument in the subjects they teach. Take advantage of your apprenticeship with these master scholars. As you learn their craft, you can build the kind of expertise that makes college worth your investment.

acknowledgments

THE AUTHORS WISH TO THANK many colleagues for their excellent contributions, including Emiline Buhler, Kathy Clarke, Jared Featherstone, Kevin Jefferson, Lucy Malenke, Karen McDonnell, Paige Normand, Justin Thurston, and Jim Zimmerman. Thanks to Garon Scott and the team at Oxford University Press for their support in publishing this second edition—and to Maya Chandler for creating original drawings to illustrate our ideas. We are indebted to Frederick Speers, development editor for the first edition, who first imagined this book and who provided wisdom and generous guidance to see it through.

We appreciate the help of many outside reviewers in strengthening the first edition manuscript, including Clark Draney, College of Southern Idaho; Christopher Ervin, Western Kentucky University; Jeff Pruchnic, Wayne State University; Brooke Champagne, University of Alabama; Greg Hagan, Madisonville Community College; Danielle Zawodny Wetzel, Carnegie-Mellon University; Megan Swihart Jewell, Case Western Reserve University; Cheryl Edelson, Chaminade University; Dave Badtke, Solano Community College; Andrew Higl, Winona State University; George Cusack, University of Oklahoma; Gina Weaver, Southern Nazarene University; Susie Crowson, Del Mar College; Anthony Cavaluzzi, SUNY Adirondack; Joe Musser, Ohio Wesleyan University; Tisha Turk, University of Minnesota-Morris; Brian Walter, St. Louis College of Pharmacy; Michael Morgan, Bemidji State University; Jessica Gravely, Prairie State College; Eileen Abrahams, Schenectady County Community College; Eleanor Welsh, Chesapeake College; Andrew Scott, Ball State University; and Stephanie Mood, Grossmont College. Thank you as well to those reviewers who helped with reviews for the second edition: Rebecca

Addy, University of Nebraska at Kearney; Jill Anderson, Tennessee State University; Diann Baecker, Virginia State University; Joshua Borgmann, Southwestern Community College; Kristi Costello, Arkansas State University; Vanessa Cozza, Washington State University; Joshua Dickinson, Jefferson Community College; Michael Donnelly, Ball State University; Marjorie Ellenwood, La Sierra University; Tyler Fleming, University of Louisville; Amanda Freeman, James Madison University; Mary Beth Kwenda, Black Hills State University; Jennifer Marlow, The College of Saint Rose; Bonnie Markowski, University of Scranton; Mark Meritt, University of San Francisco; Christine Murray, Texas A&M University–College Station; Jun Okada, SUNY Geneseo; Kelly Rivers, Pellissippi State Technical Community College; Leslie Roberts, Oakland Community College; Keaghan Turner, Coastal Carolina University; Paul Walker, Murray State University; Gina Weaver Yount, Southern Nazarene University; Eloise Whisenhunt, Young Harris College; Julia Whyde, Casper College; Gregory Winston, Husson University; and Susan Wright, William Paterson University.

We received invaluable feedback from many students in our first-year writing classes, especially Nathan Boone, Taylor Coats, Danielle Camiso, Erin Dooley, Kaitlyn Keyser, Jordan Lewis, Nick Love, Liz Mott, Will Mullery, Laura Nettuno, Trygve Rorvig, Jessie Seymour, Olivia Smithey, Tyler Young, Cameron Yudkin, and also outstanding suggestions from tutors in our University Writing Center.

We are also indebted to our past teachers and mentors who instructed and inspired us, particularly Jim Corder, Becky Howard, Bob Jacobs, Robert Keys, Joseph Petraglia, Gary Tate, Robert Carballo, Patricia King, Jay B. Landis, Janet Martin, Gretchen McTavish, Kenneth Morefield, Virginia Schlabach, and Beverly Schneller.

Finally, we want to thank our families for their encouragement, patience, and wisdom. We are especially grateful for their support and care—and for cheering us on.

CHAPTER **one**

What's the Purpose of Scholarly Writing

chapter checklist

- What does scholarly writing achieve?
- How can we use writing to improve our lives?
- What distinguishes scholarly writing?
- How can rhetoric deepen our understanding of communication?

For many students, academic writing seems awkward or pointless. Even if you've been a successful writer in school, you've probably encountered some assignments that ask you to do things that don't make much sense. What's the point, for example, of endlessly practicing five-paragraph essays? Why, you might wonder, must I use MLA citation format for my bibliography? Why does my teacher demand six sources (only two of which can be from the Internet)? And *so what* if I use Wikipedia?

We wrote this book to reveal the motivations behind academic writing and to help you understand how creating arguments, in particular, can teach you things that will be useful to you in college, in work, and in life. Writing can be empowering: it gives us a voice and an opportunity to say something meaningful and significant. When we write about something, we stretch our minds and we learn more deeply. When faced with a writing task, we have the potential to change the world in some small way—even if it's just to inspire or pester or provoke one reader—and to change our own minds about something. Writing and arguing are *active*, and they can even be fun.

So, What's the Point of Scholarly Writing?

You may not realize this, but you're already an expert communicator. You were using language before you could walk. And despite criticisms that "people don't read or write enough these days," we actually do so more than our ancestors ever did. With Google, Facebook, Wikipedia, Twitter, and text messaging at our fingertips, many of us consume and produce writing constantly, with sophistication that we're still trying to understand. So, although we might not read books the way our grandparents did, we may very well be the best information foragers and social networkers who ever walked this planet.

Our natural expertise may also be the reason why academic writing seems so baffling at times. Decades of real-world language use have taught us that authentic communication involves a genuine audience, purpose, and context—all of which academic writing seems to lack. What's the point, for example, of writing a paper about the deeper meanings of Shakespeare for your English teacher, who likely knows and cares more about literature than his students probably do? Or, why should a teacher really care about students' opinions on, say, legalizing marijuana? In either case, the reader or writer may be left wondering: *so what?*

A Scholar's Work—in College and Beyond

The *so what?* question can only be answered if you understand how and why scholarly writing works as a genuine form of communication, with real audiences and purposes. To begin, you should know that higher education has two interrelated functions:

- To *communicate* knowledge
- To *create* knowledge

Professors not only teach; many are also professional scholars who, in various ways, work to investigate humanity's endless supply of unanswered questions and unsolved problems. In fact, human progress depends on posing and answering such questions, from the most broad and consequential ("How might humans live together peacefully?") to the specific and seemingly obscure ("How does climate change affect the migration patterns of ruby-throated hummingbirds?"). Scholars, such as professors and other researchers, are experts at advancing what we know by investigating such questions. What's potentially exciting about college is that you might have an opportunity to learn from professors who literally "wrote the book" on the subjects you're studying.

College will provide you with an opportunity to *apprentice* as a scholar. Just as an artist, mechanic, or teacher might practice under the mentorship of an expert, you will learn how master scholars discover and communicate knowledge. As an apprentice, you can begin making sense of how and why scholars use writing and argument to expand the bounds of human understanding.

Why Bother?

By now, you might be wondering how you might reasonably be expected to "expand the bounds of human understanding." After all, aren't you mostly in college to learn what others have been discovering for the last few thousand years—or simply to get a good job? Who ever said that you wanted to become a professional scholar, anyway? How will all this make you a better citizen, professional, or worker?

Our answer: **You'll use the skills, knowledge, and habits that you learn as an apprentice scholar throughout college and in your personal and professional life.** As an undergraduate student, you won't really be expected to cure cancer, end world hunger, or design an income tax system that actually makes sense but rather to *practice* some of the skills that are necessary to do such things.

TRY THIS ➤ Set Some Goals for Yourself

TRY THIS exercises will give you an opportunity to practice or investigate chapter content.

For this exercise, seek outside expertise to help you set some goals for developing as a writer. Chances are good that you have friends or relatives who are established in the workplace (or maybe you have extensive work experience yourself). Whether or not they attended college, working professionals know something about what characteristics contribute to a successful career. They might even be in a position to hire new employees. Call or e-mail a few of them and ask the following questions:

- What skills would you look for when screening applicants?
- What do you think are the most important things for me to learn in college?
- What's the role of writing and continued learning in your work?

Scholarly Habits of Mind

Whether or not you plan to become a professional scholar, developing the skills and habits that scholars use can help you succeed in college and beyond. For example, you'll be more likely to notice what others overlook, to solve problems creatively, and to make decisions independently. People who are well educated, either by schooling or by years of life experience, exhibit habits of mind that others can learn.

select reliable sources, dig for better data, and recognize weak or deceptive arguments—all of which will make you a better reader and writer.

We've already been building up to the first lesson about rhetoric: To be an effective communicator, you should always **pay careful attention not just to the contents of your message but also to your intended audience and purpose.** These elements—audience, purpose, and message—are the main components of what we call the *rhetorical situation.* Rather than seeing writing simply as lifeless words and ideas on a page (or on a computer or mobile screen), scholars think of reading and writing as social activities—a conversation that involves real people and human motivations.

Analyzing Rhetorical Elements

Understanding rhetorical elements will help you become a more deliberate, adaptable communicator. Think of rhetoric as a flexible tool for problem solving: **These rhetorical principles will help you figure out how to proceed when you don't already know what to do in a communication situation.** They will help you read and write more effectively by helping you orient yourself in situations that you've never encountered before—and they will reveal things you probably never noticed about already familiar situations.

Begin by thinking of communication as an interconnected framework involving an author (writer or speaker), an audience (reader or listener), and a message (written text, speech, or image)—all interacting for some purpose within a specific social context or setting.

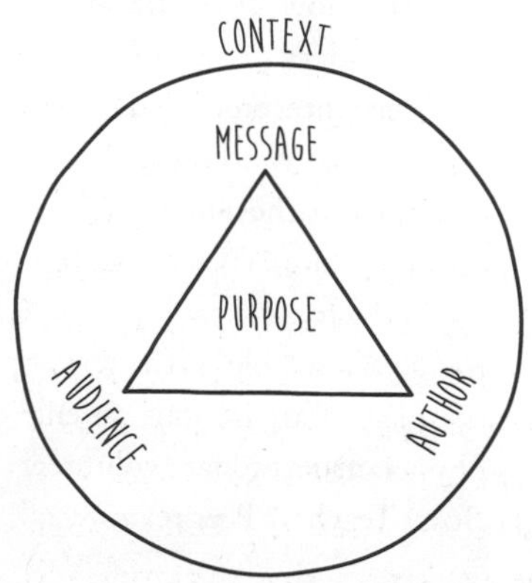

This rhetorical triangle helps us understand that meaning is not simply the contents or subject matter of a message. Authors and audiences *create* meaning by writing and reading messages, and they do so within contexts that shape that meaning.

An easy way to remember these rhetorical elements is to ask yourself the investigative questions that reporters and detectives use: *who?*, *what?*, *when?*, *where?*, *why?*, and *how?* Whenever you read or write, ask yourself questions related to these primary categories. To emphasize our attention to the *so what?* question, we begin with *why*.

Why? (*So What?*)

- *Inspiration* of the writer: What is the author's motivation? What question, problem, or other inspiration prompted him to write?
- *Purpose* of the message: How is the message supposed to affect the audience? What function does the message serve?
- *Implications* for the reader: Why is this a significant topic for the audience? What are the larger consequences and applications?

Who? (*Author, Audience*)

- *Author*: How does the author establish his credibility? What might readers already know about the author that could influence how they interpret the message?
- *Audience(s)*: Who is the intended audience? Are there other readers? What is the audience's background (age, gender, income, education, values)? What assumptions or biases might readers have about the topic?
- *Roles*: What "role" is the writer playing? For example, is he playing the part of an anxious parent? Frustrated customer? Concerned physician? Passionate volunteer? What's the audience's role? Jury? Boss? Teacher? Peer reviewer?

When and Where? (*Context*)

- *Timing*: When was the message published? Is there something about the timing that might be significant to an audience?
- *Publication*: Where was the message published? For example, did it appear in a scholarly journal, a popular magazine, or on the Internet? What does the publication venue suggest about the text's audience, purpose, and credibility?
- *Place*: In what setting and culture was the message published?

What and How? (*Message*)

- *Thesis*: Does the message contain an explicit or implied thesis, or main point?
- *Supports*: How much (and what kind of) background information does the author present? What kinds of evidence or examples does the message use?
- *Genre*: Does the message follow a recognizable genre, such as a business proposal, newspaper editorial, or research article?
- *Style*: What kind of tone do you notice? Is it serious, funny, sarcastic, scholarly, arrogant, immature, or what? Which words stick out? What hints do they give you about the author's purpose and audience?
- *Design*: What design elements are used? Does the design seem informal, playful, ordinary, formal, technical, or what? How does the message use charts, images, or other visual elements?

If you read only for content—as students often do with assigned readings—you may overlook the bigger picture and deeper meaning of what you read. You will miss the opportunity to develop more quickly as a reader, writer, and scholar if you don't slow down to examine communication as a complex social interaction.

Let's consider an example to illustrate our point: the rhetorical situation of this book. We, the coauthors, are experienced college writing teachers. We also tutor writers from all over campus, so we've helped thousands of students with all kinds of writing in many different subjects. Knowing that about us can help you understand where we're coming from and maybe even trust us more than, say, your friends or relatives, to give good advice about college writing. Wherever you, our intended audience, are right now, we are thinking about you as we write, trying to explain ideas in ways that will make sense, seem interesting, and be most useful to you.

You should also try to imagine our motivations and context. Why did we choose to write this book? On the one hand, writing is part of our occupation. To be successful in a college like ours, professors must publish. For us, though, writing this book is more than just a job. We're especially interested in the *problems* that this book attempts to solve:

- What are the most important things that students should know about writing in college and in life?
- How can we present those topics in fresh and interesting ways?
- How can we translate our expertise in writing and rhetoric into something that's useful for students who may not like to write and probably have never formally studied rhetoric?

Knowing our motivations for writing this book can help you comprehend and even evaluate our message, including our stylistic choices. If, for instance, our purposes were different—such as to provide a comprehensive description of Western rhetorical theory or to explain the advanced intricacies of argumentation—this book would read very differently. We would likely have used a more formal style and included more technical details. A change in purpose has a ripple effect on content, style, organization, and so forth.

Our point is that if any of the rhetorical variables in a situation change (such as the audience or context), so does the meaning. Failing to consider the rhetorical situation—whenever you read, whatever you're reading—means that you're missing parts of the message, and you may even misunderstand the message completely.

Scholarly Writing as a Rhetorical Activity

Examining scholarly writing through a rhetorical lens can reveal how it is similar to and different from other kinds of communication.

- **Scholarly writing has real *purposes* based in problems that interest the participants.** In Chapter 5, we discuss common categories of problems, for example: "How should we interpret X?" "What caused Y?" "What should we do about Z?" Each of these questions prompts a different kind of scholarly investigation and a distinct kind of writing designed to answer the question.
- **Scholarly writing addresses specific *audiences*.** Unlike some school writing that seems to be intended for no particular reader, scholarly arguments always address a specific group of people, often defined as a specialized academic *discipline*—for example, chemical engineers or US Civil War historians.
- **Scholarly writing belongs to larger conversations, histories, and *contexts* that determine the rules for what counts as good communication.** Lawyers use established courtroom procedures, rules of evidence, and precedents to build a case. Similarly, to establish new knowledge in a discipline, scholars must know what methods of reasoning are typical, what kinds of evidence are acceptable, and what other scholars have already said about the subject.

Along with the similarities between scholarly and everyday arguments, there are also some important distinctions to keep in mind:

- **Scholarly writing addresses sophisticated, *demanding audiences*.** Scholars will expect that you examine your subject from different angles, that you anticipate other perspectives or counterarguments, that you validate your evidence, and so on.
- **Scholarly writing pursues *knowledge, not victory*.** Unlike advertising or political campaigns, scholars use writing to communicate

and create knowledge, rather than merely to persuade their audience. Because winning isn't the ultimate goal, *how* we communicate is just as important as *what* we communicate about. In fact, in college you will often be judged more on how you develop and defend your ideas than on the ideas themselves. For instance, in a literature class, your professor will evaluate your interpretation of a poem based on the evidence you provide to support your thinking, rather than whether you arrived at a single "right" answer. Remember, your goal in college is to apprentice as a knowledge-maker. The "product" of this learning is not so much *what* you make as learning *how to make.*

Understanding these characteristics can help you make sense of why scholars make specific stylistic moves and rhetorical choices. For instance, the point of following MLA citation practices or addressing readers' counterarguments makes more sense when you remember that scholars typically write for specific, demanding audiences. The technical details of scholarly writing become much more meaningful within this framework.

So What?

Scholars read and write to answer three basic questions:

1. How do we know what we know?
2. Why do we believe what we believe?
3. How can we improve what we know and believe?

Remember throughout your scholarly apprenticeship that most professors want to hear what *you* think. They will encourage and expect you to demonstrate your knowledge, to exercise your critical thinking skills, and to take some intellectual risks. Typically, they don't want you to regurgitate old knowledge and reuse familiar formulas. We hope you'll take them up on the challenge, using writing as a tool to discover, communicate, and revise what you know, think, and believe.

In the next chapter, we will explain how you can use the rhetorical principles we've described so far to develop a more flexible, sophisticated process for reading and writing. This foundation will prepare you to read, analyze, and write in a variety of rhetorical situations. In Chapter 3, we'll describe how to select and incorporate sources that will help you engage in scholarly discussions. After that, we will begin to explore one of the main tools that scholars use to communicate and solve problems—*argument*, which happens to be a crucial but often confusing feature of scholarly writing, and is therefore the focus of the rest of this book.

What's Next

WHAT'S NEXT features will help you transfer and apply what you've learned into other classes and beyond school. Take what you've learned in this chapter and respond to the following prompts.

1. **Seeing yourself as a scholar.** Write a 1,000-word essay that introduces your intellectual interests and motivations to your instructor and your classmates. Use the following questions to get you started:
   - Think back on previous writing assignments and try to remember one that you liked the most and one that you liked the least. What inspired or discouraged you? What motivates you—or *might* motivate you—to write?
   - What do you want to know more about? What questions inspire you most? What beliefs do you want to interrogate and understand? Identify some significant questions—related to your major or to your life—that spark your curiosity.

2. **Analyzing audiences.** College classes often assign readings that were not originally intended for a student audience. To get the most out of such readings, it's helpful to imagine how the original readers might have responded to a message. We can begin by looking for

clues about those primary audience members. One kind of clue is called a *paratext*, which includes textual elements that originally accompanied the reading, for example, a book cover or other articles published within a magazine, newspaper, or website. Advertisements yield especially useful clues about intended audiences.

For this activity, select three different communication media (such as a commercial website, a television news program, and a popular print magazine). Scrutinize several of the advertisements and analyze what they indicate about the identity of the intended audience members (for example, their age, political affiliations, level of education, interests, values). Then, share your notes with a classmate, present your findings to the class, or write about your analysis for an outside audience.

3. **Writing and researching in your discipline.** Interview a professor in your discipline to learn about writing and research practices in your field. Then, write a two-page summary of your professor's comments. Some sample questions that you might consider asking are as follows:
   - What is the purpose of research?
   - How do scholars think and analyze in this discipline?
   - What "moves" (such as explicitly stating the thesis early in an argument or using personal opinion to support a claim) do you expect students to make in their papers? What features do you value most in student writing?
   - How do scholars in our discipline write? What does their writing process look like?

   If you were to present this interview to an audience, you could add a photograph of the person being interviewed or a video or audio clip. Can you think of ways that this might make your presentation more persuasive? Do you think this would add something substantive or just add unnecessary ornamentation?

CHAPTER two

How Do Scholars Read and Write

chapter checklist

- When, why, and how do we read sources?
- How do experienced writers structure their writing processes?
- How can we improve our writing processes?

Scholarly writing is a conversation. By publishing their views, findings, and arguments, scholars build on each other's work. However, before beginning a project, scholars typically review what others have said before. They "listen" awhile to get their bearings and to ensure they know what's already been established. Although scholars frequently conduct research to update or corroborate previous work, topics lose their compelling luster if others have already covered the subject sufficiently. Just as jokes become less funny when heard over and over, scholars lose interest in rehashing questions that have already been settled. That's why, **for scholars, the writing process usually begins with reading.** Reviewing the work of current and previous scholars gives us a sense of what topics interest our scholarly community, what gaps or questions still need investigation, and where we might contribute to the ongoing conversation. Therefore, scholars usually begin the writing process by reading sources (journal articles, books, and other scholarly references), which can help us:

- Verify whether our work will yield fresh understanding
- Begin collecting information to answer our research questions
- Provide context for our investigation by relating our study to other scholars' work
- Borrow methods of investigation or theories that worked for other scholars
- Identify views, assumptions, or conclusions to build on or diverge from

Starting the writing process by reading other scholars' work helps us learn what has already been said and explain how our contribution or approach is different. Ideally, then, we'll be able to offer readers some *news*.

Read Like a Scholar

In their daily routines, scholars read much more than they write. As an apprentice, your primary means of learning will be reading other scholars' work. Of course, you'll spend plenty of time listening to lectures or participating in class discussions, but much of your learning will be on your own, reading books or articles assigned by your professors. Reading is more difficult than many students realize or care to admit. Although reading for comprehension may seem simple when the content is familiar, the kind of reading required for analyzing ideas and arguments can be quite challenging. Fully comprehending scholarly writing requires careful, thoughtful, and analytical reading.

Challenges to Effective Reading

You may already think you are a good reader. These days, we seem to be reading all the time, but we read differently than our parents or grandparents did. Immersed in electronic texts, most of us have become good (although we could always become better) at "surfing," or literally, skimming along the surface of the Web. With some tweaking, the skills you use to quickly browse websites or Wikipedia will also help you handle the reading that you will likely encounter in college.

However, success at surfing may also conceal a weakness. Have you ever been reading for a long time and then suddenly realized that you can't remember what you just read? Have you ever been overwhelmed by trying to make sense of a long, complicated article or book that you were assigned? While you may excel at skimming, you may not be as good at remembering, comprehending, and analyzing what you've read.

Reading requires concentration, engagement, and a quiet mind—all of which are difficult to maintain in our highly distracting society that values technology, multitasking, and immediacy. These priorities potentially overload our attention, as Nicholas Carr argues in his provocative article "Is Google Making Us Stupid? What the Internet Is Doing to Our Brains" (*The Atlantic*, July/August 2008). Carr summarizes the views of neuroscientists, psychologists, sociologists, and writers who believe that the Internet's scattered, fast pace threatens our ability to concentrate and think deeply. We all can relate to Carr's distracted reading experience. For many of us, if something isn't highly captivating with flashy graphics, bright colors, short snippets of text, and lots of pictures, it won't hold our attention for very long. This is unsettling, given the fact that complex problems and grueling tasks require deep concentration. If Carr is correct, then we need to think carefully about how the Internet affects how we process information.

By practicing reading, you can train your brain to slow down, to focus, and to move beyond surface-level thinking. These habits of mind are essential for us to be productive members of society. We need doctors who can think through a diagnosis carefully and deliberately, without losing concentration at the drop of a hat. We need senators who can debate an issue at length, without succumbing to distraction. Furthermore, we want these habits of mind to come naturally, which requires practice. Reading is like a fitness class for your brain.

TRY THIS ➤ Reflect on Your Reading Process

To begin this exercise, find and read Nicholas Carr's article, "Is Google Making Us Stupid?" on *The Atlantic* magazine's website. Briefly summarize why Carr thinks online reading is "making us stupid" and what he thinks we should do about it. Then, reflect in writing on how technology has shaped your reading process—in positive and negative ways. Compare your responses with those of your classmates.

Reading Strategically

The first lesson in strategic reading is to **have a clear, specific purpose in mind every time you read**. Are you reading to understand new concepts for a class? Are you trying to collect background information or to answer a specific question? Or are you examining models of writing that you want to imitate?

Your answers should determine your reading pace, place, and approach. For example, if you're searching through the library or Internet databases to find sources for a paper, you might only need to scan them to decide whether you should invest more time in reading. When you find sections of a book or article to be useful, then you can layer on deeper reading and analysis techniques. The bottom line is that you shouldn't read everything the same way.

To get the most out of your reading, you'll need reading techniques that focus on concentration and repetition. If your mind is not actively engaged and you don't review what you've read, you won't remember it, let alone be able to comprehend or analyze new information and difficult arguments. Brain research indicates that **repetition enhances memory**. The more times you think about information or ideas, the better they stick. Also, repeating the information in a slightly different way each time increases your level of comprehension. So, in order to enhance and monitor your concentration, reading experts advocate a reading process that involves three different phases: previewing, reading, and reviewing.

Previewing

Before you read something, scan the table of contents, headings, tables, images, and key words to get some sense of the main ideas and organization. Think about how the reading connects to what you already know and want to learn. Also, consider the rhetorical elements we discussed in the previous chapter: author, purpose, context, and so forth.

Reading

Once you've previewed the text, you're ready to begin reading as you normally would, except now you can read much more quickly (probably twice as fast) with greater comprehension because you already know most of what the text is about. As you're reading, take notes about important concepts, along with any questions and reactions to the reading. Speed up when reading information you already know, and slow down for new or complicated material.

Reviewing

Lost concentration presents the biggest obstacle to remembering and comprehending what you read. Whenever you forget what you just read, you've lost concentration. That's why we suggest reading and reviewing in a continuous loop. Whether you pause every few minutes, every page, or every paragraph, **stop reading and recall what you**

just read. If you can accurately recall what you just read, then continue. If not, you've only wasted a few minutes of effort, so go back and read and review again.

You can also **improve concentration by limiting distractions**. Every time you stop reading to answer a text message, to check social media, or to have a conversation with a friend, you break concentration. Consider finding a quiet place and turning off your cell phone while you study—or better yet, disconnect from your wireless network. You'll end up getting better results in less time than if you allow yourself constant interruptions. You might even discover what reading was like before Google.

Write Like a Scholar

Just as scholars adapt their reading process for different situations, experienced writers customize how they write for specific purposes, audiences, and occasions. Learning a flexible writing process can be especially useful for writing outside of school where, instead of having a structured rhetorical situation (assignment guidelines), you encounter unfamiliar kinds of writing, in different contexts, for new audiences.

In the past, you may not have needed such a sophisticated writing process. Inexperienced writers use a simplified process for good reasons. Remember, when you first started driving, how difficult it was to think about turning; accelerating; braking; and navigating roads, signs, and traffic all at the same time? To avoid information overload and to simplify the writing process for students, teachers often require a formula that looks something like this. First, pick a topic. Then, research the topic, as needed. After reading enough sources, create an outline and write a first draft. Finally, revise, edit, and submit the paper. In theory, this process works reasonably well because it forces students not to skip steps and because it's easier to learn a complicated process by concentrating on one part at a time.

However, **experienced writers usually don't write in such a formulaic, straight line**. Scholars typically follow a more *recursive* process—that is, they move back and forth among the stages, often repeating steps multiple times and at different points in their process. Although they typically create a plan before they begin, scholars also allow drafting, revision, and peer feedback to reshape their ideas. Throughout the writing process, they improve and focus their ideas by imagining different audiences and purposes and by finding potential gaps in their arguments.

Learning to use a more complex writing process might seem overwhelming, but scholarly writing takes practice and persistence. Inexperienced writers sometimes have an unrealistic and unattainable view of writing—that good writing happens magically for the lucky few, with little effort, as though you're either born a good writer or not. Here's the good news: **Effective writing is not a magical or natural talent**. It can be explained and learned. In fact, research about learning indicates that people who have a "growth

CONSIDER THIS ➤ Habits and History

For this reflection, use the following questions to help you think through how you typically write for school assignments. Be honest.

1. What, if anything, do you do before you start to write a draft? Do you freewrite or use an outline? How do you generate ideas?
2. What conditions do you prefer while writing? Do you like to write at a desk—or maybe in bed? By hand or on a laptop? What time of day do you do your best writing? Do you need quiet, or does background noise or music help you focus?
3. What do you do with your first draft? What kinds of changes do you typically make before handing it in?
4. How did you learn these strategies and habits? Why do you write this way?

mindset"—meaning they believe that they can improve their abilities and increase their intelligence—are more successful at learning new things. To develop your writing ability, you only need four things: knowledge; practice; feedback; and, most important, motivation. These key ingredients can help you become a more effective writer in college and beyond.

Remember, too, that college professors expect you to *apprentice* as a scholar, not to become professors or professional writers. Keep your goals within reason, and don't let scholarly writing intimidate you. Like learning to drive, it might seem awkward and frustrating at first, but becoming proficient may be easier than you think.

The One-Draft Wonder

Despite how much teachers try to improve students' writing process, research indicates that most new college students write one draft and make few changes before submitting their writing for a grade. For practical purposes, novice scholars often hand in their rough drafts.

Why do so many students still trust their one-draft wonders? Efficiency.

If, based on your own experiences, a single draft and some light proofreading have given you the results you want (an acceptable grade or a completed assignment), then why would you expect big rewards from multiple drafts? And if no one has ever taught you how to draft and revise effectively, how could you be expected to do so?

Most writers can achieve *some* success without much planning or revising. As long as investing the bulk of your time and energy in drafting yields the results you want, that's okay for now. But if you're like us, when you encounter difficult writing projects (like a 20-page research paper, or a short but complex argumentative essay), you'll need a process that includes careful planning and lots of revision.

So our first writing process lesson is this: Adapt your writing process to fit the particular writing situation. **Experienced writers don't write the same way every time, and neither should you.**

If your teacher assigns a short argument and you can effectively organize your ideas in your head without making an outline beforehand, then go ahead. If you can write an effective short-response paper in one draft the night before it's due, that's okay. But before you think your one-draft wonders will always work in college, think back to when you first learned algebra. You probably thought "showing your work" was pointless, at least at the beginning. When the problems became more difficult, however, you learned that you could no longer solve them in your head. You needed a more complex process to solve more complex problems. The same is true in writing.

A Better Writing Process

So, what does a more complex writing process look like? We'll begin by breaking the writing process down into four parts: discovery, drafting, revision, and editing.

- *Discovery* includes tasks such as choosing a topic, identifying the right questions to ask, finding and processing outside sources, organizing ideas, and so forth.
- *Drafting* generates the first version of a complete draft.
- *Revision* involves significantly adding, deleting, or rearranging chunks of text or content.
- *Editing* polishes paragraphs and sentences for style, formatting, grammar, and so forth.

Note carefully how we distinguish between revision and editing. Think of revising as major surgery and editing as cosmetic surgery. Major surgery repairs vital organs, whereas cosmetic surgery changes a person's appearance. Good writing requires both.

We assume that since you're in college, you're willing to invest serious time and energy into your studies. Still, you can only afford to spend a certain amount of time and effort on a given assignment. Thus, the four parts of the writing process are inversely proportional to each other: **The more time and effort you spend drafting, for example, the less time you have to invest in discovery or revision.** To illustrate these proportionalities vividly, we might use a pie chart like this.

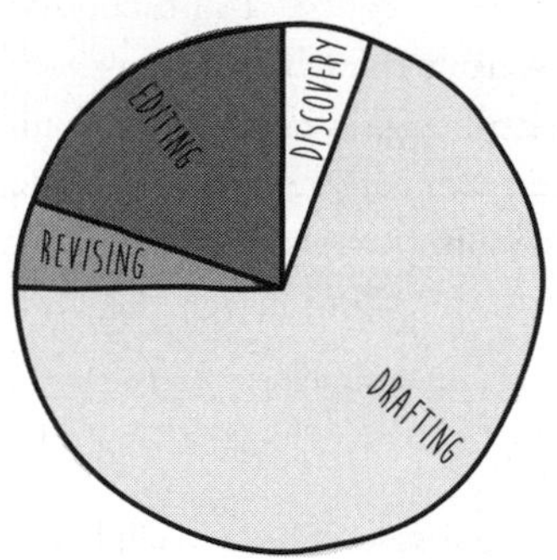

Of course, these portions are not scientifically precise, but the pie chart can help us imagine the typical writing process of one-draft wonder writers who spend most of their time drafting and editing, leaving little to invest in discovery or revision.

How might the one-draft process hinder your development as a writer? What are its potential costs? First, if you love your draft too much, you won't want to change it. After all, if the majority of your investment is drafting, then you probably won't want to redo that work, even when it's not very good. More important, **if you only write one draft, you lose the opportunity to revise and expand your thinking**—to reenvision your message, to understand your subject matter more deeply, and to discover new insights and better ways to present your ideas. Again, a simple writing process might work fine if you want a simple written product, but if you want something more substantial and sophisticated, you'll need to use a better writing process.

Rather than relying so much on a single-draft process, you might find it useful to experiment with other economical ways to invest your time and energy. For example, if you begin thinking about an assignment as soon as you get it, maybe even jot down ideas as they occur to you, then you can add discovery time with little cost. Similarly, a 15-minute visit to your instructor's office to talk about plans for the paper can pay big dividends. If you change your topic or misread the assignment at that early stage, then you haven't already "wasted" time drafting, right? Scholars do this, too, when they discuss an idea for a research article or a conference paper with a colleague who can help them brainstorm and develop a research plan. Another good time investment is using your campus writing center, where you should be able to obtain help during any stage of the writing process. All of these discovery strategies save drafting time by helping you to organize and avoid later problems. In fact, for some scholars, drafting takes the least amount of time because they do most of the hard thinking and problem solving before they compose their first paragraph and after their first draft is complete.

Experienced Writers' Processes

For complex tasks, experienced writers try to balance the elements of the process, spending more time before and after drafting to develop and refine their writing. In fact, experienced writers often spend more time thinking (discovery) and rethinking (revising) their writing than they do creating their first draft because they realize how much these activities can expand and deepen their understanding.

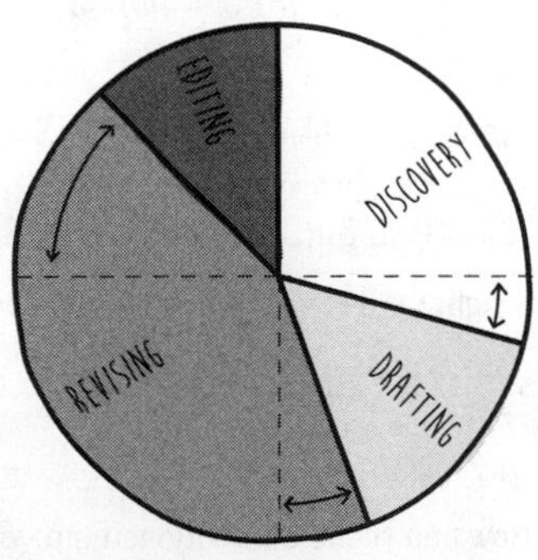

Researchers have also discovered that experienced writers customize their writing process to the task at hand. For example, a research-based project written for scholarly publication requires a significant investment of discovery and revision, whereas creating a resume may require more time drafting and editing.

TRY THIS ➤ Adapt Your Writing Process

For this exercise, consider how you would customize your writing process for different situations. Create a pie chart to illustrate how you would invest your time in discovery, drafting, revising, and editing for the following tasks:

- A resume for your dream job
- An in-class essay exam
- A group research assignment
- A science lab report

Compare your pie charts with classmates and discuss differences and similarities among your writing processes.

Set Priorities and Adapt Your Process

Experienced writers don't feel locked into a linear process, but they do set priorities. Following writing experts Paula Gillespie and Neal Lerner, we divide these priorities into higher order/global drafting and revising concerns and later order/local editing issues.

Table 2.1 DRAFTING VERSUS EDITING

DRAFTING & REVISING CONCERNS	EDITING CONCERNS
Higher order: first priority, major	Later order: later priority, minor
Global: essay or paragraph-level	Local: sentence-level
Examples: content, focus, organization	Examples: style, grammar, formatting

How can these distinctions help you adapt your writing process?

Experienced writers address higher order concerns first, not just because they're more important. **Prioritizing increases the effectiveness and efficiency of your writing process.** Trying to address everything at once is overwhelming, even for expert writers. Focusing your attention on a few issues at a time will decrease your cognitive load, which increases the effectiveness of finding and fixing problems in your writing. Prioritizing also increases efficiency. For example, before you edit a paragraph to make sure your writing is clear and correct, you should make sure that the paragraph effectively develops necessary content. If a paragraph presents information that is off topic or restates information that you already covered, then you may need to revise it. Why waste time tweaking sentences that might later be removed or substantially changed?

Another way to save time is to think carefully about your audience and purpose so you can adapt your writing process according to the needs of each particular situation. You will be frustrated if you assume that chemists write the same as economists, that every professor in your major will follow the exact same grading criteria for every

CONSIDER THIS ➤ Introducing Sources

For this reflection, examine how we introduced Gillespie and Lerner's idea of "higher" and "later" order writing issues above. We called them "writing experts" and used an "attributive tag" to introduce their terminology. Attributive tags such as these help us clearly delineate between our ideas and other scholars' thoughts:

- "According to the author, ____________________"
- "The text states ____________________"
- "The writer makes the point that ____________________"

You might also point out your sources' credentials (area of expertise, level of education, relevant accomplishments) like a lawyer would do for an expert witness. In this instance, did the amount of information we provided about Gillespie and Lerner help you trust them?

assignment, or that every job will require the same kind of writing tasks. By experimenting with different strategies, you can assemble a writing tool kit to use when you encounter new or difficult writing situations. Throughout this book, we'll present many ways of interpreting, handling, and excelling at various writing tasks.

Manage the Writing Process

Experienced writers organize their efforts to improve effectiveness and efficiency. To be successful—and to reduce unnecessary stress—we don't recommend tackling a large writing task at once, in one sitting, the night before the assignment is due. The level of thinking and writing expected in college requires us to work in stages. Remember, writing is a process. We need time for our ideas to "marinate," time to find sources, time to get feedback on drafts, and time to revise and edit. To reserve time for all of these things, try to manage writing tasks sensibly:

- **Break the assignment into a series of manageable tasks, and then assign a deadline for each task.** For example, set a deadline for completing your research and another deadline for the first draft. If you create a timeline that organizes your tasks, you can hold yourself accountable. You might use a daily planner for this, install scheduling apps on your smartphone or tablet, or find resources available online.
- **Break a long assignment into chunks.** For example, you could think of a 20-page paper as 4 shorter papers, each with its own purpose. Thinking about the assignment in this way can make a daunting task more manageable. Focusing on smaller objectives, in stages, helps us be more productive and feel less overwhelmed. Consult the Scholarly Model on pp. 177–178 for ideas on how to divide large assignments into segments.
- **Take good notes throughout the research process.** The process of sifting through sources can be overwhelming, and it's easy to

mix up your sources. That's why it's imperative to take careful notes along the way. Some writers keep all of their notes in one place, like a notebook or online research folder. Other writers like to record information about each source on separate note cards or files. When you find a particularly useful quotation, write it down in your research notebook or on a note card or type it into a document. That way, you can cut and paste quotations, along with their citations, into your paper easily and efficiently.

- **Keep meticulous records.** As you conduct your research, invest time in recording bibliographic information for all your sources: author, title, publication information, and page numbers for any quotations or paraphrases. If you keep meticulous records, you won't waste time shuffling through files or papers, trying to remember where you found a memorable phrase. Online reference management systems can help you track, organize, and format citations while you conduct your research.
- **Get feedback along the way.** Assuming it's okay with your instructor, always have someone you trust read and respond to an early draft. Your professor might be willing to do this during office hours. If you have access to a writing center, try working with a tutor who can help you think through an assignment's various parts, brainstorm ideas, develop a plan, and revise your drafts. Tutors typically see many different kinds of assignments, so they can teach you strategies and give you a different perspective than you may have considered.
- **Don't insist on following a fixed or linear plan.** Just because your paper begins with an abstract or an introduction doesn't mean you have to start on that section first. If you don't know where to begin—if you feel stuck or overwhelmed—start with something straightforward: for instance, begin with your Works Cited page. Type up quotations that you might include in the paper. Format your document. All of these simpler tasks can get you started and alleviate some fear of the blank page. Remember,

writing is difficult for everyone, and just because you're stuck doesn't mean that you can't find your way. Sometimes, in order to make progress, you have to jump around and then go back to reorganize or fill in the gaps.

Interpreting Assignments

Because scholars in most disciplines use writing to communicate their discoveries, another challenge of college writing is that it comes in many forms or genres—from scientific research articles to business case studies to artistic analysis papers. You probably won't write in every class, but you may very well write more often than you have before in classes other than English. These writing tasks will have different purposes, audiences, and writing styles, so there are no clear-cut rules or go-to formulas for every scenario. Instead, you'll need to make informed decisions by interpreting your professors' assignments thoughtfully and looking for clues in the assignment that suggest its rhetorical situation and a smart approach to take. The sections that follow provide some features to consider.

Writing with Purpose

As an apprentice, you can assume that most writing assignments will ask you to showcase your knowledge and understanding of subject matter while also using critical and creative thinking to develop some fresh understanding. Your professor might provide clues for the assignment's purpose by using specific terms to focus your attention, such as:

- *Analyze*—to take something apart to see how it works
- *Interpret*—to examine something's meaning, implications, or significance
- *Evaluate* or *critique*—to judge something according to established criteria

Whenever professors use less specific terms such as "discuss" or "examine," ask them to clarify or provide some strategies for how to meet their expectations. Think carefully about your audience and purpose, and ask yourself, should the writing:

- Persuade the audience to adopt a new position?
- Enlighten readers and give them new ideas to think about?
- Defend a controversial interpretation?

Regardless of your writing task's central aim, professors usually expect you to demonstrate what you're learning in class. Here's where you'll need to use a little gamesmanship, because you'll often find yourself explaining something to someone who already knows more than you do about a subject, or arguing a point to demonstrate that you know how to build an argument. Keep in mind that you're *practicing* scholarly writing—just as you would a sport—so your professor wants to see you make specific moves. Like a coach watching a football team run a new play, your professor is observing from the sidelines, expecting to see you demonstrate the strategies and skills you've been learning. Knowing this makes clear why you should elaborate your ideas and explain concepts, even ones your professor already understands. You need to convince your professor that *you* grasp the concept, and explaining it allows you to display the intricacies of your understanding. Think of it this way: **The paper that best demonstrates learning is the one that you could not have written before taking a course**. Write that paper.

To demonstrate learning successfully, try to exaggerate your new knowledge: refer to key terms in the textbook or mention important theories or topics covered in class. We don't mean that you should regurgitate information to the point where you dilute your own voice and thoughts. You can connect your ideas to concepts you've been studying in ways that display your new knowledge. Scholars must also "overexplain" what they're talking about sometimes because their subject matter is often so specialized and their discoveries are so original that even their expert peers need extra help to understand. Connecting prior knowledge to new ideas helps audiences understand messages more easily.

Even when it's "just practice," writing for your professor provides an opportunity for you to engage with a real audience and to get more immediate and helpful feedback than professional scholars typically receive. Seize opportunities to interact with your scholarly mentors by asking questions in class, visiting during office hours, and paying careful attention to written feedback. This experience conversing with professors and interpreting and meeting their demands can prepare you to impress future employers who might not clarify their expectations so explicitly and give feedback so generously.

Writing for Multiple Audiences

When interpreting assignments, you also need to identify the intended audience, so it's important to decipher readers' dispositions and their needs. You can imagine your audience metaphorically as a dartboard, with the bulls-eye representing your target audience and the surrounding rings signifying secondary and tertiary audiences (other readers who could also benefit from your work). Apprentice scholars usually aim for professors as their primary target audience. Professors can stand in as a proxy for the scholarly community by identifying credible sources, asking relevant research questions, and suggesting an appropriate style and format for a specific community of scholars.

Alternatively, some professors will ask you to consider your classmates as your audience, in which case you can write for peers who have a similar level of expertise and experience as you. Just as scholars use peer review to improve and validate their work, you may have the opportunity to give and receive feedback from fellow apprentices.

Sometimes, professors will ask you to imagine addressing "real" secondary audiences. For example, you might investigate tax reform and write an evaluation or proposal argument in the form of a blog post, a letter to your legislator, or an op-ed piece for your local newspaper. Each of these assignments should prompt you to consider distinct audiences, purposes, and styles. Even if you don't actually publish your work for an outside audience, such writing can be fun and useful practice—and you can still look for places to publish your work (for example, in your student newspaper or an undergraduate research journal).

Undergraduate and even graduate students often write for an audience of "no one in particular," which can leave their prose flat and uninteresting. When experienced scholars have something important to say, they try to imagine specific audiences early and often during the writing process by asking themselves:

- Who would care about my topic and findings? Who needs to know what I've learned? Who can act on what I've found?
- What writing styles will those readers expect and find persuasive?
- What publications does that audience read?

Make It Matter: The *So What?* Factor

Experienced scholars not only consider who would care about their message but also **why their message matters to them and to their readers in the first place**. Thinking carefully about the larger implications of your writing task—how it relates to your course's learning objectives, your personal goals, and other classes—can give you a clearer rationale for doing the work. Having a sense of the *so what?* question can also help you make smart decisions. For example, ask yourself:

- Why might my professor have assigned this?
- What does she hope I'll learn from doing this?
- How does this assignment relate to the readings we've discussed in class or other course material?
- What skills or habits of mind might this assignment help me practice, and how could these help me later?

Identifying the purpose, audience, and larger significance of a writing task can help you make decisions about content, length, organization, and writing style, among other things. Plus, you'll gain greater insight into the authentic reasons for writing, which can increase your motivation.

CONSIDER THIS ➤ Using First Person

For this reflection, consider the appropriateness of using the first person in scholarly writing. We argue that professors really want to hear what you think. However, teachers have probably warned you not to use "I" in formal academic writing. So, you might be wondering,

- How am I supposed to express my thoughts without using the first person?
- Can I ever use "I" in college writing? If so, when?
- When might it be inappropriate to use "I"? Why?

Considering what we've said so far, how do you think we'd answer these questions? What have you been taught before, and what do you *really* think?

(Note: We continue discussing the use of first person in Chapter 10.)

So What?

Adopting some of the reading and writing practices that scholars use can make your processes more efficient and effective. Equipped with these practices and a broad understanding of scholarly writing's unique purposes and features, you are ready to dig deeper into how we integrate sources effectively and responsibly into your own writing. Scholars are expected to write with integrity, so we explain how to borrow from sources and intertwine your ideas with those of others. We show you how to create a conversation with sources by summarizing, paraphrasing, quoting, interpreting, and elaborating on source material. We also explain some of the fundamentals of citation to help you decide when and how to cite sources in your writing.

What's Next

Take what you've learned in this chapter and respond to the following prompts.

1. **Categorize characteristics of good writing.** For this exercise, identify the distinguishing features of "good" writing, and then sort them as either global/higher order or local/later order concerns, using the following steps:
   - As a class, discuss the following question: "What are some defining qualities of 'good' writing?" List the characteristics on the board.
   - Assign each of the characteristics into one of two categories: higher order concerns and later order concerns. For example, if you decide that clarity is an important feature, which category does that fall under?
   - Discuss what you observe about labeling writing characteristics this way. Do any of the features fall into both categories? Which characteristics seem most important? What does this exercise teach you about writing?

2. **Online reading guide.** Reading on-screen is increasingly common. You might already use e-textbooks or do the majority of your reading on a laptop or tablet. Given what we've said about the importance of careful and critical reading, along with the

challenges of reading online, what problems might you encounter when reading electronic texts? Do you think e-readers help or hinder reading? What strategies could you use to combat any ill effects of reading online? What apps or resources might help you? Develop a list of strategies and resources for reading online that you can share with your classmates.

CHAPTER **three**

How Do We Select and Use Sources Responsibly

chapter checklist

- How can we find the best sources?
- What are effective strategies for summarizing, paraphrasing, quoting, and citing sources?
- How—and why—do we write with integrity?
- How do we avoid plagiarizing?

You might wonder why we're talking about sources before we've developed an argument to write about. After all, scholars use sources to back up their arguments, so we need a thesis *before* we know which sources we need, right?

Not exactly. As we've said, scholars rarely begin writing an argument before they've reviewed the work of current and previous scholars. In fact, scholars almost always contextualize their own arguments in light of what others are saying or have said in the past. So, **for scholars, nearly every paper is a research paper**. Or at least every paper presents an opportunity to conduct some kind of research, because for scholars, every paper attempts to answer a question through investigation. That's why professors care so much (sometimes it might seem like a little too much) about finding good sources and "documenting" or citing those sources in elaborate bibliographies or lists of "works cited." As scholars, we value each other's contributions and we leave a paper trail to prove it.

Sifting Through Sources

In college, most professors will expect you to include sources—at least your class readings, if not "outside" library sources—every time you write. But how do we know which sources are best? Let's begin by considering our trusty Internet pal, Wikipedia.

As you've probably noticed, many teachers dislike or distrust Wikipedia. Why do they discount "the free encyclopedia that anyone can edit" as a credible source for scholarly writing? There are several reasons:

1. **Stability.** Wikipedia content changes all the time, and therefore your readers may not be able to go back and find the same information that was there when you accessed it. Although folks are getting more used to the idea of dynamic, electronic publications, many readers still trust printed text more (although this may change with time).
2. **Credibility.** Anyone can write Wikipedia entries, and contributors often do so anonymously (known as "crowdsourcing"). Scholars care about credentials, which is why they place more trust in authors with proven expertise. If they don't know you, they don't (yet) trust you. That's why apprentices must earn credibility by borrowing it from more established sources. By selecting sources that have been peer-reviewed, apprentice scholars can appear even more credible. Scholarly publications undergo a rigorous review process through which experts scrutinize quality. Wikipedia does

have an editorial review process, but it's more organic and egalitarian. Contributors edit each other's entries and make decisions through consensus. Scholars generally don't trust unstable sources written and reviewed by anonymous crowds. So, if you're trying to impress a scholar, citing Wikipedia probably won't work (unless, of course, you're writing a paper *about* Wikipedia).

3. **Bias.** Although Wikipedia urges contributors to maintain a "neutral point of view," some articles show bias, especially when the author is motivated by his own self-interest or when he seems closed-minded or prejudiced. Keep in mind, though, that just because an author presents an argument (or "opinion") doesn't make something "biased." Bias has more to do with whether a source examines a controversy from multiple perspectives or is one-sided, or whether the investigator is open-minded or approaches a topic with a predetermined answer, regardless of what the evidence suggests. A biased scholar discovers what she wants to find, rather than letting the investigation lead toward whatever truth unfolds. Intentionally presenting inaccurate information or misrepresenting sources isn't so much biased as it is manipulative. All writers are biased to some extent because our perspectives are colored by previous experiences. However, we can limit the extent to which our bias influences our investigation by remaining informed, open-minded, and devoted to accuracy.

Despite objections about its stability, credibility, and bias, Wikipedia provides a vast, easily accessible, and *relatively* accurate storehouse of information about almost anything. In fact, here's a little secret: most of us use Wikipedia anyway—experts and apprentices alike. That's because it's a useful reference for gathering background information—a good place to get a general sense about a topic, then dig deeper into other, more credible sources. Notice that Wikipedia entries often contain extensive references and suggestions for "further reading," many of which might be trustworthy enough to use as scholarly sources.

CONSIDER THIS ➤ Wikipedia on Wikipedia

For this reflection, read Wikipedia's entry on Wikipedia and discuss the following in class:

- What other issues does the entry raise about Wikipedia's credibility?
- Which references in this entry seem most trustworthy as scholarly sources? Why?

So What's a Better Source?

As we say throughout this book, when it comes to what works in writing, everything depends on the particular audience, purpose, and context. For an audience of scholars, the most trustworthy sources are those written by other scholars in reputable publications that use a rigorous review process, such as scholarly journals. Other situations call for different sources, but generally you can follow our trusty "credibilimeter" when deciding what sources carry the most scholarly credibility.

Notice that we haven't claimed that any of these sources are necessarily invalid or incorrect. Entertainment media, for example, are sometimes true and often believable. That's just our point: **Credibility**

depends on the particular audience and situation. If you're arguing with a friend about sports, you probably don't need a scholarly source to seem convincing. *SportsCenter* will probably do.

Even if they may not be the most credible scholarly sources, social media, Wikipedia, newspapers, and other popular sites can be good places to start searching for background information or interesting topics to write about. Scholarly print publications lag behind popular and electronic media because it takes so long for scholars to complete their research and have it reviewed and revised for publication. So Wikipedia isn't necessarily a bad place to start.

Just don't stop searching after skimming the first few paragraphs on Wikipedia or the first page of Google hits, and remember to think carefully about what sources and evidence your audience will trust. Experienced scholars mistrust sources that haven't been scrutinized by experts, so if you want to communicate or argue with scholars, you need to be able to find, understand, and use academically credible references.

CONSIDER THIS ➤ Appropriate Sources

For this reflection, describe some different situations when non-scholarly sources would be effective. When might scholarly sources be ineffective?

How Do We Find Credible Scholarly Sources?

Ask other scholars. When we're initially investigating a topic and looking for the best sources, we often start by asking other scholars to identify journals, books, or articles that experts in the field know well. These books and journal articles may even be on our colleagues' shelves. From these, we find a clearer starting point, which can save us lots of time. Also, when other scholars read our work, they will expect us to reference these key sources to prove that we know what we're talking about, or at least that we've done our homework.

You should do the same.

Instructors hold office hours for a reason: to help students. Take advantage of this time and meet with a professor who is an expert in the field that you're studying. For example, if you're writing a paper on alienation and the effects of social media on teenage girls, an English professor specializing in feminist literature or a sociologist who studies gender could probably recommend some reliable and useful sources. This might seem intimidating and time consuming, but beginning your research in the right place can save you many hours of frustration.

Plus, most professors will be thrilled to help. Imagine how you'd feel if you spent years studying something like the feeding habits of Amazonian frogs, waiting patiently for that one student who showed genuine interest in your expertise.

We also consult reference librarians who can help us identify research techniques that will yield better results. Librarians work with research databases more often than we do, so they can share lots of techniques and shortcuts. For example, librarians can help you select appropriate databases for your topic or narrow your database search terms. They can also show you how to locate sources by proximity, because libraries and databases cluster sources by subject headings.

If we already have a handle on search techniques and want to work independently, we'll **explore a research database**, like Academic Search Complete. (If you don't have easy access to library databases, Google Scholar can help find scholarly articles in a pinch.) Online journals allow us to access full-text versions of most articles. Many databases only include material that has been peer-reviewed, so we can usually be confident that the articles are accurate and well researched, although they could still be biased or controversial. In addition to being credible, many articles are searchable, so we can move through them quickly using our computer's *find* function to search for relevant sections of an article.

If we're looking for more general sources, such as magazine articles or newspaper editorials, we'll **search online**. We might look at company websites, blog posts, or personal Web pages, depending on our purpose. But whenever we're viewing public sites like these, we shift our rhetorical thinking into overdrive. We ask ourselves:

- Who wrote this? What makes the authors credible?
- What are they trying to achieve? For example, is anyone profiting from this? Who? How might money-making efforts influence the content?
- How do they support their claims?
- When was this written? Will this still be here next month?

Sources need to convince us that they deserve a place in our writing. Thoughtful investigation helps us determine whether an online source is credible and worth using. We expect to do a lot of hunting

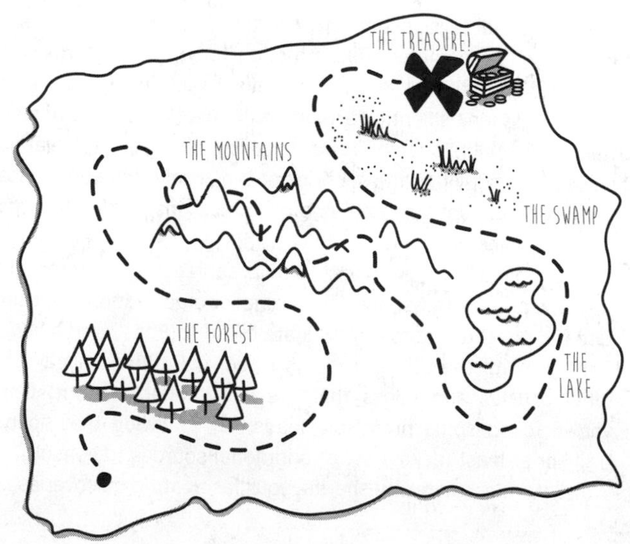

around, so we don't just settle with the first hits that our search engine picks. Settling is a rookie mistake. Unlike most online navigation that is quick and easy, searching for good sources takes time and patience. To find the prize, we must wade through forests of dense material, trek across mountains of reading, and trudge through deserts with no relevant sources in sight. Remember, the buried treasure might not appear until the final leg of the journey—or the third page of search results.

TRY THIS ➤ Practice Sifting Through Sources

For this exercise, practice searching for credible sources. As a class or in small groups, select a research topic that interests you—any topic that you're truly curious about. Then, search online for three to four credible sources.

1. If your library has access to research databases online, begin by entering search terms in a scholarly database, such as Academic Search Complete.
2. Select the full-text version of an article that seems promising and use your computer's *find* function to search for terms that will lead you to the article's most relevant sections. For example, if you find a long scientific article on the health benefits of meditation, you might search for words such as "stress" or "relationships" to quickly find the sections of the article that you're most curious about. Jot down notes on the most interesting information and points you find.
3. Search online for high-quality public sources, such as articles from a reputable newspaper, magazine, or organization's website. Use the questions above to evaluate these sources' credibility.
4. Skim each of the source's Works Cited or References page for other articles and books that are worth checking out. Once you've found some promising leads, try following that "paper trail" or at least make a list of additional sources to consult.
5. Wow your classmates by sharing your fascinating discoveries.

What's the Best Research Container?

Another criterion that you should consider when sifting through sources is *scope*. Look for the right-sized research container for the scope (the breadth and depth) of your argument. If your topic is broad, begin with a source that has enough room to meet your needs. **Big topics need big research containers.**

Here we're not talking about *Encyclopedia Britannica* or Wikipedia, either. If your topic has been studied extensively, you might find a more exhaustive and credible reference book on the subject in your school library. For example, for a topic as broad as World War II, our school's library holds several scholarly encyclopedias (including the five-volume *The Encyclopedia of World War II*) that could help you discover exactly what you want to write about.

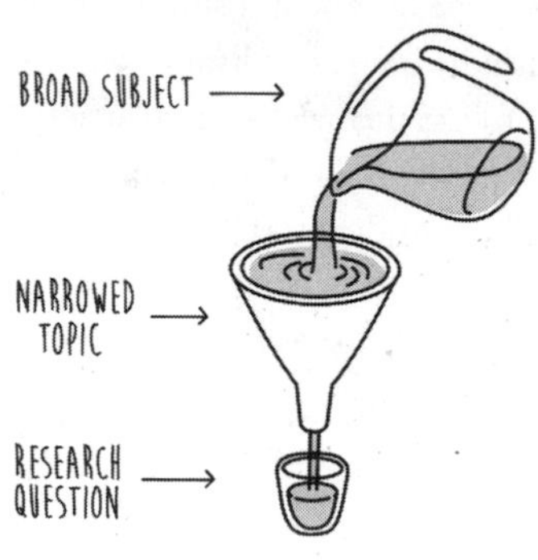

Once you narrow your topic a bit, you might search your library for more manageable, medium-sized sources. Scholarly books, which are often 200 to 400 pages, focus more narrowly than most novice scholars might think. Our library has hundreds of books on narrower World War II topics, including *The African American Experience in World War II* or *London at War, 1939–45*.

Scholarly journals publish cutting-edge research, so they usually present specialized topics for subject matter experts. Most journal articles are about 20 to 30 pages in length, with an appropriately narrow scope that "fits" into that page count. For example, a journal article about World War II would have a very specific focus, like "Replacing Battleships with Aircraft Carriers in the Pacific in World War II," published in a discipline-specific journal, *Naval War College Review*. One advantage of a recently published journal article—as opposed to a book or an encyclopedia—is that it reflects the most current debates in a field.

Novice scholars sometimes think that journal articles are the quickest to read because they are the shortest. Wrong. They might be short, but because of their specificity, they often require prior knowledge about a subject before they can be useful. That's why it's usually smart to educate yourself with a "bigger" source before diving into a specialized journal article.

If you want to write about a contemporary controversy, you might also consider starting with online sources that examine topics from multiple angles, such as *Issues and Controversies* or *Opposing Viewpoints in Context*. Much like encyclopedias for a big topic, these sources can help you narrow a broad topic. Say, for example, you're interested in comparing educational standards in public versus private schools. You might begin with *Issues and Controversies* and from there, find a book like *Keeping Them out of the Hands of Satan: Evangelical Schooling in America* or an even more specific journal article, such as "School Vouchers and Student Attainment: Evidence from a State-Mandated Study of Milwaukee's Parental Choice Program," from *Policy Studies Journal*. Following a research process like this one, which moves from "large" research containers to "smaller" ones, can help you narrow your scope, minimize frustration, and learn a lot more.

And that's the whole point. For apprentice scholars, "research" typically means learning from more experienced scholars, borrowing from the established credibility of their investigations, and using their writing as models for making arguments. "Library research" may not enable you to expand the bounds of human understanding, but it will initiate you into the habits and practices of a community that does.

Summarizing, Paraphrasing, and Quoting Sources

As we collect credible sources, we begin choosing how we want to integrate them into our writing through summary, paraphrase, and quotation (see Figure 3.1). Working closely with sources will help you better understand other people's ideas and build on them in your own writing. Often, after you read an essay or scholarly article, you'll be asked to write about it. But before you can fairly evaluate the argument or respond to it with your own ideas, you'll need to be sure that you understand the source's message.

Summary is the most important and common technique when writing about sources, and it incorporates paraphrasing and sometimes quotation. Scholars use summaries to *distill* a source—either all or part

Summarize

- To capture the whole text in a smaller amount of space
- To identify the most important parts of a larger text
- To condense

Paraphrase

- To represent a portion of the text in your own words
- To restate an idea in a different style but maintain the original length
- To translate someone else's words into your own phrasing
- To avoid quoting too frequently, in order to maintain a consistent tone

Quote

- To express a specific idea verbatim
- To credit an author's original term, phrase, or controversial statement
- To boost your credibility

Figure 3.1

The Rationale for Summary, Paraphrase, and Quotation

How would you decide when to use each of these techniques?

of a text—into a more condensed, selective version. In practice, scholars typically summarize just the parts they need, such as a source's findings or the methodology. While a summary is a scaled-down version, a paraphrase is typically about the same length as the original passage.

Why is it important to understand this distinction? Because you'll need to use the technique that best suits your purpose.

In many classes, you'll need to report on your library research by summing up major theories and significant previous research on your topic. Scholars also regularly summarize, paraphrase, and quote other scholars when they write "literature reviews" or "research reviews," which they publish with their findings to help their readers enter the conversation and share background information. When we're describing something long and complicated, a summary allows us to *select* main points and *condense* the original. However, if we're restating just a paragraph or a sentence, a paraphrase allows us to *translate* the original into our own words—not just do a synonym swap—while maintaining a similar length.

Generally, scholars prefer summarizing and paraphrasing over quoting. That's because both of these techniques allow the writer to maintain his voice and display his grasp of the material. Think about it. We can't condense or translate something unless we really know what it says, so when we summarize and paraphrase, we demonstrate that we understand the source. Simply quoting doesn't give us the opportunity to display this depth of understanding.

Quoting less also makes your writing smoother because readers don't need to transition repeatedly from your style to other writers' styles. Quoting is more acceptable or even necessary in literature or writing classes because those disciplines care most about language. On the other hand, scholars writing in the sciences or business may quote rarely, if at all. Still, you can bet that in most scholarly writing you'll be doing a lot more summarizing and paraphrasing than quoting. These techniques leave a lot more room for your own ideas and arguments than if you overwhelm your writing with quotations.

But summarizing a source can be difficult.

How Do We Summarize?

Summarizing requires us not only to understand *what* the text says but also *how* it says—how it's structured, how it builds its argument, how it achieves its purpose, and so on. After we understand the original in its entirety, we can select the most relevant details. We focus on main claims and don't get bogged down in the details. Just like someone who builds model cars or airplanes, we construct a scaled-down version of the original that will fit the size of our paper. We also have to consider the proportions of the original; if the original is 20 pages long, we can't spend one-third of our summary on the first 2 pages. We don't have room for every detail, but we can't leave out any major parts, either. So we look carefully at the original and how all of the parts fit together before we decide what to include and what to leave out.

To select the right parts, it's helpful to get in the "believing" mindset: give the author the benefit of the doubt and try to understand exactly what he is trying to accomplish. Imagine how all of the parts could possibly fit together (even if they seem unrelated). Assume that the author's intentions are logical. Withhold evaluation and see the absolute best in the text so that you can write fair and nonevaluative summaries. There's plenty of time to discount ideas, reject messages, and tear apart evidence in assignments that call for analysis or response. But, when summarizing, we try to be nonjudgmental and play the role of an objective reporter. To do that successfully, we follow these steps:

1. **Read the text** carefully, paying attention to the genre of the original and how it's organized. For example, if you're summarizing a research article and you know how that genre is typically organized (described in Appendix B), you know where to find the main claims and support. Reading is the most important step because if we don't understand what we read, we can't summarize it well.

2. **Create a "reverse outline," or schematic, of the text's layout**. This technique comes in handy whenever you're reading complicated arguments, and even when you're revising your own writing. To compose a reverse outline, first write down the main claim of each paragraph, either in the margins of the text or on a separate sheet of paper. You might be able to find a topic sentence, or you might need to express the main ideas in your own words; aim for one phrase or short sentence per paragraph. Forcing yourself to identify each paragraph's main idea helps you break down a complex argument and recognize its many parts. Then, write those points in outline form so that you can see the progression of the ideas on a single page, if possible.
3. **Select the most relevant points**. Study the reverse outline to identify the most central ideas—the blueprint of the text—which someone who hasn't read the source would need to know in order to grasp the overall argument. Don't get bogged down in the supporting details, examples, and evidence. Also, briefly **include other rhetorical elements that would help your reader understand your source's rhetorical situation**, such as the author, intended audience, purpose, genre, and publication context. (Use the first paragraph of our sample rhetorical analysis on pp. 549–55 as a guide.)
4. **Write a summary** that aims to be unbiased, clear, and proportionally accurate but shorter than the actual text. The first time you write the summary, it might still be pretty long. Don't worry about that; you can condense it further later. Just try to clearly convey all of the text's main points.
5. **Revise the summary** to make it even shorter. Now's the time to make the most brutal cuts. Figure out what deserves to be there and what can be left out. Beware also of any inaccuracies or judgmental language, and note any paraphrases or quotations that need citations.

TRY THIS ➤ Practice Summarizing

For this exercise, practice reading and summarizing the scholarly article "A Wandering Mind Is an Unhappy Mind" by Matthew A. Killingsworth and Daniel T. Gilbert (printed on pp. 435–40). The essay contains approximately 900 words. Use the techniques we've covered so far, and track your word count. Maximum words = 150, or about 15% of the original. Then, in class, compare your summaries with your peers: How similar are they? Which parts are different? How did you decide which details to include and which ones to omit? If you included any paraphrases or quotations, how did you decide which ones to use?

After comparing your notes with classmates, condense your summary even further. Try summarizing the essential contents of the article in 100 words or less.

Paraphrasing

Paraphrasing is a difficult skill for apprentice scholars to master. To paraphrase effectively, you must closely read and fully understand your source, and you must practice, using the techniques we outline in this chapter. Before we describe techniques for paraphrasing, let's look at some examples of inappropriate paraphrases and then more sufficient changes. Here's an example of paraphrases using an excerpt from later in this chapter. Compare the original text with the inappropriate paraphrase, noticing the similar—and even exact—phrasing and syntax (word order).

- **Original quotation:** "This may seem odd, but schools typically do not allow students to recycle papers. For example, you probably cannot dust off a paper you wrote in high school—however long ago that was—for use in a college class."

- **Inappropriate paraphrase:** It might seem weird, but schools typically prohibit students from reusing papers. You cannot hand in an old paper from high school in your college class.

Notice how the inappropriate paraphrase changes a few words but retains nearly the same sentence structure as the original? Simply exchanging synonyms does not make the paraphrase appropriate. The writer has just replaced a few terms and copied the syntax. Even with an accompanying citation, most colleges consider this a kind of plagiarism. Writing scholar Rebecca Moore Howard coined the term "patch-writing" to describe this "failed" paraphrasing, or what many honor codes call insufficient paraphrasing—source material that is neither quoted nor adequately rephrased. Regardless of what an honor code says, patch-writing is a poor use of source text because it does not indicate that the writer has deeply processed or even understands the source. Students use patch-writing more often when they are not familiar with the content or language of a source, so be sure to invest adequate time practicing the reading strategies from Chapter 2.

Now compare the inappropriate paraphrasing with the following two examples of proper paraphrases:

- **Proper paraphrase:** According to Schick and Schubert, colleges may consider resubmitting old assignments to be a kind of plagiarism (65).
- **Proper paraphrase with quotation:** Writing scholars Schick and Schubert warn students not to "recycle papers" from high school for college classes (65).

Notice how these versions are significantly different from the original? They reframe the original, using both different words and different sentence structure to express the same idea. They also contain needed citations, which we'll explain later.

How Do We Paraphrase?

How do we paraphrase appropriately, without running the risk of plagiarism (stealing another person's words or ideas)? The key is to represent the source closely without using the author's style or phrasing. To do so, follow these steps:

1. **Read carefully** the paragraph or sentence that you want to paraphrase.
2. **Think about what it's saying.** Mull it over. Chat with yourself about the ideas. (Experienced scholars talk to themselves all the time.)
3. **Rewrite the gist of what the source says**, without looking at the original paragraph or sentence. Resist the temptation to glance at the author's exact wording; otherwise, you might be influenced by the author's style and find it difficult to rephrase. The only reason to return to the original is to get a clearer grasp of the content. If you review the original, then repeat Step 2 before trying to write again.
4. **Double-check the original** to ensure your paraphrase is accurate but significantly different from the original—in terms of sentence structure, word choice, tone, and possibly even length.
5. **Cite the author** with an in-text citation or use an attributive tag (see p. 27). We will talk more about citation styles and practices, along with quotation techniques, later in this chapter.

Following these steps should help you maintain integrity when incorporating other people's words and ideas into your own writing, which is the focus of the next section.

TRY THIS ➤ Evaluate Paraphrases

For this exercise, compare the original quotations from "A Wandering Mind Is an Unhappy Mind" with the accompanying, attempted paraphrases. Are the paraphrases appropriate or not? Why?

1. **Original quotation:** "Many philosophical and religious traditions teach that happiness is to be found by living in the moment, and practitioners are trained to resist mind wandering and 'to be here now.' These traditions suggest that a wandering mind is an unhappy mind. Are they right?"

   Attempted paraphrase: Killingsworth and Gilbert question whether people should limit their tendency to daydream. They suggest mind-wandering may be harmful if scholars are correct that people are most content when they are fully present, living one moment at a time.
2. **Original quotation:** "In conclusion, a human mind is a wandering mind, and a wandering mind is an unhappy mind. The ability to think about what is not happening is a cognitive achievement that comes at an emotional cost."

   Attempted paraphrase: Killingsworth and Gilbert conclude by saying that a wandering mind is an unhappy mind. Although humans have a natural ability to think about the future, this ability may come at a high price.
3. **Original quotation:** "We solved this problem by developing a Web application for the iPhone (Apple Incorporated, Cupertino, California), which we used to create an unusually large database of real-time reports of thoughts, feelings, and actions of a broad range of people as they went about their daily activities."

   Attempted paraphrase: Killingsworth and Gilbert rectified this issue by creating an iPhone app, which they utilized to compile an uncommonly huge database of live reports of people's ideas, sentiments, and behaviors as they experienced their daily lives.

Revise any of the above paraphrases that are inappropriate, and then compare versions with a classmate.

Quoting and Integrating Sources

Most scholarly writing, including the kinds of assignments you're likely to encounter in college, uses published sources to support arguments.

Every time you include a summary or paraphrase or quotation, you might think of that source as an expert witness in a trial. As the trial lawyer, you might borrow the expertise and credibility of a scientist, for example, to validate or refute DNA evidence. Then you'll have a conversation with that source—and with your audience—about what that evidence means.

Unless your readers, the "jury," already know your source (if he's Einstein or Shakespeare, they might know him already), then they'll expect you to introduce your "expert witness" and explain why we should trust him. One of the best places to learn how to do this in nonscholarly writing is to study newspaper reporting.

Newspaper reporters seamlessly integrate other people's words into their articles, as Alan Schwarz does in his *New York Times* article "Attention Disorder or Not, Pills to Help in School" (Oct. 9, 2012):

> [S]ome experts note that as wealthy students abuse stimulants to raise already-good grades in colleges and high schools, the medications are being used on low-income elementary school children with faltering grades and parents eager to see them succeed.
>
> "We as a society have been unwilling to invest in very effective nonpharmaceutical interventions for these children and their families," said Dr. Ramesh Raghavan, a child mental-health services researcher at Washington University in St. Louis and an expert in prescription drug use among low-income children. "We are effectively forcing local community psychiatrists to use the only tool at their disposal, which is psychotropic medications."
>
> Dr. Nancy Rappaport, a child psychiatrist in Cambridge, Mass., who works primarily with lower-income children and their schools,

> added: "We are seeing this more and more. We are using a chemical straitjacket instead of doing things that are just as important to also do, sometimes more."

Reporters don't just assume that readers intuitively know who their sources are, so they don't just insert a quote without any warning or description of the source's identity. Otherwise, readers might be confused. They need to know the identity of the source and how the source will contribute to the reporter's story. So it's important for writers to *frame* their quotations with:

1. **An introduction**: usually an "attributive tag" (what some scholars call a "signal phrase") that clarifies who's speaking, such as "According to . . ." or "The author states . . ."
2. **An explanation** of why the source is relevant to the story

Newspaper reporters can model the basics of creating attributive tags, but they don't show us how to *converse with* sources as deeply as scholars do. As you notice in the example above, the reporter relies more heavily on the source to present information than is typical in scholarly writing. If you deleted the quotations from this excerpt, there would hardly be any content left. You can't really get away with that as a student because, as we keep saying, professors are typically more interested to hear what *you* think than what your sources say. Write like an apprentice scholar, not a reporter. In the next section, we'll describe how to create a conversation with your sources.

TRY THIS ➤ Study How Popular Publications Introduce Sources

For this exercise, collect several examples of popular sources (newspapers, magazines, etc.) and study how the authors introduce their sources. Create a list of rules or techniques that authors use.

How to Create a Conversation

When we build sources into arguments, we not only clarify who our sources are, but we also tell readers:

- Why a quotation is there
- What it means
- How it's related to, or supports, our argument

We don't expect our readers to figure this stuff out through ESP. For one thing, readers could misunderstand or misinterpret quotations. More important, readers wouldn't know what *we thought about* the quotation. We want to involve our sources and our readers in a conversation. When we introduce and elaborate on sources, we help readers clearly "hear" our sources' messages. These techniques amplify and connect sources to our argument, like plugging an electric guitar into a 50-watt amplifier. Without such wired connection, our source may be muffled or inaudible.

Instead of quoting a source and immediately moving on, we elaborate on sources in the following ways:

- **Interpret the source.** Unless a quotation's message is blatantly obvious, we typically offer some kind of explanation. Readers usually need help interpreting a quotation because we've taken it out of its original context. Especially when there's unfamiliar vocabulary or dense information, we translate the source's ideas into more accessible language. We add explanations directly after each quotation, such as:
    - "This passage suggests that . . ."
    - "In other words, . . ."
    - "Here, the writer explains that . . ."
- **Explain how the quotation relates to our argument.** Although the relationship between a quotation and our ideas might seem clear, readers often need us to highlight that

connection. We link a quotation to our paragraph's central point by telling readers exactly *why* and *how* the source is relevant. Quotations can serve as evidence that supports our point when we add commentary like:
  - "Dr. X illustrates my point exactly: . . ."
  - "The author's views are relevant because they show that . . ."
  - "All of this relates to my point that . . ."
- **Tell readers what makes the quotation significant.** Because we only quote a source when it's necessary, we should know why a quotation is important. But readers need to understand the implications, too. They need to know what is meaningful about a quotation—why it matters—and what the consequences of its ideas are. To shed light on a quotation's implications, we say:
  - "The author's ideas have important consequences, mainly that . . ."
  - "If we extend the scholar's argument, we can see that . . ."
  - "What makes this point particularly __________________ (urgent, puzzling, thought provoking, valid, etc.) is . . ."
- **Consider ways to make a source our own.** Link a source to our argument by providing our own unique example, analogy, or related experience to illustrate the idea, like this:
  - "My own learning process matches the theories proposed by John Dewey in his book, *Experience and Education*. For example . . ."
  - "Nancy Sommers says that the writing process is like a 'seed' (384). A more fitting metaphor to describe my writing process would be . . ."

These strategies allow us to talk alongside our sources, rather than expecting them to speak *for* us. We can maintain ownership of the argument by preventing our sources from overpowering our own voice. We also gain some points with our readers—especially with professors—when we show off our analytical abilities and critical thinking skills.

TRY THIS ➤ Integrate Sources More Fully

For this exercise, review a manuscript that you're currently drafting or that you recently composed and look for places where you can introduce and elaborate on your sources more fully. Use the model phrases you learned to introduce quotations and explain, interpret, and/or contextualize your sources' arguments.

Citing Sources

While integrating other writers' words and ideas into our own writing, we are careful to mark those contributions and leave a trail back to our sources. That's what citation is all about: **Scholars value accurate citations because they illuminate the genealogy of our work**. Missing or incorrect citations can hinder other scholars' efforts to evaluate the credibility of an argument or to relocate a source.

However, as important as citations may be for scholars who publish their research, experienced writers treat citations like they treat grammar and punctuation—as local, later order concerns that we described on p. 26—and you should, too. As an apprentice scholar, your writing will develop more quickly if you concentrate *first* on selecting good sources, analyzing and evaluating their content, and responsibly integrating their words and ideas into your own writing.

How Do We Know When We Need to Cite Something?

Here's the easy answer:

- **Always cite quotations and paraphrases**, and include the page number, if available.

- **Cite summaries, too.** If you're summarizing part of a source, include the appropriate page numbers. When summarizing an entire source, page numbers are not necessary.
- **Cite statistics, dates, and other details** that are not common knowledge.

Now, here's where it gets more complex: what exactly *is* "common knowledge"? We don't need to cite things that everyone already knows, right? As with most things in writing, that depends.

Before the Internet, teachers often told students that if you could find the same information in some arbitrary number of sources (three or five or however many different places), then you could consider that information "common knowledge," so you wouldn't need a citation. This general rule doesn't work so well anymore for two reasons.

First, the number of times information gets published may or may not indicate anything about it being commonly known. Websites often "borrow" information and text from each other without attribution. (Please don't follow their example.) Finding an urban legend repeated on 15 different websites doesn't make it true *or* common knowledge. Just because the Internet operates as a public domain for everyone's benefit does not exempt scholars from citing what we find there, either.

Secondly, while the five-sources-equals-common-knowledge rule may have helped students before the Internet, the rule doesn't really get at the heart of the matter, which isn't really whether we need a citation but rather *When do we need to use a source to verify information in our arguments?*

The answer, of course, depends on your topic and audience: *How confident are you that your audience already knows what you're talking about?* For example, you can probably be confident that an audience educated in a US high school already knows what happened on July 4, 1776. But even a college-educated US audience would expect a citation if you were discussing the events of October 29, 1923 (the date when, according to Wikipedia, the modern Republic of Turkey was established). You can probably find the details of Turkey's history in hundreds of books, articles, and websites, but if your audience doesn't already know it—and *you* didn't before reading your sources—then they'll expect to see where you got your information. Otherwise, they just might not believe you.

Citation Fundamentals

Many academic disciplines (such as history, engineering, or sociology) or clusters of disciplines (such as humanities, sciences, or social sciences) have created consistent guidelines for how to cite sources. Disciplines publish their "citation styles" so that everyone in their field can use a consistent, recognizable citation format. For example, humanities scholars such as literary and language specialists often use Modern Language Association's (MLA) *Handbook for Writers of Research Papers*. Social scientists (including psychology, business, education, and health sciences) typically use the *Publication Manual of the American Psychological Association* (APA). As an apprentice scholar, you will most commonly use MLA and APA styles. However, you may also encounter more specialized citation styles used by historians, journalists, lawyers, mathematicians, engineers, or other professionals.

Because there are so many different citation styles, we recommend consulting handbooks and online resources when formatting citations. However, before consulting these resources, it's helpful to know about the two main ways that scholars cite or "document" their sources: bibliographic and in-text citations.

Bibliographic citations appear at the end of a scholarly article or paper as a list of "References" or "Works Cited" or as a "Bibliography." A bibliographic citation includes everything that a reader would need to know to find the exact source that you used. Creating this list of bibliographic citations will be much easier if you collect the basic information you need whenever you encounter a new source: author, title, and publication information (when, where, and who published the source). If you remember to collect these basic elements as you conduct your research, you'll have whatever information you need to create your bibliography later. Bottom line: **Keep track of whatever details you or your reader would need to retrace your steps to find each source again**.

Brief in-text citations appear right next to where you summarize, paraphrase, or quote from your source. In-text citations point readers toward a specific source and, when needed, a specific place (page or pages) in that source.

So Many Styles . . .

Try to remember the main elements of a citation, but don't try to memorize the finer points of citation formatting. If you need to collect many sources, you might consider using an automatic formatting tool like RefWorks or EndNote. When you need to verify accuracy or format your citations manually, consult library resources, such as the MLA and APA style manuals, or a reputable writing center website, like the Purdue University Online Writing Lab (OWL).

Write with Integrity

Anyone who's been interviewed by a newspaper or television reporter knows what it's like to have his words taken out of context or used to prove a point that he really didn't intend to make. Even if reporters try to use their sources responsibly, when they distill a long interview down to a pithy sound bite, the person being interviewed can feel cheated.

Scholars maintain their integrity by making a good faith effort not to "cheat" the authors whose words and ideas they borrow. That's why we work so diligently—using the techniques for careful reading and analysis that we've discussed in this book—to fully understand our sources' content, intended purpose, and persuasive strategies *before* we critique them, disagree with them, or use them to support our own arguments.

As a community of scholars, we must be able to trust each other's work and trust that our colleagues will use our work responsibly. That's where the idea of plagiarism comes from. Yes, plagiarism is a kind of stealing (in fact, the word "plagiarism" comes from the Latin term for "kidnapping"). But more important, plagiarism violates the trust of the scholarly community. How can we build on each other's discoveries if we cannot trust the integrity of the work done to produce and communicate those discoveries?

Because we never know how our work will influence others, we take scholarly integrity very seriously. The results of "cheating" sometimes have obvious and immediate consequences. Imagine, for example, the potential health and safety risks caused by a medical researcher who takes shortcuts in testing a new drug. And think of all the previous research on which that medical innovation depended. Faulty research by a previous biologist or chemist or physicist might also have indirectly tainted the development of the new drug.

The credibility and integrity of our scholarly work is therefore *networked* and *interdependent*, which is why we cite our sources. We didn't design citation styles just to torture scholarly apprentices. Our specialized referencing systems (MLA and APA, for example) enable us to exhibit scholarly genealogies for our discoveries. Scholars who review our work can judge its credibility, in part, by scrutinizing the lineage of our work, which we present to readers through citations and bibliographies. So even though we don't expect you, as a scholarly apprentice, to begin "expanding the bounds of human understanding" just yet, we do expect you to acknowledge your sources from the beginning.

So far, we've been justifying why scholars cite their sources. The last, and perhaps most obvious rule of writing with integrity is simply that you do the work yourself and don't copy from other writers. Learning requires practice. **Copying from others denies you the opportunity to learn.**

Plagiarism

Most schools have formal honor codes that define various kinds of cheating. The term "plagiarism" typically means copying someone else's words or ideas without giving attribution, or explicit acknowledgment. Buying a paper off the Web or copying someone else's writing is deemed the most serious of offenses and often carries the strictest penalties, such as failing the assignment or the course, or even expulsion from school.

You will also get into trouble for copying a passage from a source without quoting it. Remember to mark all quotations and provide proper citations as we described earlier.

Students are often less familiar with other kinds of honor code violations, which may include unauthorized collaboration and recycled writing.

Unauthorized Collaboration

Scholars rarely write alone. They usually discuss their ideas with others and ask colleagues to critique their writing. You should do the same whenever possible, with one caveat. **Always ask your instructor, in advance, about what kinds of collaboration she allows.**

Most professors, most of the time, will appreciate that you're using every available (ethical) means to improve your writing. However, there may be occasions when you'll be expected to complete your work alone to demonstrate your own, individual learning. Seeking help from writing center tutors is usually acceptable, but to be safe, consider asking your professor first.

Recycled Writing

This may seem odd, but schools typically do not allow students to recycle papers. For example, you probably cannot dust off a paper you wrote in high school—however long ago that was—for use in a college class. This rule may not seem fair (after all, the paper is your intellectual "property," so you're not really stealing someone else's work), but handing in the same paper twice violates the primary purpose of academic integrity policies: **You can't learn something new if you don't do the work.**

If you want to reuse some words or ideas from a previous paper, ask your professor for guidance. He can probably help you think of ways to expand on your previous work. Scholars do this all the time as part of an evolving "research agenda," when they develop ideas over a series of research projects and publications. Tough questions and problems often take years to resolve.

Tips for Avoiding Plagiarism

- **As you read, pay careful attention to how writers use their sources.** Practice by imitating various styles. More skill with using sources will increase your confidence and lower the risk of plagiarism.
- **Maintain careful notes as you read and conduct research.** When taking notes, mark quotations with quotation marks, and keep track of page numbers and which material comes from which source.
- **Don't be tempted to write your paper and *then* go back to fill in the citations.** Doing so will only generate more work

(retracing your research steps) and increase the risk of inadvertent plagiarism.

- **Don't procrastinate.** Looming deadlines cause anxiety that can cloud judgment. Don't be tempted to take shortcuts, and don't fool yourself into thinking that you write best under pressure. If, for some reason, you cannot complete your work on time, discuss your situation with your professor. Be honest, don't make excuses, and know that the sun will rise again tomorrow.
- **Get to know your honor code** so you'll know how your school handles academic integrity. Ask questions when in doubt. Ignorance of the rules is typically not an excuse for breaking them.

TRY THIS ➤ Investigate the Honor Code

For this exercise, find and review your school's policies for academic integrity. Then, answer the following questions:

- How does your school's policy compare to the honor codes you encountered in schools you attended previously?
- Are there any inconsistencies between your honor code and the guidelines we provided in this chapter?
- What are the implications or applications of academic integrity policies outside of school?

So What?

We create arguments from sources by responsibly borrowing and building on the words and thoughts of other scholars. When in doubt, cite what's not already in your head. You won't be accused of plagiarism for citing too much. And remember, your writing should demonstrate *your* thinking. Use sources to support your ideas; don't let them dominate your writing.

Now that you know something about how scholars read, write, and use sources, you're ready to learn more about *argument*: the essential tool that scholars use to explain their ideas. In the next chapter, we introduce the ways that arguments work in college and in life. We explain how arguments grow out of problems and controversies, and how they use research and evidence to answer significant questions. We describe how to locate weak spots and assumptions in arguments in order to make a compelling case. And we reveal how effective arguments are built on a strong basis of agreement with shared knowledge, values, and beliefs. This overview will give you a strong foundation for creating arguments that matter—those that answer the important *so what?* question, connect with audiences, and improve our understanding of the world.

What's Next

Take what you've learned in this chapter and respond to the following prompts.

1. **Using sources in scholarly and nonacademic work.** Find a scholarly journal article in your field on a subject that interests you, and investigate how the author uses sources. In three different colors, highlight quotations, paraphrases, and summaries. Then, find a magazine or newspaper article that also uses outside sources. Use the same colors to highlight the different ways the author uses sources. After you finish color-coding the articles, estimate the percentages and create a pie chart or other graphic to show your results. Compare your results with a classmate and reflect on the following:
   - How much does each author use each technique?
   - How much of the article is the author's argument?
   - How do the scholarly arguments use sources differently than the nonacademic ones?

2. **Citation systems.** Look up the citation system that your discipline uses and practice formatting a few different bibliographic citations.

For variety, format a book, a scholarly article, and a credible website. Then, compare your citations with a few classmates:

- What differences do you notice among styles?
- What disciplinary values might influence these different details, such as the date placement?

3. **Trace a scholarly genealogy.** Killingsworth and Gilbert credit a number of sources in their bibliography on which they built their research—their scholarly ancestors, so to speak. If you can access the online version of the article via your library's website, their citations are hyperlinked to the sources. Also on the website is a listing of subsequent research that grew out of Killingsworth and Gilbert's research—their scholarly descendants.

   Read one of the subsequent articles (scholarly descendants) listed on the website under the heading "This Article Has Been Cited by Other Articles." (If you can't access their article online, you can search Google Scholar for links to sources that cite the article.) Consider how the article builds off of Killingsworth and Gilbert's research, and reflect on the following:

   - Where in the article do the authors cite Killingsworth and Gilbert?
   - How is the article related to "A Wandering Mind Is an Unhappy Mind"?
   - Can you imagine how Killingsworth and Gilbert's article might have been an inspiration for this article?

   Then, write a one-page summary of the article, describing how it continues the scholarly conversation. Share your summaries in class to discuss the different threads that Killingsworth and Gilbert's "scholarly descendants" take up. If you're interested in pursuing this further, read one of Killingsworth and Gilbert's "scholarly ancestors" to see how their work influenced "A Wandering Mind Is an Unhappy Mind."

CHAPTER four

How Do Arguments Work

chapter checklist

- How do people use arguments in school and beyond?
- What are the elements of arguments, and how do we build them?
- How do we locate underlying assumptions, gaps, and weak spots?
- How does investigation inspire arguments?

When you hear the term "argument," you might first think about kids squabbling over whose turn it is to sit in the front seat of the car, or you might imagine you and your parents fighting over how late you can stay out. "Argument" may also conjure visions of television lawyers presenting their case before a jury, or senators debating over the particulars of a new energy regulation. For us, the term "argument" signifies a tool that helps us explain *what* we think and *why* we think so. A thesis states what we think, and the rest of the argument shows why. Arguments influence our audiences' knowledge, beliefs, or actions, and they can also clarify or enhance our own thinking. Scholars use argument to justify their discoveries.

Effective arguments enact significant purposes. They are a means of doing work in the world, not a process of fighting or persuading others that we're right. Compelling arguments respond to questions or problems that seem urgent, controversial, or significant to writers and their audiences. They help us create and communicate answers and solutions, and they influence us to modify what (or how) we know, believe, think, or act.

Arguments use different structures, depending on their purposes, but they typically include four main elements: a claim, support, rationale, and some explanation of why the argument matters. Some forms of argument are easy to spot, such as editorials, proposals, and advertisements. However, other forms may not appear argumentative, even though they contain common elements of argument. Let's look at some examples in different situations that you might not immediately recognize as arguments.

What Does Argument Look Like in Different Contexts?

Arguments originate from a gap or imperfection, an unknown answer, or an unsolved problem—an inspiration that matters to the writer. The problem could be as simple as an employee facing financial difficulty or as complicated as the federal deficit. We design arguments that respond to these practical or theoretical controversies.

Let's consider some examples from school and the world beyond that illustrate how arguments can be used to achieve various purposes.

- **Scholars** use arguments to explain and improve our world. In recent years, for example, increased occurrences of school shootings in the United States have led us to ask why these tragedies *occur*, what *causes* people to do such terrible things, and what might be *done* to prevent future violence. Researchers in psychology, sociology, criminal justice, and other disciplines conduct investigations and build arguments to help us understand and address problems like these.

- **Government and military intelligence experts** use arguments to inform politicians. Analysts piece together information from limited or incomplete sources, compare different versions of what might be happening, make judgments, and draw conclusions about what they think. Their answers help justify foreign policy actions of all kinds.
- **Criminal trial lawyers** use arguments to establish guilt or innocence. Juries decide questions of guilt or innocence based on the cases presented by prosecution and defense attorneys in the courtroom. The justice system seeks the truth about the case, but regardless of what actually happened, the verdict determines a defendant's fate.
- **Scientists** discover evidence through research, which others use to build compelling cases for new laws or regulations. For instance, in the 1920s, a German scientist posed the research question: What diseases might be linked to cigarette smoking? Other scientists conducted follow-up research and gathered mounting evidence about the dangers of smoking, which eventually led governments to require health warnings on cigarette packaging.

These examples illustrate a defining feature of arguments: All arguments—whether they intend to solve practical problems or simply deepen our understanding of an issue—**begin with a question or uncertainty and use some method of investigation and case building to arrive at a conclusion**. That is, honest jurors, politicians, and scholars examine the evidence *before* drawing conclusions.

Creating strong arguments requires careful thinking and consideration of others. Arguments have serious implications when they influence decisions that affect people. In government, arguments can determine whether programs receive funding or soldiers go to war. A trial can determine a defendant's freedom or death. Jumping to conclusions can lead to bad decisions that harm others, which is why ethical writers and readers don't take shortcuts.

CONSIDER THIS ➤ Starting with Questions

For this reflection, consider the following: we believe the scholarly approach of case building increases the chances of finding the truth or the best decision/answer possible. However, this process (starting with a question and withholding judgment until investigation is complete) might be different from how you have been taught to develop arguments:

- When you write, when do you come up with a thesis?
- When were you taught to consult sources?
- How do you think the writing process might affect scholars' ability to discover accurate information, to think objectively, and to build ethical arguments?

Thinking through these questions can make you more aware of your writing habits and can help you develop new and better practices. Reflecting on your writing process can also give you insight into potential problems in your approach. For instance, if you always look for sources after you develop a thesis, you might overlook compelling evidence that contradicts your argument.

What about Specialized Scholarly Arguments?

Right about now, you might be thinking that some scholarly arguments you've read or heard about don't seem to have purposes that are obviously significant, practical, or urgent. In the examples we listed earlier, the issues are clearly important to the world. In contrast, scholars often work in such narrow specializations that their arguments may seem insignificant or impractical to people outside their scholarly community. However, such work is significant and compelling to those writers and their audiences. In fact, a scholarly community signals the importance of such work by publishing arguments for everyone to hear.

Of course, scholars don't always address problems of great urgency or practical significance, but even when their work is theoretical or esoteric, their arguments respond to questions or problems that matter to them and to their audience. For example, scholars might:

- Discover a disciplinary question that puzzles them
- Feel aggravated by a problem in their teaching
- Vehemently disagree with another scholar's findings
- Notice something new that contradicts previous experience

Such topics compel scholars to investigate and to write arguments for others in their field to consider and build on. Some of these arguments may ultimately influence people outside of academia, while others might more immediately affect specific disciplinary fields.

Here are some specific examples of arguments that scholars make to each other:

- A literary scholar, on the basis of textual evidence, biographical information about an author, and historical information about the time and place of a publication, argues for a new interpretation of a famous novel.
- An education scholar, using theories about learning and results of experimental teaching, argues for a new method of effective instruction.
- A nursing scholar synthesizes previous studies to argue for standardizing a "best practice" medical technique.

Apprentice scholars can feel more motivated and be more successful when they identify similar gaps and imperfections. If you can find a question or problem that really interests you—something you want to figure out—you can get a taste for what it's like to solve a scholarly puzzle. The next few chapters explain how to discover arguments that ignite your curiosity. Finding a *purpose* to write (beyond completing the assignment) will help you develop as a scholar. It might even feel less like practice and more like something that matters.

How Do Scholars Create Arguments?

Now that you know what scholarly arguments are, you might be wondering how scholars develop an idea. Experienced scholars tend to follow a process that looks like this:

1. **Begin with a very specific problem or question** within your discipline that interests you.
2. **Review scholarly publications** to make sure that your question is worth asking or that your problem still needs solving, so that fellow scholars won't be wondering *so what?*
3. **Design and conduct some kind of investigation** to solve the problem or answer the question, such as conducting an interview or distributing surveys. Chapter 6 includes additional guidelines for conducting original research.
4. **Report results of the research**, in the form of an argument, to colleagues in your discipline via a scholarly conference presentation and/or publication.

Because scholars create arguments *from* previous scholarship, original data, practical experience, and other inspirations, **writing typically follows research** for experienced scholars. However, here's a little secret: experienced scholars often dread writing as much as students do. Most scholars find answering questions and solving problems more stimulating than writing papers about what they discover. Once they've answered their question, scholars can get bored and just want to move on to the next problem. The last thing they want to do is worry about APA citation styles and manuscript formatting, but they know they have to publish their work so others can use it—and they understand that they must present their work in certain established forms (genres and styles) that their readers recognize and value.

Apprentices can begin to practice scholarly writing by investigating problems and questions through the work that others have done. Often the problems will be assigned by instructors who (a) already know the key issues and background well and (b) can provide relevant sources through course readings.

Other times, you can choose your own questions and engage in what we call "library research." Rather than collecting and analyzing raw data (a "primary" source), scholarly apprentices mostly use information that has already been examined and reported by others ("secondary" or "library" sources). As you mature as a scholar, you might even conduct original experiments or study historical artifacts or archives as primary source materials.

Argument as Investigation and Case Building

As you may recall from the first chapter, scholars use arguments to seek truth and justify discoveries that result from careful investigation. This means that scholars often don't know their thesis when they begin but rather *discover* it through investigation and research.

Imagine an archaeologist who unearths some petrified bones. She might suspect that the bones belong to a dinosaur, but she must continue digging, analyzing, and assembling the skeleton to discover the animal's identity. If you've seen a dinosaur skeleton in a museum, you probably noticed plastic "bones" and wires that the archaeologists added to complete the puzzle and hold everything together. Writing an argument requires a similar process of finding sources and evidence and assembling them to create a coherent message.

Sometimes, this process takes decades. Consider, for example, the smoking example that we cite earlier in the chapter. When scientists initially questioned the health effects of cigarette smoking, they began

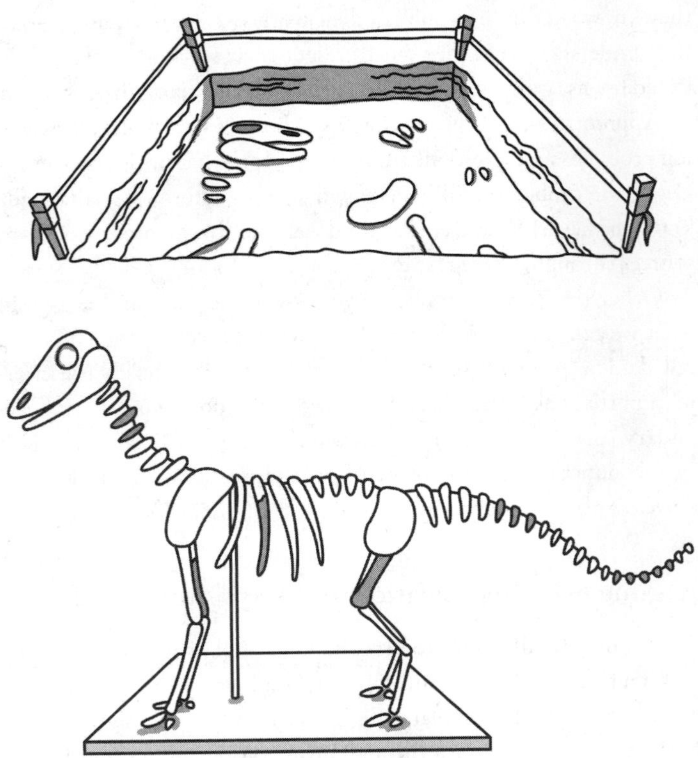

their research process with a question or a hypothesis; they suspected that smoking might not be good for us. *After all,* they thought, *you're inhaling smoke.*

By investigating piles of medical records and discovering that many people suffering from lung cancer were, indeed, heavy smokers, scientists began to assemble compelling evidence to build a case against smoking. As evidence of cigarettes' danger mounted, the US government's warnings (or arguments) grew proportionally stronger, from a statement in 1966 that sounded more like opinion ("Cigarette smoking may be hazardous to your health") to statements of fact like ones we see now ("Smoking causes lung cancer, heart disease, emphysema, and may complicate pregnancy").

In other words, the thesis intensified as the evidence became stronger: "We *suspect* this might be hazardous," then "We *think* this is dangerous," and finally "We *know* that cigarettes can kill you!" The thesis, which originated in a question, became more "certain" and convincing as the support accumulated.

Implications and Applications

The smoking example demonstrates how arguments can gradually change the way we think about issues over time. Much of what we know, think, and believe evolves through investigation, new experiences, and persuasive arguments.

If you don't think that arguments can influence what we know, think, and believe, consider the effects of:

- Arguments made by civil rights leaders who changed how we think about equality
- Arguments made by feminists who influenced the way American families function
- Arguments made by activists who demanded health care reform
- Arguments made by respected mentors who inspired you to question a previously held opinion

These examples illustrate how arguments can have tangible effects on our daily lives. Can you think of more examples of arguments that have influenced what you know and how you live?

Indeed, the best arguments are the ones that have important *implications* and *applications*—consequences or effects that answer the *so what?* question. For instance, arguments can inspire readers to reconsider their position, to modify their behavior, or to open themselves up to another possibility. Or arguments can evoke a change in the writer himself: for example, when he develops a deeper understanding of an issue or problem, when he encounters new viewpoints, or when he experiences the peace of mind that comes from validating his beliefs and values.

As with the writer's purpose or inspiration, implications can be stated explicitly or inferred by the reader. Sometimes we tell audiences how and why our arguments matter so they won't miss the impact. Research articles often begin with a section that contextualizes the study's significance (called a Research or Literature Review) and conclude with a section that discusses the larger implications of the research findings. Whether or not we tell our readers outright how and why our arguments matter, we at least hint at some implications so they're not left to wonder, *so what?*

Compelling arguments have significant implications that not only change what audiences think but also inspire follow-up questions and arguments. In this way, the process is circular. For example, we might read a *Science* magazine article that concludes that we are less happy when our minds wander. One implication of this argument might be that we should pay more attention to what we're doing while we're doing it. Discovering this might lead us to ask, "What techniques can we use to quiet our minds?" Now, we have some inspiration for research that might ultimately lead to an argument about the benefits of meditation. See how the process works?

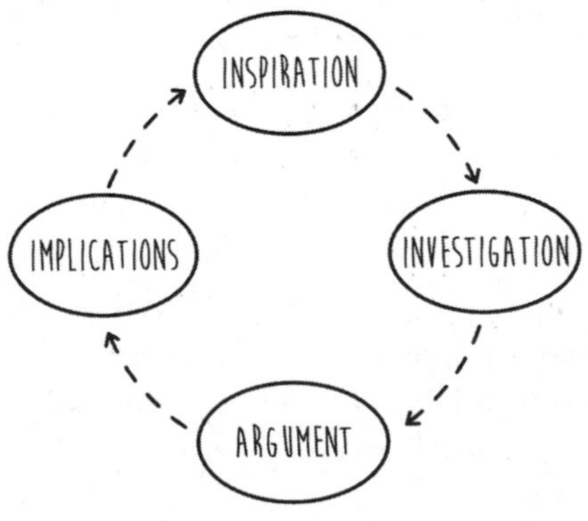

TRY THIS ➤ Use Precise Vocabulary

For this exercise, take a break from the chapter's content to examine and experiment with some language choices that writers make.

We have attempted to write this book in an engaging, straightforward, and informal style. That includes not overwhelming readers with technical jargon or unnecessarily complicated words. However, you'll notice that we occasionally choose less familiar terms to express precise meaning. (On p. 73, for example, we described some scholarly work as "esoteric.")

Part of what makes language marvelous—and writing potentially fun—is gathering a deep pool of available vocabulary. Whenever you read, keep a dictionary or smart phone app handy so you can acquire new words for your own use.

Beware, though. Scholars who use big words just to sound smart do no favors for themselves or their readers. If we need a complex word to convey a complex idea, that's fine, but often we don't.

Effective writing is deliberate and precise—not overcomplicated.

What do you think of our choice to use "esoteric"? What other words or ways of expressing this idea would work as well or better? To reflect on the effects of using sophisticated vocabulary, experiment with the following:

1. Write a simple sentence.
2. Consult the thesaurus to rewrite the sentence with more sophisticated words.
3. Revise the sentence to strike a tasteful balance between sophistication and clarity. Then, compare with a peer and explain your word choices.

How Do We Build Arguments?

Imagine an argument as a bridge between a writer and reader. The **thesis** is the roadway, built by investigation and thinking. The road will not stand alone without displaying our investigation and thinking for readers to scrutinize. We must build **supports** to hold the road up and **rationales** to link everything together.

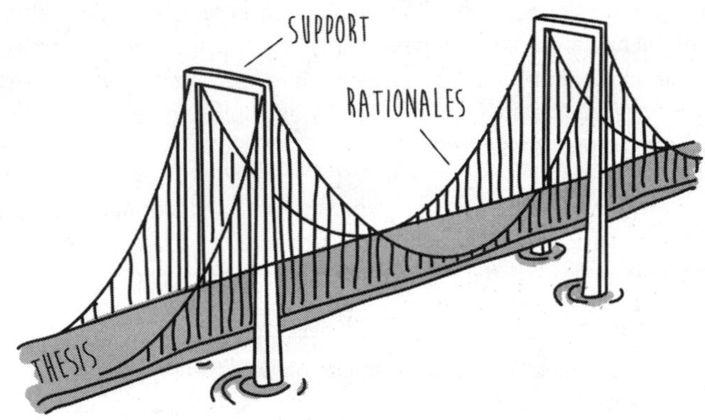

The thesis is our argument's central **claim**, a debatable or controversial idea that we're proposing to our audience. A thesis can be stated explicitly or implied. Although it often appears in the beginning of an argument, sometimes we state our thesis most clearly in the conclusion, because that's what it really is: the conclusion or result of our investigation and thinking. Sometimes the thesis can be more like a hypothesis (used in experimental or scientific method), when it's a tentative thesis that needs to be tested and validated through investigation and argumentation.

Supporting Claims

Because claims are controversial or open to question, we pair them with some kind of support that our audience will trust. The basic structure looks like this: [Claim] because [support]. For example,

Claim: You should keep reading BECAUSE
Support: this chapter will be really useful.

In everyday arguments, we call this kind of support a "reason," but a reason is actually another kind of claim that our audience might question (like "this chapter will be really useful"). Rather than relying only on reasons, scholars seek the firmest, most well-developed supports they can find, ones that critical audiences will trust. The three most common categories of support used by scholars are evidence, verification, and illustration (see Table 4.1).

Evidence includes anything we can observe. During an experiment, for example, we might observe a chemical reaction or response from a plant that we're studying. We can also use evidence acquired through personal experience, as when we witness an event or observe a film or work of art. When writing a literary analysis, we can use quotations from a poem or novel as evidence for our interpretation. As we discuss in Chapter 6, we typically use evidence to activate our audience's sense of logic or reasoning.

Verification includes things we can look up. Students often support arguments by summarizing, paraphrasing, and quoting from scholarly articles or books to corroborate their claims. Lawyers refer to laws and legal precedents as verification. Scholars rely on

Table 4.1 KINDS OF SUPPORT

EVIDENCE Something you can observe	VERIFICATION Something you can look up	ILLUSTRATION Something you can imagine
• Empirical data • Personal experience • Textual evidence	• Previous research • Law or precedence • Established theory	• Fictional narrative • Hypothetical example • Analogy or metaphor

When might these different kinds of support activate reasoning, build credibility, or evoke emotion?

established theories and previous research to verify their work. Verification often determines the credibility of an argument.

Illustrations involve things we imagine. For example, we might offer a hypothetical example or fictional narrative to support our thesis. Like other illustrations, figures of speech such as analogies and metaphors can evoke an emotional response from the reader.

Scholars typically use specialized terminology to categorize different kinds of support:

- Evidence is a **primary source**, something that you can collect and analyze yourself.
- Verification is a **secondary source**, which means someone else has already analyzed or interpreted the evidence.
- Illustration is an **original source**, one that you create or borrow for a particular argument.

Of course, some kinds of support can cross over into more than one category. For example, sometimes personal experience can be used as evidence but also carry emotional impact. A hypothetical example can either evoke emotion or activate reasoning. Sometimes empirical data or statistics can build credibility. What's most important is that we think carefully about what we want a particular support to accomplish: Do we want it to build credibility, activate reasoning, or evoke emotion? We select the appropriate kind of evidence for our specific purpose.

Evidence tends to be the strongest kind of support because we trust most what we can observe. Evidence connects most clearly and certainly with reality and truth. Evidence also works well for different audiences, whereas verification may be culturally specific. For example, the US Constitution would provide convincing verification for an audience of US citizens but probably not for Canadians. Likewise, sociologists might not trust or find relevant the theories and research used by literary scholars. As the most speculative form of support, illustrations can evoke the most inconsistent but potentially powerful effects on audiences. We discuss ways to support arguments in much greater detail throughout the rest of the book.

For an argument to be successful, our audience must accept the support we present. Whenever an audience doubts or considers our support controversial, the bridge collapses. Sometimes collapses occur when the audience doubts the accuracy of evidence or misunderstands an illustration, but most commonly, supports fail when we haven't linked our claims and supports with a strong rationale.

Linking Support to Claims

We can walk, swim, run, and sit up straight because our musculature and skeletons work together. But these functions would be impossible without the tendons that connect our muscles and bones. Similarly, a rationale connects claims and supports together so they can function as an argument:

[Claim] BECAUSE [support].

A **rationale**, also known as a premise, explains the "because" part of an argument. Often, these rationales go unstated, but they are always present, whether or not we make them explicit. For example, we might argue that people shouldn't smoke *because* smoking is unhealthy. The unstated or assumed rationale is that *people should not do unhealthy things*. You might think that rationale is obvious or "common sense," and so it doesn't need to be stated explicitly, but you've probably heard what can happen when you assume. In this case, we shouldn't assume that rationale is obvious or uncontroversial when so many people who know the risks of smoking do so anyway. Countless doctors and government officials have warned people about the dangers of smoking, yet many people continue to smoke. Why? Because many people disagree with the notion that people should not do unhealthy things. For them, the rationale is open to question—another claim that needs support.

TRY THIS ➤ Practice Articulating Rationales

For this exercise, provide missing rationales for the following arguments:

- You're feeling sick (*support*), so you should go see a doctor (*claim*).
- Trendy jeans are worth the money (*claim*) because they're so stylish (*support*).
- American citizens should learn Spanish (*claim*) because there are so many Spanish speakers in the United States (*support*).
- Our candidate is tough on crime (*support*), so she deserves your vote (*claim*).
- Universities should pay student athletes (*claim*) because they earn substantial revenue for the school (*support*).
- Fraternities promote unhealthy behavior (*support*), so they should be shut down (*claim*).

Compare your answers with a classmate. Then, explain how you might support your rationales if your audience questioned them.

Rationales are just as important to arguments as claims and support. In fact, a distinguishing characteristic of scholarly argument is the extent that scholars go to scrutinize rationales and make them visible. That's why scientists use elaborate statistical calculations in their research: to validate the strength of linkages between evidence and the conclusions of investigation. In Chapters 5 and 8, we explain more fully how to develop and test rationales.

Table 4.2 ARGUMENT ELEMENTS AND THEIR FUNCTION

ELEMENT	FUNCTION
Purpose	The *inspiration* of the writer, the *functions* of the message, and the *implications* for the audience
Thesis or central claim	A debatable or controversial idea
Support	The *evidence*, *verifications*, and/or *illustrations* used to defend the claim
Rationale	An explanation of how a support holds up a claim

Can you imagine how these elements come together to form an argument?

An Everyday Argument

To illustrate the basic components of an argument, let's consider an example of an everyday workplace argument. Like many everyday arguments, this example begins with a claim supported by reasons. But remember, reasons are actually claims themselves—debatable statements—not evidence, verification, or illustration. As soon as the reader or listener disagrees with a reason, we must provide better support.

Everyday arguments often stack claims on top of other claims with little support. This kind of argument can work when we argue with friends or acquaintances who share extensive background knowledge, but whenever we encounter points of disagreement, we must support our claims with evidence, verification, and/or illustration. We must eventually base the argument on something that we agree about, something that's not open to question. This is especially true with arguments written for a demanding, sophisticated audience. In a later section, we'll show how a scholarly argument does just that.

Let's imagine a scenario where an employee is feeling financially strapped, so he approaches his boss to build a case for a pay raise. The dialogue goes like this:

EMPLOYEE: "I deserve a raise." (*thesis*)
BOSS: "Um, so do I. But why should I give *you* more money?"
EMPLOYEE: "Because I work hard, I'm indispensable, and I'm underpaid." (*reasons*)

The employee's argument should seem familiar, because the layout resembles the kind of argument that most of us learned in high school. His main claim, or thesis, asserts that he deserves more pay. To support his thesis, the employee gives three reasons that he thinks his boss will accept. **Effective arguments always build on some basis of acceptance or agreement.** If the boss agrees that her employee is hard working, indispensable, and underpaid, she's likely to give him a raise (if she has the authority to do so, her budget allows, and so forth). However, as we can see from the dialogue, the argument only works if the boss accepts the reasons provided. Note that the employee has not yet offered evidence or verification to support his claims:

BOSS: "I agree that you're a hard worker, but tell me more about how indispensable you are."
EMPLOYEE: "Well, I have more experience doing this work than anyone else in this office, and I'm a good problem solver." (*more reasons*)
BOSS: "Can you give me some examples of problems that you've solved that nobody else could?"
EMPLOYEE: "Sure. Remember that time. . .?" (*evidence*)
BOSS: "Okay, so now I see how you're a hard worker and sometimes indispensable. But so is everyone else. Why do you think you're underpaid?"
EMPLOYEE: "Because other employers keep offering me more money."
BOSS: "Can you show me some of those job offers?" (*verification*)

Getting to the Bottom of Things

Do you notice how difficult it may be to get to the "bottom" of an argument? Whatever reasons the employee provides, the boss can always dig deeper, asking for more support. With an especially complicated or controversial argument—or when addressing a demanding audience—this process might go on for a long time before reaching the bottom or finding some basis of agreement.

Let's look at the original argument once more in a graphic format that highlights how its structure can unfold (see Figure 4.1).

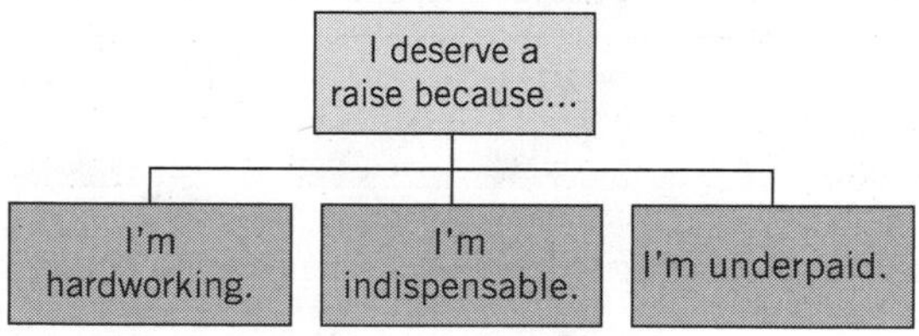

Figure 4.1

An Employee's Argument for a Raise

Notice that the employees three reasons are really claims.

Again, if the boss agrees with the basis provided, she might be persuaded. If not, the employee must dig deeper to build a stronger, more elaborate foundation for his argument, like the one shown in Figure 4.2.

Thus, we can imagine a brick building, where the thesis must rest on a strong foundation of support. Any block that's doubted or not accepted by the audience can cause the argument to teeter or crumble like a tower of blocks (think of the game Jenga). As we provide better reasons and more evidence to meet the needs of our audience, the basis of our argument grows larger.

In scholarly arguments, we drill down until we find much more solid ground to support our arguments. You can see how an everyday argument might work when both the person arguing and the audience share extensive background knowledge. But in the workplace example, the employee might need to provide evidence of his work productivity or examples of his contributions. Or he may need to verify that he has received job offers from other companies. His foundation would have been stronger if he had built these supports into his argument from the beginning.

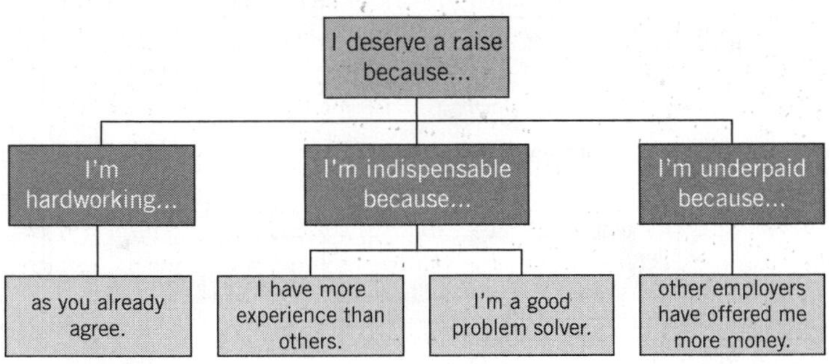

Figure 4.2

An Employee's More Developed Argument.

Can you imagine what evidence or verification the employee could use to support her claims?

TRY THIS ➤ Assemble the Elements of an Argument

For this exercise, practice building the elements of an argument. To identify a topic, brainstorm with other students about a problem or question at your school. Propose a potential solution (stated as a thesis) to resolve the problem, and think of what kind of support would convince faculty or administrators to implement your plan. Then create a block structure like Figure 4.2 to represent how you could present your proposal.

Learning to anticipate and meet the needs of a demanding audience (the way scholars try to do) can help you make more compelling and convincing everyday arguments, too.

Making Assumptions

Assumptions are any elements of the argument that either the writer or the audience are thinking but not saying. Assumptions can include things such as

- Evidence, verification, or other background knowledge that we assume our audience already knows ("You've seen my work, so you already know I'm a good problem solver.")
- Rationales ("You value hard work.")
- The inspiration or implications of the argument ("You know I've been struggling financially, and you can imagine how much harder I'll work if I get a raise.")

Assumptions lurk below the surface, like the immense base of an iceberg that is much larger than its visible top. Indeed, what's assumed in an argument is usually greater than what's said or written. That is, **assumptions make up the bulk of the total argument**, even though they're typically hiding, unstated, below the surface.

Of course, we always have to make some assumptions when creating an argument because we can never say everything we mean. In everyday arguments, we often leave most of our assumptions "submerged" when we argue with people we know well. We can rely on shared background knowledge, familiar culture, and so forth. When the employee in our everyday argument example provides reasons disguised as support, he is making assumptions. In this case, however, he wrongly assumes that the boss will not question his reasons or need additional support. And that's the problem: **Arguments often break down not because of what we've said but because of what we (wrongly) assume our audiences already know or believe.**

Let's examine another example: many politicians argue that wealthier citizens should pay more taxes in the interest of fairness. In this argument, politicians might assume a variety of things, for example:

- That economic equity creates "fairness"
- That fairness means that those who can afford to pay more taxes should owe more taxes
- That wealth causes political disparity and therefore higher taxes support equality by limiting the accumulation of wealth

It's easy to imagine how others may find these assumptions controversial or want additional support or explanation. Again, unless we know our audience well enough to anticipate what readers already know and believe, we must make our assumptions more explicit and possibly defend them.

When we engage in scholarly arguments, we're arguing with strangers—readers who don't know or trust us already and who will scrutinize our arguments carefully. (In fact, rigorous scholarly "peer reviews" are normally "double blind"—that is, the author's and reader's identities are not known to each other during the editorial process.) Scholarly arguments therefore seek to be as complete as possible so that readers can critique our work. Scholars know that writing is different from speech; we can't clarify, reword, add more detail, or respond to objections once we've published or "turned in" the argument. So we work diligently to ensure that our support is as solid and complete as space allows, that our rationales are clear, and that our "bridge" is fortified.

One way to avoid making assumptions is to make our unstated assumptions (reasons, inspirations, prior knowledge, and so forth) explicit. Metaphorically speaking, we raise as much of the argument above the water as we can.

"Above-Water" Arguments

Because arguments have the power to change our minds, behaviors, beliefs, and actions, scholars scrutinize their arguments carefully. As an apprentice, you might find the task of finding and fixing faults in your arguments daunting, and you might think they'll become too long or overexplained. But scholars leave little to chance. Every sentence in the argument is there for a reason, whether it be to prevent an objection, to answer a question, or to fully explain a controversial point. As much as is practical, we make our support and rationales visible to our audience. **Arguments that anticipate disconnects—that is, objections and unshared assumptions—have the best chance of changing our audience's mind.**

Taking the time and space to design a complete argument that will satisfy a skeptical audience usually pays off. Doing so not only helps

TRY THIS ➤ Build Support

For this exercise, take what you learned about making assumptions and apply it to a hypothetical situation.

1. Imagine that you're a teenager who wants to stay out later than usual for a party, but you need to persuade your parent to let you do so.
   a. What claims and support might your audience accept?
   b. What unstated assumptions must your audience share for your argument to work?
2. Now imagine that you're the parent, trying to convince your teenager that staying out late is a bad idea. What support and shared assumptions would make your argument work?
3. Based on how you answered 1 and 2, where are these arguments most likely to break down? What are the potential sources of disagreement or unshared assumptions?

us persuade readers, but we're also more likely to understand our subject in more depth and detail.

Rookie Mistakes and How to Fix Them

For apprentice scholars, one of the most difficult parts of college writing is imagining how much is safe to assume and how much must be made explicit. In other words, how much of our iceberg do readers need to see? As a general rule, **increased controversy requires increased explanation.** A truly "original" thesis will contradict what the audience already thinks, so we have to work harder to earn their agreement.

Here are three of the most common rookie mistakes made by apprentice scholars:

1. **Arguing the obvious**, or arguing about something the audience already knows or agrees with. Here, the writer wastes lots of effort supporting a conclusion (thesis) that really doesn't need to be argued.
2. **Arguing without support**, or underestimating how controversial a statement is—stating something *as though* readers already know or agree with it when, in fact, they don't. Rookie writers often use unsubstantiated claims to support an argument.
3. **Supporting without arguing.** Sometimes apprentice scholars present evidence, verification, or illustrations without telling the audience what point they're trying to make. Expecting that your audience will reach an unstated conclusion is a trick that works fine in everyday arguments, advertising, or politics. (For example, advertisers expect that handsome men can "sell" products to women.) However, experienced scholars state their claims clearly and explicitly.

So how do we avoid making these mistakes?

- **To avoid arguing the obvious:**
  a. **Read more.** When scholars think they have an original idea, they review other scholars' work to make sure that their research question or tentative argument isn't old news. (We discuss Research or Literature Reviews more in Appendix B.) You can do the same by consulting scholarly sources; if you find lots of sources that have made your argument already, you might need to find a new angle.
  b. **Ask an expert.** A good shortcut is to ask a scholarly mentor, such as your instructor, if the idea seems fresh and interesting. She'll tell you if she's already read too many papers about a "tired" subject like lowering the drinking age.

- **To avoid arguing without support:**
  a. **Highlight your argument.** Read your draft and mark the thesis and supporting claims in color (on your computer or with a highlighter). Then review the parts that aren't highlighted. Do the claims need more support? Is there anything that your audience might question?
  b. **Consult a reader.** Ask a trusted classmate, writing center tutor, or your instructor to review your draft with an eye for assertions that need more evidence or explanation.

- **To avoid supporting without arguing:**
  a. **Use topic sentences.** Like mini-thesis statements, topic sentences can alert your reader to the reason or claim that you're about to develop. Good writing doesn't always need topic sentences, but they can help weary readers (and you) keep track of your points. We discuss more organizational strategies in Chapter 8.
  b. **Search for stranded support.** Make sure that you have clearly linked your claims and support together. Is it clear what point you're trying to support with that evidence?

So What?

Arguments use evidence, verification, and illustration (what is known or invented) to support claims (what is unknown or controversial). In effective arguments, the writer's inspiration and the implications for the audience converge to answer the question: *so what?*

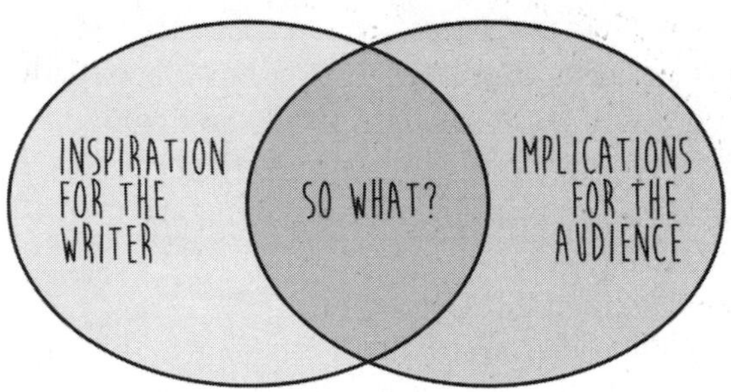

Now that you know that arguments are a complex network of inspirations, claims, support, rationales, assumptions, and implications, you might wonder how you can analyze arguments carefully enough to detect all of these features. Indeed, before we give any more advice on developing compelling arguments, we'll offer useful strategies for analyzing and responding to arguments. Responsible scholars wait to advance their own arguments until they have fully listened to what others have said. In order to develop persuasive arguments, we must first discover the most reasonable answers and the best courses of action for our audience. After all, our own thinking might be flawed, and it's certainly limited, so we need to take into account the intellectual work of others. Chapter 5 describes analytical techniques that you can use to understand others' arguments deeply so you can participate as an informed apprentice scholar.

What's Next

Take what you've learned in this chapter and respond to the following prompts.

1. **Practice question and argument.** Integrate the various parts of an argument by creating an outline or graphic that develops one of the following questions:
   a. What major should I choose?
   b. Which profession should I pursue after college?

   Once you've selected a question, state your tentative answers to the question in the form of a thesis, such as "I should major in [Biology, Business, or Basket Weaving] so that I can get a job that is profitable and prestigious." Now, make a list of the kinds of support you would need to convince a friend or relative who thinks you should decide something different. Can you think of some evidence, verification, and illustrations that would answer the question more definitively?

2. **Explore current arguments.** For this exercise, explore the arguments surrounding a current social or political issue that interests you, like the local food movement. Read a few popular sources, such as newspapers or magazine articles, and at least one scholarly article, and then discuss the following in class:
   - Who are the various stakeholders in this issue (for example, individuals, organizations, and governments who have an interest in the matter)? What are their concerns? What arguments do you hear them making?
   - What questions or controversies do these arguments raise?
   - What characteristics of your community context promote or limit these discussions? For example, arguments about the local food movement might be different if you live in a farming community or a large city. What economic or cultural

factors might influence the stakeholders? What is the dominant political affiliation, and how does that affect people's views on the issue?

Analyzing an argument in this way helps us understand an issue and its context more deeply. We can better recognize the complexities of an issue; understand the people involved and their different perspectives; and appreciate how the issue relates to other topics, values, beliefs, cultures, and customs within a social context.

CHAPTER five

How Do We Analyze Arguments

chapter checklist

- How can we analyze rhetorical elements?
- How do we identify an argument's central controversies?
- How should we respond to arguments?

As you read more scholarly writing, you will begin to see texts not merely as unquestionable, lifeless, purely objective collections of facts and ideas, but as part of conversations that writers and their audiences use to create and recreate knowledge—and you will begin to participate in that discussion yourself. Closely studying an argument's rhetorical elements can deepen your understanding of its message.

Analyzing Rhetorical Elements

To read and analyze a text rhetorically, we break down the argument to see how it works, without judging or agreeing or disagreeing. The guiding questions of analysis are as follows:

- How is the argument designed?
- What choices did the author make in designing the argument?
- Why did she make those choices?

For example, why did she choose to open the essay with that particular illustration, or why did she choose that kind of evidence? Analyzing texts this way helps us read other writers' work as models for our own. In the next section, we will discuss additional rhetorical elements to examine while reading.

So What? The Inspiration, Purpose, and Implications

As we discussed in the previous chapters, authors write because they are responding to some ***inspiration*****: a problem, question, or gap in understanding**. Something *motivates* them to write. Maybe they read something and disagreed with the author's argument. Or they discovered a problem that needed a solution. Or they became curious about a question. Something happened. We can better decipher a writer's inspiration if we ask ourselves: What happened? What is this writer responding to? Where did this idea originate? Why did this topic matter to him? Whether or not the writer explains or implies an inspiration, effective arguments usually leave clues about the author's motivation to write.

If the inspiration is the cause of the argument, the ***purpose*** **is its desired effect**: what the writer hopes his argument will accomplish. In general, arguments influence how our audiences think or act, so an argument's purpose will be to modify the knowledge, beliefs, or behavior of the reader.

Implications **involve the larger outcomes of an argument**: indirect and unforeseen consequences that go beyond its immediate purposes. Let's consider an everyday example that ties these elements together. Suppose someone becomes irritated about teenagers speeding through her neighborhood (*inspiration*), so she writes a letter to the editor of her local newspaper to raise awareness of the problem (*purpose*). After reading the published complaint, the chief of police sends a patrol car to the neighborhood to set up a speed trap (*implication*).

Now here's a scholarly example. A professor who tutors in a writing center notices many students who seem to obsess too much over "later order" concerns in their writing, such as grammar, punctuation, and citation formatting (*inspiration*), so he experiments with different tutoring techniques that shift students' focus to higher order issues, such as designing compelling arguments. He shares the results of his investigation in a journal read by faculty at other writing centers, hoping to enhance their tutoring practices (*purpose*). A few readers hold workshops for faculty across disciplines who want to improve how they teach writing, and the tutoring techniques are translated into strategies for teaching peer review in business courses, science labs, and so on (*implications*).

TRY THIS ➤ Practice with Inspiration, Purpose, and Implications

For this exercise, take what you've learned and try to imagine two or more possible inspirations, purposes, and implications for each of the following examples. Compare your results with a classmate.

- An editorial that criticizes a local politician
- A cigarette package that warns about the health risks of smoking
- A college academic department website
- A consumer survey that polls residents about their spending habits
- An in-class exercise in which you practice thinking about inspirations, purposes, and implications

Author and Audience

Knowing something about an author's credentials and background can give us insight into her assumptions, motives, biases, and credibility. We might investigate her background (by searching online) to learn about her expertise and what else she's written. We might also search for information about her political, personal, and community affiliations, if we think these factors might influence her argument. Similarly, we imagine the argument's intended audience—background and demographics (age, gender, income, education, political preferences), values, assumptions, and biases—because all of these elements can influence a writer's choices and an audience's reactions.

CONSIDER THIS ➤ Yourself as the Audience

For this reflection, think about what factors might influence how you interpret an argument. What are your values, assumptions, biases, and background? How might personal factors—such as your age, gender, ethnicity, education, income, or political preferences—influence how you interpret and respond to arguments? For example, how might your perspective on arguments differ from someone significantly older or younger than you?

Genre

Think of a genre as a **typical, recognizable *form* or *means* that achieves some *function* or *purpose*.** For example, to transport people from one location to another, humans have designed different types or "genres" of vehicles, such as bicycles, motorcycles, cars, trucks, trains, and planes. Each of these genres has a recognizable form. When we see an automobile, we immediately recognize it as an automobile, we know what it's designed to do, and we can distinguish it from a spaceship or unicycle or other kind of vehicle.

You already know about literary genres, such as plays, poems, or novels. Like vehicles, we immediately recognize their forms and functions because they're designed according to unwritten "rules" or conventions that audiences recognize and expect. Argument genres are no different. For example, we know that an editorial (*genre*) typically expresses a viewpoint about a current event (*inspiration*) in order to change public opinion (*purpose*). Or, we recognize a warning label (*genre*), written in response to a known health risk (*inspiration*), that cautions consumers about the dangers of using or misusing a product (*purpose*).

Arguments surround us, often in places we don't usually consider. For instance, think about stoplights as a kind of argument: their purpose is to *persuade* you to stop, go, or slow down. In contrast, exit signs merely *inform* you where you can exit a highway (or building). Their purpose is not to persuade anyone to exit—that's what billboard advertisements are for (EXIT HERE FOR THE BEST BARBECUE YOU EVER TASTED!).

Understanding the relationship between purpose and genre can dramatically improve our reading comprehension and give us an efficient starting point for analyzing an argument's effectiveness. When we recognize an argument's genre and purpose, we can evaluate it according to established, although often unwritten, rules and expectations. For example, when you watch a horror movie, you expect to be scared and startled—maybe even disgusted by blood and gore. There might also be some drama and humor, but like all genres, a horror movie has to follow the rules, mostly, or audiences will be disappointed. There's nothing worse than a comedy that isn't funny or a mystery with no surprises. Later chapters discuss expectations for appropriate styles, organizational patterns, and design features for genres of scholarly writing.

Context

In some situations, understanding an argument's content and genre will be enough to comprehend the message. But we've all communicated and miscommunicated enough to know how important the context can be. For instance, have you ever shown up to a party and realized that you were terribly overdressed? The style you wore last time was clearly too formal for this occasion. The context changed, so your choice was no longer appropriate.

Messages mean different things in different contexts. When reading something written long ago or far away, we may not be able to fully understand a text's meaning or purpose unless we know something about the time period, culture, community values, controversies, current events, and so on. Thinking about these elements gives us a richer picture. Arguments become more meaningful when we consider where and when they were created.

TRY THIS ➤ Examine a Scholarly Journal

For this exercise, find a physical copy of a scholarly journal and examine its features. Your school library should have copies of scholarly journals related to your major discipline. Find one, flip through it, and answer the following questions:

1. What do the article titles and topics indicate about the journal's intended audience?
2. What can you tell about the context or current scholarly conversations that are important?
3. Who publishes the journal, and how might that affect the journal's credibility?
4. How would you describe the genre and style of most articles?
5. Besides articles, what other kinds of content does the journal contain?

Identifying the Controversy

Beyond the basic elements of the rhetorical situation, rhetoric provides more sophisticated tools for reading and writing arguments. The most powerful tool of rhetoric, which we call the Controversy Categories, provides a systematic way to understand and create different types of arguments based on what kinds of disagreements an argument addresses. Because Controversy Categories are new to most college students, we introduce them here and provide opportunities for more practice in subsequent chapters. Table 5.1 describes the Controversy Categories in detail, but first we'll walk through an example to give a general sense of how this system works.

Our example is a murder case. During the trial, the first controversy that must be resolved is what actually happened—the facts of the case. If the prosecution does not have sufficient evidence to establish that, for example, the defendant was the person who stabbed his girlfriend (or his boyfriend, spouse, companion, or neighbor) to death, then he will go free. Once the prosecutors prove that fact, then they must establish that the accused person's actions fit the legal definition of murder. The cause (motive) and circumstances might affect the definition: Was it premeditated? A crime of passion? An accident? And the definition—first- or second-degree murder, involuntary manslaughter, and so forth—will determine the penalty or action to be taken according to the law.

In a trial, it doesn't make sense to skip steps and decide whether an accused person should receive the death penalty before we determine whether he was the person holding the knife. Indeed, that's why many countries, including the United States, base their justice systems on the presumption of innocence (innocent until proven guilty)—to guarantee citizens due process before enforcing penalties. The process doesn't always work, but if you were accused, would you rather face a lynch mob?

Note how the trial example shows the *sequential* or *hierarchical* progression of controversy categories. Until we agree about the facts, definitions, and interpretations (what's happening and what it means), there's no sense in finding solutions (enacting policies and

Table 5.1 CONTROVERSY CATEGORIES

CONTROVERSY CATEGORY	QUESTIONS FOR INVESTIGATION	EVERYDAY EXAMPLE	SCHOLARLY EXAMPLE
Existence or fact	Is it true? Did it happen?	Does country X have nuclear weapons capability? How do we know?	Do scholarly apprentices struggle with the demands of college-level reading?
Definition or interpretation	Does this case fit the definition? How do we interpret this information?	What kinds of weapons does country X possess?	What kind of reading problems do college students have?
Cause, consequence, or circumstance	What caused this? Was it intentional? Are there extenuating circumstances?	What prompted country X to develop nuclear weapons?	Why do college students struggle with scholarly readings?
Evaluation	Is it right or wrong? Is it serious enough to warrant our attention?	Do country X's nuclear capabilities pose an imminent threat to global security?	Do students' reading difficulties present a serious obstacle to learning?
Jurisdiction, procedure, policy, or action to be taken	What, if anything, should we do about it?	How should we respond to country X as a nuclear threat?	What actions might professors and students take to improve reading skills?

What controversy are you currently debating with friends, and which category would that issue fall under?

procedures). To further illustrate this logical progression, think about skipping a rock over water. Sometimes, the rock skips several times, and sometimes it just goes plunk.

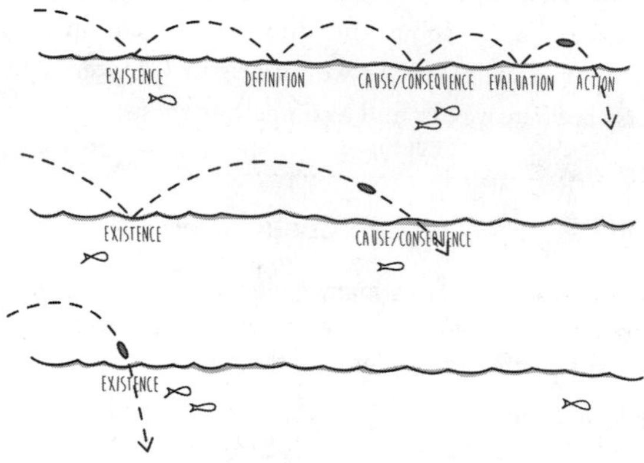

Like a skipping rock, arguments that address fewer controversies can go deeper below the surface. Sometimes, writers skip over controversy categories that have already been resolved. For example, if the prosecution provides a video recording that clearly shows an act of murder and the identity of the accused and the victim, then defense counsel may concede that her client "did it" but argue about the circumstances or build a case for temporary insanity.

Sorting and prioritizing controversy categories allows us to skip over what's already well-established and focus our attention on the heart of the matter, or to locate places where multiple, competing disagreements have accumulated. Most complicated debates, such as gun control or abortion, involve multiple categories of disagreement. Complex arguments like these can be difficult to resolve because participants cannot agree to resolve a common "sticking point." For example, advocates for gun rights might focus too much on definitions (such as rights) and values (freedom to bear arms), whereas gun control advocates might fixate on competing values (safety) and policies (control measures).

Controversy categories can help us methodically navigate complex issues to get at the heart of the matter—the main controversy or point of disagreement. After all, arguments are designed to *resolve* controversies, so we can argue more effectively and efficiently if we can settle what we already agree about and direct our attention (argument) toward what matters most. As we discuss in Chapter 7, the main controversy is where we can find a compelling thesis.

TRY THIS ➤ Practice with Controversy Categories

For this exercise, identify as many controversies as you can for the following topics. Create a table with three columns: topic, stakeholders, and controversies. Here are the topics:

1. Grade inflation
2. Violent video games
3. Military conscription (draft)
4. [Choose a controversial topic that interests you.]

A Guided Analysis of a Scholarly Argument

Now let's put everything together to examine a scholarly argument by carefully analyzing the main elements of the rhetorical situation: author, audience, message, purpose, and context. As we go along, think of how the elements connect with each other, as illustrated in this diagram that we introduced in Chapter 1.

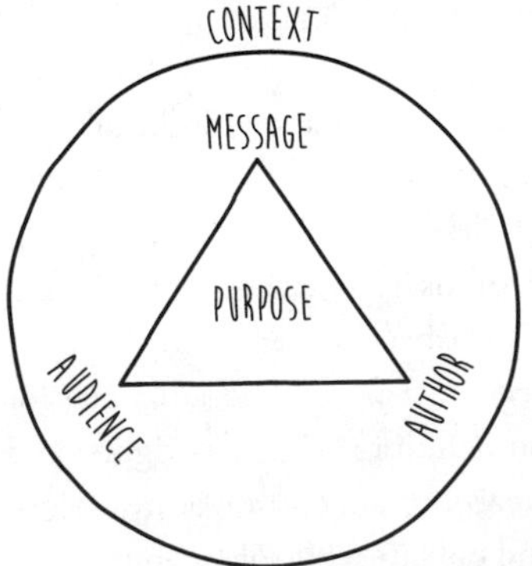

Before we begin, read the article "A Wandering Mind Is an Unhappy Mind" by Harvard psychologists Matthew A. Killingsworth and Daniel T. Gilbert (reprinted in this book on pp. 435–40). Then, follow along in the essay as we model the analysis.

Identify the Audience and Context

Before we begin reading, we take note of the argument's publication information (where and when it was originally published) to help us identify the audience and understand the larger context. To identify Killingsworth and Gilbert's audience, we might ask ourselves:

- What do we know, or what can we find out, about the original publication context?
- Who are Killingsworth and Gilbert trying to reach? Who will read this article, and why?

This article originally appeared in the journal *Science*, which, according to their website, is "the world's leading journal of original scientific research, global news, and commentary." Journals like *Science* publish scholarly, peer-reviewed articles that typically attract particular kinds of readers (scholars and scientists). Knowing this information gives us some sense of the audience's level of education and expertise. We can assume that Killingsworth and Gilbert are writing for highly educated readers with a scientific background.

Identify the Author and Inspiration

A quick Google search for Killingsworth and Gilbert indicates that they are experts in their fields. They work at prestigious universities and regularly publish research in psychology. Their status influences their approach to the topic, their perspectives, and their purpose—and builds their credibility with *Science* readers.

In order to identify the authors' inspiration, we ask ourselves three important questions as we're reading the article:

- What initially motivated Killingsworth and Gilbert to investigate the connection between mind wandering and happiness?

- What gap in research or unanswered question prompted their attention?
- Why did *this* particular problem or question matter to these psychologists?

The researchers cite two pieces of information that stirred their curiosity and led them to hypothesize, or tentatively claim, that mind wandering might interfere with happiness. We can locate these statements in the first paragraph of the article. Can you find them?

If you still can't figure out the researchers' inspiration, look for an important clue in the introduction by asking yourself:

- What is their research question?

Identifying what prompted Killingsworth and Gilbert's investigation helps us understand how and why they developed their hypothesis, and how this led them to investigate people's thoughts and feelings. The inspirations and hypothesis that we detected are shown in Figure 5.1.

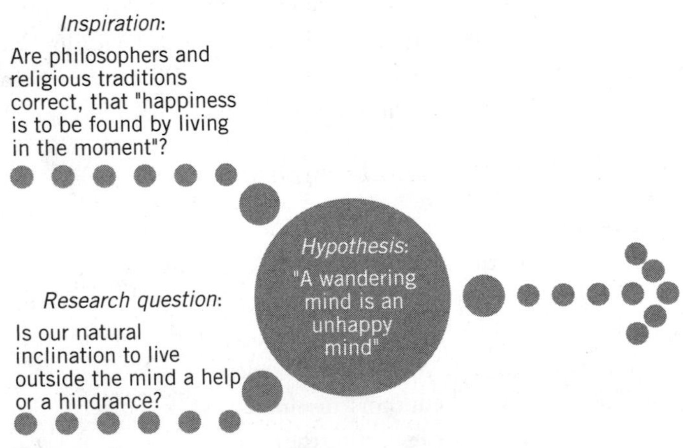

Figure 5.1

Do you notice how the psychologists' hypothesis responds to their initial questions or inspiration?

Identify Parts of the Message

An argument's message contains various components, including the thesis, support, genre, and style. For this sample analysis, we'll focus on thesis and supports. (Consult Appendix B for additional discussion about the generic layout of a research article.)

Identify the thesis. Arguments often state their thesis, or main debatable idea, in the introduction. Research articles like this one usually begin with a hypothesis, or tentative thesis. A hypothesis or thesis is simply the writer's answer to their research question. To locate the thesis or hypothesis, we ask ourselves:

- Where is a potentially controversial, overarching idea that Killingsworth and Gilbert will need to support?
- What controversy categories does the article address? How do the authors support their conclusions?

Knowing the thesis or hypothesis in advance helps us to evaluate the quality of the argument as we read along, because we already know what the writers are trying to discover or "prove." As we continue reading Killingsworth and Gilbert's methodology and results, we can be asking ourselves whether their research validates their hypothesis or not. In a research article like this one, the "conclusion" really is the thesis: the results or findings of the investigation. So, if the title didn't make the thesis clear, then the conclusion certainly should.

Identify the support. Although we typically find an argument's inspiration and thesis early in an argument (and perhaps again at the end), the body of the argument usually contains the support. In the case of empirical research like this study, the support is whatever information or data the writers collect to answer the research question. To find the support, we look for examples of evidence, verification, and/or illustrations that hold up the thesis. In "A Wandering Mind Is an Unhappy Mind," we note that the support is primarily evidence, in the form of empirical data (statistics), which provides "the results of observation and experimentation" (*Oxford English Dictionary*). When we diagram the elements of the argument, we see a strong base of support (see Figure 5.2).

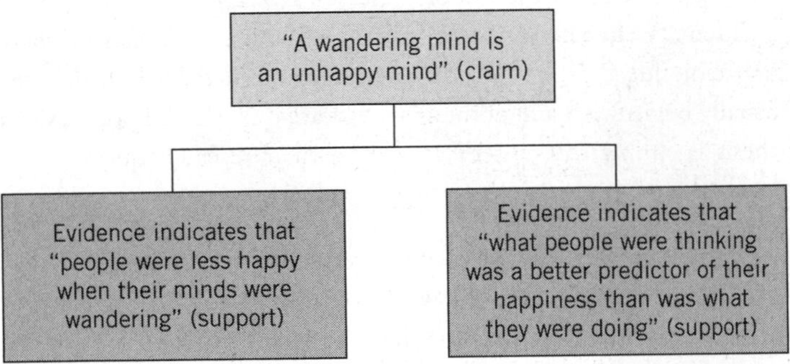

Figure 5.2

The Elements of the Argument in "A Wandering Mind Is an Unhappy Mind"

What are some possible implications of these findings?

CONSIDER THIS ➤ Missing Support

For this reflection, find one claim in "A Wandering Mind Is an Unhappy Mind" that is not supported with evidence, verification, or illustration, and think about why the authors did not offer support. In order to understand this choice, ask yourself:

- Who is the original audience and what background knowledge would most readers have?
- How controversial or "open to question" is the claim for that target audience?

(*continued*)

Then, compare your answers with a peer and discuss the following:

- When writing, how do we decide whether claims, evidence, and rationales are open to question and therefore need support?

Develop a list of criteria for assessing whether we need to support claims.

Identify the rationale. Finally, we can identify rationales in the *Science* article when we look for places where the authors connect their statistical findings with their claim that "a wandering mind is an unhappy mind." To find these, we ask ourselves:

- Where do Killingsworth and Gilbert explicitly discuss the connection between their thesis and their research results—in order to tie up any loose ends?
- How do they help readers interpret the statistics they present?
- Where do they correct potential misunderstandings about how their data support their conclusion?

We often spot rationales at the end of paragraphs because that's an effective place to remind readers explicitly how the support verifies, illustrates, or provides evidence for a claim. As is common in many research articles, Killingsworth and Gilbert help readers interpret their data so that we can see how they have drawn their conclusions.

Identify the Author's Purpose

Knowing Killingsworth and Gilbert's audience, inspiration, and message helps us imagine their purpose—or the goal of their argument. Remember that a writer's purpose and thesis are *not* the same thing. The thesis is the main point that the writer attempts to support, whereas the purpose is the desired outcome of the argument—usually, how the writer wants to change the audience's understanding, beliefs, or behavior. To identify Killingsworth and Gilbert's purpose, we ask ourselves:

- What did Killingsworth and Gilbert hope to accomplish by publishing their findings?
- How could these findings change readers' behaviors or beliefs?

We imagine that Killingsworth and Gilbert wrote this article *to inform* or enrich readers' understanding about the consequences of mind wandering and *to convince* readers of its seriousness using empirical data. These actions (to inform or to convince) were likely their purposes. They may also have sought *to impress* their scholarly community or *to challenge* the thinking of other researchers who disagree with them. We suspect these latter purposes could be possible, knowing Killingsworth and Gilbert's intended audience and their chosen publication.

Identify the Implications

A scholarly argument's implications may be stated or implied. If they are stated, we usually locate them in the conclusion. But Killingsworth and Gilbert do not explicitly address the consequences of their argument or suggest specific changes readers should make (like learning to become more focused). To identify unstated implications, ask yourself:

- What are the potential consequences or effects of the argument?
- What is the larger significance of the argument? Why does it matter? *So what?*

Deciphering an argument's implications helps us discover what the writer wants us to *do* with the argument. We can also identify questions for further research, issues we might take up in our own writing, and other potential "leads" (inspirations).

Table 5.2 IDENTIFYING AND INTERPRETING A SCHOLARLY ARGUMENT'S COMPONENTS

ELEMENT	QUESTIONS TO ASK YOURSELF	PLACES TO LOOK
Audience	• Who is the author writing for? Who will read this argument? • Where was this argument originally published?	Publication context and writing style (word choice, organization, sentence structure, tone)
Inspiration	• What gap, problem, or unanswered question prompted the writer's attention? • Why did this problem or question matter to this writer?	Introduction
Thesis or central claim	• What is a potentially controversial, overarching idea that requires support and directly responds to the inspirations? • What controversy categories does the argument address?	Title, introduction, and conclusion
Support	• What evidence, verification, and/or illustrations hold up the thesis?	Body paragraphs
Rationale	• Where does the writer explicitly discuss the connection between a claim and support, in order to tie up any loose ends? • Where does the writer correct potential misunderstandings that readers might have about the link between the claim and support?	Near the end of all paragraphs and in the conclusion
Implications	• What are the consequences, effects, or larger significance of the argument (stated or implied)? • Is there a call to action?	Conclusion

How might this table help you read complicated arguments?

Analyzing Visual Arguments

Up until now we've discussed techniques for analyzing written arguments, but we haven't delved into the details of image-based arguments. Since many arguments that we encounter on a daily basis include visual elements, let's discuss ways of interpreting images and using them in arguments.

Often a picture, graphic, or video can be more persuasive than words alone. Advertisements, social media, television, and websites are only a few of the sources of visual messages we encounter. We use the same principles to examine visual arguments that we would to analyze and evaluate print-only arguments:

- Who is the author? Who is the intended audience?
- What is the controversy or debatable claim?
- What support does the argument contain?
- What is the purpose of the argument?
- How does context affect its meaning?

The strength of visual arguments—their vividness—can also be a weakness. Vividness makes these arguments memorable or "sticky," as advertisers say, and vividness can also evoke emotional responses easily. However, because images are often used as illustrations rather than evidence or verification, their success depends on them evoking the intended response, which doesn't always happen. Claims and rationales are often more implicit, so we must ask ourselves:

- What is missing from this argument? What has the author left to my imagination?
- What connotations, symbolic meanings, or cultural assumptions am I supposed to supply?

Let's examine the following visual argument, a cigarette warning label created by the US government. Figure 5.3 is one of a series of labels developed in 2011 to replace the surgeon general's warning.

When analyzing visual arguments, as with any others, it's useful to begin with the basic elements of the rhetorical situation. In this case, the label's purpose is to discourage women from smoking during pregnancy. From the stated reason, "Smoking during pregnancy can harm your baby," we can infer that the thesis of the label is "Don't smoke when pregnant." There may also be secondary claims, such as (a) "Don't smoke around pregnant women" and maybe even (b) "Don't smoke in the presence of babies." The illustration of an apparently unhealthy baby implies a connection between smoking and harm to infants, either born or unborn.

Figure 5.3

Cigarette Warning Label

How does this label activate reasoning, build credibility, and evoke emotion?

The primary audience is likely women who are pregnant or who are considering pregnancy, because the label explicitly warns about potential harm to "your baby." The label may also warn others about the dangers of secondhand smoke, particularly fathers, who might smoke in the presence of infants or pregnant women. To appeal to a younger audience, the creators may have chosen to use a comic book style, instead of the graphic photographs that other antismoking ads and labels use. Note, too, that unlike the old cigarette warnings, the surgeon general's verification is not emphasized. Instead, a small copyright of the US Department of Health and Human Services (HHS) appears in the background. Because the copyright is so small, the author of the government's warning appears to be the cigarette company or brand itself, whose name appears in large font at the bottom of the label. Suggesting that the message comes from the manufacturer rather than the government might be more persuasive for some audiences.

In this advertisement—as in many visual arguments—illustrations and emotion dominate the argument. In fact, the only support offered by the label is an illustration, a drawing of a distressed newborn baby in an incubator. The baby faces the viewer, crying out, with a breathing tube and electrodes. This disturbing illustration may evoke a strong enough emotional response to provoke action from smokers who probably already know about associated health risks—even though the argument presents no evidence or elaborate verification.

One implication is that people quit smoking around babies. Beyond that, by including a phone number, 1-800-QUIT-NOW, the label connects its message to a larger antismoking campaign and clearly states what the audience should do.

What other implications or questions does the label raise? For example, how might people respond to an argument that's literally in their hands? Would this label be powerful enough to dissuade consumers from buying a pack of cigarettes? Would it be powerful enough to persuade smokers to call the QUIT NOW hotline or stop smoking around children? Why might this labeling campaign be considered controversial?

TRY THIS ➤ Analyze a Visual Argument

For this exercise, find a compelling print or video advertisement that argues with words and images, and then analyze the visual argument, using the following questions:

- What claims does the ad state or imply?
- What kinds of support are provided?
- How do the visual elements (images and document design features such as color and font) work together with the words?
- What makes the argument effective (or not)?

Responding to Arguments

Although reading may be your primary means of learning in college, writing is what typically provides evidence of that learning. Your teachers will often assign papers to test how well you comprehend what you read. They also expect that you can deepen your understanding *as you write* about a text, so they will ask you to "respond" or "critique" or "analyze." You should begin by asking your professor what he means by these terms, but a typical response assignment asks you to figure out what the text is arguing, either subtly or explicitly, and develop some kind of reply.

To respond effectively, you should think of your reading as a source for inspiration. A good place to begin such a response is by evaluating the argument made by your source. Evaluation is not the same thing as summary, which—as we explain on pp. 49–50—is a recap of what an author says. Sometimes apprentice scholars summarize an argument (that is, restate its most important parts) instead of evaluating it because they're reluctant to critique a published author, or they don't know how to evaluate an argument, or they simply prefer the easier task. Instead of regurgitating the gist of a message, evaluation involves judging whether the writer's strategies were effective for her intended audience and purpose (or for other audiences and purposes). Again, when evaluating an argument, we're still not arguing with the writer, but rather using her argument as a model from which we might learn what choices are more or less effective. Once we're done analyzing and evaluating, we will understand our source well enough to argue with it, to respond to it with our own opinion by agreeing or disagreeing—or, preferably, by adding something new.

It's important to realize that simply agreeing with your sources doesn't yield especially interesting results. Disagreeing is a bit more interesting, but we want to avoid a simplistic "I'm-right-you're-wrong" kind of debate. So, whenever we're responding to an argument, we agree or disagree in order to *extend* the argument and contribute something new. Think about it—in any conversation, the most interesting person is the one who introduces a new idea, a fresh perspective on the topic.

However, you might believe you have little to say in response because you don't know much about the topic. Or you might have been trained only to comprehend an argument, not to engage in a conversation with it. Summary, analysis, and evaluation enable you to dig deeper into *understanding* your sources (what other scholars have already said) in ways that can yield something fresh to say. Another way to come up with a significant response is to do some brainstorming. The "Believing and Doubting Game" can deepen your understanding of what you read and, at the same time, give you plenty to write about.

Play the "Believing and Doubting Game"

This strategy offers an efficient place to begin because you start with what you already know and think, focusing your attention on the writer's arguments. The questions are inspired by a brainstorming and peer review technique called the "Believing and Doubting Game," which was developed by writing expert Peter Elbow. The "Believing and Doubting Game" helps you think more carefully about how you relate to an argument as an individual reader (see Table 5.3).

The technique works like this. First, you "believe" the text fully by asking yourself questions that help you understand and extend the writer's ideas. Then, you "doubt" the text by asking yourself questions that help you challenge and even refute the writer's ideas. Running through these questions whenever you read can prepare you to design an argument of response, or even just to have more to say during class discussions of a reading.

Table 5.3 THE BELIEVING AND DOUBTING GAME

"BELIEVING" QUESTIONS	"DOUBTING" QUESTIONS
• What are the text's strengths? What does it do well? • Which claims do I agree with? • Which underlying values or beliefs do I share with the author? • How does the argument relate to my life? • What other ideas, examples, or scenarios fit the writer's argument?	• What are the text's weaknesses? • Which claims do I disagree with? • What are the writer's biases? • What does the writer overlook? What questions are left unanswered? • What claims need more support? • What rationales are faulty or missing?

Can you think of more questions that you could use to "believe" and "doubt" an argument?

TRY THIS ➤ Play the "Believing and Doubting Game"

For this exercise, practice playing the "Believing and Doubting Game":

1. Read the essay "With Liberty and Justice for Some" by apprentice scholar Emanuel Grant (reprinted on pp. 507–16). Then, spend 30 minutes playing the believing game, in response to his essay. Practice responding to the argument by answering questions that help you extend Grant's ideas.
2. Spend 30 minutes playing the doubting game. Answer resistant questions that help you challenge Grant's ideas.
3. Write a blog post that responds to Grant's argument and designs an argument of your own. You won't be able to address all of Grant's points, so select a few that interest you and compose a response that extends the conversation about this topic.

Mind and Mine the Gaps

Arguments can never address a controversy exhaustively. Writers inevitably leave unanswered questions, alternative interpretations, missing links, and things unsaid. These are opportunities for readers to join the conversation. We recommend that you "mind these gaps" just as subway riders do in New York City. *Minding the gap* means watching out for logical holes, missing examples, discrepancies, questions—spaces for you to insert your opinion. Along the same lines, once you find a gap, you can *mine* it: dig deeper, excavate the argument, and search for new idea "gold." When you plunge your shovel into the argument's holes, you can discover hidden gems and valuable, never-before-seen insights.

So What?

Keep in mind that we can't enter scholarly conversations (make our own arguments) until we're familiar with *what* others have said and *how* and *why* they've said it. The concepts and techniques we've introduced in this chapter can help you become a more efficient and effective scholarly apprentice who analyzes arguments carefully by categorizing controversies, looking for gaps in arguments, and developing interesting responses.

The next chapter explains how we collect and incorporate various kinds of support (verifications, evidence, and illustrations) to create messages that are more credible, logical, and emotionally appealing.

What's Next

Take what you've learned in this chapter and respond to the following prompts:

1. **Identify Controversy Categories.** Expand our "Guided Analysis of a Scholarly Argument" (pp. 106–114) by identifying the

controversy categories that Killingsworth and Gilbert address in their article, "A Wandering Mind Is an Unhappy Mind" (pp. 243–247). Use Table 5.1 to guide your analysis.

a. Create a two-column chart, listing all five controversy categories in the left column. In the right column, list as many specific controversies as you can find in the article. Write the controversies as questions, following our examples in Table 5.1.
b. Which controversy categories does the article not fully address? Which of these gaps could inspire further investigation? What kinds of research could you use to answer those questions?

2. **Multimedia presentation.** Go online to the TED Talks website (http://www.ted.com/talks) and find a video of Matt Killingsworth's presentation, "Want to Be Happy? Stay in the Moment." The presentation covers many of the same arguments he and his coauthor made in their article, "A Wandering Mind Is an Unhappy Mind." Watch the video and answer the following questions:
   a. What did the presentation accomplish that the article could not? How did it do so?
   b. Did seeing and hearing the author make his arguments more or less credible? Why?
   c. What kinds of multimedia did he incorporate, and how did that enhance his arguments?

3. **Analyze an argument rhetorically.** Analyze an argument's rhetorical elements in order to understand the author's choices. Follow these steps:
   a. Select a persuasive text (such as a magazine article, blog post, or even an advertisement) that interests you. Choose wisely by selecting something that has interesting rhetorical elements that you can detect and describe. It's generally best to stay away from strictly informative genres (like newspaper reports) and instead look at editorials, opinion pieces, and other persuasive genres.

b. While reading the article, analyze the argument's rhetorical elements:
   - Audience and author
   - Context: timing, publication
   - So what: inspirations, purposes, implications
   - Message: genre, style, thesis, supports, rationale

Refer to the list of questions on pp. 8–9 for guidance on completing a thorough analysis. Also, take note of the controversies that the author addresses. You might even list 5 to 10 of the main issues he discusses, and then categorize them according to the kind of controversy they are (existence/fact, definition, cause, evaluation, and jurisdiction/policy).

c. Write a three-page *rhetorical analysis* of the article. Your goal is to fully describe the argument's rhetorical elements and to explain *how* the text makes its argument. You can write for an audience of peers who have already read the essay (so you don't need to summarize the article). For assistance organizing your essay, read ahead in Chapter 8. You can also review the sample rhetorical analysis on pp. 549–55 and read the annotated article on pp. 307–14 to see the kinds of comments you might want to make.

CHAPTER **six**

How Do We Support Arguments

chapter checklist

- How do we build credibility, activate reasoning or logic, and evoke emotion?
- How can apprentice scholars incorporate original research?
- When do different kinds of support work best?

In this chapter, we'll explain some techniques that scholars use to collect and present various kinds of support. As we've discussed, scholars expect higher standards of evidence and reasoning than you might find in campaign advertisements or infomercials, but that doesn't mean that scholarly arguments can't include other kinds of persuasive techniques. Everyday arguments build credibility and evoke emotions that cannot be scientifically measured or predicted according to black-and-white rules of logic. Here again are the kinds of support that we introduced in Chapter 4.

Table 6.1 KINDS OF SUPPORT

VERIFICATION Something you can *look up*	EVIDENCE Something you can *observe*	ILLUSTRATION Something you can *imagine*
• Previous research • Law or precedence • Established theory	• Empirical data • Personal experience • Textual evidence	• Hypothetical example • Analogy or metaphor • Fictional narrative

Can you recall how different kinds of support activate reasoning, build credibility, or evoke emotion?

Building Credibility

Before most readers will trust new information that we present, they must consider us or our arguments to be *credible*. We've already discussed how audiences find some texts more credible than others. For example, scholars take the *Oxford English Dictionary* more seriously than Dictionary.com. They see scholarly journals as more credible than Wikipedia.

Credibility, or what the ancient Greeks called *ethos*, usually comes from three sources:

1. **Verification**, borrowed from trustworthy sources. Verification relies on "secondary" sources, which means someone else has already analyzed or interpreted the evidence. By integrating verification into our arguments, we demonstrate that we've read and understand what experts have already said (as in a Research or Literature Review). We assume that our audience will trust us only after we prove that we know what we're talking about.
2. **Reputation**, or what the audience already knows and thinks about the author before starting to read (for example, if he's a respected scholar or celebrity washout). Readers trust authors whom they recognize as experts. Similarly, readers trust arguments that appear in respected publications even before they begin reading.

3. **Presentation**, which involves using a style that's suitable for your audience and purpose. You wouldn't wear cutoff jeans and flip flops to a formal business interview. In scholarly writing, we can project credibility by using an appropriate style (effective tone, correct grammar and spelling, etc.) and by adhering to scholarly genres (using logical organization and support). Precise editing also demonstrates that we care about our writing and our audience. Additionally, we demonstrate trustworthy character by considering different perspectives (including counterarguments), by acknowledging weaknesses in our own arguments, and by treating sources respectfully (summarizing, quoting, and citing accurately).

Activating Reasoning or Logic with Evidence

Credibility helps us connect with readers by gaining their trust, but evidence and reasoning provide the strongest foundation for arguments.

To understand why, we must consider the concept of reliability, which indicates how closely the results of investigation come together to form a pattern. For example, if several professors graded the same paper differently, then we would consider their evaluation results to be unreliable. Reliability is a measure of consistency.

Audiences respond to evidence more reliably than they respond to credible or emotional appeals. Just as we all use different credibilimeters in different situations, we don't all laugh at the same jokes or cry at the same movies. But with the aid of instant replay and digital video, we can all agree when we see a football player stepping out of bounds. (Of course, without instant replay, referees generate lots of controversy.)

We're most "certain" of what we can observe and count because observing and counting don't seem like acts of interpretation. For instance, we're probably more confident in the conclusions we might reach if we conduct a biological experiment in a lab with carefully controlled methods than we might be confident in predicting next month's weather or developing a definitive interpretation of a Renaissance poem.

Quantitative Evidence

To seek reliable conclusions, scholars develop careful methods of investigation that will yield similar results each time. Scholars who engage in quantitative investigation use statistical analysis to test the quality of their results, which helps make evidence much more persuasive. Statistics also seem more precise. Compare, for example, the following statements:

- Most of Greenland's ice sheet has melted.
- Nearly 97% of Greenland's ice sheet shows evidence of surface thawing.

The apparent precision of the second statement seems more believable, right? The first statement sounds anecdotal—like something you might have heard from a friend who had a sister who knew some guy in Greenland who noticed a lot of melting. The second statement seems like something written by a scientist who might have planted a bunch of precise little instruments across Greenland, or, in this case, had access to sophisticated thermal satellite imagery. Also, "surface thawing" is more precisely stated than "melting." Statistics bring otherwise ambiguous information into sharp focus, like glasses that correct blurry vision.

Qualitative Evidence

Please don't think of evidence only as quantitative data. What "counts" as evidence varies across disciplines. Qualitative evidence includes information that must be interpreted, rather than counted.

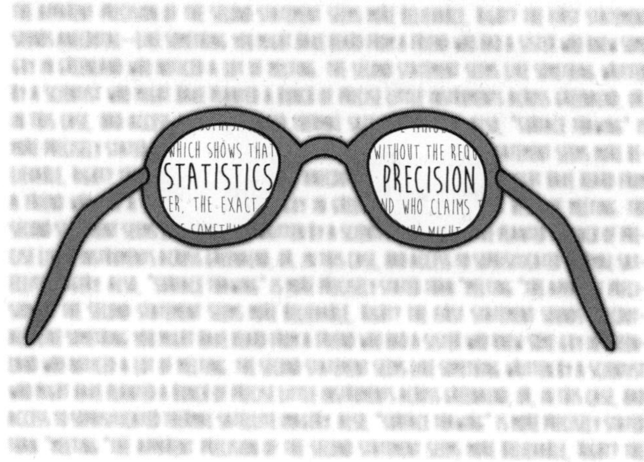

In literary studies, for example, evidence might be actual words (quotations) from a novel, or known biographical information about an author. Similarly, scholars of theater, music, or visual arts might use a performance or a painting as their primary "data." Sociologists and psychologists might observe and interpret human behavior.

Whatever their discipline, scholars are careful to design reliable and precise methods for collecting, analyzing, and reporting evidence. As you continue your scholarly apprenticeship, pay careful attention and ask your professors lots of questions about what "counts" as evidence in their disciplines and how they determine whether that evidence is trustworthy.

Incorporating Original Research

Apprentice scholars often rely heavily on "library research" to support their arguments with verification. However, scholarly arguments become more interesting when we can collect some evidence for ourselves. To do so, we use a reliable research methodology, present and analyze our results, and draw conclusions.

Research Methods

Many scholars use empirical research—that which is based "on the results of observation and experiment"—to support their arguments (*Oxford English Dictionary*). Scholars collect empirical data in the lab and in the field through various means, such as experiments, observations, and case studies. Even if you can't carry out elaborate investigations, you can conduct interviews and observations or distribute surveys to practice gathering reliable data.

You'll find it helpful to consult with a more experienced scholar, such as your professor, when developing your research methodology. The research question will determine the appropriate methodology. For example, if you wanted to learn how a scientist approaches the writing process in general, you might interview a biologist, a physicist, and a chemist using somewhat open-ended questions. To answer a more specific, narrowly focused research question (such as "How much time do scientists typically invest in drafting a research article?"), you might survey several dozen different kinds of scientists.

To enhance credibility, we follow legitimate methods of data collection. Disciplines have specific guidelines and rules for conducting empirical research, which you might learn when assisting specific professors in their research. However, for many apprentice scholars, using legitimate methods mostly means following common sense:

- **Interviews.** Be courteous and respectful of your subject's time and expertise. Plan extensively beforehand, with carefully constructed questions, a clear sense of your purpose, and background knowledge about your interviewee. Record the interview, with permission, so that you can quote and paraphrase accurately.
- **Surveys.** Write clear and calculated questions that get at your research question but don't lead your audience too much. Invite a few peers to read over a survey before you distribute it to the masses so that you can catch any confusing phrases, misleading questions,

or errors. Collect enough survey responses to have a representative sample size.
- **Observations.** When possible, remain inconspicuous and limit the amount of influence your presence creates. When drawing conclusions about an observation, consider the possible effects your presence might have had on the behavior you observed.

Keep in mind the strengths and limitations of different methodologies. Surveys may yield high reliability (consistent results) but low accuracy. If a question is leading or confusing, the results might not really mean what we think. On the other hand, an interview or case study might yield high accuracy but low reliability or generalizability.

When conducting research that involves human subjects, most universities require a formal review and approval process to ensure that research is conducted with integrity, protects privacy, and keeps participants safe. Before beginning such research, consult with your scholarly mentor to learn more about the process and procedures.

Analysis

Once you've collected some data, you can begin to analyze it by asking yourself:

- What does this evidence suggest? What might it mean?
- How could this information help me answer my research question?
- Do these responses align with what other scholars have found, or are the results different?
- What questions remain unanswered? What else needs to be studied?

Be careful not to interpret your research results overzealously. Scholars hesitate to claim that their evidence "proves" their conclusions. Instead, they typically make limited claims about what their results "suggest." Again, remember the basics of argumentation: **Your claim can only be as strong as your evidence.** For example, interviews can help you collect rich, detailed data, but their results cannot be easily generalized. And even if you survey 100 college students and they all respond "yes" to the same question, you can't generalize this response to say that "all college students agree." You can say, "100 out of 100 college students responded 'yes,' which *suggests* that this is a popular response among college students; however, more research is needed."

Again, more experienced scholars can help you with analytical techniques.

Evoke an Audience's Emotions

Evidence and verification provide the foundation for scholarly writing, but like any form of human communication, scholarly arguments may also contain elements that arouse readers' emotions.

In everyday arguments, emotion often dominates. Consider, for example, television commercials that solicit donations for animal shelters by showing sickly, pathetic looking kittens and puppies. In fact, the term "pathetic" has roots in the ancient rhetorical name for a persuasive emotional appeal, *pathos*, which is also the root of the words "sympathy" and "empathy."

Emotion can be a powerful but dangerous force. Advertisers and politicians sometimes use emotional appeals to cloud their audience's judgment, to get them to act irrationally or to "go along" even when offered no evidence or logical reasons to do so. For example, cigarette advertisements might make teenagers think it's cool to do something that has potentially dangerous consequences. Political propaganda often uses emotions to motivate citizens to actions that are oppressive, violent, or not in their best interest.

The potential abuse of emotional appeals makes scholars cautious about using them. Writers who attempt to manipulate their audience's emotions risk losing credibility.

Besides, emotional appeals tend to be the most subjective, unreliable kind of "proof" available because emotional responses tend to vary so widely among different individuals and cultures. Using facts and knowledge as evidence builds a more solid, objective basis for argument because most everyone trusts them and finds them persuasive. If we built a pyramid of persuasive appeals, we'd place evidence at the bottom, then credibility, with emotion at the top.

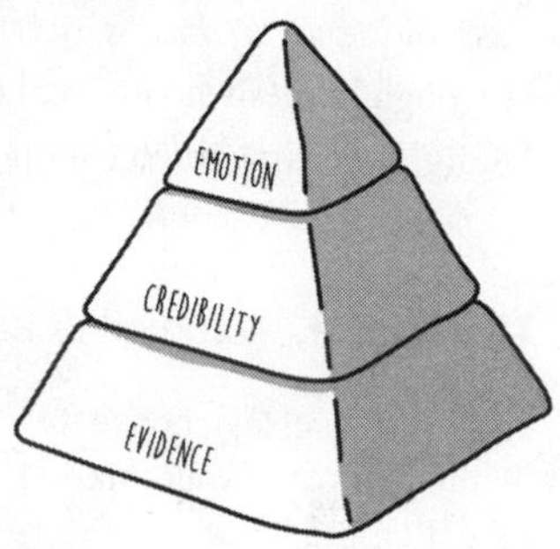

Think of this like a food pyramid: use emotion carefully, in small amounts. Just like sugar, butter, or seasonings in a recipe, a little goes a long way. In limited doses, emotion can amplify an argument, especially if you want your audience to *do* something, like admit you to college or adopt a business proposal.

What are some safer ways to use emotional appeals in scholarly writing?

- Use vivid language and concrete imagery to illustrate your argument. Precise, fresh, lively words can stir interest and evoke a powerful response, even if the content isn't pulling at anyone's heart strings.
- As long as you build the core of your argument with evidence and verification, you could consider adding a touching example in your introduction or conclusion that arouses your audience's emotions.
- Perhaps the most efficient means to evoke emotion is to use symbolic cultural references that you know will resonate with your audience. For example, you might arouse a US audience's patriotic values with an iconic reference, either an image (Mount Rushmore or the American flag) or a verbal metaphor ("as American as baseball and apple pie"). Ancient Greeks characterized this persuasive

technique as *mythos*, which still resonates with us, for example, through heroes who are real (Abraham Lincoln or Martin Luther King, Jr.) or imagined (Wonder Woman or Captain America).

TRY THIS ➤ Credibility and Emotion

For this exercise, choose two current TV or magazine advertisements that pique your interest. As you examine the advertisements, reflect on the following:

- How do these advertisements build credibility or play audiences' emotions?
- Who would find these advertisements most persuasive? Why?
- How might these advertisements fail?
- What differences do you find between how these advertisements appeal to their audiences?

Share your analysis with some classmates. What do you notice about the roles that credibility, reasoning, and emotion play in advertising?

Crossover Effects

Supports often carry "crossover" effects. For example:

- We often use verifications, such as previous research or expert testimony, to build credibility. However, we might also use such sources as evidence (to activate reasoning) by borrowing another researcher's data set or using an eyewitness account of an event.
- Even when an audience cannot understand or judge the legitimacy of data or statistics, presenting gobs of such evidence can make an author or argument seem more credible.
- Illustrations can not only arouse emotions but also activate reasoning. Consider, for example, arguing that "the wars in the Middle

East are just like Vietnam." That statement uses an illustration to make a logical point. The reverse is also true: consider how we used pie charts in Chapter 2. Usually, these graphics represent data, but we used them as illustrations to help you imagine different versions of the writing process.

The most interesting and sophisticated crossover support might be personal experience.

Personal Experience as Support

Arguments often use personal experience to enhance credibility or emotion. In our first chapter, for example, we explained that we (the authors) are both experienced writing teachers and tutors, assuming that information would increase your trust that we know enough to write this book. In professional and everyday arguments, people often mention their experiences as credentials for speaking on a subject (though this is less common in scholarly writing). Personal experience can also amplify an argument's emotional appeal by creating a vivid illustration or by demonstrating empathy for your audience.

In scholarly arguments, perhaps the most common use of personal experience is as evidence. For example, someone writing an argument proposing improved support systems for students with learning disabilities might describe her experiences with dyslexia. We're careful not to overgeneralize from personal experience—after all, our sample size is only one—but personal experience can bring a depth of detail and perspective that other sources cannot.

As a scholarly apprentice, you can use personal experience as a powerful primary source of evidence, credibility, and emotion. Just be sure to use it carefully and ask your audience (if available) when you have questions about whether it's appropriate for the kind of argument you're trying to create.

Narrating

One way to incorporate personal experience, to use a more intimate voice, and to captivate readers is to compose a narrative, which uses elements of storytelling. For example, you might have written a personal narrative statement for admission to college. Narratives like this contain implicit arguments (for example, "You should admit me to college because of A, B, and C"). You might use narrative in a creative writing class, in a cover letter, or in a graduate school application essay.

Researchers also sometimes think of their writing as a kind of narrative. A good research report "tells a story": we found this problem, designed this experiment, and discovered these results. Scholars also use "micro" narratives to arouse emotion or interest, especially in their introduction or conclusion. When using storytelling this way, narrative becomes a kind of evidence or illustration. For example, if arguing about homelessness, a writer might begin with a story about a real person and his experiences living on the streets. Such graphic examples can serve as compelling evidence and can highlight the real world implications of an otherwise dry scholarly argument.

Using narrative elements may seem like a no-brainer, but it actually presents its own set of challenges:

- **You can't forget the audience.** When you're telling a story, particularly a personal one, it's easy to get wrapped up in what you already know and care about. But you have to connect with readers and make your experience relatable and meaningful to them so that the implications are evident. The story needs to be captivating, with a source of tension, a *so what?* Just because an experience is life changing for you doesn't mean that readers will see its significance. That means you have to think about your audience the entire time, asking yourself:
    - Why should readers care?

  - What's the larger significance here?
  - What's the takeaway message (implications) that readers haven't already heard a hundred times?

  To keep your attention focused on your audience's needs, you might consider answering some of these questions explicitly by articulating clear claims and rationales, at least in your draft. If, in the final revision, you're confident that the audience will get your point, you can always remove those statements.

- **You still need evidence.** You may think that a personal story doesn't require proof, but all arguments need support. Whenever you're trying to convince readers of something—to think differently about an issue, to change their attitude, to embrace your message—you're writing an argument that requires support. Narratives typically incorporate evidence in more subtle ways, but it's still there. Usually, it's in the details. Elements of the story help to support the conclusion, the overarching thesis or argument. To incorporate this evidence, ask yourself:
  - What story elements illustrate my message?
  - What details can serve as evidence to prove my point?

  Be sure to layer in these details so that you're not only saying something enlightening but supporting it, too.

Select Support According to the Controversy Categories

We can use the controversy categories as building blocks for larger arguments. Each category calls forth a particular kind of argument. For example, if we're writing an argument about women's changing roles since the turn of the 21st century, we recognize that we're writing an argument about *fact or existence* (because we would be answering the question "Have women's roles changed since 2000?") and *definition* (because we would be answering the question "In what ways have women's roles changed?"). Once we identify what kind of argument we're developing, we can select the techniques that correspond to that category.

Arguments about Existence and Fact

Existence arguments can be difficult because audiences tend to hold stubbornly to what they already believe or think they know. Typically, existence arguments rely on observable evidence for support. Consider, for example, how emphatically people who have witnessed UFOs believe in extraterrestrial life, whereas people who have not seen flying saucers tend to remain suspicious. Even within the scientific community, an experiment must be repeated again and again before there's consensus about a major discovery.

Not everyone has a laboratory or can observe phenomena across the world. Therefore, we often rely on verification to support existence arguments; we trust others to observe evidence for us. How else would we know about galaxies or subatomic particles that we cannot see for ourselves? So, if an apprentice scholar were writing an existence argument, say about President John F. Kennedy's assassination, she might draw from different historical accounts to speculate on what really happened.

Sometimes existence can be presented through illustration, as is the case with science fiction and fantasy art that, for example, develops a political critique or proposes an alternative future (recall *The Hunger Games*). Michelangelo illustrated, through his drawings, the existence of flying machines long before we sent anyone to the moon. Illustrations can support arguments to bring into existence things we can only imagine.

Arguments about Definition

Many arguments begin with disagreements about how we define a term or concept. Arguments about abortion policy, for example, become bogged down before they begin if parties to the argument cannot agree about whether abortion is "murder." And arguments about whether abortion is murder also depend on when we define an embryo or fetus as "human"—that is, when human life begins. (Note how we use quotation marks to call attention to terms in dispute.)

Public controversies often hinge on the definition of a word or phrase. In a famous White House scandal, President Bill Clinton famously asserted that he "did not have sexual relations with that woman, Miss Lewinski," prompting vigorous debate about what specific kinds of physical interactions constitute "sexual relations."

Knowing that vaguely defined terms can cause arguments to stall, scholars tend to be very careful about the language they use, often explaining potentially controversial terms in the beginning of their arguments. Often, we present small definitional arguments as building blocks for larger arguments. For example, in order to argue against "corporal punishment," we would need to define what we mean by the term. Does spanking of children by their parents fit the definition? In most states, parents can legally use "reasonable force" to discipline their children. But what actions are "reasonable"? It's worth thinking through any terms that might be open to question before proposing a larger evaluation or proposal argument.

Usually, we argue whether a case fits an existing definition. But sometimes we discover a case that doesn't fit existing definitions, or we can't agree on a definition and need to create one. For example, we might redefine the term "marriage" by comparing different types of marriage and looking for patterns across groups.

Some definitional arguments can be so interesting, significant, and substantial that they can take an entire essay or even book to examine adequately. For example, rhetoric scholars Celeste Condit and John Lucaites wrote a book-length study of definitional arguments about the term "equality" in American history. Their book, *Crafting Equality: America's Anglo-African Word*, traces how public arguments transformed the very meaning of equality—from how the US

Continental Congress referred to equality ("all men are created equal" but not women or slaves) to the present.

To craft a definitional argument, we must first settle on a definition that our audience will accept. Sometimes we can simply define a term explicitly and hope that the audience will accept our definition, as in "for the purposes of this argument, we will define 'reasonable force' as physical contact that does not cause bodily harm or long-term emotional damage."

Another strategy is to verify a definition with a credible source. Sparingly, we might use an everyday dictionary to validate our meaning: "*Merriam Webster's Dictionary* defines murder as. . . ." For a scholarly audience, a more credible place to start would be the *Oxford English Dictionary*, or *OED*, which gives a richer set of definitions and some historical background of how a word has been used over time. (Sometimes it's also interesting to see where words came from, what they originally meant, and how their meanings have evolved.)

For a more specialized scholarly audience, we consult specialized encyclopedias, such as Thomas Sloane's 837-page *Encyclopedia of Rhetoric*. Scholarly encyclopedias are written by experts who provide extensive discussions and bibliographies to help sort out the nuances of key terms and concepts in a specialized subject. Check your local library's reference section for a range of scholarly encyclopedias, from the *Encyclopedia of Paleontology* to the *Encyclopedia of Management*.

Once we've established an agreeable definition, we then explain how our subject "fits" that definition using evidence and illustration. For example, a law that bans assault rifles will clearly define its characteristics so we can determine whether the Colt AR-15 fits the legal definition. If we wanted to argue that energy drinks are dangerous or unhealthy, we would need to explain what we mean by "dangerous or unhealthy" and then cite evidence that energy drinks have those effects.

TRY THIS ➤ Write a Definition

For this exercise, brainstorm with peers to identify an issue that is controversial because of people's conflicting definitions. For example, public funding for art sometimes raises the controversy of "What counts as art?" After you select an issue, write a one-page argument that develops and defends a specific definition of a term or phrase that is central to the controversy. Afterward, compare your definitions with your peers and discuss the implications of your definitions.

Arguments about Cause and Consequence

Arguments that try to establish a causal link are one of the most difficult cases to make. That's because it's difficult to definitively link a cause and effect without confusing cause with correlation. Often, when writers try to argue about cause and consequence, they commit logical fallacies like the ones we discuss in Chapter 9. However, you may have read persuasive essays or watched documentaries that build compelling cases against social or environmental problems, such as *Food Inc.* or *An Inconvenient Truth.* If you look back at these films, you might notice that they are causal arguments.

Arguments about Evaluation

Like definitional arguments, evaluation arguments sometimes stand alone and sometimes become part of larger arguments. For example, an argument proposing a solution to international copyright infringement would probably begin by describing the problem and then evaluate why copyright violations are wrong and deserve our attention. This last part is especially important because ethical issues can help motivate an audience to act by highlighting an argument's implications.

TRY THIS ➤ Examine a Causal Argument

For this exercise, select and analyze an essay or a film that makes a causal argument. To find an example of a causal argument, think about topics that yield debates about cause and consequence. Then, read or view the argument to identify and analyze specific techniques the author uses to build her case. As you analyze the argument, consider the following questions:

- How does the author organize the argument? Why do you think she chose that structure and sequence of ideas?
- How does the author build a case that the consequences or effects are not merely coincidental?
- How effective is the argument, overall?

We begin evaluation arguments by establishing criteria by which we will judge the case at hand. Those criteria must be based in values shared by the audience. Let's consider the argument against corporal punishment that we discussed earlier. In this example, the definition hinges on the phrase "reasonable force," which we defined as "physical contact that does not cause bodily harm or long-term emotional damage." Here, we're making a kind of evaluation argument, counting on our audience to share our belief that causing bodily or emotional damage to children is morally unacceptable.

Because evaluation arguments depend so much on values and beliefs, they tend to be complex and compelling, especially when they involve competing values. For instance, most Americans value national security and individual human rights, but the use of aggressive interrogation techniques on suspected terrorists (defined by critics as "torture") places security and rights in apparent conflict. In cases like this, we must argue why we hold one value more dearly than another.

To fully evaluate an issue, we might have to compare (find similarities among) and contrast (find differences among) components of the controversy. In fact, many arguments compare and contrast theories, texts, artifacts, events, concepts, and so on. For example, a research or literature review compares sources in order to describe and analyze the scholarly "conversation" about an issue. When using this mode of analysis, it's important to synthesize—bring items together in a new, enlightening way so that readers learn something new about a subject—rather than just look at each item or subject separately. **The structure we choose can help promote synthesis.** For example, if we compare similar items alongside each other, perhaps even within the same paragraphs, we're more likely to show off our good thinking by explaining exactly how we've arrived at our evaluation. Doing so can help us avoid the worst kind of comparison/contrast analysis—the one that says little more than "These things have some things in common but are still different." When we compare and contrast items in close proximity to each other, we can examine the intricacies of each, as they relate to the other.

TRY THIS ➤ Evaluate a Film or Restaurant

For this exercise, choose a film or restaurant that you want to evaluate. Before viewing the film or dining at the restaurant, identify a list of criteria against which you will evaluate your subject. Then, write a 500-word review of the film or restaurant. Post your evaluation on a blog or a social network for others to read and comment on.

Arguments about Policy

When we write a proposal argument, we typically (a) describe a problem, (b) present potential solutions, and (c) justify a course of action. We might not spend equal time on every section but instead think about the primary source of disagreement. For instance, if readers already understand the severity of a problem, we can focus more on the solution and justification sections. However, if readers don't recognize a problem, we need to spend more time proving that there's actually cause for concern. To determine which controversies you can skim or skip, do your research, test your arguments on a real audience (such as a classmate or a writing tutor). Or ask your professor: How much can I assume my audience already knows or agrees with my argument?

So What?

Effective scholarly arguments use reasoning and evidence and connect with an audience through credibility and emotion. However, each rhetorical situation requires a different dose of these supports. Scholars typically prefer evidence over credibility and emotion, but that's not to say that values don't influence how we investigate and reach conclusions—or that we shouldn't pursue questions that involve human emotion. As Aristotle taught, we must appeal to the whole person; although evidence provides a stable foundation, it doesn't always motivate people as powerfully as credibility or emotion.

In the next chapter, we argue that the best way to develop a compelling argument—one that your audience will want to read—is to pursue a stimulating question. We offer concrete strategies for finding important and inspiring questions, and we detail the steps of refining and narrowing a thesis to make it more complex. This chapter also recommends some arguments to avoid and gives alternative options like the evolving thesis and ones with a stylistic flair.

What's Next

Take what you've learned in this chapter and respond to the following prompts.

1. **Analyze an everyday argument.** Find an everyday argument or persuasive text that interests you, such as an advertisement,

political cartoon, letter to the editor, or magazine article. Map out the uses of evidence, verification, and illustration, and then consider how well they work. Are you persuaded? Why or why not? You might also consider creating a pie chart or another graphic representation that illustrates the ratio of evidence to illustration to verification.

2. **Debate.** Practice debating a controversial issue. As a class, list several potential issues, and then vote on the most interesting one. Some topic suggestions might include genetically modified foods, salary caps, grading practices, drones, paid college athletes, adolescent plastic surgery, and single-sex schooling. Next, divide into groups for each position on the controversy, and develop a plan for your argument. Develop a potential list of evidence, verification, and illustrations that support your position. You might spend time outside of class gathering more support and then present your arguments to the class. After each group defends its position, take some time to develop and present rebuttal arguments.

3. **Evaluate a persuasive campaign.** Watch a couple short films from Dove's Beauty Campaign, such as *Dove Evolution*, *Beauty Pressure*, or *Body Evolution*. Discuss the following questions with a peer and then as a group:
   - What and where is the thesis (argument)?
   - How does the film develop credibility? Is the use of credibility effective for its intended audience and purpose? Is it relevant and sufficient?
   - How might this use of credibility fail?
   - How does the film arouse emotion? Is the use of emotion effective?
   - How might this use of emotion fail?
   - How does the film use evidence and reasoning? Is the use of evidence and reasoning effective? Is it relevant and sufficient for supporting the argument?

- How might this use of evidence and reasoning fail?
- What additional techniques do you notice? How effective are these?

After analyzing the films, write a 1,000-word response to the arguments presented in these films, or write a rhetorical analysis essay. We explain the purpose and features of this kind of essay on p. 122.

CHAPTER **seven**

How Can We Create a Compelling Thesis

chapter checklist

- How do we find a question worth pursuing?
- What are the right questions to ask?
- Can (and why should) you change your thesis?
- How can you jazz up your style?

Even though you might have been taught to decide on your thesis *before* you start writing your argument, experienced scholars typically begin with a really good question. Remember, every argument answers a question.

Every Great Thesis Grows from a Stimulating Question

Scholarly investigation builds new knowledge or understanding by posing questions, gathering information (conducting research), and processing that information to draw conclusions. When scholars publish their discoveries, they must "show their work" by building a case to support those

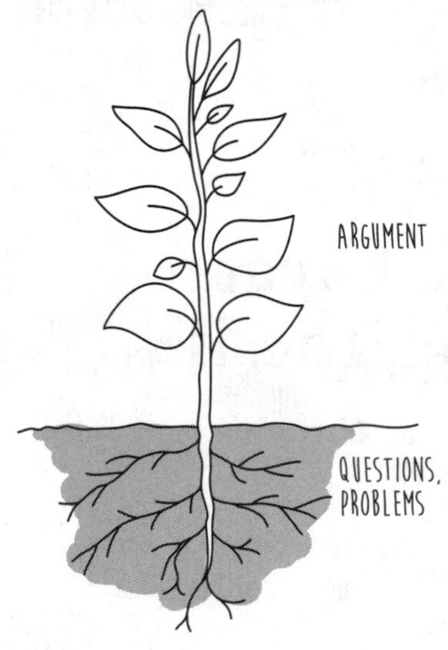

conclusions. In their introduction or research review, scholars often tell the audience explicitly what question they were trying to answer so readers can focus their attention on whether scholars have "earned" the conclusion by providing adequate support.

Ideally, questions grow organically from the work that scholars do. Scholars notice gaps in previous research, such as a historical archive or literary work that has never been examined, or an experiment that needs to be extended or updated using the latest scientific techniques. This kind of problem solving also applies to work outside of school, such as when a business manager develops a model for promoting her services to a new audience or an engineer designs a factory to be as safe, sustainable, and cost effective as possible. Although we may not always get to solve problems as significant or practical as curing Alzheimer's disease, scholars and professionals use similar methods to answer questions that matter to them and their readers.

Notice, though, that scholars, engineers, and business managers already have extensive training and experience in their field, which means they have the expertise to identify and solve these important problems. The originality of their arguments depends on that expertise. It's easier for a medical scientist to discover a cure for cancer if he's intimately familiar with state-of-the-art research trends and methods.

Lacking this expertise, how can an apprentice such as yourself know what question to ask or problem to solve so that you can create an original thesis? How can you possibly develop an argument that experienced scholars, like your professors, have not already fully considered?

- **Keep reading.** Remember, scholars write from sources. Ask your scholarly mentor to recommend readings on your topic. Once you find a good source, scour its bibliography for related readings that will take you deeper or in new directions.
- **Apply your perspective.** You undoubtedly have knowledge or life experiences that your professor does not. Use that expertise to bring fresh perspective to a subject. Realize, too, that ignorance (meaning lack of information, not lack of intelligence) can be a strength. Knowing little about something may help you to ask questions or see things that are invisible to experts.
- **Make your own luck.** Just like seasoned scholars, apprentices sometimes stumble accidentally on a research topic, a piece of evidence, or an insight that others have overlooked. Discovery often happens by mistake, so be brave and curious.
- **Challenge yourself.** Arguments demonstrate evidence of thinking. Discovering something for yourself can lead to a good thesis, even if it's not "news" to the experts.
- **Talk with others.** Conversation often sparks great ideas. Talking with trusted friends and mentors helps us refine fuzzy ideas and discover more original angles from which to approach a topic.
- **Try free writing.** (See the following TRY THIS exercise.)

TRY THIS ➤ Freewriting

For this exercise, experiment with a technique called *freewriting*, which simply means drafting with abandon. When freewriting, we don't plan ahead or stop to edit; we just write. Freewriting works well for getting started when you're not sure what you want to write about, or when your brain gets clogged with too many ideas. Freewriting can also cure writer's block (which often happens to perfectionists who

(*continued*)

edit too much while composing). Here's a technique inspired by Peter Elbow's classic book *Writing Without Teachers* that you could try alone or in class:

Step 1: Open a new document in your word processor. Save it with an awesome manuscript title.

Step 2: Turn off your computer monitor and write for 15 to 20 minutes. (Laptops: swivel the monitor flat or cover with paper.) Don't stop writing for anything.

Step 3: Turn on the monitor. Save your work. Check your word count to see how much you've written. Gloat.

Step 4: Repeat Step 2 for another 10 minutes; then repeat Step 3.

Step 5: Spellcheck the document so it's readable. Do not edit. Save again.

Step 6: Close the document and take a 10-minute break.

Step 7: Return to your computer and read the document. Do not edit. Locate the most interesting, controversial, or promising sentence. Cut and paste that sentence into a new document and begin again at Step 1. Repeat until you become lightheaded or you complete your first draft.

Ask the Right Questions

Scholars cannot always identify significant questions and problems without some help. A great tool for getting started is to explore the kinds of controversies that arguments address, as we explained in Chapter 5. These five categories are all that we need to discover a great question because most every argument you can think of belongs to one of these categories. To illustrate how to use these questions to discover an argument or a thesis, let's work through an example.

Imagine that you want to write an argument about the media's influence on body image, but you don't know how to come up with a compelling thesis. You initially thought that you could write a thesis like "The media negatively influences teenage girls' self-image," but your professor told you that such an argument would be a cliché, because most people already know that. You're frustrated, and you don't know how to develop an alternative focus. Here's where you might start:

Use the five controversy categories to brainstorm potential questions about your topic. Write down as many questions as you can. Your goal is to examine the topic exhaustively so that you can find a question worth pursuing. Just like with freewriting, when brainstorming a list of questions, try to "catch" as many ideas as you can. You don't need to decide right away about whether your questions or thoughts are stellar or weak. Like a fisherman trawling the ocean for as many fish as possible, your goal is to sweep up every last sardine.

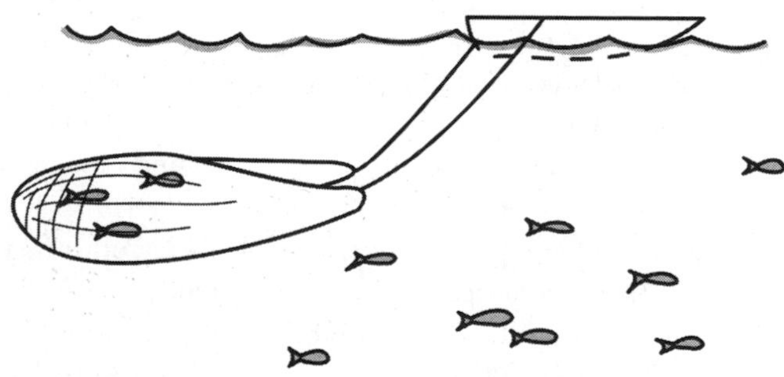

A preliminary list of controversy questions might look like the ones found in the next section.

Potential Questions about the Media's Influence on Body Image

Controversies of existence or fact (Is it true? Did it happen?)

- Does the media actually influence teenage girls? How do we know?
- Who else does the media influence?
- How much influence does the media have on teenage girls?
- Has the media always influenced teenage girls? Did this influence accelerate at a certain point?

Controversies of definition or interpretation (Does this case fit the definition? How do we interpret this information?)

- What kind of "influence" are we talking about? Does the media influence girls' thoughts, choices, feelings, aspirations, values, or something else?
- What are the signs of media influence?
- What kinds of media (magazines, film, television?) are most influential?
- What other cases would fit the definition of media influence?

Controversies of cause, consequence, or circumstance (Was it intentional? Are there extenuating circumstances?)

- Who is to blame?
- Does the media intentionally target teenage girls? Why are teenage girls profitable targets?
- Do current problems such as exercise addiction and eating disorders also result from the media's influence?
- Why are teenage girls particularly vulnerable? What other factors affect the media's influence?
- What are the consequences of this problem? What are the effects of a poor self-image? What other personal and societal problems are related?
- What theories (maybe from psychology) help explain why the media can have such a strong influence on teenage girls?

Controversies of evaluation (Is it right or wrong? Is it serious enough to warrant our attention?)

- Are the media's influences good or evil?
- Should the media take some moral responsibility for its influence?
- Is this problem more serious than other issues adolescents face?
- Is the problem serious enough to deserve immediate action?
- Do we have a moral obligation to address this issue?

Controversies of jurisdiction, procedure, policy, or action to be taken (What, if anything, should we do about it?)

- Should the government regulate media more closely?
- What can parents do to protect their teenage girls?
- How can teenage girls avoid or counteract the media's influence?
- What existing laws, policies, or solutions developed for similar controversies might apply?
- Should magazines develop a rating system like films do (G, PG, PG-13, R, NC-17) to limit adolescents' exposure to harmful messages from the media?

Once you develop a long list of questions, select the questions that are most stimulating and original. These are your starting points. From here, you can speculate on the answer to a question (develop a hypothesis or tentative thesis statement), or you can begin reading other scholars' views (verification) or collecting data (evidence). We describe methods for data collection in Chapter 6.

TRY THIS ➤ Practice Using the Controversy Categories

For this exercise, reflect on which controversy categories are most compelling, and then develop a list of questions yourself.

1. Review the media influence example and identify which questions are most interesting.
   - What makes these questions particularly thought provoking?
   - Which controversy categories seem to yield the most interesting possibilities? Why do you think so?
2. Following our example, select a topic that interests you, such as an issue related to your major or a problem that you have observed on your campus, and develop a list of questions using the controversy categories. Organize the questions in a table that outlines the controversy categories and then lists four to six

(*continued*)

questions per category. For example, you could brainstorm questions for any of these topics:

- Cost of higher education
- College admissions criteria
- Extracurricular funding in college (for example, student clubs or athletics)
- Relationships in college
- Campus diversity
- Characteristics of "good" writing

You might find it helpful to imagine stakeholders—potential audiences who care about this issue and would be affected by its implications. For example, students, parents, employers, legislatures, college administrators, and lenders might raise different questions about college funding.

So What's a Good Question?

Believe it or not, you *can* ask a bad question, at least when it comes to creating a thesis. Some questions just won't lead you down a path toward an interesting argument. Bad questions can be too simple, too obvious, or just plain boring. Good questions—ones that lead to good answers (strong thesis statements)—are challenging, compelling, and controversial. Keep these three Cs in mind when developing research questions.

Challenging questions. Scholars prefer thoughtful questions that require more sophisticated proof, scientific data, or investigation. These questions challenge scholars and their readers intellectually because they inspire careful, critical, and creative thinking. For example, compare the following:

- Too easy: "Do students abuse Adderall and Ritalin to improve concentration and test performance?"
- Better: "Are universities morally obligated to create educational programs and policies that prevent students from abusing prescription drugs?"

Compelling questions. Good questions have significant consequences or implications for real people or real situations, even if the effects are mostly theoretical. Scholars can appeal to larger audiences when they investigate issues of greater significance.

- Trivial: "Is the cafeteria's food service on weekends convenient for on-campus residents?"
- Better: "What are the economic costs and benefits of colleges providing accessible and convenient services (beyond academic support)?"

Controversial questions. Great questions don't need to be scandalous (although they can be), but they usually inspire some degree of disagreement among readers concerning the best solution to a problem or answer to a question. Selecting a question that has a spark of tension can lead to a more provocative argument.

- Pointless ("No duh"): "Is smoking unhealthy?"
- Better: "If smoking poses a public health risk, shouldn't it be illegal?"

CONSIDER THIS ➤ Using Examples

For this reflection, consider the difficulty of choosing effective examples, which is something we tried to do in this last section.

Examples help us "show" our ideas, rather than only talk about them abstractly. But we have to think carefully about how audiences will interpret our examples, or they'll misfire. Consider the previous examples of "better" questions. Do you think they work? Do you understand and agree that the "better" examples are actually stronger? Can you think of more vivid examples than the ones we provided? How might you use examples in your own writing?

When you're brainstorming possible research questions, see whether they fit the criteria of stimulating questions by asking yourself:

- Which questions are most controversial, interesting, or complicated to answer?
- Which questions already have obvious, simple, or commonly known answers? (Avoid these.)
- Is this question expansive and sophisticated enough for me to fulfill my assignment's page requirement, yet narrow enough for me to investigate it deeply within the page limit?
- How might I answer this question? What methods (for example, surveys, interviews, library research) could I use?
- Do I have the time and resources—such as access to relevant books and articles, labs, contact with experts—that I'll need to answer this question?

These practical questions help us determine what we can accomplish within the *constraints* of a writing task, which are:

- Available time (for thinking, reading, research, drafting, revising)
- Available knowledge (about methods, background information)
- Available space (literally, constraints of page and word counts, plus assignment guidelines, genre and style conventions)

When writers select a question or thesis that's simply too big, their arguments typically lack *focus*. Apprentice scholars often think they need a huge problem to fill the pages, but really they need a small problem to investigate deeply. Our advice: **Dig narrow and deep, rather than broad and shallow**. Burrow into the shores of the beach, not the confines of a sandbox.

It's difficult to demonstrate much thinking (develop a really good idea) if you're only scratching the surface of a problem. You'll likely just say things most people already know (obvious or uncontroversial thesis) or leave readers hanging (advancing a thesis that's more controversial than

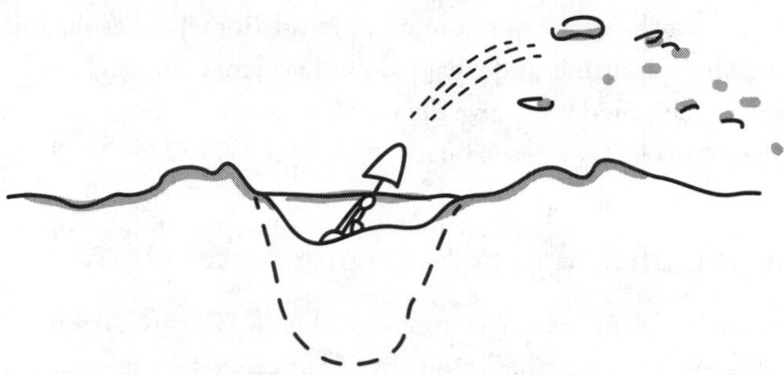

you realize, leaving holes in your argument). Instead, you need to select a focus that gets to the heart of an issue by unraveling layers of complexity.

"Great," you might say, "but how do I do that?" More insight into the controversy categories can help.

Picking Juicier Questions

As you might have noticed, controversies move from yes/no questions involving controversies of fact or existence (for example, "Do students cheat a lot? Check yes or no") to more complicated and usually more interesting questions involving definition, cause, evaluation, and policy (such as "Why do students cheat so much?" "Is cheating really unethical?" "What can or should be done about it?").

Questions from the latter categories are typically the ripest for picking because they're sweeter and more complex. Consider, for example, a yes/no question that examines a controversy of existence versus a question that involves policy:

- Simple question: "Should the drinking age be lowered to 18?"
- More complex question: "What kind of public policies might protect young adults from the dangers of drinking while safeguarding their civil rights?"

The second question gets at the heart of the matter, the *so what?* Plus, it gives the writer a much clearer plan of attack. You can imagine exactly what the writer might research in the library, what she might include in her outline, and what pieces of evidence she might collect. The first question doesn't give the writer a specific focus, so she probably wouldn't know where to start.

Turning Clichéd Arguments into Better Ones

Clichéd arguments restate common wisdom ("We can learn important lessons from tragedies in our lives") or rely on an overused idea ("Capital punishment is unethical"). Clichés don't work in scholarly writing because their life has already been sucked dry; there's nothing left to discover or add to the discussion. Also, clichéd arguments don't answer the *so what?* question. They may be interesting, but they don't solve an important problem or get to the heart of the matter. Your passion for a topic may not be enough to motivate your audience. Professors often discourage students from writing about clichéd subjects such as abortion, gun control, or the death penalty—not because such topics are uncontroversial but because it's so difficult to tell your audience anything they haven't already heard many times before.

Choosing a clichéd topic can also lead to *confirmation bias*. If you have already made up your mind about your topic, then you might only consider information that confirms your existing viewpoint rather than approaching the subject from a fresh or objective perspective. Most people will stop listening to someone who thinks his viewpoint is the only one that matters. Besides, *what if you're wrong?*

You might gravitate toward familiar topics because you know them well or can easily find plentiful sources. If you discover that other writers have already addressed your topic the same way, then your planned argument may bore your readers. You can still discuss something familiar if you can find a fresh or unique "take" on the subject that will transform a cliché into something more compelling. Using the controversy categories to focus and complicate your topics can help.

Let's walk through an example. Many students are concerned about their right to drink alcohol. Therefore, essays that argue for a lower drinking age are painfully common. Unfortunately, most of these arguments will be overly familiar to your audience. The problem you face, then, is trying to write about something that interests you but needs an angle to engage your audience. Starting with a less familiar question can help. We can use the controversy categories to develop more compelling, complex questions, such as the following examples:

- What's the real problem: underage drinking or alcohol abuse? (*Existence/fact*)
- How should Americans define an "adult"? What are the underlying assumptions about adulthood in American culture, and what are the implications of these assumptions? (*Definition/interpretation*)
- If young people have wanted to lower the drinking age for many years, why hasn't anything changed? What causes political apathy among 18- to 21-year-old voters? (*Cause/consequence*)
- Is the real problem that the legislative process takes so long? Should we be worried that many citizens are unhappy with the government but apathetic about change? (*Evaluation*)
- How can we encourage young adults to become more politically active? How can we make the process of enacting new laws more efficient and possible? (*Policy*)

Through investigating related issues using the controversy categories, we can find underlying issues that are more compelling and fresher for our audience.

So, to sum up: you can find the strongest thesis statements by doing the following:

1. Investigating a controversy thoroughly to identify the best questions that people haven't answered fully yet
2. Selecting challenging, compelling, and controversial questions
3. Focusing on the later controversy categories

Use Sources to Generate Ideas

The controversy categories can help us discover an inspiration and begin collecting support for a potential thesis. However, you don't have to develop thesis statements entirely on your own. Conducting library research and reading other scholars' work can also help you develop ideas for a thesis. The following techniques help us generate ideas:

1. **Play the "Believing and Doubting Game"** with sources to discover new applications and arguments. Get in the habit of asking yourself the questions that we describe on pp. 118–119 every time you read a new source. Reading actively in this way can inspire new ideas in response to existing ones.
2. **Find a source with which you strongly disagree.** Reading alternative viewpoints can help you clarify your own perspective.
3. **Create a table that compares and contrasts various sources.** You can use this table to do a number of things: (a) to outline diverse perspectives; (b) to identify the heart of the matter, according to these sources; (c) to find points that the sources overlook; (d) to highlight central disagreements; and so forth.
4. **Pair two sources in conversation with each other.** Imagine what two authors might say to each other if they were together. Imagine what new insights they might reach, given the chance to converse. Predict the answers that one author might give to the other author's questions, given their respective positions.
5. **Look at one source through the "lens" of another source.** This strategy allows you to do a couple of things: (a) apply a theory that one source describes to another source's examples or case studies or (b) consider the implications of one scholar's argument on another scholar's position. For example, in order to discuss how cloning might enable survival of the fittest, you could apply Darwin's theory of natural selection to an anticloning article.

All of these strategies can prompt an original thesis. However, keep in mind that some of these strategies require you to speculate and build a case for your interpretation. In those instances, you'll need to explain and support your thinking.

TRY THIS ➤ Use Sources

For this exercise, select two reliable and useful sources on a topic of your (or your instructor's) choice. Then, use one of the five techniques we outlined for using sources to generate ideas. Record your brainstorming by taking notes, freewriting (see pp. 147–148 for a description of this technique), or creating an outline or table.

Alternative Competing Hypotheses

Sometimes scholars develop multiple tentative answers, or hypotheses, to answer their research questions. For example, following the scientific method, early researchers may have used the following hypotheses concerning tobacco use:

1. Smoking improves health.
2. Smoking is unhealthy.
3. Smoking has no significant effect on health.

Next, researchers might collect evidence—by studying correlations between disease and smoking via health records, experiments on rats, or maybe just sitting around smoking a lot—and then measure which hypotheses have the most and least amount of support. The amount of support, of course, determines the strength of the conclusion (thesis). As evidence accumulates, the hypothesis intensifies from a possibility to a probability, evolving from something we *suspect* to something we think we *know*.

Investigating simultaneous, competing hypotheses helps scientists reduce bias. Even if a researcher favors a particular conclusion, the scientific method allows the evidence to speak for itself. Good researchers generate as many potential hypotheses as they can to increase their chances of discovering the best possible answer, which is sometimes something truly original.

Can I Change My Thesis?

Yes. Not only can you change your thesis, but you often should. The purpose of investigation is to *discover* knowledge—not just to reinforce what we already think. Experienced scholars allow their investigations to change their perspectives on a subject, which is why we begin with questions and hypotheses, rather than making up our minds before we begin our research.

Many inexperienced writers think that they should select a thesis early in their writing process and then stick with it at all costs. They see the thesis as an unchanging guide for the paper's direction. But this notion of a fixed thesis disregards the writing process that experienced writers follow. Scholars typically have a tentative thesis or hypothesis in mind when they begin researching and writing, but they refine and change their views as they encounter better evidence and other scholars' findings. Their thesis ultimately *evolves.*

For example, a writer might begin her first draft with a fairly simple thesis, like "SAT scores are unfair and unreliable predictors of college-level success." After some preliminary research, she discovers evidence that higher SAT scores do often correspond to higher college grades, so she revises her thesis: "Although SAT scores can predict many students' college-level success, universities should not value SAT scores over other aspects of a student's application, such as grades and extracurricular activities."

Then, in her next draft, she might refine those ideas even further by developing a solution, or proposal argument (a genre that we describe in Appendix B), for a specific audience of university policy makers:

> Colleges should use new technologies such as FaceTime and Skype to interview applicants online, rather than relying primarily on outdated assessment tools that reflect students' abilities in very

> limited contexts, such as exam environments. To gain even more perspective on the "whole student," admissions offices might even employ current students to assist with the selection process.

Notice how the writer's final thesis is more specific and more original? It demonstrates the writer's *thinking* on the issue. Also, notice that this final thesis falls under the last category of controversies (controversies about jurisdiction, procedure, policy, or action to be taken). Not surprising—given what we said earlier about picking juicy topics. This final category is where you'll find your strongest thesis statements when readers already agree on the issues in the previous categories. Here's why. Facts, as the basis of argument, are often based in the past; there's less to argue about because we know more about the past than the present and the future, which are still unfolding. Knowledge and beliefs (controversies about definition and evaluation) are juicier because we're still struggling to get a sense of them right now. Controversies about what we should do in the future are juiciest because we really don't know what will happen (it's anyone's guess).

In the case of our example, many readers would already know that SAT scores are imperfect predictors of college-level success, but they might be unsure about alternative criteria. The writer's evolved thesis would address the heart of the issue: "What should we do about this problem?" In her final draft, the writer may show how her thesis evolved, or she may just revise the original thesis by changing the introduction. Readers may never even know her previous thoughts on the topic. What's important is that she remains open to different ways of seeing a controversy so that she can understand its complexity and select a thesis that takes into account multiple perspectives and objections.

Why Would I Change My Thesis?

You might oppose such a flexible stance because of the extra time involved. After all, if you write your paper with one thesis in mind and then change your argument, you could face extra hours of researching and revising. How will you ever finish a paper if you keep shifting the focus of your argument?

Remember, the point of scholarly argument isn't only to finish a paper but also to discover and communicate knowledge. Scholars don't write for the sake of writing; they write to communicate (and sometimes discover) what they think. **Settling on a thesis before writing closes off opportunities to learn.** Usually, you're not really *changing* your argument so much as *focusing* and *refining* so you can learn more.

How can you do so more efficiently? Spend more time reading and thinking and brainstorming *before* actually writing a formal draft. Anticipate problems in your thinking and objections to your position before they pop up in your paragraphs. Keep in mind, too, that for scholars, writing grows out of investigation.

Moreover, let's be honest: most of us have trouble identifying exactly what we're trying to say until we talk it out. Drafting can achieve that. We might have a blurry idea of a thesis but once we start writing, we realize we really mean to say something different. Embrace that process. Allow yourself to discover first and organize later.

Peer review can also help us identify a good thesis. When someone reads a scholarly draft, the best question to ask is this: What do you find most interesting? (Consult Appendix A on "How to Benefit from Peer Review and Collaboration" for advice and additional questions to guide peer review.) Often, the most interesting—and thus potentially best thesis—lurks somewhere toward the end of a draft. This makes sense, if a thesis is really the conclusion of your thinking, right?

Because conventional scholarly arguments lead with the thesis, once you find it, all you have to do is put it at the beginning and pretend you knew that all along. It's as if you're saying: here's what I discovered, now let me show you how I arrived there and why you should believe me. Alternatively, if you change your thesis midway through your writing process, you might want to tell readers how and why you've arrived at a new conclusion. You can do this with the "evolving thesis."

Writing an Evolving Thesis

You might be pleased to hear that there are other options available than leading with your thesis.

We're all familiar with the five-paragraph essay that keeps a consistent thesis throughout. Historically, though, the "essay" was exploratory and evolving. (The French word *essai* literally means an "attempt," "test," or "experiment.") Similarly, an argument with an evolving thesis builds and becomes more complicated, narrow, or detailed as the paper progresses. This kind of thesis offers different advantages, such as:

- **Showing readers your evolving thoughts.** If you want to illustrate exactly how you've reached a particular conclusion, you can begin your paper with your initial hypothesis and then introduce counterarguments, evidence, or verification that influenced your thinking. By showing what has expanded and changed your perspective, you can take your readers on the intellectual journey that you followed while investigating the issues.
- **Building a complicated argument.** Sometimes you simply can't articulate your entire conclusion before you've explained its various subpoints. In these cases, you need to explain or prove one part of the thesis before moving on to the other parts. The evolving thesis allows you to defend each claim separately and then—like a staircase—to build to the precipice, your overarching thesis. This strategy can make your logic clearer for your reader to process and understand.
- **Developing a controversial argument.** When you take a controversial stance, one that your readers might reject outright, it's smart to begin from a position that your readers are more likely to accept. That way, you can establish some common ground. Then, you can gradually evolve your thesis by proving claims one at a time, in the same way that you would develop a

complicated argument. With this strategy, you essentially say to readers: "We can agree on X. Now let me explain Y. . . . After you agree with me about Y, I'll support Z. . . . Once you understand why I think Z is true, you might reconsider your position." The evolving thesis is useful when you need to persuade your audience gradually and methodically, when you want to get them on your side before fully exposing your position. For example, Charles Darwin used this technique in his groundbreaking book *On the Origin of Species by Means of Natural Selection*. Can you imagine why?

- **Keeping the reader interested or surprised.** You can introduce an element of surprise and engage readers when you initially hold back a bit. We're not advocating that you mislead your audience or intentionally frustrate readers, but you can unravel your ideas dramatically, like a ball of yarn. For example, instead of giving your full position in the first paragraph, you might give readers a taste of it but leave out the complicated details. Then, you can incorporate the intricacies of your thesis as the paper evolves. This strategy is especially enticing when your audience expects you to take one position and you actually support a different one or when your topic might otherwise be dull.

As you might suspect, thesis statements raise ethical implications. On the one hand, showing your cards at the beginning of an argument can be more ethical because it's less sneaky. Because the readers already know where the argument is going, they can evaluate evidence within that context, according to that purpose, as they go along.

On the other hand, the deferred or evolving thesis can also treat the audience as a partner investigator. If you present evidence without telling readers how to interpret it, they're free to draw conclusions for themselves. Of course, audiences might not reach the same conclusions as you do, so you lose some "control" over the argument. But that's okay if you consider your audience to be equals and remember that the point of arguing isn't just to win but to seek understanding and make the best decisions together.

The bottom line is: **Wherever you place it, the best thesis is somewhere you arrive, not a place to begin.** A thesis states the results of thinking. Sometimes you need to investigate a topic, consider the controversies that surround it, weigh evidence, and activate reasoning before you know what to think. After all, jumping to conclusions often gets people into trouble.

Thinking carefully and considering all the available evidence and viewpoints? That's the work of scholars.

TRY THIS ➤ An Evolving Thesis

For this exercise, study the structure and the strategies of an evolving thesis by reading the apprentice scholar's essay "With Liberty and Justice for Some" (on pp. 249–257) and discuss the following questions in class or with a peer:

1. What is the thesis? How does it change? To answer this question, mark each time the writer's thinking seems to shift.
2. What makes this evolving thesis effective?
3. What, if anything, doesn't work for you as the reader? What could the writer do differently?

Infuse a Little Style

Thesis statements can engage readers through their ideas and through their form. **We aim for thesis statements that are both provocative and clear**: vivid in their expression and evident in their meaning. Actually, thesis statements can be more than one sentence long, and they don't have to be as dry and tasteless as a cafeteria sheet cake. When we write—and rewrite—thesis statements, we search for words that convey our meaning clearly and precisely, using language that will stimulate readers. We talk more about writing with style in Chapter 10, but for now, we want to encourage you to avoid boring, tasteless, and overly general statements that don't invigorate your reader.

"Although" Statements

One concrete way to engage readers is to use an "although" clause in your thesis statement, which positions your idea against an opposing idea. A thesis with an although clause looks like these samples:

- "Although many scholars support ________________, new data suggest that, in fact, ________________ is more accurate."
- "Although you might at first believe ________________, once you see evidence to the contrary, you'll be convinced that ________________."
- "Although it is true that ________________, the real issue is ________________, which many scholars have overlooked."

Try Something Unexpected

Another way to make your argument stand out is to select a purpose, style, or genre that your reader may not expect. If you're having trouble writing a thesis statement because you can't find something interesting (original) to say, try to find an interesting way to say it. Specifically, try a style or genre that's different (such as satire, or using a metaphor to structure your argument), or maybe pick a different purpose—for example, to amuse your readers or even to provoke them. You could direct the argument toward an overlooked audience who doesn't yet know they have a stake in the issue. Any of these strategies would put a different spin on the topic and bring something new to the conversation.

Checklist for Thesis Statements

After you've composed a thesis statement, test its quality by making sure it meets these criteria:

- Answers a challenging, compelling, and/or controversial question
- Gets at the heart of the controversy
- Breathes new life into an issue and avoids overused, common wisdom
- Is appropriate for the argument's audience, purpose, and context
- Engages readers with specific and interesting content and style

So What?

How many times have you heard a friend make an argument that you've already heard a dozen times before? Contrast that feeling of boredom or exasperation with the way it feels to hear something new and think, "I've never thought about it *that way* before." Developing a significant question and compelling thesis is about finding that slightly different angle, fresh perspective, or personal twist that will give readers a beautiful "aha" moment.

With a compelling inspiration, you're ready to begin developing an argument. We recommend doing some preplanning before you start drafting, and in the next chapter, we offer several organizational strategies to use throughout the writing process. We encourage you to experiment with these and adapt them according to your (and your audience's) needs. We describe organizational "moves" that scholars typically use, such as referencing other scholars' important discoveries, controversial claims, or shared knowledge at the beginning of an argument or proposing solutions at the end. Additionally, we offer techniques for developing and expanding arguments to fill in gaps and improve coherence.

What's Next

Take what you've learned in this chapter and respond to the following prompts.

1. **Analyzing arguments.** Select a controversy debated in your community. Find two arguments (editorials, blog posts, opinion pieces, etc.) that express opposing viewpoints, and try the following:
   - For each argument, outline the author's main claims and identify which controversies each claim addresses. For example, what is the author's first main point, and is it an argument about fact, definition, cause, evaluation, or policy?
   - Compare the authors' claims. Do they address the same categories of controversy? Or are they arguing about different things (for example, one is an argument of fact, whereas the other is an argument of policy)? In other words, are they arguing effectively with each other, or are they arguing past each other?

2. **Using sources as inspiration.** Practice using sources as inspirations for your own argument. Pick a controversial topic that you might be interested in writing about. Find two to three sources that approach the topic from different vantage points or perspectives. While reading the sources, ask yourself:
   - How do these essays relate to each other?
   - What ideas, questions, viewpoints, and so on, do they have in common?
   - What issues are they both interested in?
   - What might the authors agree on?
   - Where might the authors disagree?
   - What new questions or issues do you want to explore?

   Then, develop three to five research questions, new angles, or controversies that you could explore in an essay.

CHAPTER eight

How Do We Organize and Develop Arguments

chapter checklist

- What strategies can we use to organize and reorganize our ideas?
- What are some typical organizational patterns?
- How can we develop and expand our arguments?

Communicating ideas accurately is incredibly difficult. That's why, when writing or speaking to others, we work hard to structure our ideas as clearly and deliberately as possible. Thoughtful organization and development aim to reduce our readers' *cognitive load*, making it easier for them to access our good ideas. Our goal is not to oversimplify or "dumb down" arguments but to make them easier to follow by carefully organizing and elaborating, as needed by our audience.

Rather than just following rules and templates, imagine elements of organization and development as tools for reducing readers' workload. Using these techniques can help us cultivate a more creative and purposeful writing process. For example, rather than thinking of an introduction as paragraphs that just fill space at the beginning of our argument, we think of what we can *accomplish* with an introduction: introduce our topic and inspiration, provide background information, establish our credibility, and forecast our argument's main claims.

Although we can arrange claims, supports, ideas, and paragraphs in many different ways, we design arguments deliberately by **putting everything in its place for a reason**. Generally, we use two guiding principles to reduce reader workload (and thus increase coherence and readability):

1. Move from known to unknown information, general to specific ideas, and accepted to controversial arguments.
2. Create smooth connections and fill in any gaps that might interrupt the "flow."

Following these guidelines will not only help you organize your writing but also help your readers process your ideas more easily.

Organizing Rhetorically

Because there are many ways to arrange an argument, we must think carefully about our audience, purpose, and message in order to select the best structure. We don't have prescribed formulas that work in all

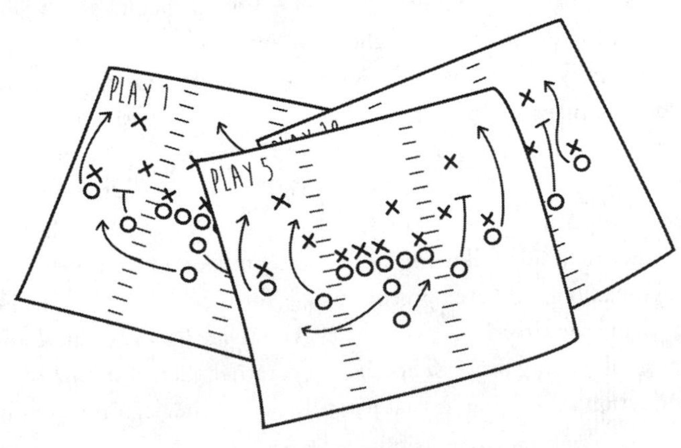

cases, and we don't make things up as we go along. Instead, we can use moves that have been practiced before, like the "plays" that sports teams use for practice and competition.

You might even consider your time as an apprentice scholar as a scrimmage, an opportunity to practice plays that pros in your academic discipline use. With time—and especially in the big game when it really counts—you can begin to adapt the playbook to specific situations, even calling "audible" modifications when circumstances change.

Eventually, you may outgrow certain basic plays. For example, sometimes apprentice scholars get stuck on the familiar five-paragraph essay format. That's a useful foundation for writing, but most college writing requires more than five paragraphs, and most arguments involve more than three main claims. Complex concepts and complicated arguments demand more sophisticated structures that allow us to expand our ideas, explore subclaims, and address readers' objections.

Before we start drafting—while we're still brainstorming, freewriting, and outlining—we begin thinking about the best way to arrange our ideas to suit a particular audience and purpose. We analyze our rhetorical situation and ask ourselves:

- What's my purpose? What am I really trying to accomplish (for example, to change readers' opinions, to offer a solution, to help readers understand a concept or event)?
- What role am I playing? What persona do I want to create?
- What's my audience's stance toward this issue? Will readers likely welcome or resist my ideas?
- How do writers typically organize this kind of argument? What kind of organization will my readers expect? Should I try to meet these expectations or "bend the rules"?
- Should I conduct original research, such as collecting data or performing experiments? How will I organize and present my results?

Rather than just picking a pattern that worked well last time, we think strategically about our purpose and audience: what we want our message to accomplish and who we're trying to reach. We then select a structure to meet our readers' needs and help us achieve our purpose.

Techniques for Organizing Your Thoughts

Different writing situations call for different strategies of organization. Sometimes we know most of what we want to say before we start writing. In those cases, we can compose an outline and mostly stick to it. Other times, we may lack a clear sense of our argument, so we need to begin writing, see where that takes us, and design a logical structure later. Still other times, we need to use creative organizational techniques that help us arrange and assemble our thoughts. Let's look at a few of those techniques next.

Visualize Your Organization

Every writing toolbox needs some techniques for conceptualizing your argument visually. One way is to imagine your paper as a building that has various rooms, each with a different function. We envision how the rooms (ideas, paragraphs) connect together in a way that will make sense to our readers. For example, if we imagined our argument as a museum that displayed ancient Egyptian artifacts, we could arrange the rooms chronologically (separate rooms for each time period), or we could organize the rooms topically. Either way, in the first room of our museum, we would want to greet visitors, arouse their interest, introduce our main ideas, and preview the tour. After all, we want to motivate our audience from the start and keep them from getting lost.

In addition, we would need to post clear signage (transitions and rationales) throughout the building to help visitors move easily through the exhibit. This would help the audience see how the rooms connect and how the contents of each relate to each other.

Finally, we'd want to conclude our audience's experience in some meaningful way. If, like many museums, our exhibit potentially overwhelmed our visitors with complexity and detail, we might want to synthesize what they saw—tying everything together so they didn't miss the point. We might also want to elaborate on the implications of our argument, perhaps by showing ancient influences in present-day Egypt, or even how ancient Egyptian art and culture has influenced the rest of the modern world.

Thinking metaphorically and visually about our argument helps us to imagine how its various parts fit together and to consider the argument from our audience's perspective so that they don't become lost, sidetracked, or overwhelmed.

CONSIDER THIS ➤ Using Metaphor

For this reflection, take a break from the chapter's content to examine and experiment with some choices that writers make.

We chose to use a museum metaphor to explain organizational concepts for two reasons. First, similes and metaphors allow us to illustrate a concept using something that's already familiar, or relatable, to the audience. Second, metaphors are vivid. "Showing" rather than "telling" will help our audience "see," understand, and remember an idea more accurately.

Using metaphors can be risky, though, because our audience might not recognize what we're referencing, or they may think we've oversimplified the issue. In our case, you might not be familiar with the typical layout of a museum. Even worse, you might apply the metaphor strictly and decide that all arguments are organized chronologically or topically. Despite these risks, we decided that the

(continued)

benefits of vivid illustration outweigh the potential risk of misguiding our readers.

Do you think the museum metaphor works? Is it placed wisely, or is there a better place in the chapter for the metaphor? Can you think of another metaphor that would illustrate this concept? What does this example teach you about the complexities of using metaphors in your writing?

Experiment with Maps, Graphics, and Software

Maps, cluster diagrams, or technology can be helpful tools for arranging our ideas while brainstorming. We might simply sketch out ideas on paper or use a word processor to design a graphic. Visuals can help us explore a topic in depth, discover key issues, find missing rationales, and tighten connections among our claims.

We can also use presentation software to visualize our argument. For example, traditional software can help us generate a plan for organizing our argument if we think about each of our main points as a slide. We add subclaims and support in bullets under each slide's main claim. Then, we can rearrange the slides according to the most logical outline. We can transform our presentation blueprint into a paper by adding rationales and more in-depth support. Newer online presentation software alternatives can also be used for planning purposes because they allow us to organize ideas with more complicated structures and interconnections. For example, we can illustrate how one claim connects to three subclaims that are all components of a larger idea.

TRY THIS ➤ Create a Visual Representation

For this exercise, create a concept map or other graphic as a way of developing and organizing an argument that interests you.

Patterns for Organizing Arguments

While drafting an argument, you can also experiment with some common "moves"—steps and strategies—that scholars use to develop arguments. For starters, you can follow the conventional argument structure used by many disciplines. In the sciences and social sciences, for example, scholarly research articles typically contain eight major sections:

1. Abstract
2. Introduction
3. Literature (or research) review
4. Research methods
5. Results or findings
6. Analysis and discussion
7. Conclusion
8. Bibliography

We describe the purpose of each of these sections more below and in Appendix B, but this outline provides a good starting guide, based on the typical way that many scholars arrange ideas and information.

Start with What Others Have Said

After introducing the topic of investigation, most scholarly arguments provide some background by highlighting related work by other scholars. We do this for three reasons:

1. To familiarize readers with the subject's context and to place our argument within a scholarly conversation
2. To verify our assumptions, methods, or the research question, as in a research or literature review
3. To demonstrate that we've done our homework by reviewing previous research. Neglecting to cite or at least refer to previous,

relevant scholarship damages our credibility within the scholarly community.

The length and style of the research review depends on the paper's length and on the audience's familiarity with our topic. A formal review of previous research (or "literature review") can span several pages, or it might only appear in an opening paragraph that contextualizes the argument. Regardless of what the review looks like, **scholars rarely assert their own position before they've first acknowledged what others have said**. They situate their perspective within the larger scholarly "discussion" about a topic. For example, a writer might begin an argument by citing predominant theories that inform an issue and quoting important viewpoints. We describe these techniques for verifying arguments in Chapter 6.

These strategies allow us to present what is already known about a subject before complicating it. That is, we can establish what others have already "said"—what our audience knows to be true—before we challenge these perspectives, add our own discussion to the mix, and explore new questions. Moving from known to unknown also reduces cognitive load, as mentioned above.

Follow Scholarly Models

As we've discussed, scholarly investigation proceeds from a question or problem toward an answer or conclusion—also known as a thesis. Scholars often don't know what their thesis will be when they begin investigating, but they lead with the thesis when reporting their results, as if to say, "Here's what I've discovered. Now let me show you how I got there."

Although not all forms of writing follow this conventional structure, many of them still use the generic moves and structure of the classical argument, which was developed by ancient Greeks and Romans. If you grew up in Europe or the Americas, this form of thesis-first argument probably seems familiar. Other cultures sometimes meander toward their conclusions or don't proceed through their points in a straight line, allowing their arguments to unfold more like a narrative journey. In fact, some non-Western cultures think we're rude for being so blunt, but American academic and professional audiences generally expect to hear the "bottom line up front"—a familiar move that also reduces cognitive load. Learning to get to the point early will serve you well not just in scholarly writing but also in business and scientific communication, where audiences don't want to work too hard or wait too long for you to answer the question, *so what?*

The conventional structure we offer next provides many potential moves we can make to organize an argument, but we never follow these lockstep. Rarely do we make *all* of these moves, or even sequence the sections in this exact order; rather, we thoughtfully select the ones that suit our particular rhetorical situation. Think of this structure not as a detailed outline to follow strictly but as a series of options to use according to your audience's needs. Imagine the format as a menu to select from—deliberately and thoughtfully—when you're determining what your audience might need. Notice how the Scholarly Model is compatible with the scholarly research framework described above.

The Scholarly Model

1. **Introduction**
    - Identify the controversy, problem, or research question and its significance and relevance (inspiration, implications).
    - Establish your qualifications to write about the topic.
    - Create common ground with readers.
    - Demonstrate fairness.
    - Arouse readers' attention and interest, often with a vivid illustration or a personal narrative.
    - State or imply the thesis.
    - Forecast the structure of the argument.

2. **Background**
   - Summarize important sources and previous research on the subject.
   - Describe the topic's history and its theoretical foundation.
   - Give an overview of the situation or problem.
   - Explain the process you used to answer a research question or to study a problem (for example, methods used to collect and analyze data, or theories applied to a particular subject).
3. **Support**
   - Present verification, evidence, and illustrations that support the thesis, organized in a clear and thoughtful pattern.
   - Report and tabulate data and results gathered through investigation, sometimes using figures and charts.
   - Explicitly link subclaims and support back to the thesis.
   - Analyze, interpret, and apply research findings.
4. **Consideration of alternative arguments**
   - Examine alternative points of view.
   - Note advantages and disadvantages of alternative positions.
   - Acknowledge limitations of your research or viewpoint.
   - Explain why your argument is better.
5. **Conclusion**
   - Briefly summarize and synthesize the overall argument.
   - Identify the implications of research findings.
   - Make clear what readers should think or do.
   - Add a strong emotional or ethical appeal.
   - Raise questions for further research.

Remember: this structure is a useful starting point that we approach creatively, adapting the template to particular rhetorical situations. It's not a cookie-cutter model for all arguments.

Also, there is no prescribed formula for how long each section should be. We might devote several pages to one part and only a few paragraphs to another. We select a ratio and scope that meets the needs of our purpose and audience. As an apprentice, try to notice these moves while reading and practice them yourself in different genres as you learn what your audiences expect.

TRY THIS ➤ Design an Argument Based on the Scholarly Model

For this exercise, begin organizing an early draft of an argument using the menu of options offered by the Scholarly Model. Answer the following questions to help you decide what to include in your argument:

- How many of the Model's main sections will my audience need? For instance, will they expect to hear about alternative arguments? Are readers already familiar with the topic, or will they need extensive background information?
- What other "moves" will you need to make in order to develop your argument?
- Do you need separate sections for all of these "moves," or can some be combined?
- Which moves will be most effective in the conclusion?

Highlight or list all the points on the outline that you may want to include in your argument.

Use the Controversy Categories

Exploring an argument's various controversies, like we do when we're brainstorming, can also help us decide where to begin a paper and how to arrange our ideas. The hierarchy of these controversy categories (outlined in Table 5.1) offers a natural progression to follow. We can organize an argument around these categories by first addressing controversies about fact or existence, then discussing definitions and consequences, then evaluating, and finally offering solutions.

Organizing with controversy categories creates a logical progression of ideas and allows us to focus on the issues that are most controversial and interesting. In fact, we typically don't cover all of these categories: we skip over the issues that our audience already agrees with, knows, or understands. For instance, if we're writing about global warming, and we know readers agree:

- That climate change actually *exists*
- That it is *defined* as "an alteration in the regional or global climate" (*Oxford English Dictionary*)
- That it is *caused* by excessive carbon emissions

Then we skim over the first three kinds of controversy (existence, definitions, causes) and get right to the heart of the matter to discuss:

- Whether climate change is *serious enough to deserve our attention* (evaluation)
- Which *solutions* would be most realistic and effective (policy)

TRY THIS ➤ Use the Controversy Categories to Brainstorm and Organize

For this exercise, develop a list of questions about a topic that you are writing about, using each of the controversy categories (Fact/existence, Definition, Cause/consequence, Evaluation, Policy). Then, select key questions or points from each category, and create an outline that follows the order of the controversy categories. For a refresher on how to use the controversy categories to develop ideas, consult Table 5.1.

Techniques for Organizing Paragraphs

The following techniques are useful when organizing your argument overall (macrostructure) and when arranging individual paragraphs (microstructure). You might use these techniques when you're drafting your argument for the first time or when you're revising. Keep in mind that organization isn't only something we work on before we start writing. Often, when a professor asks you to revise your essay, one of the primary changes she expects is improved organization. Here are some ways to improve an argument's organization while you're drafting and revising.

Highlight Agreement before Disagreement

As mentioned previously, sometimes we skim over issues that our audience already knows. However, jumping into the center of the controversy may be a strategic mistake when making arguments that are especially divisive or when we imagine that an audience will resist our thesis. In such cases, we first try to build some common ground with our readers.

For example, we might begin by acknowledging opposing arguments to show our readers that we respect their perspective. This move is typical in Rogerian argument (inspired by American psychologist Carl Rogers, who coined the phrase "unconditional positive regard"), which focuses on negotiating and empathically listening to another side. Rather than blindly starting with our own position, Rogerian argument starts with the audience—prioritizing their views and building bridges to reach consensus—rather than pushing our own agenda in order to win or prove we're right. This organizational move shows how our organizational choices can enable or undermine our purpose and invite or alienate our readers.

Stick to the Point

As we discussed in Chapter 5, scholars dig deep rather than shallow when creating arguments. Focusing on the main argument helps readers, too. Try to keep things simple for you and your reader by eliminating irrelevant information. To figure out what's needed and what's tangential, use your thesis as your guide. Ask yourself "Is this point directly related to my thesis?" or "Does this information directly support my argument?" You might find it helpful to think of your thesis as an umbrella: Does every claim and detail support the spokes and fabric of the umbrella? Or is something better suited under a different umbrella—and therefore another argument?

Repeat Key Terms

When editing, we can highlight connections and create a sense of unity by repeating key words throughout an argument. Weaving in terms that are central to our argument can create a more consistent and memorable message. Successful orators often use this technique, such as in Martin Luther King, Jr.'s "I Have a Dream" speech.

We're careful not to overdo it, though. In limited doses, repetition can reinforce and unify our argument. For example, throughout this book, we've used the term "strategic" frequently to remind readers that writing should be deliberate. Has this word stuck out to you? Does it unify and reinforce our message, or has it been too repetitive?

Create a Reverse Outline

A "reverse outline" can show us how well paragraphs come together to form a coherent, well-organized whole. This outline looks very similar to a prewriting outline, but it's called a "reverse outline" (described on p. 50 in Chapter 3) because it's composed *after* a draft is written. To write a reverse outline, list the main points of each paragraph, which will give you a schematic of your draft's layout. You might also list the function of each paragraph within your draft, using the Scholarly Model as a guide. (For example, mark where you review previous research or examine alternative points of view.) Reverse outlines function like rearview mirrors; they help us navigate our way forward by showing where we've already been from a different perspective.

Once we create the outline that reflects what we've already written, we can see whether our paragraphs are focused, our main claims are evident, and our ideas progress logically. Then, we can make adjustments to keep us on the right track. Our goal here is to improve our argument's *coherence*; we don't want our audience to struggle through making sense of an incoherent message.

TRY THIS ➤ Disassemble a Draft

For this exercise, disassemble a draft to improve its organization. Print a draft of something that you're currently writing and cut it into separate paragraphs. Mix up the paragraphs and play with different sequences to decide which arrangement works best. Then, trade your piles with a classmate to ask for feedback on paragraph sequence and discuss possible transitions.

How to Develop and Expand Arguments

Organizing and reorganizing a draft will likely expose gaps and disconnects among ideas. Arguments "flow" better not only if we arrange each part carefully but also if we make sure to weave our ideas together and fill in any missing parts for our audience. Let's look at some ways of tying ideas together and eliminating gaps.

Build Transitions

When revising, we look for places that lack explicit transitions between paragraphs or sections of an argument. Think of transitions as signposts that direct the reader. Like a travel guide who points out important landmarks along the tour or a road sign that indicates when drivers need to exit, a writer guides his audience through his argument with strategically placed signposts. These markers tell readers, either explicitly or implicitly:

- What's coming next
- How ideas are connected
- When a change in subject or tone will occur
- How to interpret the argument

Signposts make our writing clear and readable so that readers don't need to work too hard to follow our meaning. Signals can be as simple as transitional words or phrases such as "however," "moreover," "similarly," and "on the other hand," or they can be as sophisticated as lengthy sections that clarify the relationship between one idea and another. What we don't want to do is just insert a transition whenever we sense a gap. Transitional words are powerful tools, but they won't magically create a connection where one does not exist. They're not love potions.

To create tighter connections among ideas, we consider the hierarchy of our claims—how they relate to one another—and we use signposts to highlight that relationship. It's important that we send the signal that communicates exactly what we mean. For example, we don't want to write "in addition" (which would connect two equally weighted ideas), when we mean "accordingly" (which would indicate a cause and effect). To be precise, we ask ourselves:

- How are these ideas related? What is their relationship?
- Are these claims equal, or is one a subpoint of another?

In addition to linking sentences, signposts can help readers move smoothly from one paragraph to the next. Paragraphs typically begin by referring back to something familiar, such as a previous paragraph, a concept explored earlier, or the thesis. Readers become confused when they encounter paragraphs that don't clearly relate to something they've seen before. We can help readers feel comfortable in a new paragraph by beginning the paragraph with something *old*—something touched on earlier—and then using this reference as a bridge to *new* material. For example, review our previous paragraph, where we began by saying: "To create tighter connections between ideas, we consider the hierarchy of our points." Note how the first part of this sentence is old information (because we made this point earlier). The second part of the sentence introduces the new material, which is easier for readers to interpret within the context of the familiar statement. Imagine how the sentence would read without a reference to something already known.

Add Metacommentary

You can also develop your argument by incorporating *metacommentary*, explicit statements about your intended meaning that clarify your message and address any confusion readers might have. Scholars use metacommentary to talk explicitly about their data collection methods, their rationales, and their thought processes. For example, we might say:

- What I mean by that is . . .
- The point I'm trying to make is . . .
- I'm not saying ________________. What I am saying is . . .
- Let me clarify: ________________ is my central argument.
- The gist of the matter is . . .
- In other words . . .

These statements allow us to interrupt the flow of our writing and step in as "the author" to clarify any misunderstanding or speak directly to the reader, which is what narrators do when they interrupt a movie scene to explain something to viewers. We use metacommentary sparingly, though. Like any snazzy trick, we don't overuse it, for fear of diluting its power.

TRY THIS ➤ Look for Metacommentary

For this exercise, review your favorite chapter in this book to find examples of metacommentary. Look carefully for places where we incorporated statements to clarify our meaning or address any confusion readers might have. As you investigate, think about the following:

- What effects does this metacommentary have?
- Why do you think we chose to incorporate these statements where we did?
- What gaps in our logic would remain, without this metacommentary?

Provide Rationales to Fill in the Gaps

When arguing, scholars typically provide a *rationale* or explanation of how their evidence, verifications, or illustrations support their thesis. When writers leave out this important ingredient—the metaphorical glue or linkage that holds the argument together—readers must make logical leaps on their own. For example, imagine that a writer argues that "We should invest in clean energy (claim) because 97% of Greenland's ice sheet shows surface thawing (evidence)." The argument is difficult to follow because the audience has to supply the missing rationale, such as "Clean energy will reduce carbon emissions, which cause climate change that results in melting ice sheets. So, if the ice begins to melt, we should invest resources in clean energy development and maybe avoid an environmental apocalypse."

In contrast, a scholar might connect his claim and evidence by saying, "We should invest in clean energy [claim] because excessive carbon dioxide is causing climate change [rationale], as demonstrated by the fact that 97% of Greenland's ice sheet shows surface thawing [evidence]." **Rationales connect claims with their supports.**

One of the best ways to develop rationales is to probe an argument for missing controversy categories. In the climate change example above, we provided a fact (thawing) to support a proposal (for clean energy). The missing explanation is a subclaim about cause and consequence: "excessive carbon dioxide [causes] climate change." Readers need this rationale to understand how the evidence supports the main argument. If we think they may not make that leap, we provide the rationale for them. And why take the risk that they may not make that leap?

Again, scholarly argumentation is case building. We want to "show our work" as much as possible so that the audience can follow along with less cognitive load and less chance of misunderstanding.

TRY THIS ➤ List and Define Key Terms

Often, arguments lack shared definitions of key terms. For example, in order to argue about "justice," you may need to explain what you mean by the term, which also may require some discussion of "freedom," "equality," and other related terms.

For this exercise, brainstorm a list of 5 to 10 terms that you think are central to an argument that you're currently writing. Decide whether you will need to define any of these unfamiliar or controversial terms for your audience. Consult pp. 136–138 for a description of how to write definition arguments.

Aim for Reader-Centered Writing

One way to show our work is to transform our arguments from *author*-centered writing (stuck in the writer's head) to *audience*-centered writing (focused on readers' needs and expectations). Audience-centered writing anticipates readers' needs: places where they could stumble, disagree, misinterpret, or need more explanation.

Experienced writers view their writing from this audience perspective and build or clarify rationales to link their claims and evidence. They also watch out for (a) supports without claims and (b) claims without support. When these elements are missing, arguments can fall apart because readers can't see the logical pathway that guides our thinking.

Adding rationales makes our assumptions more explicit, and they elucidate implications for claims. To see what we mean, look at the following example of a paragraph from a job application essay (or "personal statement"). This first draft doesn't offer much rationale at all, and many claims are missing:

> I am qualified for this job because I am hard working, work well in teams, and have top-notch experience in the field. During my senior year in college, I worked as an intern at Awesome & Super-Awesome Law Firm. During that time, I conducted research for one of the senior partners, filed confidential papers, and represented the firm at college fairs. I also have experience working extensively with my peers in group projects, and I studied abroad for six weeks during the summer.

The writer cites impressive experiences as evidence, but she expects the reader to understand *why* these experiences are valuable and *how* they make her a competitive candidate. She doesn't make an argument that would translate her experience into something meaningful.

The writer could improve her argument by adding rationales that explain why her claims matter. For example:

1. (Claim) My self-reliance and my ability to handle adversity blossomed
2. (Support) . . . when I studied abroad . . .

3. (Rationale) . . . [and you should care because] my self-reliance will be an asset to your company in a position like this, which operates independently of the main office.

Now, see how adding rationales and missing claims (marked in boldface) can enhance the paragraph:

> I am qualified for this job because I am hard working, work well in teams, and have top-notch experience in the field. During my senior year in college, I worked as an intern at Awesome & Super-Awesome Law Firm. During that time, I conducted research for one of the senior partners, filed confidential papers, and represented the firm at college fairs. **The fact that the partners trusted me to preserve client confidentiality demonstrates that I am reliable, honest, and responsible.** Moreover, the experience I gained as a company representative refined my presentation skills, **which shows that I am articulate and comfortable speaking in public.** I initially developed these professional social skills by working with my peers in group projects. **These assignments developed my ability to work independently and as part of a team, showing that I am both a self-starter and a collaborator. My self-reliance and my ability to handle adversity blossomed** when I studied abroad for six weeks last summer, **which required me to manage my own time, adapt to a new culture, and live independently.**

See the difference? Now readers know exactly why she is qualified for the job. The writer added revealing explanations that support her argument ("You should hire me because . . ."). These details fill in the gaps of her logic so that readers interpret her experience more like the writer intends. The evidence no longer stands alone, without any bridge to her implied thesis.

This elaboration adds something else, too: length. It is not meaningless filler but substantive additions to the paragraph that also increase the word count. That's a win-win outcome, since many apprentice scholars worry about meeting an assignment's length requirement.

TRY THIS ➤ Incorporate Reader-Centered Writing

For this exercise, select a paragraph in a paper that you are writing or have written recently (for this or another class). Imagine the paragraph from your readers' perspective, and ask yourself:

- Is it clear what I mean exactly?
- Where might the reader be confused? What could be misleading?
- How does this information support my thesis?
- Where do I need to provide additional rationales?

Explain Relevance and Sufficiency

Scholars and other well-educated thinkers use two kinds of powerful rationales to evaluate and develop arguments: relevance and sufficiency.

Relevance indicates the quality, or qualitative strength, of a connection between a claim and its supports. For example, grades are supposed to measure learning, but are they a *relevant* measure? Do grades accurately reflect learning? In the sciences and social sciences, scholars carefully explain the relevance of evidence by making clear distinctions among correlation, causation, and coincidence. Just because, for example, parents see a correlation (or connection) between increased use of vaccines and increased rates of autism doesn't mean that we can claim for certain that vaccines *cause* autism. In this case, the evidence is circumstantial. And as we all know, any good defense lawyer will object to the relevance of circumstantial evidence against his client because the evidence might indicate something different.

Sufficiency reflects the quantitative strength of a rationale. We cannot claim more than we have evidence to support. Again, think about a courtroom trial. A jury will only find someone guilty if the prosecution offers sufficient evidence. In fact, in a criminal trial, where the defendant is "presumed innocent" until proven otherwise, guilt must be established "beyond a reasonable doubt." Civil trials have different rules and standards. For example, sufficient support in a civil case is the "preponderance of evidence." Can you imagine why a criminal trial requires an overwhelming majority of proof, whereas a civil case needs only a simple majority of evidence to render judgment?

Invest in a Good Title

Apprentice scholars oftentimes underuse compelling titles. Titles are important because they are our first chance to capture the audience's attention and to inform readers about the argument's content. A strong title tells what the paper is about (topic) and arouses the reader's interest (with a hint toward conclusions or implications). That's why titles like "Paper 1" or "Rhetorical Analysis" don't work well—they're neither specific nor interesting. Scholars frequently use two-part titles with a main title that engages readers and a subtitle that states the main idea. Another option is to write a title that poses a compelling question or that states the thesis explicitly. Here are a few examples of titles that we like:

- "Seeing Red? The Mind-Bending Power of Colour" (by Tom Chivers)
- "Accents and Ebonics: When the Hood Goes to College" (by Taylor Callwood)
- "Will We Use Commas in the Future?" (by Matthew J.X. Malady)

- "Get Stadiums out of Our Churches" (by Alan Levinovitz)
- "Let's Give Chivalry another Chance" (by Emily Esfahani Smith)

In these examples, we can predict what the argument might be about, and we're inspired to read further.

Elaborate

Writers can never cover an issue entirely, so we can always find more room for development. As readers, we can mine these gaps to discover unanswered questions, missing evidence, and places to insert our ideas. As writers, we can identify gaps in order to expand and refine our arguments. For apprentice scholars who struggle to meet an assignment's page length requirement, gaps are a productive place to expand a draft. Keep in mind that if you don't have enough material to fill the pages, chances are good that you need to develop your argument by conducting more research or digging deeper into your analysis. But if you're absolutely sure that you have selected an appropriate scope for your writing task, you can use the following strategies to enhance your argument. (Note that the last three suggestions can help you answer the *so what?* question, too.)

1. Incorporate more examples.
2. Respond to more objections.
3. Relate the argument to real-life contexts.
4. Discuss the larger implications of your argument.
5. Make connections to other related issues.

Although these strategies help us expand our points, we do not "pad" arguments with unnecessary fluff. Like most audiences, professors typically would prefer that you get to the point and, if necessary, write less. Busy readers value conciseness almost universally.

So What?

Effective writers use structure to ease their readers' cognitive load and reduce misunderstanding. They consider their audience's needs and put everything in its place for a reason. And they present their arguments as completely as possible by providing rationales to connect claims with relevant, sufficient supports.

We can use various strategies to structure arguments effectively for particular audiences. For instance, creating an idea map might reveal connections among our thoughts, adapting a recognizable structure might ease your readers' cognitive load, and reverse outlining our points might help us rearrange the argument. Because there are many techniques for organizing ideas, we recommend experimenting with different strategies to find ones you're most comfortable with. The larger your tool bag of options, the more likely you will be to find a technique that works when you get stuck or that gives you a starting point when you encounter a new writing task.

In the next chapter, we explain how to locate an argument's weak spots. Faulty reasoning and misuse of credibility and emotion can undermine a writer's purpose and deter readers, but they can also present opportunities for improvement. When we notice gaps and faults in our argument, we can investigate holes to fill, new ideas to explore, and other hidden possibilities.

What's Next

Take what you've learned in this chapter and respond to the following prompts.

1. **Examining a publication.** One of the best ways to learn about effective organization is to study examples. To see how scholars in your discipline typically arrange their arguments, find a scholarly article that is published in one of your discipline's prominent journals.

Your library most likely has access to these scholarly journals online; if so, you can begin by searching in a database such as Academic Search Complete or EBSCOhost. You might also ask your advisor or a professor in your major to recommend an article that represents the typical features of scholarship in your field. For example, if you wanted to know what scholarly articles look like in writing studies, we would recommend examining articles in the journal *College Composition and Communication*.

Once you've selected an article, look carefully at the organizational moves the argument makes and discuss the following in class or with a peer:

a. How does the author begin? What "moves" does she make? For example, does she reference other scholars, raise important questions, or define key terms?
b. How and where does the author address the argument's *so what?*
c. Is the paper divided into different sections with headings?
d. Are there major shifts in the paper between different topics? How does the author transition between different ideas?
e. How does the author handle potential objections or different perspectives on the topic? Does she give voice to any opposition? Where?
f. Are there graphics and charts? How do they relate to the text?
g. Are there footnotes or endnotes? What purposes do these serve?
h. What moves does the author make in the conclusion?

Now, write an e-mail to an incoming student who is planning to major in your discipline. Give him some tips for writing in your discipline, particularly for organizing and formatting scholarly papers. Provide links to useful resources and examples.

2. **Proposal arguments.** Watch the documentary *An Inconvenient Truth* to investigate its techniques and evaluate it as a proposal argument. Consider the following questions:
   a. How is the film organized? Why do you think the film's creators chose this arrangement? What effects does the order have on the audience?
   b. Who is the intended audience for this documentary? What clues in the film hint at this audience?
   c. How does the documentary convince viewers that a serious problem exists? Are you convinced by the support?
   d. What unstated assumptions does the film rely on? What values and beliefs must the audience share?
   e. How well does the film respond to opposing views?

CHAPTER **nine**

How Can We Find Faults and Gaps in Arguments

chapter checklist

- What are fallacies, and how do we avoid them?
- How much can we rely on credibility and emotion?
- How do we anticipate and respond to objections?

Whenever we buy a product we don't need because of some advertising gimmick or use a lame excuse to avoid a traffic ticket that we know we deserve, we participate in arguments that persuade when they should not. Most of us do so often, and all of us do so sometimes.

Why are weak arguments so appealing? According to social psychologists, we use mental shortcuts to save energy. For example, we generalize what we observe. When we notice a pattern—say, several drivers from a neighboring state driving like maniacs—we conclude (or argue) "people who live in [insert neighbor state here] are terrible drivers."

Of course, we shouldn't make such a sweeping claim after observing such a small sample of drivers from a neighboring state, many of whom probably drive more responsibly. But you can certainly imagine making this kind of reasoning mistake without giving it much thought. Hasty generalizations like this are mental shortcuts that we rely on to make sense of the world with whatever limited information we have at hand. Often, the conclusions we reach also involve preexisting biases or emotional reactions that further cloud our thinking.

Shortcuts work okay when the consequences are slight. You probably won't go bald because you bought a bottle of lousy shampoo based only on a celebrity endorsement. However, shortcuts certainly matter when an argument can send a person to prison; create a new law; or, in the case of news reporting or scholarly arguments, change how we view the world.

Scholars since Plato have warned against the potential abuses of rhetoric as a tool for poor decision-making, manipulation, and tyranny. That's why, from ancient times to the present, a key function of education has been to improve the quality of arguments that we make or follow. Lawyers, legislators, and scholars have developed rigorous standards to minimize the potential abuses of argument. They scrutinize each other's claims and support, honing their reasoning and accounting for multiple perspectives so their arguments will be more acceptable to demanding audiences.

Fallacies and Critical Thinking

Rooted in the critical reading skills described in Chapter 2, this chapter presents methods to locate gaps and faults in our own and others' arguments. Fallacies reflect poor thinking. Learning how to identify fallacies, qualify claims, and anticipate and respond to alternative views will strengthen your arguments and your thinking. Knowing how to avoid fallacies can make you a better learner, communicator, consumer, and citizen.

Written arguments provide your audience with a window to view your thinking. Being able to build fallacy-free arguments will demonstrate effective critical thinking and make you more credible in school and in professional settings. Arguments based on sound reasoning can withstand harsher scrutiny, and in most cases they can help us find better answers to our questions and solutions to our problems.

When reading or listening, recognizing fallacies can also make us smarter consumers of arguments made by advertisers, politicians, bosses, and so-called friends. Learning about fallacies can inoculate citizens against being manipulated by others because we'll be more likely to think twice (or more) about whether we should believe an argument—especially when we're already inclined to do so.

Fallacious Arguments

Fallacies are arguments built on unsound rationales. In other words, a fallacious argument weakly, or even mistakenly, connects a claim and support.

Let's consider an everyday example. How often do you buy more expensive name-brand products instead of cheaper generic alternatives? The underlying argument might look something like this:

Smucker's Grape Jelly is better than its generic equivalent (CLAIM)

→ *because* (UNSTATED RATIONALE)

it carries a brand name (SUPPORT)

In this case, we assume that, in general, name-brand merchandise has superior quality compared to generic products. Indeed, Smucker's advertising tag line says so: *With a name like Smucker's, it has to be good.*®

But wait. How did we ever make the connection that name brand equals quality? What's our unstated rationale? Have we tried Smucker's Concord Grape Jelly in a side-by-side taste comparison with, for

example, Walmart's generic Great Value equivalent? Have we compared ingredients on the labels? (Hint: the ingredients and nutritional information are identical.) If not, then what do we base our conclusions on: that our grandmother always bought Smucker's, that we've had a few bad experiences with other generics, that we don't want to be seen buying or serving "off brands," or that we've seen one too many Smucker's commercials? In each of these cases, our rationale is weak, and we may be wasting our money.

Educated consumers resist fallacious arguments because they impair our best thinking. **Fallacies may seem persuasive, but they do not build the best possible case for reaching a conclusion.** Regardless of their potential persuasiveness, arguments can and should be evaluated more carefully when based on a weak rationale.

Scrutinizing assumed rationales is what most people mean by the phrase "critical thinking." You can learn about dozens of different kinds of fallacies in critical thinking or philosophy classes or via books and websites on the subject. In this chapter, we focus on describing some general categories and how they work rather than trying to cover every type of fallacy. In general, fallacies typically follow one of three patterns:

1. Faulty use of reasoning or logic (activated by evidence)
2. Faulty use of credibility (built with verification, reputation, or presentation)
3. Faulty use of emotion (often evoked by illustrations)

Faulty Reasoning

Mistakes in reasoning are the most common fallacies, but they are often easy enough to find and correct.

Jumping to Conclusions

You already know one of the most common fallacies—the overgeneralization, sometimes called a "hasty generalization." The faulty rationale here involves *insufficiency*: reaching a conclusion before sufficient evidence accumulates, as in the case of horrible drivers discussed above.

Again, it's human nature to seek patterns and sort our experiences into categories. But when generalizations become stereotypes that influence how we treat others, they raise serious ethical issues. The best way to counteract the risks associated with "jumping to conclusions" is to slow down and scrutinize an argument's rationale—especially when it's unstated.

CONSIDER THIS ➤ Sufficiency Fallacies

For this reflection, consider these three generalizations, and then reflect on the bulleted questions that follow.

1. Students are lazy.
2. Professors lack common sense.
3. High school graduates make less money than college graduates.

- How do you think someone could reach each of these conclusions? What evidence would they use?
- What rationale would make each of these statements persuasive?
- Which audiences would find these most persuasive, and why?

Qualifying Your Claims

You can avoid sufficiency fallacies in your arguments and in your own thinking by *qualifying* your claims. **A qualification is a stated restriction that limits a claim's strength.** For instance, you might say something like "I don't know about *all* [neighbor state] drivers, but I've seen lots of knuckleheaded ones in my neck of the woods." Qualifying claims helps us avoid exaggerating our conclusions.

Let's consider ways to qualify the claim "Students are lazy." We could do one or more of the following:

1. Weaken the verb: "Students *seem* lazy."
2. Narrow the subject: "*Some* students seem lazy."
3. Limit and clarify the modifier: "Some students seem *to devote inadequate efforts to studying*."
4. Add verification: "*Recent research indicates that* some students devote inadequate efforts to studying."

Note that in these examples, the precision and length of each statement increases as the scope of the claim decreases. It's almost as if scholars use more words to say less—but really, we're just careful not to overstate our claims.

One qualification that bothers many scholars is using the phrase "I think" to introduce a claim. (Even worse may be using "I feel" when discussing what you think or believe, rather than your feelings.) Beginning claims with "I think" is probably why many English teachers ban "I" from student writing. It's not that they necessarily discount students' thoughts or experiences, either. As we discussed in Chapter 6, personal experience can provide very persuasive evidence. Teachers dislike "I think" because the phrase often precedes an *assertion*, or unsupported opinion. Students sometimes think they can avoid the work of building an argument (supporting their ideas and providing strong rationales) if they simply qualify their claims as "personal opinion." Also, characterizing an assertion as "just my opinion" can shut down conversation for people who believe that "everyone's entitled to her own opinion." For public arguments, especially scholarly arguments, audiences agree that everyone is entitled to her opinion—but they expect that writers will provide support and rationales for the audience to scrutinize.

Really, every claim contains an implied "I think" before it. Trust that your readers will know that: take ownership of your arguments rather than "hedging" your claims.

TRY THIS ➤ Qualify Claims

For this exercise, use the techniques you've learned here to qualify the other two claims from the previous CONSIDER THIS.

Fallacies of Relevance

Another main category of reasoning errors involves *relevance*. Even when there's sufficient support, the linkage between that evidence and the claim or thesis may be weak.

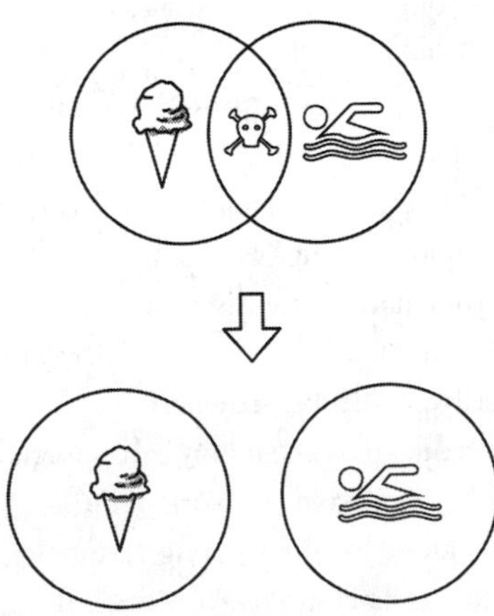

Correlation versus Causation

A common kind of relevance fallacy confuses correlation with causation (initially described on p. 139). A famous example involves ice cream sales and drownings. As you can imagine, both phenomena increase during the summer, so we might imagine that there is a *correlation* between increased ice cream sales and drownings.

But that doesn't mean that increased sales of ice cream in the hot summer months actually *cause* more drownings. Folks just like to swim more when it's hot. And more people frolicking in pools and ponds means more drownings.

Scientists and other researchers who use data to answer research questions employ statistical analysis to test the strength of the relationship between variables (like ice cream sales and drownings, or smoking and lung cancer). When a correlation becomes more than coincidental, the evidence becomes "significant." Scholars and others who have been well educated about quantitative methods habitually scrutinize scientific findings by asking questions such as:

- How large was the sample size?
- What's the margin of error?
- What other variables may be involved?

Changing the Subject

A second type of relevance fallacy intentionally introduces information that's only weakly related to the conclusion. Politicians often use this fallacy, changing the subject to avoid answering a question:

REPORTER: Can you describe your proposed tax plan?

POLITICAL CANDIDATE: We need a tax program that supports the middle class and creates new jobs.

REPORTER: Yes, but can you talk specifically about how your plan will accomplish those goals?

POLITICAL CANDIDATE: We must work together, across political parties, to solve these issues. I believe my track record demonstrates my ability to get things done in Washington.

In this case, the candidate simply changes the subject, or controversy category, so as to avoid providing any specifics, drifting from the original question of *how* the tax plan will work to *what* it should accomplish to *why* he's the person who can make things happen.

Philosophers who study informal logic or reasoning sometimes call the "changing-the-subject" technique a kind of "red herring" fallacy (after the distractingly stinky fish). Experienced scholars avoid extraneous information that might sidetrack or mislead their audiences.

Other Reasoning Fallacies

In addition to fallacies of sufficiency and relevance, there are several common mental shortcuts that educated communicators are careful to avoid.

Straw Man Arguments

A "straw man argument" presents an oversimplified, exaggerated, or simply inaccurate version of an opposing argument to make alternative perspectives seem weak, foolish, and easily refutable—like a scarecrow that we could easily knock over. One of the most common straw man techniques is to misquote or use someone's words out of context. Another popular trick is to misrepresent or oversimplify opposing views. Think about the following examples of claims, drawn from straw man arguments we see and hear around us daily:

- "Pro-life advocates don't care about women's rights."
- "If you're not with us, you must be against us."
- "My opponent's tax plan will target the poor and destitute, while giving the wealthy a free ride."

We look out for the straw man whenever we encounter arguments, especially opinion pieces, political ads, campaign speeches, and product advertisements. These sneaky moves tell us a lot about a writer and his message, mainly that his case probably isn't very strong if he has to weaken the other side in order to look good. We also scour our own arguments for faults like these.

CONSIDER THIS ➤ Mistreating Opposing Views

For this reflection, think of a time when you or a friend treated each other's perspectives unfairly during a disagreement. Reflect on the consequences of mistreating different perspectives. How did this affect the way that you responded to the argument? What kind of character did you or your friend exhibit? Was the argument improved at all by downplaying the other side?

Slippery Slope Arguments

Sometimes we get caught up in dire predictions about the future. If, for example, you ask someone for a date and she or he rejects your offer, then you might conclude that there's probably no future in that relationship. And if that relationship won't work, then maybe none ever will and you'll eventually die alone, miserable that you could never find love.

Obviously, we try to take rejections less seriously. And we should also question political, social, or economic arguments based on some rationale that the worst will inevitably happen, or that the present so definitively determines the future. The future is, after all, unknown. Ask any weather forecaster.

CONSIDER THIS ➤ Using Humor

For this reflection, weigh the costs and benefits of using humor in your writing.

You may have noticed our occasional attempts at humor, such as suggesting that someone might interpret rejection as a sign that he will "eventually die alone." We try to use humor to enliven the text and give our reader a break from otherwise serious discussions.

(*continued*)

Although most people enjoy a chuckle, humor also incurs risk. The audience may read literally and become confused, or they might interpret the tone as inappropriate and not take us seriously.

Do you think our (sometimes lame) attempts at humor work? How do they affect how you read or process our ideas? How does humor affect the style of a piece of writing? (We continue discussions of style in Chapter 10.)

False Dilemmas

Also known as an either/or fallacy or binary thinking, a false dichotomy is a kind of oversimplification. For example, in a special State of the Union address in September 2001, President George W. Bush famously stated that "You're either with us or you are with the terrorists." Obviously, there were probably groups who favored neither terrorists nor the US, and maybe even some who sympathized with both. (And to be fair and not create a straw man argument by taking this often quoted statement out of context, Bush's next sentence made his position somewhat less extreme: "From this day forward, any nation that continues to harbor or support terrorism will be regarded by the United States as a hostile regime.")

Scholars try to imagine many possibilities, rather than basing arguments on the rationale that there are only two choices when there obviously are more.

Circular Reasoning

Sometimes people back up a claim with the exact same claim, disguised as support. For instance, someone might say, "That food is unhealthy because it causes cancer" or "That action will be beneficial because it will help you." In both examples, the reason given is the same as the stated claim. This fallacy is also called "begging the question" (although you may notice that many people mistakenly use that expression when they actually mean "raising a question").

Truth as Support

Truth is a special category of support. Here we're not talking about facts or reality but about a "Truth" that's not really open to question, such as religious beliefs or patriotism. Verifying an argument with a Truth can be very tricky; those who believe the Truth will probably believe the argument, but of course, not everyone believes the same Truths. Truths, after all, are usually matters of faith more than logic or evidence.

Invoking a Truth often shuts down arguments, because once a discussion gets down to matters that are not "open to argument," there's little left to debate. Furthermore, in the United States, where we generally consider matters of faith to be private, scholars typically refrain from supporting arguments with Truths.

Whenever scholars can, they build their arguments on the least controversial, most accepted support available. When invoking values, public sources of verification make more effective scholarly arguments because they build on commonly held agreement. For example, Martin Luther King, Jr. condemned racial injustice by invoking shared American values that had previously been articulated by the nation's founders and Abraham Lincoln. For an audience who shares those values, King's arguments were, and remain, quite persuasive.

Relying Too Much on Credibility

Writers and readers commonly make mistakes with credibility, just as they do with evidence.

We must be careful about using shortcuts to assess a source's credibility. For example, a website domain (.com, .edu, .org, .gov) is not sufficient for determining its trustworthiness. You may have been taught to be more suspicious of .com websites because they only want to sell their brands or products, but company websites can be informative, if biased, sources for researching a business and its products or services. Also, don't jump to the conclusion that other websites (like .orgs) have no agendas. One look at organizations such as the NRA, PETA, MADD, and MoveOn proves different.

We misuse credibility whenever we trust or agree with an argument because of the author's reputation, rather than the verification and evidence presented. We might make this mistake, for example, when thinking that everything we read in a textbook (like this one) must be correct. It wouldn't have been published otherwise, right?

Advertisements often use this kind of *false authority* fallacy because they know that consumers will buy products based on celebrity endorsements, rather than on what they know about the quality of the product itself or whether it really works. Of course, endorsements like these can backfire with disastrous effects when a celebrity's reputation changes (think of Lance Armstrong or other sports heroes gone bad).

There's good reason not to be swayed or try to persuade others by relying too much on credibility. Think about it. **Credibility is a kind of oversimplification.** Reputations are often inaccurate or not well deserved, and they can change or even be faked fairly easily.

Credibility can also be used in deliberately or inadvertently negative ways. An ad hominem, or "against the person," fallacy intentionally emphasizes negative credibility, rejecting an argument just because of the arguer's reputation. This happens in politics when diehard Republicans or Democrats refuse to consider the other side's arguments because of party affiliation, rather than evaluating the strength of support provided. Another credibility fallacy is the "bandwagon effect," when we decide to do something just because it's popular with others. Here, our unstated rationale is that "what's good for others must be good for me." The fashion industry frequently exploits the effectiveness of the bandwagon effect in its advertising with the implied rationale, "Buy this product in order to belong."

One of the most commonly used credibility fallacies is an appeal to tradition, when we support present or future actions not on good reasoning but on what's been done before. These arguments often seem appealing, but their rationales are weak—often some nostalgia for the past or fear of change. In either case, doing things the same old way without question inhibits progress and does not represent strong critical thinking.

As we discussed in our chapter on supports, credibility is the gateway to persuasion: Before most audiences will trust new information that we present, they must consider us or our arguments to be credible. Indeed, Aristotle identified credibility, and especially the perceived character of the speaker or writer, as the most authoritative form of persuasion. Even experienced scholars are not immune to the lure of credibility. Scholarly journal articles are sometimes wrong, despite rigorous review by disciplinary experts. And despite being written mostly by novices, Wikipedia articles are mostly accurate and often well supported.

As with other kinds of fallacies, we should always ask two questions. How sufficient and relevant are these supports? Are these rationales strong enough to connect these claims and supports?

Getting Emotional

Emotions provide the least reliable but typically most compelling kind of support. Consider how much money charities raise by showing cuddly puppies or starving children to evoke sympathy. Emotion can make the difference between an audience agreeing with an argument and doing something about it. However, emotion can also cloud good judgment. Consider the last time you became overly emotional in an argument. Did you make the best decision possible?

As we discussed in the chapter on supports, arguments often arouse emotions with vivid examples, narratives, or personal experiences that may not represent the larger picture. Such illustrations may seem persuasive, but on closer inspection, they are insufficient supports when they represent small sample sizes, ignore substantial counter evidence, or hide faulty reasoning.

TRY THIS ➤ Identify the Fallacies

For this exercise, use what you've learned about fallacies to explain why the following statements might not persuade your professor. What rationales does each of these statements assume, and why might those rationales be fallacious?

Sample claim: None of the other writing classes are this hard and their teachers give all A's.

Assumed rationale: Classes can and should all be equally difficult and grade the same way.

Problem: Just because one person does something a certain way doesn't mean others should automatically follow suit (bandwagon appeal).

1. My mom said this paper was really good.
2. I'm an "A student"; I don't deserve a B for this course.
3. This paper is just as good as the ones that earned me As in high school.
4. Maybe my paper isn't that good, but I tried *really* hard.
5. What did you expect? I'm a math major.
6. If you fail me, it'll ruin my life.

Answers

1. Rationale: What mom thinks is relevant. Problem: Appeal to false authority—your mother isn't teaching this class.
2. Rationale: Past performance guarantees future results. Problem: Relevance/overgeneralization—just because you get good grades in most classes doesn't mean you'll earn them in every class.
3. Rationale: High school is the same as college. Problem: Relevance—college is not high school.
4. Rationale: Efforts should count more than quality. Problem: Relevance—quality counts.

(*continued*)

5. Rationale: Math majors are not good writers. Problem: Hasty generalization/stereotype or relevance—being good at math doesn't limit your writing ability.
6. Rationale: Consequences are relevant to evaluating performance in a course. Problem: Manipulative emotional appeal based in weak reasoning (slippery slope). This one's especially complex because it can be interpreted as any of three different fallacies: (a) an emotional fallacy, playing on the pity of the teacher not to harm the student with a bad grade; (b) a sufficiency fallacy, because one course grade typically does not cause success or failure in life; (c) a relevancy fallacy, because grades reflect performance in a course, not success or failure afterward.

Hidden Benefits of Studying Fallacies

Humans don't simply operate according to cold, hard logic like robots or Mr. Spock. In fact, fallacies are often quite effective (that is, persuasive), even when audiences pay close attention. It takes practice and constant attention to recognize fallacies in everyday life, and, as humans, we often believe what we choose to believe. This isn't to say that you should willfully use fallacies to manipulate an audience, but you should also not reject arguments outright when they contain weak reasoning, either. Just be mindful of these faults as part of the larger picture.

Remember, too, that **fallacies aren't necessarily false.** Making a hasty generalization or invoking a Truth may very well be an error in reasoning, and using such techniques may cause a critical audience to question your conclusions. However, just because such fallacies use weak reasoning doesn't mean that they're false. For example, consider the fallacy "If you fail me, it will ruin my life." We can certainly imagine a situation where this might be true. Perhaps a student is at risk only for failing this particular course, he needs this course to graduate, and he's been offered the job of a lifetime but cannot be hired without the degree in hand. Still, his grade depends on his performance in the course, not the consequences of that performance.

Finally, consider the usefulness of fallacies as gems for further research. For example,

- You might think of a hasty generalization as a hypothesis worth testing.
- You might notice red herrings as potential issues to investigate further.
- You might introduce evidence to support an argument that typically evokes only emotion.
- You might search for credible sources to replace the false authorities that a weak argument relies on.

Anticipate and Respond to Opposing Views

In addition to avoiding fallacies, we can make arguments stronger by addressing alternative perspectives. When we fail to anticipate our audience's objections, readers are left thinking, "Yes, but what about ____________________?" or "How could you overlook the fact that ____________________?" These omissions can annoy readers or imply that we haven't thought through our argument fully. At the very least, readers won't be fully convinced. At the worst, they'll be offended, angry, or unwilling to read any further.

Sometimes we feel this way when we view political advertisements that only show one side of the story, such as when a candidate attacks her opponent for one poor decision while disregarding all the good work he's done. This kind of ad hominem attack can diminish our trust in the candidate's good will. Writers can make similar mistakes, whether they mean to or not. There are several ways to avoid misrepresenting the other side.

Anticipate Objections

Imagining potential objections is one of the best ways to fortify our arguments against resistance. After all, it's much better to anticipate readers' objections while we're drafting an argument than it is to hope that our readers won't think of that one counterargument that could unravel our whole case. Unlike in conversation, writing can't be supported or clarified any further once it's published. Once it's in print, we can't add or take anything back, so we use strategies such as the following to *anticipate* objections.

Walk in the Reader's Shoes

In Chapter 8, we introduce Rogerian argument, which teaches us the importance of honoring our audience's perspective and their life experience. Whether or not we're writing a Rogerian argument to a resistant audience, we imagine what readers will think as they're interpreting our argument, what they value, what they know, and how they might respond to claims. We examine each of the argument's components from the reader's perspective and identify places where readers might object, asking ourselves:

- What elements of support are weakest and most vulnerable?
- What might readers have to say in response? If I were reading this aloud to another person, where might he stop me and say, "Wait a minute! What about ____________________?"

Identify the Potential Controversies

To avoid missing a key component of an argument, we make sure we've covered all our bases. We explore an issue comprehensively and identify different ways of approaching it by examining all five controversy categories, which we outlined on p. 104. We figure out the heart of the issue—the place where our readers will likely disagree with us—before we start writing, or we review the various controversies as we're revising to identify alternative viewpoints.

Play the Devil's (or the Angel's) Advocate

Peter Elbow's "Believing and Doubting Game" that we mention in Chapter 5 helps us explore controversies from perspectives that differ from our own. It's worth spending time getting in the mindset of someone who thinks very differently from us because it can help us see an issue's complexity more clearly—rather than through our limited tunnel vision. We also ask trusted readers to play devil's advocates for us by directly challenging our ideas, pretending to support an opposing position, and pushing us to consider all the implications of our claims.

TRY THIS ➤ Locate Missing Objections

For this exercise, review a piece of writing that you have recently composed or are currently working on. Use the first two strategies we recommend (walking in the reader's shoes and identifying the controversies) to discover alternative viewpoints and possible objections. Then, work with a partner to play devil's advocate for each other. Help each other identify possible gaps and faults in your arguments.

Respond to Objections

Once we pinpoint the objections readers could raise, we acknowledge and respond to them. Doing so demonstrates to readers that we've done our homework and understand the complexity of the controversy. Also, if readers have reasonable objections, we need to show how we've thought through those issues and reconciled our views. Basically, we have two ways of responding:

1. **We can concede.** When our readers' objections are valid, we typically acknowledge their legitimacy. We don't think of conceding as "giving in" or undermining our argument; rather, we concede to

show readers that we're honest, open-minded, and reasonable. However, we're careful about the way we frame the concession so that we don't *sound* weak or unsteady in our position. We use statements such as the following to acknowledge the alternative view and then explain why our argument still works, despite an objection:

a. Scholars who claim ________________ make a good point because ________________; however, what they overlook is ________________. This is actually more important because ________________.
b. I concede that ________________, but I still maintain my position because ________________.
c. Although ________________ is a relevant concern, the heart of the issue is ________________, which means ________________ needs to happen.
d. It is true that ____________________. However . . .

Notice how many of the above statements contain words such as "however" and "although"? These terms are *conjunctive adverbs*. Also, most of the sentences contain two parts: a deemphasized portion (the first "although" part, called a *dependent clause*) and an emphasized portion (the second part where our message comes through—the *independent clause*).

These examples show that sentence structure and word choice can bolster our message. We can emphasize our position by using conjunctive adverbs and a sentence structure that basically says, "I'll give you this minor thing, but look at what's more important." Subtle but effective, don't you think? We talk more about stylistic choices like these in Chapter 10.

2. **We can refute.** If we disagree with our readers' objections, we can explain how we've arrived at an alternative position. We describe an opposing view and then present the evidence, verification, and illustrations that convinced us to think differently. We imagine this refutation as a mini-argument that needs support. Still, we

maintain a respectful tone and treat others' objections fairly, without oversimplifying or inaccurately representing their views. Usually, this means that we summarize the opposing view in a way that shows we understand where scholars are coming from, like this:

a. Some scholars argue ________________ because they interpret evidence to mean ________________.
b. Many well-intentioned people have said ________________, which is understandable because ________________.
c. Another way of viewing this issue is ________________.

After we give voice to the opposition, we explain and defend our point of view. This refutation may take a few sentences, a paragraph, or an entire section. It all depends on how relevant the objection is to our central argument. To decide how much attention to give it, we consider the building blocks of our case and what claims our readers must accept in order to move forward in the argument.

So What?

People don't change their minds easily. An audience that disagrees with an argument naturally tends to pick apart the argument, whereas when audiences hear arguments they already agree with, they tend to think less critically about the quality of the rationale and support.

What's difficult about creating arguments is knowing how picky or objective an audience will be. Generally speaking, we assume that scholarly audiences will be "neutral"—that is, rigorous but open-minded. Recognizing fallacies can help us scrutinize arguments and avoid taking shortcuts with our thinking. Finding faulty rationales while reading can make us less gullible. Filling gaps while writing can make our arguments more convincing for demanding audiences in school and beyond. Although we can't always see the faults and blind spots in our own arguments, we can ask others to review our work and help us refute counterarguments or elaborate and build stronger rationales.

Throughout the book, we've described writing as deliberate and flexible. Similarly, in our final chapter, we describe how to adapt your writing style to different rhetorical situations. Rather than prescribing strict rules, we explain the effects of stylistic and grammatical choices. We answer specific questions such as "What is passive voice?" and "Can I bend the rules on purpose?" as well as share fun techniques you can try to vary your sentences, liven up your language, and add some pizzazz to your prose. Finally, we offer proofreading and editing advice that you can use on your own or with a trusted reader.

What's Next

Take what you've learned in this chapter and respond to the following prompts.

1. **Fallacies scavenger hunt.** Fallacies can be found everywhere. (Okay, maybe that's an overgeneralization.) Spend a day noticing as many fallacies as you can find—in the news, in advertisements, and in your daily conversations. Collect and analyze the most interesting examples. Bring your artifacts to class and discuss which ones you think are most persuasive and why.

2. **Critical thinking.** Imagine yourself in a job interview. Your potential employer asks you about your critical thinking skills. To help you prepare for this question, write a page about how finding and fixing faults in arguments can help you solve workplace problems.

3. **Satirical argument.** Write a short, satirical argument that relies heavily on fallacies. Here's an example that one of our

students, Trygve Rorvig, wrote. Before writing your own satirical argument, try to identify each of the fallacies in this example:

The drinking age of America is too high because everyone who endorses it is horrendous. The legislators of Virginia should change it back to 18, like it was at first. Other countries have a lower drinking age so we should, too. Charlie Sheen drinks alcohol, and that man is a legend so it should be legal for 18-year-olds. If we legalize a lower drinking age, the students in college will have higher morale, which will cause less depression, which will cause higher life satisfaction for all. So if you're not for a lower drinking age, you are for the depression of 18-year-olds. Some people say 21 is a good age, but I might offer a rebuttal by sharing the many kinds of alcohol there are, such as wine, beer, liquor, or moonshine (which should be legal, too). Legalization of a lower drinking age will be beneficial to America because it will be good for the people of the United States. Almost all 18-year-olds want a lower drinking age, so they cannot be wrong.

CHAPTER ten

What about Style

chapter checklist

- What are the features of style?
- How can we develop a range of styles?
- How do we edit and proofread?

You may have learned "never" to use the first person ("I") in academic writing. But what should you do when a professor asks you to write about your personal experiences? When faced with a question like this, or another stylistic dilemma, keep in mind that "rules" for good writing are not universal or unchanging, because what works in one context for a specific audience and purpose might not work for another. In other words, **writing is a series of strategic choices**.

Writing with Style

What is stylistically appropriate in one argument might be a faux pas—or even a colossal blunder—in another situation. Just as you wouldn't wear pajamas to the club or a bathing suit to a presentation, you probably shouldn't use slang in a lab report. But you might use popular colloquialisms in an article for the student newspaper because such language could help you connect with readers. As with fashionable attire, what constitutes a smartly chosen writing style depends on the rhetorical situation.

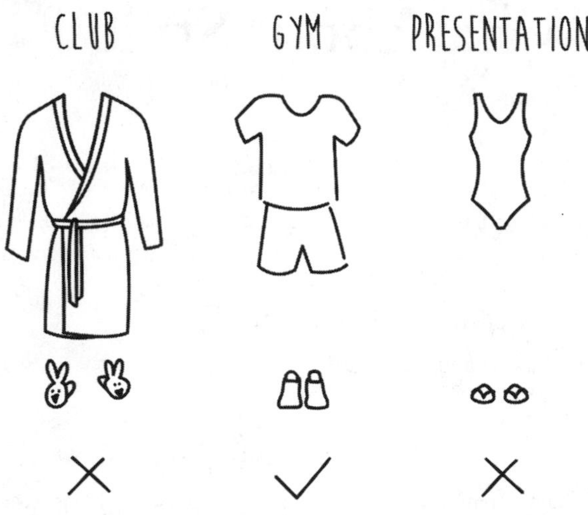

Therefore, we define style as "thoughtful flexibility"—the ability to customize our writing for different situations and expectations. With practice, style is something that you can change and adapt according to the needs of different audiences, purposes, and contexts.

To be clear and precise, scholarly style doesn't have to be boring, nor does it require unnecessarily fancy expression. The universal rule for good style, in scholarly writing or elsewhere, is for it to *seem deliberate*, with every word and sentence carefully chosen for its particular audience, purpose, and situation. Effective scholars try to **write compelling prose that reduces your reader's workload**.

Although we can't offer foolproof advice for every writing situation, this chapter will help you think deliberately about your stylistic choices. Before we delve into the details of style, let's focus on some fundamental terms and concepts.

CONSIDER THIS ➤ Style for Different Occasions

For this reflection, consider how writers adapt their style for different audiences, purposes, and contexts.

1. How would you describe the overall style of this book? How does our style compare to other textbooks you've read?
2. You probably use different styles in different situations. Describe your favorite writing style, and explain why it's your favorite.
3. What elements of style have you noticed in the scholarly writing that you've read? Create a list of common characteristics.

Compare your answers with those of a classmate.

Clarity and Vividness

Imitating good writing can be an effective technique for improving style, but it often backfires when apprentice scholars try to emulate the dense, highly technical style that they read in published scholarship. Trying too hard to sound smart can sacrifice clarity. The result is often wordy, convoluted, confusing prose that overworks readers.

Remember, the primary goal of writing is to communicate. If our style interferes with our ability to communicate, we've adopted the wrong style. To avoid an overly academic, pretentious style and reduce your readers' fatigue, consider the following suggestions.

Start Easy

As we discussed in Chapter 8, how we sequence information affects our reader's cognitive load. Generally speaking, we can reduce their workload by easing them into content that is newer or more complex. This works at the essay level when we state our thesis in the introduction ("bottom line up front") before introducing supporting details. This works at the paragraph level when we use topic sentences to announce the main idea of a paragraph. And it works in sentences when we make the most general "big" idea the subject of the sentence. Consider, for example, the following sentences:

A. Trauma to the face that damages capillaries near the eye causes a black eye, or periorbital hematoma.
B. A black eye, or periorbital hematoma, is caused by trauma to the face that damages capillaries around the eye.

Which do you prefer? Which is easier to read? These sentences both contain the same information. Sentence B begins with the concept or term, and then provides details. For most readers, sentence A is more difficult to read. (Notice, too, that sentence B uses the passive verb construction, "is caused," which in this somewhat rare case enhances clarity.)

Remember, Less Can Be More

While explanations and descriptions are necessary to communicate our full arguments, most readers appreciate when we spare them from wading through more words than necessary.

Use Strong Verbs

Sometimes writers nominalize verbs by turning them into nouns. For instance, "express" becomes "expression," and "communicate" becomes "communication." Nominalized sentences can become clunky or unclear because they are overloaded with prepositions and excessive words. Helen Sword from *The New York Times* (July 23, 2012) calls nominalizations "zombie nouns" that "cannibalize active verbs," leaving the sentence desiccated and lifeless.

To see what we mean, consider which of the following sounds better:

- "The study of rhetoric *is the investigation of* how persuasion and communication work."
- "Rhetoric *investigates* how persuasion and communication work."

Nominalized verbs sometimes help us express abstract ideas or vary our sentence structure, but nominalizations can also make our writing less lively, concise, and readable than using the original verbs.

Notice, too, how the first example sentence uses the verb "is" with the nominalization "investigation." The verb "to be" is not inherently evil, but it rarely enhances clarity. As a general rule, editing "to be" out of our writing can help us avoid using nominalizations and passive

TRY THIS ➤ Eliminate Nominalizations

For this exercise, practice translating nominalizations into active verbs, and then look for nominalizations in a draft that you're currently writing.

To practice reviving stilted language, turn the following sentences into more lively constructions:

1. The demonstration of her character was shown through her consideration of others.
2. The examination of multiple views made the essay interesting.
3. The discussion of the issue was resolved through consideration of everyone's viewpoints.

Now, look for nominalizations in a draft that you're currently writing. Replace as many nominalizations as you can find with more lively, precise verbs. To make the process easier, try using the "find" function in your word processor to search for word endings such as *-tion*, *-ism*, and *-ity*.

voice, which we discuss later in this chapter. Replacing "to be" with more precise verbs that reflect our exact meaning makes our writing more engaging and fluid.

Use Vivid and Precise Language

Descriptive language can help you incorporate details into your writing that help readers feel, see, and experience your message. However, this style doesn't work in every situation. When the audience values brevity and clarity, as is often the case in business or scientific writing, literary flourishes fail. Chemists don't want flowery lab reports, and bosses don't necessarily appreciate business proposals that rhyme.

We are very careful not to overembellish our writing if the genre or audience calls for concision, but that doesn't mean that we can't use vivid and precise language. In fact, readers generally prefer specific and clear phrasing, details, and examples that express ideas precisely—so long as every detail is there for a reason. For example, consider a vague word like "beneficial," which communicates very little substance. If we said, "Our class was beneficial," readers wouldn't know exactly what made it beneficial. Was it informative? Intellectually challenging? Motivational? Transformative? (Who knows?)

We use descriptive language to select words that transmit our exact meaning without interference or distortion. Think of this as "showing" readers exactly what we mean, rather than just "telling" them. The difference is in the level of detail. When we "show" readers, we give them something concrete to grasp—evidence of our intended meaning. When we "tell" them, we claim more abstractly.

Telling and showing come together like a claim and support. For example, if you "tell" your audience to vary their vocabulary, then they might need for you to "show" them how.

Telling: "You might use synonymous phrases . . ."

Showing: ". . . for example, refer to a puppy as a 'wee canine.'"

Showing is more precise and lively because it's less abstract.

Mechanics

Often we hear students clump all local concerns together under vague headings such as "grammar" or "flow," but these imprecise terms don't convey *exactly* what students are referring to—punctuation, transitions, sentence structure, grammar, or something else. Accurate, precise terminology can enable writers to think and communicate more carefully about their writing. For example, writers can ask for specific assistance from peer reviewers or tutors when they use terms that communicate their exact needs. Writers who talk vaguely about their writing often are less sure about what they really need to improve. To be more precise, we use the term *mechanics* to refer to sentence-level concerns, which include spelling, punctuation, capitalization, grammar, and usage.

Errors and Mistakes

Even though hardly anyone speaks or writes with perfect mechanics all the time, most educated readers expect standard academic English in formal writing. Sometimes mechanical errors do significantly affect meaning. For example, you've probably seen the T-shirt or poster that says: "Let's eat grandma." This statement implies serious bodily harm, whereas the corrected version is an invitation: "Let's eat, grandma."

Although punctuation may not actually "save lives," as these comical T-shirts claim, mechanics can certainly modify meaning. Punctuation, in particular, can be a powerful tool that affects a message. Consider, for example, the following versions of a sentence:

- A woman, without her man, is nothing.
- A woman: without her, man is nothing.

Do you notice how these sentences mean something very different? This is the main reason why educated readers value proper mechanics;

they value precise meaning and want readers to say what they mean clearly and deliberately. **Errors add confusion**. Errors cause readers to work harder to make sense of what we're trying to say.

Even when they don't seriously impair meaning, **mistakes can diminish credibility** because of the potential for imprecision or miscommunication. Educated readers will likely interpret mistakes as signs of laziness (like the writer didn't edit carefully and therefore don't care about our work) or ignorance (as though the writer doesn't know the rules). Just as when preparing for a job interview, when submitting a final draft, we make every effort to make sure our appearance is polished and professional. There's no reason to lose the job over a bit of toilet paper stuck to your shoe or an errant apostrophe.

With that being said, deviations from standard academic English can result from nonstandard dialects and written accents, not from "mistakes." What may look like a grammatical mistake may actually be an accepted form in another English dialect. We like to think that people are becoming more open-minded about variations of English, but we also know that standard English carries power in many circles. Those of us who are multilingual writers or speakers of nonstandard dialects need to decide when to use standard academic English and when to use other dialects. It's generally helpful if writers can use these dialectical differences intentionally, so becoming well versed in the rules of standard academic English can make you a more versatile writer.

Grammar versus Usage

Grammar and usage are not the same, and experienced writers know the difference. Simply put, "grammar" involves the rules for how we use language traditionally or formally, whereas "usage" is how most people actually use language in everyday conversations.

Here's an example that explains the distinction. In Chapter 1, we mention that many scholars avoid sexist language by alternating between "she" and "he," or just using "she" (since "he" had his turn for hundreds of years). The same usage formula applies to the other forms of third-person singular ("him," "her," "his," and "hers").

Third-person plural makes matters more complicated. Grammatically speaking, personal pronouns should "agree" in number with the noun to which they refer. In the previous sentence, for example, "they" refers to and "agrees with" the word "pronouns." This gets tricky, though, when a pronoun refers back to a singular noun phrase. Take, for example, this sentence: "Every student should bring [insert possessive pronoun] laptop to class." From a strictly grammatical perspective, "every student" is singular, so the pronoun should be "his" or "her": "Every student should bring *her* laptop to class." However, because gender-neutral language has become accepted usage for writers and speakers who are less finicky about grammar, people now commonly say, "Every student should bring *their* laptop to class." Experienced writers know this distinction and deliberately shift between formal and informal registers, or language styles, according to the particular audience, purpose, and context. Also, sometimes, writers use "their" as a singular pronoun to refer to a person in gender-neutral terms for political or social reasons. Although the singular "their" is becoming increasingly

CONSIDER THIS ➤ The Politics of Language

For this reflection, consider how language choices can carry political and social implications. Language use is complicated, especially because the words we use shape our perceptions. For this reason, people debate instances when language use causes "microaggressions," everyday offenses that intentionally or unintentionally target minority groups. For instance, consider the following examples and discuss the political and social implications of these language choices:

- Names of athletic teams, such as the Washington Redskins and the Atlanta Braves

(*continued*)

- Terms such as "homeless," "foreigner," "opposite sex," "elderly," "disabled," and "American"
- The practice of standard and nonstandard English
- Other language issues you have encountered

accepted in everyday conversation and in writing, writers need to be aware of how their audiences may respond to their language choices.

When you think about it, many mistakes don't significantly impair meaning. Because we usually read words and punctuation in the context of sentences, paragraphs, and pages, we can often understand what a writer's trying to say even if a word is misspelled, missing, or incorrect (substituting "their" for "there," for instance). However, if you're writing something more formal, especially for a professor who knows and cares that "every student" is singular, then try to conform to standard academic English, or you might damage your credibility. In either case—informal or formal writing—try to avoid mistakes that confuse your readers and increase their workload.

You can find detailed discussions of mechanics in style handbooks and credible resources online, such as Oxford Dictionaries Online and Purdue University's Online Writing Lab (OWL). Even if you're not ready to memorize the rules for using *who* versus *whom* or avoiding dangling modifiers, we highly recommend finding helpful resources that you can consult on a regular basis.

Punctuation

Punctuation marks, such as commas and colons, make our writing more readable; we can prevent confusion and reading fatigue by correctly punctuating sentences. But punctuation marks do more than help us communicate clearly—they can even help us emphasize our argument and persuade readers subtly. When deciding how to punctuate a sentence, we ask ourselves:

- How are the ideas in these sentences related?
- What level of connection do they have with each other?

Punctuation marks create a spectrum of connections among ideas. For instance, periods offer complete separation, whereas commas produce a tighter relationship between similar ideas. If you think of a paragraph as a group of people, imagine how sentences mingle with and relate to each other.

1. A **period** fully separates ideas. Each sentence can stand on its own, independently.
   EXAMPLE: "Experienced writers know that sometimes they have to write first to discover what their argument will be. Often, they allow writing to inspire their thinking, rather than the other way around."
2. A **dash** separates—especially to emphasize or to elaborate—one portion of a sentence from another. Often, dashes direct the reader's attention toward the end of a sentence, but they can also highlight the middle portion of a sentence (as in the previous sentence). Writers can also use commas or parentheses to mark off a part of a sentence, but the dash has a different effect. Putting commas or parentheses around something suggests that it's less important, while dashes are used to *emphasize* the separated portion.
   EXAMPLE: "Scholars typically take advantage of every opportunity to have someone read and respond to their work in progress—either their real audience or a peer who can play substitute."
3. A **colon** is used in two main ways: (a) to introduce a list (as we're doing right now) and (b) to combine two independent sentences, where the first part of the sentence introduces the ideas of the second part. The colon is placed after the introduction or the "spoiler" regarding what comes next.

EXAMPLE: "A similar phenomenon occurs with writing: practicing effective habits can help them feel more natural, but practicing bad habits will further instill them."

4. A **semicolon** connects two sentences that express closely related ideas. The semicolon allows the writer to elaborate or clarify one idea with another closely related one.
   EXAMPLE: "You can build knowledge about writing through practice; however, practice alone won't make you a better writer."

Bending the Rules

As you've probably noticed through reading this book and elsewhere, writers sometimes bend or break the mechanical rules—especially rules of usage—for dramatic effect. This can be appealing, stylistically, as long as the audience knows you're doing so intentionally (and as long as it's appropriate for your purpose and context).

Like this, for example.

Sometimes we use incomplete sentences, extra punctuation, one-word answers, or even miniature paragraphs because the prose reads better with the intentional deviation. We like the way it sounds. Or the alterations actually enhance the meaning or clarity of our message. We make these choices deliberately, after we've considered the full effect of our style selection, based on how we expect our audience to respond. However, because professors normally expect proper mechanics, apprentice scholars should intentionally "break the rules" sparingly and only when the effect will magnify the message.

Like any writer who reads her audience carefully, you have to figure out whether your creativity will be praised or scorned. Stylistic decisions provide practice for the choices you have to make when composing work e-mails, communicating with clients, or writing online in public spaces. The style you choose determines the way you present yourself, and carefully selected rule violations can demonstrate your rhetorical dexterity. To be on the safe side, you can show your professor that you know what you're doing by pointing out intentional mechanical variations in your paper (mark them with asterisks, or add footnotes or penciled comments to explain), or you can always get permission ahead of time.

Active Voice

You've probably heard teachers talk about finding your authentic "voice" when you write. Readers in the humanities often like to "hear" a human voice as they read. In other disciplines, such as the sciences, audiences commonly expect a more objective-sounding, "voiceless" style. Neither approach is wrong. In fact, the more styles writers can master, the more flexibility they have to adapt to different situations.

Verbs make a big difference in how readers "hear" our writing. Scholarly writing often employs active voice, where the doer of the action (the actor) comes before the object that is acted upon (the action receiver), like this:

EXAMPLE: "The scientist (*actor*) conducted (*action*) the experiment (*action receiver*)."

Passive voice reverses the sentence order, placing the object that is acted on before the action and the actor, like this:

EXAMPLE: "The experiment (*action receiver*) was conducted (*action*) by the scientist (*actor*)."

Neither order is grammatically incorrect, but **many readers prefer active voice because it's usually clearer and easier to read**. In active voice, the action progresses in the order that it occurs—from the actor, through the action, to the object—rather than placing the result before the cause. This linear order creates a steady rhythm that keeps readers moving forward. On the other hand, passive voice is usually wordier, which increases the reader's workload and slows him down.

In addition to being cumbersome, passive voice can be vague when the actor is missing because we may not know who performed the act. At its worst, passive voice intentionally hides the person responsible for the action. Consider, for example, the notorious statement "Mistakes were made," which doesn't indicate *who* made mistakes. The culprit can evade blame.

The bottom line is that scholarly writing values agency, clarity, and full disclosure. We aim to write sentences that help readers move smoothly and understand both what happened and who is responsible.

You can pinpoint passive voice in your own writing by spotting sentence structures like the example above (action receiver–action–actor). Another trick is to notice the way the verb changes in passive voice. Passive voice always uses a "to be" verb (am, is, are, was, were, be, being, been) along with another verb in its past participle form (usually ending in -ed or -en). You can also set most word processor's grammar and style checker to help you identify instances of passive voice.

To transform passive voice into active voice, ask yourself: Who is responsible for this action? Who is performing this action? Then place the doer, or the cause, before the action or result.

TRY THIS ➤ Transform Passive Voice into Active Voice

For this exercise, practice transforming the following sentences into active voice.

1. Well-educated people know that everyone's perspective, including their own, is limited by ignorance and bias.
2. In college, you will often be judged more on how you develop and defend your ideas than the ideas themselves.
3. Arguments are built on a basis of acceptance or agreement.

(*continued*)

4. Opinions can be shared by many, but are understood as subjective, or open to interpretation, debate, and revision.
5. As an apprentice, you will get to practice the same active approach to reading that scholars take—one that is fueled by curiosity, authentic motivation, and a desire to respond.
6. If your mind is not actively engaged, you will not remember what you read, let alone be able to comprehend or analyze new information and difficult text.
7. Experienced scholars mistrust sources that haven't been scrutinized by experts.
8. Scholars don't want to repeat research that has already been conducted or pursue questions that have already been answered.

Does changing voice change the meaning? If so, how? Which versions sound better? Why?

Now, inspect a piece of your own writing for signs of passive voice, and rewrite sentences that would be clearer in active voice.

Creative Choices We Make to Improve Style

The best news about improving style is that it's something you can practice on your own.

Imitation

One way to develop a range of styles is to practice imitating other writers whom you admire. Imitation is an ancient and useful technique for learning to write. Imagine, for example, that you were going to apply for a job but had never written an application letter or resume. Unlike in school writing, your audience (a prospective employer) would likely not provide detailed instructions for this assignment. Your best bet would be to ask someone who's recently been on the job market (and who scored a good job) to borrow her application documents to use as a guide.

Scholars often do the same thing when they want to write an article. Once they find a journal that their intended audience reads and that fits their topic, they study articles in the journal to create a set of instructions:

- What's the typical length of articles?
- How are they usually organized? For example, how much space do authors devote to reviewing previous research?
- What style is typical? Do writers tend to write more or less formally? Are there lots of graphs or charts?

TRY THIS ➤ Practice Imitating

For this exercise, select a short piece of writing by an author whose style you admire. Study the passage carefully, noticing the author's voice, word choices, and tone. Then, write a paragraph about any topic of your choosing, trying to adopt the author's style. In class, compare imitations and describe the style you were trying to mimic.

Sentence Variation

Another technique for improving style is sentence variation, which was popular during the Renaissance and used by great writers such as Ben Franklin. You can begin with a statement (like "I love ice cream") and then write multiple versions of the sentence, changing the style each time. Here are a few strategies for revision:

- **Rhetorical variation**: Change the audience, purpose, or context.
- **Amplification**: Elaborate; exaggerate; or use an analogy, metaphor, or simile (EXAMPLE: "I pine for ice cream just as reality stars crave drama").

- **Linguistic variation**: Substitute vocabulary or rearrange the order (EXAMPLE: Yoda from Star Wars might say, "Ice cream, I love" to emphasize the object of his affection).
- **Genre translation**: Rewrite the sentence in verse or as a Tweet (EXAMPLE: "Can't wait to eat this bowl of Rocky Road! #homemadeicecream").

Sentence variation helps writers assemble a richer stylistic tool kit, which can help them write more engaging prose. It also helps writers develop effective paraphrasing skills. And sentence variation can make writing more fun. Even with boring assignments, playing around with style can make the writing process more stimulating. If you can't write something interesting, write interestingly.

Figures of Speech

Rhetorical "figures" are useful tools for enriching style. You probably learned some of these while studying literature, for example:

- Metaphor: "the stench of fear"
- Analogy: "quiet as a mouse"
- Hyperbole or exaggeration: "a pea-sized brain"
- Sarcasm: "I never let schooling interfere with my education" (Mark Twain)

Brigham Young University's "Forest of Rhetoric" website (*Silva Rhetoricae*, http://rhetoric.byu.edu) provides scores of other examples and explanations to expand your repertoire.

Figures of speech can incur also some risks, such as:

- **Reference failure.** Much figurative language depends on the audience being familiar with specific cultural references. The common analogy "as annoying as nails on a chalkboard" may no longer make sense to younger readers who've only used whiteboards and digital projectors in school.

- **Inappropriate style**. Using figurative flourishes in a lab report might not go over well with an audience that wants an objective tone and "just the facts."
- **Misinterpretation**. Attempts at humor, especially through sarcasm, can fail when the audience takes them literally.
- **Clichés**. Because audiences expect figurative language to explain something in fresh terms, overused expressions can seem stale and bland.
- **Offensiveness**. Phrases like "neat freak" or "grammar Nazi" may seem harmless, but imagine how someone with obsessive-compulsive disorder would feel about being labeled as a "freak," or whether a Holocaust survivor would want grammar scrutiny equated with mass genocide.

Despite these potential pitfalls, figures of speech can be powerful argumentative devices, useful for more than stylistic embellishment. Scholars often use metaphors and analogies to introduce radically new concepts to each other or to explain specialized ideas to nonscientists (for example, explaining atomic structure as a solar system of subatomic particles).

Figures of speech can create fresh understanding and even be used beyond the sentence level as argumentative techniques. For instance, *anticategoria*, the "I'm-rubber-you're-glue" argument, turns a thesis back on the person making it. After the 9/11 attacks, for example, President George W. Bush condemned al-Qaeda as terrorists, to which Osama bin Laden responded by accusing the United States of acts of terrorism in the Middle East. This example raises the most important risk of using rhetorical figures:

- **False comparison**. Using figures of comparison to make an argument may provide a new way to make sense of your topic (for example, "America's involvement in the Middle East is like the Vietnam conflict"). However, such comparisons might also cause an audience to claim that you're using fallacious reasoning (that is, you're using irrelevant support for your argument).

In any case, think carefully about your audience's background and expectations when using figures of speech. If you think there's a chance that your figures will misfire, provide more explanation—or maybe just take it down a notch.

Revise Globally and Edit Locally

As we discussed in Chapter 2, experienced writers typically concentrate on big-picture concerns in early drafts and more minute concerns later. Like painters, they select the "tool" that best suits the job: a large paint roller for the wide strokes and a fine brush for the details and touch-ups.

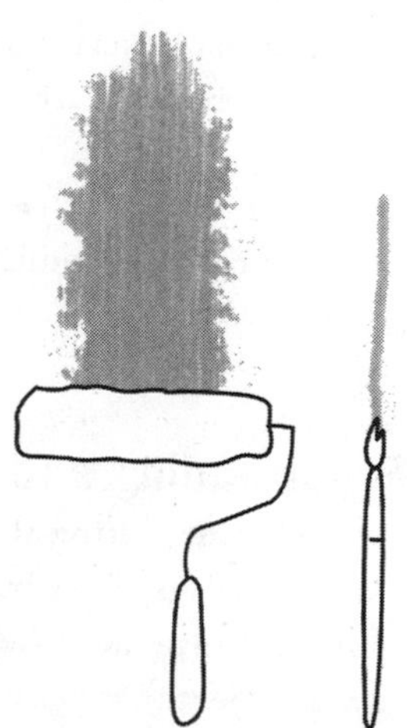

Revision focuses on global (or "higher order") concerns—such as focus, development, organization, and whether ideas make sense. Successful scholarly writers invest ample time in revising before editing for local (or "later order") concerns, such as grammar, punctuation, and so forth. Here are three good reasons not to worry about polishing your prose until you have your ideas carved out.

1. **Perfectionism can cause writer's block**. Your mind has enough to do without trying to articulate your ideas perfectly the first time, especially when you're grappling with complex concepts and arguments. As an alternative, we like to freewrite during early drafts, which allows us to develop and organize our ideas before we

nitpick over punctuation and sentence-level choices. (We describe this technique of drafting without editing in Chapter 7.)

2. **Polishing can waste time and energy** while you're still sculpting. Every time you reorganize, add, or delete content, you'll have to refinish your writing.
3. **Editing while drafting is less effective** because it's difficult to concentrate on everything at once. Returning to our writing after putting it down for a day or more gives us a fresh perspective, which helps us find more mistakes and opportunities to improve style.

Remember that you don't have to proceed through the writing process in a linear, lockstep way. Still, we do recommend that you prioritize and try not to do everything at once. We prefer to read for content and organization first, giving less attention to mechanics. Then we can pay more attention to style and grammar, targeting the quality of writing. Once we're ready to edit and proofread, we review our writing multiple times, always with a specific, focused purpose.

Proofreading and Editing

Reading your writing aloud is a very effective technique that doesn't require much expertise but yields great results. Doing so slows down your reading and exercises more parts of your brain and body (eyes, ears, and mouth), so you can be more successful editing for clarity and correctness.

Hearing your own sentences can also help you better imagine how your reader will experience your writing. Reading aloud may be unnerving at first, but it can be a tremendously helpful way to detect confusing sentences, grammatical mistakes, or just an awkward tone.

Reviewing with Others

You can also **invite a trusted friend, classmate, or writing tutor to read your work aloud**. You can check whether your main points come across clearly by asking the reader to pause after each paragraph and paraphrase or summarize what he just read.

We also ask reviewers questions such as:

- How does the writing "sound"? Is the tone appropriate?
- Are there any sentences that are confusing, awkward, or otherwise unclear?
- Are there any word choices that are vague, confusing, or overly technical?
- Where can the writing be more concise? Where can I reduce unnecessary wordiness?
- Where should I combine or divide sentences?
- Where do you see mistakes, such as missing commas, subject-verb agreement problems, or misspellings?
- Where, if appropriate, might I add more personality, through humor or vividness or other stylistic devices?

Appendix A, "How to Benefit from Peer Review and Collaboration," offers more guidance for giving and receiving feedback.

Using Technology

Technology can help with editing, too. Spellchecking tools can be useful, though they usually won't catch things like homophones (their/there) or misused contractions and possessives (its/it's). For help with that, some word processors offer advanced proofing features, with options for activating grammar and style checking. In the settings, look for where you can select features you want your word processor to check, from spacing after punctuation to passive verbs and clichés. Some style checkers will also find sentences overloaded with prepositions (of, to, for, with . . .), accidental instances of "I," and other oversights. Just be sure to **think carefully before you take your word processor's advice**. Computers are careful readers, but they're not as smart or subtle as we are when it comes to writing.

Speaking of which, be very careful with your word processor's thesaurus. Synonyms carry similar but not equivalent meaning. **Don't use words unless you know how to use them.** Trying to sound smart by using words you really don't know often has the opposite effect.

We also use the "find" function to identify boring verbs (is, are, have . . .) and grammatical mistakes we are likely to make, such as incorrect uses of "their" or "affect." The "find" function will search for any of these examples, giving us the opportunity to make changes.

Taking these extra steps makes it less likely that we'll annoy or exasperate readers. We all know readers who experience a visceral reaction when they encounter a split infinitive or a rogue apostrophe.

Developing More Style

Good writing connects with its reader. We begin creating that connection when we select a question or problem that matters to us and our audience and then write an argument that generates fresh understanding. However, in school or at work, we often cannot choose to write about a topic that naturally inspires our audience or us. Still, what appeals to readers almost universally—and can make any writing more compelling to write or to read—is craftsmanship.

There's beauty in an instruction manual that explains how to assemble a barbecue grill with precision and clarity. A research assignment about a topic that seems uninteresting can become elegant when we imagine it as an opportunity to learn a particular style or a genre shared by a community of scholars, a way of making sense of the world that we would not have otherwise known.

Successful writers never stop collecting and perfecting their tool kit of writing skills and knowledge. You can grow as a writer throughout your life through continued practice.

- Always *read as a writer*, mining everything you read for new argumentative moves, organizational patterns, sentence structures and stylistic techniques, and vocabulary and punctuation.
- Always *write as a reader*, considering how your intended audience will respond. Take every opportunity for others to read your work and help you to improve its effect.

So What?

Style is part of the message, and it's central to how we connect with audiences. Although many of the components of style are "local" concerns, their impact can be just as powerful as an argument's organization or support. Improving writing style is a lifelong pursuit, one that you can continue developing by experimenting, practicing, and exposing yourself to new genres and audiences.

What's Next

Take what you've learned in this chapter and respond to the following prompts.

1. **Magazine profile.** Investigate the style of a magazine that you like to read, and then compose a report that describes and analyzes the stylistic conventions of this magazine. To write your report, scrutinize the magazine overall and read a few sample articles. Consider the magazine's purpose and audience, along with the following features:
   a. Tone
   b. Voice

c. Use of intentional stylistic improvisations
d. Level of detail and vividness
e. Figures of speech
f. Visual design

You might also compare the print version of the magazine with its online version, if available. Then, compose a two-page report that informs your classmates how to vary their style in order to write for this magazine.

2. **Style makeover.** Select some writing that you want to dramatically alter in style. Use many of the strategies we describe in this chapter to edit the punctuation, voice, language, sentence structure, figures of speech, and other stylistic elements. To help you focus, you might begin by changing your purpose or audience.

3. **Sentence variation**. For this exercise, rewrite the sentence "This assignment is challenging" in at least 30 different ways, keeping similar meaning but changing the style at least 50% each time. Try using several of the sentence variation techniques we described in this chapter. Then, share your work with several classmates, compare your results, and discuss how you varied each sentence.

Readings

SECTION 1
HOW DO WE KNOW WHAT WE KNOW?

"Does the Internet Make You Smarter?"
by Clay Shirky

> **Clay Shirky** is a professor of journalism and a prominent writer and scholar who studies the Internet's effects on society. He is the author of *Here Comes Everybody: The Power of Organizing without Organizations* (2008) and *Cognitive Surplus: Creativity and Generosity in a Connected Age* (2010). His articles have appeared in *Business 2.0*, *The New York Times*, the *Harvard Business Review*, *Wired*, and *The Wall Street Journal*, which published this article in 2010.

Digital media have made creating and disseminating text, sound, and images cheap, easy and global. The bulk of publicly available media is now created by people who understand little of the professional standards and practices for media.

Instead, these amateurs produce endless streams of mediocrity, eroding cultural norms about quality and acceptability, and leading to increasingly alarmed predictions of incipient chaos and intellectual collapse.

But of course, that's what always happens. Every increase in freedom to create or consume media, from paperback books to YouTube, alarms people accustomed to the restrictions of the old system, convincing them that the new media will make young people stupid. This fear dates back to at least the invention of movable type.

As Gutenberg's press spread through Europe, the Bible was translated into local languages, enabling direct encounters with the text; this was accompanied by a flood of contemporary literature, most of it mediocre. Vulgar versions of the Bible and distracting secular writings fueled religious unrest and civic confusion, leading to claims that the printing press, if not controlled, would lead to chaos and the dismemberment of European intellectual life.

These claims were, of course, correct. Print fueled the Protestant Reformation, which did indeed destroy the Church's pan-European hold on intellectual life. What the 16th-century foes of print didn't imagine—couldn't imagine—was what followed: We built new norms around newly abundant and contemporary literature. Novels, newspapers, scientific journals, the separation of fiction and non-fiction, all of these innovations were created during the collapse of the scribal system, and all had the effect of increasing, rather than decreasing, the intellectual range and output of society.

To take a famous example, the essential insight of the scientific revolution was peer review, the idea that science was a collaborative effort that included the feedback and participation of others. Peer review was a cultural institution that took the printing press for granted as a means of distributing research quickly and widely, but added the kind of cultural constraints that made it valuable.

We are living through a similar explosion of publishing capability today, where digital media link over a billion people into the same network. This linking together in turn lets us tap our cognitive surplus, the trillion hours a year of free time the educated population of the planet has to spend doing things they care about. In the 20th century, the bulk of that time was spent watching television, but our cognitive surplus is so enormous that diverting even a tiny fraction of time from consumption to participation can create enormous positive effects.

Wikipedia took the idea of peer review and applied it to volunteers on a global scale, becoming the most important English reference work in less than 10 years. Yet the cumulative time devoted to creating Wikipedia, something like 100 million hours of human thought, is expended by Americans every weekend, just watching ads. It only takes a fractional shift in the direction of participation to create remarkable new educational resources.

Similarly, open source software, created without managerial control of the workers or ownership of the product, has been critical to the spread of the Web. Searches for everything from supernovae to prime numbers now happen as giant, distributed efforts. Ushahidi, the Kenyan crisis mapping tool invented in 2008, now aggregates citizen reports about crises the world over. PatientsLikeMe, a website designed to accelerate medical research by getting patients to publicly share their health information, has assembled a larger group of sufferers of Lou Gehrig's disease than any pharmaceutical agency in history, by appealing to the shared sense of seeking medical progress.

Of course, not everything people care about is a high-minded project. Whenever media become more abundant, average quality falls quickly, while new institutional models for quality arise slowly. Today we have The World's Funniest Home Videos running 24/7 on YouTube, while the potentially world-changing uses of cognitive surplus are still early and special cases.

That always happens too. In the history of print, we got erotic novels 100 years before we got scientific journals, and complaints about distraction have been rampant; no less a beneficiary of the printing press than Martin Luther complained, "The multitude of books is a great evil. There is no measure of limit to this fever for writing." Edgar Allan Poe, writing during another surge in publishing, concluded, "The enormous multiplication of books in every branch of knowledge is one of the greatest evils of this age; since it presents one of the most serious obstacles to the acquisition of correct information."

The response to distraction, then as now, was social structure. Reading is an unnatural act; we are no more evolved to read books than we are to use computers. Literate societies become literate by investing extraordinary resources, every year, training children to read. Now it's our turn to figure out what response we need to shape our use of digital tools.

The case for digitally-driven stupidity assumes we'll fail to integrate digital freedoms into society as well as we integrated literacy.

This assumption in turn rests on three beliefs: that the recent past was a glorious and irreplaceable high-water mark of intellectual attainment; that the present is only characterized by the silly stuff and not by the noble experiments; and that this generation of young people will fail to invent cultural norms that do for the Internet's abundance what the intellectuals of the 17th century did for print culture. There are likewise three reasons to think that the Internet will fuel the intellectual achievements of 21st-century society.

First, the rosy past of the pessimists was not, on closer examination, so rosy. The decade the pessimists want to return us to is the 1980s, the last period before society had any significant digital freedoms. Despite frequent genuflection to European novels, we actually spent a lot more time watching "Diff'rent Strokes" than reading Proust, prior to the Internet's spread. The Net, in fact, restores reading and writing as central activities in our culture.

The present is, as noted, characterized by lots of throwaway cultural artifacts, but the nice thing about throwaway material is that it gets thrown away. This issue isn't whether there's lots of dumb stuff online—there is, just as there is lots of dumb stuff in bookstores. The issue is whether there are any ideas so good today that they will survive into the future. Several early uses of our cognitive surplus, like open source software, look like they will pass that test.

The past was not as golden, nor is the present as tawdry, as the pessimists suggest, but the only thing really worth arguing about is the future. It is our misfortune, as a historical generation, to live through the largest expansion in expressive capability in human history, a misfortune because abundance breaks more things than scarcity. We are now witnessing the rapid stress of older institutions accompanied by the slow and fitful development of cultural alternatives. Just as required education was a response to print, using the Internet well will require new cultural institutions as well, not just new technologies.

It is tempting to want PatientsLikeMe without the dumb videos, just as we might want scientific journals without the erotic novels, but that's not how media works. Increased freedom to create means increased freedom to create throwaway material, as well as freedom to indulge in the experimentation that eventually makes the good new stuff possible. There is no easy way to get through a media revolution of this magnitude; the task before us now is to experiment with new ways of using a medium that is social, ubiquitous and cheap, a medium that changes the landscape by distributing freedom of the press and freedom of assembly as widely as freedom of speech.

For Analysis

1. Shirky begins his argument with analogies (comparisons) between Internet writing and previous technological advances. Do you think this introductory "move" is effective?
2. Shirky does not address many counterarguments. What claims and support could you use to dispute Shirky's argument?
3. Near the end of the article, Shirky recommends the following: "Just as required education was a response to print, using the Internet well will require new cultural institutions as well, not just new technologies." What are some solutions and actions (or "cultural institutions") that the public could adopt to improve Internet use?

For Writing

Other writers have also explored how the Internet affects us. In fact, Shirky's commentary responds directly to Nicholas Carr's well-known article "Is Google Making Us Stupid?" which was published in *The Atlantic* magazine two years earlier. Read Carr's argument (available at theatlantic.com) and find a few others that explore issues related to the Internet's influence on humanity. Then, write an argument that supports your perspective on these issues.

"How to Know What to Believe Anymore"

by Bill Kovach and Tom Rosenstiel

Bill Kovach is a journalist and former editor of *The New York Times*. **Tom Rosenstiel** is a media journalist and Executive Director of the American Press Institute. They have written several books, including their co-authored book, *Blur: How to Know What's True in the Age of Information Overload*. In this first chapter from *Blur*, Kovach and Rosenstiel imagine how today's media would report chaotic and competing accounts of an American catastrophe like the 1979 Three Mile Island nuclear accident. They use this illustration to exemplify the problems inherent in the new journalism and to challenge readers to evaluate information more critically.

Melanie Moyer first senses something is wrong when she arrives to pick up her father at the hospital.

At the nurses' desk, she overhears a doctor telling people he has already sent his wife and children north to New England. "If we start taking in all kinds of people, I don't want to have to worry about my family at home," he says.[1]

Taking in all kinds of people from what, she wonders?

"I got into the car and turned on the radio and started hearing that there was an 'incident' at the plant," a nuclear power facility nearby, she recalls later.

Across town, Maureen Doherty first sees something on the TV news. "I remember thinking I was going to die," she says later.[2]

As word spreads, workers at the plant begin contacting family and friends to warn them that something very serious is wrong. Many, like the doctor Moyer overhears, advise their families and friends to assume the worst and react accordingly.

These people, in turn, begin e-mailing others about their plans to flee. Grainy cell phone images and video of emergency vehicles, worried officials, and panicked plant employees begin to appear on local

TV and then on cable news. Experts, uninvolved but supposedly knowledgeable, are invited on the air to speculate on the possibility of a nuclear meltdown. Video clips from the movie *The China Syndrome* are played and go viral on YouTube.

The message, offered sometimes in apocalyptic terms and other times more cautiously, is that there's a problem in the reactor core, which threatens to spew radioactive particles into the atmosphere, turning a local electricity plant into an international nuclear nightmare. The entire mid-Atlantic region of the United States is at risk. Roughly a third of the U.S. population could be contaminated.

The blogosophere moves even faster than TV news and YouTube. Within moments, established bloggers begin to expound on the safety of nuclear power. Soon new blogs, including some by former plant employees, are launched and linked to by others. Within hours, competing blogs appear, some defending the role of nuclear power, and some of these include inside information. The plant's owner also creates a blog. Then three sites appear that present themselves as independent information providers but in reality are controlled by political groups, including one by the nuclear power industry, and are designed to counteract the critics. Their backers spend hundreds of thousands of dollars in keyword fees to make sure that in any Google or Yahoo search, these are the sites Americans would likely see.

The news on more-conventional news Web sites is fragmentary and often contradictory. The mix of messages is hard to sort through and depends on which site one visits and when.

On drive-time radio that afternoon, the nuclear event, still only a possible disaster, becomes a political wedge issue about power, the environment, and federal policy in the war of words among talk radio hosts on the left and the right. The same stylized talking points play out again on cable talk shows in prime time later that night. The message on cable news is particularly confusing. One channel seems to tilt toward the idea that the government is covering up the seriousness of the incident. A rival channel, in a manner equally hard to pin down but just as unmistakable, seems to infer that there is no incident at all and that the whole thing may be a rumor designed to destroy the U.S. nuclear power industry all over again, just as it was finally getting back on its feet after a generation of misguided and exaggerated claims about safety. A third cable channel seems to veer in both directions, inviting familiar political advocates along with various hazily identified experts to debate the meaning of the event that is unfolding.

As for print editions of newspapers (whose staffs are down by roughly 30 percent from ten years earlier) and for network news (where cuts in news gathering have been even steeper), they offer careful reportage but seem slow and out of step—appearing late in the day or the next morning.

The people around the nuclear site itself operate in still another world, buffeted by rumors electronic and in person that create randomly fragmented communities of information. One neighbor is convinced that a nuclear catastrophe is at hand, another that a minor incident has occurred. Others anxiously trying to weigh contradictory messages consider leaving the area but worry that could become deadlier than the nuclear threat if choked roads turn mass evacuation into mass hysteria.

Welcome to the Three Mile Island nuclear accident imagined in the age of the Internet.

This is not how the story played out. The reactor core of the nuclear power plant near Hershey, Pennsylvania, did overheat in 1979, but the incident occurred in a very different information world.

Melanie Moyer is real, and she did first hear about the accident at the hospital and then rushed to listen to her car radio. So is Maureen Doherty, who first learned about it on the local TV news. As they and people everywhere waited and watched, almost everything they learned about the incident was filtered through a mainstream news media at arguably the height of its prestige, trust, and influence in American history. On television, a handful of anchormen, whose networks did not expect their newscasts or their news divisions to make a profit, told the country what they knew without trying to dramatize for ratings. Newspapers, most of them flush with cash after vanquishing their rivals and becoming a monopoly in their markets, sent their reporters to nail down a single accurate account for that day's edition. It was an industry that all but controlled the news, took that responsibility seriously, and by and large did not recognize its own shortcomings. As such, it tended to speak to the public with a tone of authoritative reassurance. It did not, generally, shout or even raise its voice to attract attention.

Though it did not know it, Three Mile Island would become one of the last great domestic emergencies the media covered before the age of cable news, the concept of the "message of the day," the reinvention of the word "spin," and the notion that "mainstream media" could be a slur. And what occurred showed how the gatekeepers of public knowledge could verify the news before publication or broadcast and help calm a panicky nation with facts.

The crisis began at about four A.M. on Wednesday, March 28, 1979. A valve in the plant's cooling system got stuck in the open position, letting water that would have cooled the reactor leak out. Without the coolant, the reactor core began to overheat and the nuclear fuel pellets began to melt. At nine fifteen A.M., the White House was notified. At eleven A.M., plant officials ordered all nonessential personnel off the plant's premises. With that, word of "an event" at the plant began to filter out through the surrounding community. Workers called family and friends and neighbors with the news, which sputtered through the grapevine, often growing ominously with retelling. By midday, helicopters hired by the plant's owner, General Public Utilities Nuclear, and others from the U.S. Department of Energy could be seen circling above the plant, sampling the radioactivity in the atmosphere.

The worst, witnesses recalled, was grappling with the unknown. The fear generated by rumors and confusion was more intense for those nearby than for those further away. "The situation changed hourly," Maureen Doherty said. "I lived three miles away, in Hershey,

PA. Evacuation routes were slid under the door to my apartment." But that information helped little. As it turned out, she said, "There was no gas available at the gas stations. The highways were jammed with people trying to escape."

Unable to flee, Doherty began to rationalize: "I was very afraid, but resigned to the situation. Dying of radiation poisoning was not how I wanted to die, but I felt that it was already too late; we had already been exposed. I remember putting white sheets over the windows—I'm not sure why."[3]

That night, the nation's most watched newsman began his broadcast in a tone that was serious but not panicked. "It was the first step in a nuclear nightmare. As far as we know at this hour, no worse than that," CBS anchor Walter Cronkite said in opening his evening newscast. "But a government official said that a breakdown in an atomic power plant in Pennsylvania today is probably the worst nuclear accident to date."

The news reports also recalled the harrowing scenes of the hit movie *The China Syndrome,* starring Jane Fonda, Jack Lemmon, and Michael Douglas, which had opened nationwide to huge audiences only eleven days before. People knew from the movie the possible result of a nuclear plant meltdown: Molten reactor core products could burn through containment and into the Susquehanna River, creating a steam cloud that would produce radioactive fallout over the entire region. Eerily, the movie even had a scene in which gauges in the control room showed water levels in the reactor core rising to high levels. The scene exactly paralleled the event being described in the news.

With all those scenarios in mind, for the next two days a carefully restrained mainstream news media nonetheless conveyed a sense that the situation was an accident but not yet a disaster. The reactor had not melted down. The area had not been evacuated. "We'll stay here," Sue Showalker, the mother of two children and pregnant with a third, told reporters. "They won't let us rot under the sun."[4]

Then on the morning of Friday, March 30, plant operators released a significant dose of radiation from an auxiliary building. The maneuver was a gamble. It relieved pressure, which would maintain the flow of coolant to the core. But it was also possible that the hydrogen released could burn or even explode and rupture the pressure vessel. If that occurred, it would mean a full-fledged radiation disaster. The governor of Pennsylvania, Richard L. Thornburgh, in his first year in office, consulted with the Nuclear Regulatory Commission about evacuating the population near the plant. He decided to evacuate those most vulnerable to radiation and publicly advised pregnant women and preschool-age children within a five-mile radius of the plant to leave the area.

On the ground, rumors swirled. One night, around nine P.M., all the lights in town went out. "We later found out that a car struck a utility pole, but no one knew that then," an eyewitness told the *Washington Post*. "Within minutes, most of my neighbors had loaded their cars with prepacked suitcases, and were leaving. The sense of fear and uncertainty that night was incredible."

The press, however, remained cautious. "Networks held meetings to choose among words like accident, incident or disaster," a reconstruction of the media's behavior reported. "ABC decided never to use an adjective that had not been used by authorities. Americans everywhere had a solid dose of information about nuclear energy and radiation. Useful features included glossaries of nuclear terminology, medical stories on the impact of radiation on humans, advisories for pregnant women, reports on nearby reactors, analyses of low-level radiation studies and even a report on how to decontaminate a reactor ('very carefully' advised the *New York Daily News*)."[5]

Finally, on Sunday, April 1, experts determined that the hydrogen bubble inside the plant could not burn or explode after all. There was no oxygen in the pressure vessel to make it flammable or explosive. The utility company had also managed to reduce the bubble's size. To register a sense that experts now considered the crisis averted, President Jimmy Carter visited the plant and, accompanied by TV cameras and reporters, casually walked through the control room where the incident had begun.

After four fear-ridden days, during which most of the media stayed on the story around the clock, radio and television stations stopped their continuous news updates and resumed regular programming, a signal, unmistakable to Americans, that life had returned to some sense of normal. Newspaper headlines now deemed events in distant places more important. People around Three Mile Island began picking up the threads of their lives.

A generation later, how would the Three Mile Island incident play out? Is the scenario we imagine far-fetched? No matter what one thinks of the changes technology is bringing, it is certainly hard to imagine such a relatively orderly or homogenous process of information dissemination. It is easier, rather, to see something more chaotic. The question is how each of us, as consumers and citizens, will make sense of information about the next crisis. And how will we understand even the day-to-day events that play out more incrementally? How will we decide what information to believe and what sources to trust? And what, increasingly, will be the role of the old press? In other words, what is the future of truth and how as citizens are we to discern it?

That is what this book is about.

Some people observing the media landscape today have wondered whether truth even matters anymore. Perhaps, they speculate, in the new information age reality is simply a matter of belief, not anything objective or verified; now there is red truth and blue truth, red media and blue media. Perhaps gatekeepers such as Walter Cronkite have been replaced by cheerleaders such as Bill O'Reilly and Keith Olbermann; rather than trying to find out what is going on, they have already decided. Perhaps, in a sense, we have already moved from the age of information to the age of affirmation.

What is really occurring is different. Most of us have not retreated to ideological corners for our information. Not yet. At least so far, as we end the first decade of the new century, the old brands of journalism, and the old journalistic norms they represent, dominate the new information ecosystem. The problem these institutions face is that the

Internet has decoupled advertising from news. Advertisers, including individuals connecting with one another through Web sites like Craigslist, no longer need the news to reach consumers. Old journalism's problems have much more to do with a loss of revenue due to technology than a loss of audience.

The most fundamental change is that more of the responsibility for knowing what is true and what is not now rests with each of us as individuals. The notion that a network of social gatekeepers will tell us that things have been established or proven is breaking down. Citizens have more voice, but those who would manipulate the public for political gain or profit—be it corporations or the government—have more direct access to the public as well.

Utopians have heralded this as the end of journalism and the information monopoly of elites and see a citizen media culture that instantly self-corrects—a kind of pure information democracy. Critics see a world without editors, of unfettered spin, where the loudest or most agreeable voice wins and where truth is the first casualty.

We think both of these views are overwrought. The reality of the change is not the end of one media and the rise of a new "we media" culture but a blending that is tending toward a new way of knowing.

This new way of knowing is no longer a lecture by professional authorities but rather a dialogue, with all the strengths and weaknesses that implies. It is a partnership between all of us as consumers of news and information and the former gatekeepers we once relied on to verify and vet information for us.

This is an enormous change. In many ways, it even redefines what we mean by the idea of citizenship. The old idea, operating for the past three hundred years, was that people engaged periodically. They might vote in elections, attend the occasional town meeting, or work through other mediating institutions to pick leaders or monitor government. That old idea is giving way to something new. Rather than relying on the press, Congress, esteemed commissions, or other social authorities to filter information for them, citizens increasingly will filter information for themselves from a competing array of sources. Though we may little understand how, we are all assuming more control over what we know about the world beyond our direct experience. We are becoming our own editors, our own gatekeepers, our own aggregators.

The problem is that much of what this implies about our responsibilities as citizens is unresolved. What is the role of the new citizen—a realistic role, not a utopian one? What responsibilities does it convey? What are the skills we need to be our own editors? What is required of us in the new way of knowing?

There is no code written down. There are no mathematical equations for good citizenship. Whatever the skills required, they have been left largely and curiously untaught, even unexamined. As a society, we preach the virtues of an informed public. The corporations that profit from the business of media claim to champion its cause. The government and many of our best thinkers justly applaud technology for giving us more tools to engage. But generally our culture does little to teach what those skills might be. Our educational system by and large has not imagined them. Many of our journalism schools would be hard pressed to catalog, even for their own students, how to test the veracity of the news they produce. Those skills, however, can be identified. If we look at those who have been in the business of empiricism—people in journalism, law, intelligence, science, medicine, and elsewhere—we will see a set of common concepts and skills that have developed over generations. There is a discernible discipline of mind. Those skills and that discipline amount to what could be called a tradecraft of active skepticism. This book is an attempt to distill that tradecraft. It draws on the skills that were once the province of experts in discerning the truth about public life and outlines a method that citizens can use themselves—a new role for consumers in the do-it-yourself information world. Those skills center on knowing how to evaluate information from the press and other sources so that people can become participants in the new age of information rather than its victims.

It is important to know first that this kind of disruptive technological change has happened before. We can identify a half dozen similarly major advances in technology that have transformed communication and human learning. Each occurrence has, in sometimes larger or smaller ways, redefined the role of citizenship. And each occurrence has seen certain patterns repeat themselves, patterns that we can see today, including disrupting social orders, creating new authorities, and reviving simmering tensions in the two major approaches to learning about the outside world.

Today, as it occurs anew, it is critical to know how to cope with what might otherwise be a sense of chaos or, worse, the feeling that the truth is becoming irrelevant, a casualty to prejudice and to the might of those whose rhetoric is loudest or simplest, or whose marketing and spin are cleverest. There are, we submit, six steps in what can be called the "way of skeptical knowing," the discipline and skills required of a discriminating citizen. The first step is identifying what kind of content one is encountering. There are several distinct models of producing journalism in the contemporary culture—with different and in some ways competing sets of mores. Many of the new forms of dissemination, from social networking to blogs to citizen journalism, may involve any one of them. As consumers, we must first recognize what we are looking at.

The second step is identifying whether a news account is complete. Next comes the question of how to assess sources, something even many journalists have approached too hazily. Discerning consumers have often perceived this and have questioned how journalists work. Lawyers, doctors, police, social scientists, and those who work in other realms of empirical knowledge often have more refined ideas about sourcing, which some of the best journalists have adopted.

The fourth step in evaluating the news involves assessing evidence. This book will explain the difference between observing and understanding and the difference between inference (forming a hypothesis about what something means) and evidence (proving or establishing that this inference is true). Next we will explore how the more recent news models tend to use or interact with evidence, and how that is often a key way of establishing what kind of journalism you are encountering.

The last step in the process of evaluating the news involves exploring whether we are getting what we need from the news more generally. There are several tests and telltale signs that journalists themselves have used or identified to question the news they encounter. These bits of hidden tradecraft can be a key to discovering and creating great work.

Finally we also must ask what should become of journalists and the press. The dominant metaphor used to describe journalism in the twentieth century, that of the press as gatekeeper, no longer works when the press is only one of many conduits between newsmakers and the public. A new descriptive metaphor is required. What is it? What is the role of journalism in the twenty-first century? And how do the new journalist and the new citizen work together? We will outline what we call the "next journalism." We will describe what we think citizens require of journalists. We will offer ideas about how newsrooms must change to provide it. And we will describe a newer, broader definition of journalism's function in a community that suggests a window into new business models and a path to a commercial reinvention of journalism.

The outline we offer here of how citizens can function as their own more demanding and discriminating editors is not a strict formula. It is intended, rather, to describe ideas, to open a way of thinking about information. We hope it may start people on a path to being more conscious of their consumption and evaluation of news, whether they are journalists or not—in much the same way that studying algebra or chemistry or English in school helps us navigate the activities of our lives, even if we do not become mathematicians or chemists or English professors. People who are more conscious of how the news is put together will find themselves talking back to the television set, stopping and rereading paragraphs of text, or commenting on the quality and content of news accounts to friends. To these seemingly odd behaviors, we say bravo.

The issues are vital. The future of knowledge is the overriding question in our new century, as we struggle again between modernism and medievalism, between information and belief, between empiricism and faith. These forces in the end must coexist.

They have in the past. Haltingly, often against the interests of a powerful status quo, the march of the human family through history has been toward a more accurate understanding of the world. Sometimes, with two steps forward and one step back, risking imprisonment, even death, with wars fought over the progress, we have learned that the earth moves around the sun, the secrets of the atom, and that people can rule themselves rather than believing their rulers talk to god.

Key to this march have been professionals who work at the boundaries of knowledge, who consider themselves part of a trained cohort, schooled in certain methods and techniques and dedicated in their particular disciplines to learning what is true. In medicine, it is the doctors who fight disease. In knowing the stars, it is the astrophysicists who study how our universe came to be. In biology, it is the geneticists who study the building blocks of life. They study, err, share, and debate, striving for an objective search, which they call the scientific method. As theories become accepted realities, their knowledge is embraced by a more general population.

It has been an accumulation of ever-increasing knowledge of the world around us. Each generation builds on the information amassed by the preceding one, instituting new explosions of knowledge. The process is now becoming overwhelming. At the beginning of this century, it was forecast that more new information would be created in three years than had been created in the previous three hundred thousand years.[6]

The question of the new century is how will that process work? How will we as citizens learn what is true? How will we find out what information we can trust in an age in which we are all our own experts and power has been ceded to everyone?

Notes

1. Recorded on the Center for History and New Media, George Mason University Web site, http://echo.gmu.edu/tmi.
2. Ibid.
3. Ibid.
4. Peter Goldman et al., "In the Shadow of the Tower," *Newsweek*, April 9, 1979, p. 29.
5. Arlie Schardt et al. "Covering Three Mile Island," *Newsweek*, April 16, 1979, p. 93.
6. Walter Truett Anderson, *All Connected Now: Life in the First Global Civilization*. Westview Press, Boulder, 2001.

For Analysis

1. How do Kovach and Rosenstiel demonstrate the "so what?" factors of this issue? Where specifically do they draw readers' attention to the implications of information overload?
2. Which controversy categories do Kovach and Rosenstiel address? Where in the chapter do you see the authors elaborate on specific categories?
3. According to Kovach and Rosenstiel, what should citizens do to distinguish between accurate and bogus information? How does their advice compare to the suggestions we give in Chapter 3?

For Writing

Write a 1,500-word argument that describes the responsibilities and characteristics of the "new citizen." First, summarize what Kovach and Rosenstiel advise; then, build your own case by verifying your argument with other scholars' views, and/or conduct original research by interviewing trusted peers or mentors.

"When Prior Belief Trumps Scholarship"

by Charles R. Marshall

Charles R. Marshall is a professor of integrative biology and the director of the Museum of Paleontology at the University of California, Berkeley. Marshall has published his research in scholarly journals such as the *Proceedings of the National Academy of Sciences, Nature, Journal of Paleontology*, and *Evolution*. The following book review of *Darwin's Doubt: The Explosive Origin of Animal Life and the Case for Intelligent Design* appeared in *Science* in 2013.

The power of scientific reasoning derives from the complex interplay between the desire to know, the ability to reason, and the ability to evaluate ideas with data. As scientists, we have learned how to make ideas dance with reality, and we expect them to be transformed in the process. We typically add to what we already know, often showing along the way that old ideas are incomplete or, occasionally, wrong. And so we collectively build an understanding of the world that is accurate, reliable, and useful.

In *Darwin's Doubt*, Stephen Meyer (who runs the Discovery Institute's Center for Science and Culture) also tries to build. He aims to construct the philosophical and scientific case for intelligent design. I am not a philosopher, so I will not attempt to evaluate his philosophical argument that in principle it might be possible to recognize the action of a designer in the history of life. But I am willing to evaluate his scientific case for the participation of such a designer. It centers on one of the most remarkable events in that history, the relatively rapid emergence of animal phyla in the Cambrian.

Meyer's scientific approach is negative. He argues that paleontologists are unable to explain the Cambrian explosion, thus opening the door to the possibility of a designer's intervention. This, despite his protest to the contrary, is a (sophisticated) "god of the gaps" approach, an approach that is problematic in part because future developments often provide solutions to once apparently difficult problems.

Darwin's Doubt begins with a very readable review of our knowledge of the Cambrian explosion. Despite its readability and a plethora of scholarly references, however, there are substantial omissions and misrepresentations. For example, Meyer completely omits mention of the Early Cambrian small shelly fossils and misunderstands the nuances of molecular phylogenetics, both of which cause him to exaggerate the apparent suddenness of the Cambrian explosion.

I like to read the arguments of those who hold fundamentally different views from my own in the hope of discovering weaknesses in my thinking. And so even after reading the flawed first part of his book, I dared hope that Meyer might point the way to fundamental problems in the way we paleontologists think about the Cambrian explosion.

However, my hope soon dissipated into disappointment. His case against current scientific explanations of the relatively rapid appearance of the animal phyla rests on the claim that the origin of new animal body plans requires vast amounts of novel genetic information coupled with the unsubstantiated assertion that this new genetic information must include many new protein folds. In fact, our present understanding of morphogenesis indicates that new phyla were not made by new genes but largely emerged through the rewiring of the gene regulatory networks (GRNs) of already existing genes (*1*). Now Meyer does touch on this: He notes that manipulation of such networks is typically lethal, thus dismissing their role in explaining the Cambrian explosion. But today's GRNs have been overlain with half a billion years of evolutionary innovation (which accounts for their resistance to modification), whereas GRNs at the time of the emergence of the phyla were not so encumbered. The reason for Meyer's idiosyncratic fixation with new protein folds is that one of his Discovery Institute colleagues has claimed that those are mathematically impossibly hard to evolve on the timescale of the Cambrian explosion.

As Meyer points out, he is not a biologist; so perhaps he could be excused for basing his scientific arguments on an outdated understanding of morphogenesis. But my disappointment runs deeper than that. It stems from Meyer's systematic failure of scholarship. For instance, while I was flattered to find him quote one of my own review papers (2)—although the quote is actually a chimera drawn from two very different parts of my review—he fails to even mention the review's (and many other papers') central point: that new genes did not drive the Cambrian explosion. His scholarship, where it matters most, is highly selective.

Meyer's book ends with a heart-warming story of his normally fearless son losing his orientation on the impressive scree slopes that cradle the Burgess Shale, the iconic symbol of the Cambrian explosion, and his need to look back to his father for security. I was puzzled: why the parable in a book ostensibly about philosophy and science? Then I realized that the book's subtext is to provide solace to those who feel their faith undermined by secular society and by science in particular. If the reviews on Amazon.com are any indication, it is achieving that goal. But when it comes to explaining the Cambrian explosion, *Darwin's Doubt* is compromised by Meyer's lack of scientific knowledge, his "god of the gaps" approach, and selective scholarship that appears driven by his deep belief in an explicit role of an intelligent designer in the history of life.

References

1. D. H. Erwin, J. W. Valentine, The Cambrian Explosion: The Construction of Animal Biodiversity (Roberts and Company, Greenwood Village, CO, 2013); reviewed in (3).
2. C. R. Marshall, Annu. Rev. Earth Planet. Sci. 34, 355 (2006).
3. C. J. Lowe, Science 340, 1170 (2013).

For Analysis

1. What do you think of Marshall's writing style? Would you expect to find such informal elements in a scientific journal? How does his style affect his credibility? How does it enable him to connect with his readers?
2. If you can access the article online (via your library's website), review the posted comments, including a response by the book's author, Stephen Meyer. What techniques does Meyer use to refute Marshall's critique?
3. Find another book review in a reputable newspaper, such as *The New York Review of Books*. Compare that review with Marshall's. What similarities and differences do you notice?

For Writing

Using Marshall's review as a model, create a one-page template or set of instructions for how to write an effective scholarly book review.

"How Does Our Language Shape The Way We Think?"

by Lera Boroditsky

Lera Boroditsky is a professor of cognitive science at the University of California, San Diego. She publishes in popular media, such as *The Wall Street Journal* and *The Economist*, and in scholarly journals, such as *Psychological Science*. In the following 2009 essay, which was originally published in *Edge*, Boroditsky blends logic and research to argue that "people who speak different languages do indeed think differently."

Humans communicate with one another using a dazzling array of languages, each differing from the next in innumerable ways. Do the languages we speak shape the way we see the world, the way we think, and the way we live our lives? Do people who speak different languages think differently simply because they speak different languages? Does learning new languages change the way you think? Do polyglots think differently when speaking different languages?

These questions touch on nearly all of the major controversies in the study of mind. They have engaged scores of philosophers, anthropologists, linguists, and psychologists, and they have important implications for politics, law, and religion. Yet despite nearly constant attention and debate, very little empirical work was done on these questions until recently. For a long time, the idea that language might shape thought was considered at best untestable and more often simply wrong. Research in my labs at Stanford University and at MIT has helped reopen this question. We have collected data around the world: from China, Greece, Chile, Indonesia, Russia, and Aboriginal Australia. What we have learned is that people who speak different languages do indeed think differently and that even flukes of grammar can profoundly affect how we see the world. Language is a uniquely human gift, central to our experience of being human. Appreciating its role in constructing our mental lives brings us one step closer to understanding the very nature of humanity.

I often start my undergraduate lectures by asking students the following question: which cognitive faculty would you most hate to lose? Most of them pick the sense of sight; a few pick hearing. Once in a while, a wisecracking student might pick her sense of humor or her fashion sense. Almost never do any of them spontaneously say that the faculty they'd most hate to lose is language. Yet if you lose (or are born without) your sight or hearing, you can still have a wonderfully rich social existence. You can have friends, you can get an education, you can hold a job, you can start a family. But what would your life be like if you had never learned a language? Could you still have friends, get an education, hold a job, start a family? Language is so fundamental to our experience, so deeply a part of being human, that it's hard to imagine life without it. But are languages merely tools for expressing our thoughts, or do they actually shape our thoughts?

Most questions of whether and how language shapes thought start with the simple observation that languages differ from one another. And a lot! Let's take a (very) hypothetical example. Suppose you want to say, "Bush read Chomsky's latest book." Let's focus on just the verb, "read." To say this sentence in English, we have to mark the verb for tense; in this case, we have to pronounce it like "red" and not like "reed." In Indonesian you need not (in fact, you can't) alter the verb to mark tense. In Russian you would have to alter the verb to indicate tense and gender. So if it was Laura Bush who did the reading, you'd use a different form of the verb than if it was George. In Russian you'd also have to include in the verb information about completion. If George read only part of the book, you'd use a different form of the verb than if he'd diligently plowed through the whole thing. In Turkish you'd have to include in the verb how you acquired this information: if you had witnessed this unlikely event with your own two eyes, you'd use one verb form, but if you had simply read or heard about it, or inferred it from something Bush said, you'd use a different verb form.

Clearly, languages require different things of their speakers. Does this mean that the speakers think differently about the world? Do English, Indonesian, Russian, and Turkish speakers end up attending to, partitioning, and remembering their experiences differently just because they speak different languages? For some scholars, the answer to these questions has been an obvious yes. Just look at the way people talk, they might say. Certainly, speakers of different languages must attend to and encode strikingly different aspects of the world just so they can use their language properly.

Scholars on the other side of the debate don't find the differences in how people talk convincing. All our linguistic utterances are sparse, encoding only a small part of the information we have available. Just because English speakers don't include the same information in their verbs that Russian and Turkish speakers do doesn't mean that English speakers aren't paying attention to the same things; all it means is that they're not talking about them. It's possible that everyone thinks the same way, notices the same things, but just talks differently.

Believers in cross-linguistic differences counter that everyone does not pay attention to the same things: if everyone did, one might think it would be easy to learn to speak other languages. Unfortunately, learning a new language (especially one not closely related to those you know) is never easy; it seems to require paying attention to a new set of distinctions. Whether it's distinguishing modes of being in Spanish, evidentiality in Turkish, or aspect in Russian, learning to speak these languages requires something more than just learning vocabulary: it requires paying attention to the right things in the world so that you have the correct information to include in what you say.

Such a priori arguments about whether or not language shapes thought have gone in circles for centuries, with some arguing that it's impossible for language to shape thought and others arguing that it's impossible for language not to shape thought. Recently my group and others have figured out ways to empirically test some of the key questions in this ancient debate, with fascinating results. So instead of arguing about what must be true or what can't be true, let's find out what is true.

Follow me to Pormpuraaw, a small Aboriginal community on the western edge of Cape York, in northern Australia. I came here because of the way the locals, the Kuuk Thaayorre, talk about space. Instead of words like "right," "left," "forward," and "back," which, as commonly used in English, define space relative to an observer, the Kuuk Thaayorre, like many other Aboriginal groups, use cardinal-direction terms—north, south, east, and west—to define space.[1] This is done at all scales, which means you have to say things like "There's an ant on your southeast leg" or "Move the cup to the north northwest a little bit." One obvious consequence of speaking such a language is that you have to stay oriented at all times, or else you cannot speak properly. The normal greeting in Kuuk Thaayorre is "Where are you going?" and the answer should be something like "South southeast, in the middle distance." If you don't know which way you're facing, you can't even get past "Hello."

The result is a profound difference in navigational ability and spatial knowledge between speakers of languages that rely primarily on absolute reference frames (like Kuuk Thaayorre) and languages that rely on relative reference frames (like English).[2] Simply put, speakers of languages like Kuuk Thaayorre are much better than English speakers at staying oriented and keeping track of where they are, even in unfamiliar landscapes or inside unfamiliar buildings. What enables them—in fact, forces them—to do this is their language. Having their attention trained in this way equips them to perform navigational feats once thought beyond human capabilities. Because space is such a fundamental domain of thought, differences in how people think about space don't end there. People rely on their spatial knowledge to build other, more complex, more abstract representations. Representations of such things as time, number, musical pitch, kinship relations, morality, and emotions have been shown to depend on how we think about space. So if the Kuuk Thaayorre think differently about space, do they also think differently about other things, like time? This is what my collaborator Alice Gaby and I came to Pormpuraaw to find out.

To test this idea, we gave people sets of pictures that showed some kind of temporal progression (e.g., pictures of a man aging, or a crocodile growing, or a banana being eaten). Their job was to arrange the shuffled photos on the ground to show the correct temporal order. We tested each person in two separate sittings, each time facing in a different cardinal direction. If you ask English speakers to do this, they'll arrange the cards so that time proceeds from left to right. Hebrew speakers will tend to lay out the cards from right to left, showing that writing direction in a language plays a role.[3] So what about folks like the Kuuk Thaayorre, who don't use words like "left" and "right"? What will they do?

The Kuuk Thaayorre did not arrange the cards more often from left to right than from right to left, nor more toward or away from the body. But their arrangements were not random: there was a pattern, just a different one from that of English speakers. Instead of arranging time from left to right, they arranged it from east to west. That is, when they were seated facing south, the cards went left to right. When they faced north, the cards went from right to left. When they faced east, the cards came toward the body and so on. This was true even though we never told any of our subjects which direction they faced. The Kuuk Thaayorre not only knew that already (usually much better than I did), but they also spontaneously used this spatial orientation to construct their representations of time.

People's ideas of time differ across languages in other ways. For example, English speakers tend to talk about time using horizontal spatial metaphors (e.g., "The best is ahead of us," "The worst is behind us"), whereas Mandarin speakers have a vertical metaphor for time (e.g., the next month is the "down month" and the last month is the "up month"). Mandarin speakers talk about time vertically more often than English speakers do, so do Mandarin speakers think about time vertically more often than English speakers do? Imagine this simple experiment. I stand next to you, point to a spot in space directly in front of you, and tell you, "This spot, here, is today. Where would you put yesterday? And where would you put tomorrow?" When English speakers are asked to do this, they nearly always point horizontally. But Mandarin speakers often point vertically, about seven or eight times more often than do English speakers.[4]

Even basic aspects of time perception can be affected by language. For example, English speakers prefer to talk about duration in terms of length (e.g., "That was a short talk," "The meeting didn't take long"), while Spanish and Greek speakers prefer to talk about time in terms of amount, relying more on words like "much," "big," and "little" rather than "short" and "long." Our research into such basic cognitive abilities as estimating duration shows that speakers of different languages differ in ways predicted by the patterns of metaphors in their language. (For example, when asked to estimate duration, English speakers are more likely to be confused by distance information, estimating that a line of greater length remains on the test screen for a longer period of time, whereas Greek speakers are more likely to be confused by amount, estimating that a container that is fuller remains longer on the screen.)[5]

An important question at this point is: Are these differences caused by language per se or by some other aspect of culture? Of course, the lives of English, Mandarin, Greek, Spanish, and Kuuk Thaayorre speakers differ in a myriad of ways. How do we know that it is language itself that creates these differences in thought and not some other aspect of their respective cultures?

One way to answer this question is to teach people new ways of talking and see if that changes the way they think. In our lab, we've taught English speakers different ways of talking about time. In one such study, English speakers were taught to use size metaphors (as in

Greek) to describe duration (e.g., a movie is larger than a sneeze), or vertical metaphors (as in Mandarin) to describe event order. Once the English speakers had learned to talk about time in these new ways, their cognitive performance began to resemble that of Greek or Mandarin speakers. This suggests that patterns in a language can indeed play a causal role in constructing how we think.[6] In practical terms, it means that when you're learning a new language, you're not simply learning a new way of talking, you are also inadvertently learning a new way of thinking. Beyond abstract or complex domains of thought like space and time, languages also meddle in basic aspects of visual perception—our ability to distinguish colors, for example. Different languages divide up the color continuum differently: some make many more distinctions between colors than others, and the boundaries often don't line up across languages.

To test whether differences in color language lead to differences in color perception, we compared Russian and English speakers' ability to discriminate shades of blue. In Russian there is no single word that covers all the colors that English speakers call "blue." Russian makes an obligatory distinction between light blue (goluboy) and dark blue (siniy). Does this distinction mean that siniy blues look more different from goluboy blues to Russian speakers? Indeed, the data say yes. Russian speakers are quicker to distinguish two shades of blue that are called by the different names in Russian (i.e., one being siniy and the other being goluboy) than if the two fall into the same category.

For English speakers, all these shades are still designated by the same word, "blue," and there are no comparable differences in reaction time.

Further, the Russian advantage disappears when subjects are asked to perform a verbal interference task (reciting a string of digits) while making color judgments but not when they're asked to perform an equally difficult spatial interference task (keeping a novel visual pattern in memory). The disappearance of the advantage when performing a verbal task shows that language is normally involved in even surprisingly basic perceptual judgments—and that it is language per se that creates this difference in perception between Russian and English speakers.

When Russian speakers are blocked from their normal access to language by a verbal interference task, the differences between Russian and English speakers disappear.

Even what might be deemed frivolous aspects of language can have far-reaching subconscious effects on how we see the world. Take grammatical gender. In Spanish and other Romance languages, nouns are either masculine or feminine. In many other languages, nouns are divided into many more genders ("gender" in this context meaning class or kind). For example, some Australian Aboriginal languages have up to sixteen genders, including classes of hunting weapons, canines, things that are shiny, or, in the phrase made famous by cognitive linguist George Lakoff, "women, fire, and dangerous things."

What it means for a language to have grammatical gender is that words belonging to different genders get treated differently grammatically and words belonging to the same grammatical gender get treated the same grammatically. Languages can require speakers to change pronouns, adjective and verb endings, possessives, numerals, and so on, depending on the noun's gender. For example, to say something like "my chair was old" in Russian (*moy stul bil' stariy*), you'd need to make every word in the sentence agree in gender with "chair" (*stul*), which is masculine in Russian. So you'd use the masculine form of "my," "was," and "old." These are the same forms you'd use in speaking of a biological male, as in "my grandfather was old." If, instead of speaking of a chair, you were speaking of a bed (*krovat'*), which is feminine in Russian, or about your grandmother, you would use the feminine form of "my," "was," and "old."

Does treating chairs as masculine and beds as feminine in the grammar make Russian speakers think of chairs as being more like men and beds as more like women in some way? It turns out that it does. In one study, we asked German and Spanish speakers to describe objects having opposite gender assignment in those two languages. The descriptions they gave differed in a way predicted by grammatical gender. For example, when asked to describe a "key"—a word that is masculine in German and feminine in Spanish—the German speakers were more likely to use words like "hard," "heavy," "jagged," "metal," "serrated," and "useful," whereas Spanish speakers were more likely to say "golden," "intricate," "little," "lovely," "shiny," and "tiny." To describe a "bridge," which is feminine in German and masculine in Spanish, the German speakers said "beautiful," "elegant," "fragile," "peaceful," "pretty," and "slender," and the Spanish speakers said "big," "dangerous," "long," "strong," "sturdy," and "towering." This was true even though all testing was done in English, a language without grammatical gender. The same pattern of results also emerged in entirely nonlinguistic tasks (e.g., rating similarity between pictures). And we can also show that it is aspects of language per se that shape how people think: teaching English speakers new grammatical gender systems influences mental representations of objects in the same way it does with German and Spanish speakers. Apparently even small flukes of grammar, like the seemingly arbitrary assignment of gender to a noun, can have an effect on people's ideas of concrete objects in the world.[7]

In fact, you don't even need to go into the lab to see these effects of language; you can see them with your own eyes in an art gallery. Look at some famous examples of personification in art—the ways in which abstract entities such as death, sin, victory, or time are given human form. How does an artist decide whether death, say, or time should be painted as a man or a woman? It turns out that in 85 percent of such personifications, whether a male or female figure is chosen is predicted by the grammatical gender of the word in the artist's native language. So, for example, German painters are more likely to paint death as a man, whereas Russian painters are more likely to paint death as a woman.

The fact that even quirks of grammar, such as grammatical gender, can affect our thinking is profound. Such quirks are pervasive in language; gender, for example, applies to all nouns, which means that it is affecting how people think about anything that can be designated by a noun. That's a lot of stuff!

I have described how languages shape the way we think about space, time, colors, and objects. Other studies have found effects of language on how people construe events, reason about causality, keep track of number, understand material substance, perceive and experience emotion, reason about other people's minds, choose to take risks, and even in the way they choose professions and spouses.[8] Taken together, these results show that linguistic processes are pervasive in most fundamental domains of thought, unconsciously shaping us from the nuts and bolts of cognition and perception to our loftiest abstract notions and major life decisions. Language is central to our experience of being human, and the languages we speak profoundly shape the way we think, the way we see the world, the way we live our lives.

Notes

1. S. C. Levinson and D. P. Wilkins, eds., Grammars of Space: Explorations in Cognitive Diversity (New York: Cambridge University Press, 2006).
2. Levinson, Space in Language and Cognition: Explorations in Cognitive Diversity (New York: Cambridge University Press, 2003).
3. B. Tversky et al., " Cross-Cultural and Developmental Trends in Graphic Productions," Cognitive Psychology 23(1991): 515–7; O. Fuhrman and L. Boroditsky, "Mental Time-Lines Follow Writing Direction: Comparing English and Hebrew Speakers." Proceedings of the 29th Annual Conference of the Cognitive Science Society (2007): 1007–10.
4. L. Boroditsky, "Do English and Mandarin Speakers Think Differently About Time?" Proceedings of the 48th Annual Meeting of the Psychonomic Society (2007): 34.
5. D. Casasanto et al., "How Deep Are Effects of Language on Thought? Time Estimation in Speakers of English, Indonesian

Greek, and Spanish," Proceedings of the 26th Annual Conference of the Cognitive Science Society (2004): 575–80.

6. Ibid., "How Deep Are Effects of Language on Thought? Time Estimation in Speakers of English and Greek" (in review); L. Boroditsky, "Does Language Shape Thought? English and Mandarin Speakers' Conceptions of Time." Cognitive Psychology 43, no. 1(2001): 1–22.
7. L. Boroditsky et al., "Sex, Syntax, and Semantics," in D. Gentner and S. Goldin-Meadow, eds., Language in Mind: Advances in the Study of Language and Cognition (Cambridge, MA: MIT Press, 2003), 61–79.
8. L. Boroditsky, "Linguistic Relativity," in L. Nadel ed., Encyclopedia of Cognitive Science (London: MacMillan, 2003), 917–21; B. W. Pelham et al., "Why Susie Sells Seashells by the Seashore: Implicit Egotism and Major Life Decisions." Journal of Personality and Social Psychology 82, no. 4(2002): 469–86; A. Tversky & D. Kahneman, "The Framing of Decisions and the Psychology of Choice." Science 211(1981): 453–58; P. Pica et al., "Exact and Approximate Arithmetic in an Amazonian Indigene Group." Science 306(2004): 499–503; J. G. de Villiers and P. A. de Villiers, "Linguistic Determinism and False Belief," in P. Mitchell and K. Riggs, eds., Children's Reasoning and the Mind (Hove, UK: Psychology Press, in press); J. A. Lucy and S. Gaskins, "Interaction of Language Type and Referent Type in the Development of Nonverbal Classification Preferences," in Gentner and Goldin-Meadow, 465–92; L. F. Barrett et al., "Language as a Context for Emotion Perception," Trends in Cognitive Sciences 11(2007): 327–32.

For Analysis

1. What methods does Boroditsky's team use to answer their research questions?
2. How persuasive is the data that Boroditsky's research team collected? Is the data sufficient and relevant? Which research findings are most compelling?
3. Where does Boroditsky draw conclusions from the data? Underline specific claims about what the data "shows" or "suggests."

For Writing

Boroditsky acknowledges that some scholars believe that "It's impossible for language to shape thought." Find a scholar who supports this opposing position. In 500 words, summarize his or her views and the evidence that he or she cites to argue that language does *not* directly influence thought.

Excerpt from *Introduction to Real Enemies: Conspiracy Theories and American Democracy, World War 1 to 9/11*

by Kathryn S. Olmstead

Kathryn S. Olmstead is a history professor at the University of California, Davis. Olmstead has written several books and articles about 20th-century U.S. history, with an emphasis on espionage and political conspiracies. This excerpt introduces her 2009 book, *Real Enemies: Conspiracy Theories and American Democracy, World War I to 9/11*.

Introduction

IF YOU SEARCH for "9/11 conspiracies" on the Google Video Web site, you can learn some shocking things. You can learn that there were no commercial airplanes involved in the September 11, 2001, terrorist attacks—just drones and cruise missiles. You can link to Web sites that claim that the World Trade Center towers fell because bombs were secretly placed in their air ducts, not because planes, commercial or military, manned or not, crashed into them. You can watch documentary films that allege that 9/11 was an "inside job" perpetrated by the George W. Bush administration to justify its invasions of Afghanistan and Iraq. If you look at the information on the most popular of these documentaries, called Loose Change, you will see that at least ten million people have already viewed it, and thirty-five thousand of them have written reviews, giving it an average rating of four and a half out of five stars.

These opinions may seem to belong on the fringe, but in fact millions of Americans hold them. Polls show that 36 percent of Americans think the Bush administration either planned the 9/11 attacks or knew that they were coming and did nothing to stop them. A majority of Americans between the ages of eighteen and twenty-nine believe these theories.[1]

In many ways, the popularity of 9/11 conspiracy theories is a mystery. What can explain this profound distrust of the U.S. government? Why, in one of the world's oldest constitutional democracies, would more than a third of the people believe that officials of their own government plotted to carry out terrorist attacks on U.S. soil to trick the people into war?

Here's one reason: it has happened before.

In March 1962, at the height of the cold war, the U.S. Joint Chiefs of Staff presented Secretary of Defense Robert McNamara with a plan to deceive Americans into supporting a war on Fidel Castro's Cuba. Their proposal: to conduct terrorist attacks in the United States and blame them on Castro in order to provide "pretexts" for "US military intervention in Cuba." They wanted to develop "the international image of the Cuban government as rash and irresponsible, and as an alarming and unpredictable threat to the peace of the Western Hemisphere."[2]

The military chiefs planned to explode bombs in U.S. cities, sink boatloads of Cuban refugees approaching U.S. shores, and gun down Cuban dissidents in the United States. They even suggested blowing up John Glenn's rocket during his historic flight as the first American in space. In each case, the chiefs proposed to plant fake evidence that would frame Castro as the guilty party.

In their most fantastical plan, they planned to shoot down a civilian airliner. The chiefs plotted to load an airplane with unsuspecting passengers and then secretly divert it to Eglin Air Force Base in Florida. Meanwhile, a drone painted to look like the civilian aircraft would fly across Cuba, where "Cubans" would shoot it down.[3] The chiefs were so eager for war with Castro's Cuba that they were willing to stage attacks on their own citizens to justify it.

There is no record of McNamara's response, but three days later President John Kennedy bluntly told the chairman of the chiefs that he did not intend to invade Cuba anytime soon.[4] "Operation Northwoods," as the military dubbed the plot to confuse anyone who stumbled across it, never made it off the drawing board.

Forty years later, the Northwoods plans, which had been declassified in the late 1990s, were featured in the opening scenes of *Loose Change.*[5] Somewhat improbably, these decades-old historical documents popped up in books, movies, and on Web sites popular with skeptical twentysomethings who were born some two decades after Kennedy rejected the chiefs' plans. After September 11, conspiracy theorists saw in Northwoods the "precise template for the remote control and plane-switching theory that is able to explain so many discrepant facts about 9/11—down to the final detail of feigned cluelessness."[6] Others believed that it proved U.S. officials' willingness to do anything to achieve their goals.[7]

In the wake of 9/11, the evidence of real government conspiracies from the past was used to support the conspiracy theories about the government of the present. To understand contemporary theories, we need to examine the history of *proven* government conspiracies, because for all their seeming outlandishness, the successive generations of antigovernment conspiracy theorists since World War I have at least one thing in common: when they charge that the government has plotted, lied, and covered up, they're often right.

A CONSPIRACY OCCURS when two or more people collude to abuse power or break the law. A *conspiracy theory* is a proposal about a conspiracy that may or may not be true; it has not yet been proven. Scholars refer to the tendency to see conspiracies everywhere as *conspiracism,* and this tendency long ago spread from the margins into the main body of American political culture. Government officials, even presidents, sometimes propose conspiracy theories, giving official sanction to the paranoid interpretation of history.

Americans have a special relationship to conspiracy theory. Because immigrants bring a new mix of religions and ethnicities and histories to their land, Americans have worried that their country is especially open—and vulnerable—to alien subversion.[8] Over the past two hundred years, frightened Americans have targeted Catholics, Masons, Mormons, and Jews because these native groups were allegedly guided by the instructions of an alien power. The historian Richard Hofstadter argued that there was a "paranoid style" in American politics, prompted in part by Americans' need to define themselves by casting out the "un-Americans."[9]

Throughout the nation's history, many Americans have particularly feared that their federal government would fall victim to one of these conspiracies—or become a tool of conspirators. As the historian David Brion Davis has said, "Americans have been curiously obsessed with the contingency of their experiment with freedom."[10] Ever since the nation's founding, they have worried that the great instrument of the people's will would be turned against them. The philosophers of early America knew their ancient history and their Shakespeare, and they were always looking over their shoulder for potential Caesars. From the Illuminati scare of the late eighteenth century to rumors of a Catholic revolution in the nineteenth century, Americans feared that alien forces aimed to take over their government.

This book argues that American conspiracy theories underwent a fundamental transformation in the twentieth century. No longer were conspiracy theorists chiefly concerned that alien forces were plotting to capture the federal government; instead, they proposed that the federal government itself *was* the conspirator. They feared the subversive potential of the swelling, secretive bureaucracies of the proto–national security state. In effect, the institutionalized secrecy of the modern U.S. government inspired a new type of conspiracy theories. These theories argued that government officials lied to citizens, dragged the peaceable American people into foolish wars, and then spied on and oppressed the opponents of war.

Such portrayals were born out of a time when the federal government first grew powerful enough to accomplish these nefarious goals. This book, therefore, traces the fear of conspiracies within the U.S. federal government from the birth of the modern state in World War I to the current war on terror.

World War I was a watershed in the development of the U.S. government: it marked the moment when the government gained the power to carry out real conspiracies against its citizens—and when it began to use that power. During the conflict, the U.S. federal government drafted millions of its citizens, commandeered factories and railroads, and spied on and imprisoned dissidents. Through the newly established central bank, the president could control the ebb and flow of American money across the oceans to belligerent countries. The government criminalized dissent with the Espionage and Sedition Acts and encouraged Justice Department agents such as the young J. Edgar Hoover to hound antiwar radicals.[11] Sinister forces in charge of the government could do a lot more damage in 1918 than they could have done just a few years earlier; in fact, in the view of some conspiracists, the state *was* the sinister force.

The powers of the state continued to grow throughout the twentieth century, especially after the cold war began. The fear of communist plots inspired the U.S. government to adopt the conspiratorial tactics of its enemy. Determined to combat this international communist conspiracy, the CIA teamed up with the mafia on murder plots, the FBI spied on civil rights leaders who it feared were secret communists, and President Richard Nixon took governing conspiracies to a new level by conspiring to use state power to punish his personal enemies, whom he saw as the nation's enemies. Paradoxically, the end of the cold war did not ease these worries but instead prompted many Americans to redirect their fears from the Soviets to their own government. This suspicion of the government continued to climb after 9/11, as President Bush's attempts to centralize power in the presidency and his administration's deceptions about the Iraq war led many Americans to believe him capable of the worst crimes imaginable.

Most conspiracy theories about the U.S. government focus on wartime decision making or tragic national events. Theorists have tried to explain what they saw as the inexplicable: why the U.S. started or joined a war, or why it suffered a catastrophe or sudden reversal. They saw the war decisions as historical mysteries that American citizens needed to solve. Why, they wondered, did the United States join the Great War in 1917, after a majority of voters had reelected President Woodrow Wilson partly because he kept the country out of war? Why, in 1941, was the nation so woefully unprepared for the Japanese attack on Pearl Harbor? Could the president have known the attack was coming—and decided to allow it to take place for his own diabolical reasons? Why did the United States, for a brief time the world's only nuclear superpower, win World War II but then lose its atomic monopoly? Why, in 1963, could an American communist gun down the president in the middle of a major city in broad daylight? And, more recently, how could a handful of Arabs destroy the World Trade Center towers and crash a plane into the Pentagon?

In all of these cases, government officials took the conspiracy theory seriously enough to investigate it. Sometimes the official storytellers rejected a conspiracy, as they did in the Kennedy assassination; sometimes they suggested a conspiracy, as when Bush administration officials implied that Iraq secretly gave the 9/11 terrorists the help they needed to carry out their attacks. When government officials proposed a conspiracy, they became conspiracy theorists.

The officials also became storytellers. Social scientists argue that by constructing narratives, we make sense of other people's motives and behaviors; we can also begin to understand and cope with our own feelings and actions.[12] "We tell ourselves stories in order to live," the essayist Joan Didion has said.[13] Conspiracy theories are easy ways of telling complicated stories. Official conspiracy theorists tell one story about an event; alternative conspiracy theorists doubt the stories told by public officials, and then, to make sense of the world, they tell their own.

The history of conspiracy theories is often the story of the struggle over the power to control the public's perception of an event. Government officials try to control this narrative. President Wilson proclaimed that he was fighting a war to make the world safe for democracy; President Franklin Roosevelt insisted that the U.S. government had received no warning of an imminent Japanese attack on December 7, 1941. Conspiracy theorists challenge this official story, proposing counternarratives to the government's history of an event.

Early in the twentieth century, ordinary citizens found it difficult to distribute their alternative histories to a wide audience. Jacob Abrams, an anarchist who believed in a capitalists' conspiracy behind U.S. intervention in the Russian revolution, used a small printing press to publish his own antiwar leaflets and urged his friends to toss them from the third floor of a Manhattan building onto the heads of surprised pedestrians. The government found the pamphlets to be seditious and put Abrams and his comrades in prison for their efforts.[14]

In the first half of the twentieth century, American elites—men with cultural authority and access to the media—had more success in spreading their theories. Skeptical reporters wrote stories in newspapers opposed to the administration in power; revisionist historians found small presses willing to publish their work. Most significantly, members of Congress could launch an official investigation of a conspiracy theory, usually when different parties controlled Congress and the presidency. Republican Senator Joseph McCarthy squared off against Democratic President Harry Truman; Democratic Senator Frank Church challenged Republican President Gerald Ford. Congressional investigators used their subpoena power to pry loose documents from a secretive White House. In these and other cases, members of Congress investigated the alleged misdeeds of the president, while the president countered that the investigators were endangering the nation's security by revealing its secrets. The two-party system, combined with the democratic checks and balances created by the Constitution, produced a dynamic that fed the conspiracist imagination, which sought to explain real or purported failures of American democracy.

Although elites continued to confront the president throughout the twentieth century, by the 1960s ordinary citizens gained more power to challenge the secret actions of the national security state. With the passage of the Freedom of Information Act in 1966, all Americans were now empowered to examine previously classified government documents—the raw materials of history—and construct their own alternative stories of events. In effect, information became more democratized, though officials still blacked out huge sections of documents and refused to let go of others altogether. This governmental ambivalence about freedom of information—releasing, say, a Northwoods memo, but keeping other documents secret—sometimes had the effect of frightening citizens rather than reassuring them.

Changes in the media also led to the dispersion of cultural authority to challenge the government's narrative. Though fewer owners controlled newspapers and radio and television networks, conspiracy theorists found other media to spread their theories. Researchers of the John F. Kennedy assassination, for example, used grassroots citizen groups, guerrilla theater troupes, and even pornographic magazines to tell other Americans about their theory that U.S. government officials—perhaps even the current president—had conspired to kill President Kennedy. Hollywood was a powerful disseminator of conspiracy theories. Its community included *JFK* director Oliver Stone and *X-Files* writer/producer Chris Carter, who could construct powerful visual arguments and expose millions to their counter-narratives. The Internet further leveled the playing field for proponents of alternative conspiracy theories. Anyone in the world could broadcast a personal theory to a potential audience of billions and form a virtual community with fellow skeptics. The Internet provided the Jacob Abramses of the twenty-first century with the tallest building in the world.

This book traces successive generations of these modern skeptics of the government. It introduces senators from the heartland who believed that Wall Street financiers had connived with treacherous agents in the White House to push an unwilling country into World War I. It recovers the story of the World War II admiral who believed that he had been scapegoated by an interventionist president who knew much more about the Japanese attack at Pearl Harbor than he was willing to say. It reconstructs the atmosphere of fear in the country after the United States won World War II but lost its monopoly on the bomb.

These stories of conspiracy often had surprising consequences. A Nobel Prize–winning scientist may have missed out on making his most important discovery because the conspiracy theorists at the FBI believed he threatened national security. This scientist then turned his genius to proving that other secret government agents had conspired to kill the president he believed was working for peace. A senator from the rural West, outraged over CIA domestic spying, was driven to try to expose the government's lies of the past. This senator was the ultimate liberal—a proud believer in the tenet that a strong government could help its least advantaged citizens—yet his investigations inadvertently fueled antigovernment anger by teaching millions of Americans to despise and distrust their elected officials.

The last two chapters introduce the swashbuckling journalist who dared to charge that the CIA allowed some of its anticommunist allies to bring drugs into the United States—and his dismissive colleagues in the press who forced him to pay a stiff price. Finally, these chapters link this history to the citizens of today who are trying to make sense of the war in Iraq, sometimes by discerning a pattern of treason behind official failures and deceptions.

My goal is not to try to prove or disprove the conspiracy theories discussed in this book. Some are impossible to prove; others have been effectively rebutted by experts.[15] Instead, I examine why so many Americans believe that their government conspires against them, why more people believe this over time, and how real conspiracies by government officials have sparked these conspiracy theories about the government.

WHO BELIEVES THESE alternative conspiracy theories? The tendency to believe in conspiracy theories transcends race, class, and even political ideology. Black separatists often embrace conspiracy theories, and so do white supremacists. Right-wingers are receptive to conspiracy theories, but so, too, are leftists.[16] Men love conspiracy theories, but women aren't immune to their charms. Before the 1960s, most leading conspiracy theorists were men, but women began to play significant roles as conspiracism became democratized with the John Kennedy assassination. Yet no one admits to being a conspiracy theorist. As the filmmaker Michael Moore has said, "I'm not into conspiracy theories, except the ones that are true or involve dentists."[17]

Unlike Hofstadter, I do not try to psychoanalyze these theorists and determine which elements in American culture and history led them to become "paranoid." I see these antigovernment conspiracy theories as an impulse, as an understandable response to conspiratorial government rhetoric and actions. But though the impulse behind conspiracy theories is often understandable, that does not mean that the conspiracy theories themselves are logical or free from internal contradictions. Conspiracists come to believe in their theories the way zealots believe in their religion: nothing can change their mind. When new evidence surfaces, or when experts insist that, say, towers *can* collapse if airplanes hit them and fires burn hot enough, the conspiracy theorists dismiss the experts as blinded by their own preconceptions at best, or part of the conspiracy at worst.

Conspiracy theorists are not only rigid, but are also at times susceptible to the arguments of charlatans who sense an opportunity to profit from fear of conspiracy. A Jim Garrison, the New Orleans district attorney who prosecuted a Louisiana businessman for plotting to kill John Kennedy, or a Joseph McCarthy, the demagogue who gave his name to an era, can sometimes manipulate their fears with surprising effectiveness and tragic results.

But most of the ordinary conspiracy theorists in these pages were not motivated by personal gain. On the contrary, most of them believed, in all sincerity, that their country faced an imminent and existential threat. They believed that they needed to act, and act quickly, to save America. The republic was always in peril, and they, personally, were the ones to save it.

These conspiracy theorists were authentic patriots, convinced that they needed to do what they did for the sake of the country. The official conspiracy theorists always justified their surveillance by linking domestic dissidents with foreign plotters. They said that they needed to spy on these citizens because these Americans took their orders from the nation's enemies. The dissidents were *un-American*.

The dissidents, on the other hand, maintained that *they* were the true patriots who were defending their country from un-American forces. From those who decried a war fought on the "command of gold" in 1917 to the anti-Bush activists of the twenty-first century, they believed that their country would perish without their efforts to find the Truth. "I wouldn't be a patriot if I didn't try to prove the government's story is preposterous," said Barbara Honegger, a former Reagan administration official and a member of the 9/11 Truth movement.[18] This is the story of the patriots in the government and the patriots who distrust the government, and how they have combined to create an escalating spiral of fear.

Notes

1. Thomas Hargrove and Guido H. Stempel III, "Anti-Government Anger Spurs 9/11 Conspiracy Belief," Scripps Howard News Service, August 2, 2006, available at http://newspolls.org/story.php?story_id=55, viewed February 2, 2008.
2. Chairman, Joint Chiefs of Staff, "Justification for US Military Intervention in Cuba," March 13, 1962, cover memo and appendixes, available at http://www.gwu.edu/~nsarchiv/news/20010430/. For analysis of Northwoods, see Bamford, *Body of Secrets,* 82–91.

3. Joint Chiefs of Staff, "Justification for US Military Intervention in Cuba."
4. Memo by General Lansdale, "Meeting with the President, 16 March 1962," available at http://www.gwu.edu/~nsarchiv/bayofpigs/press3.html, viewed March 20, 2008.
5. See *Loose Change,* directed by Dylan Avery, at http://video.google.com/videoplay?docid=7866929448192753501, viewed March 20, 2008.
6. Tarpley, *9/11 Synthetic Terror,* 99.
7. Daniele Ganser, "The 'Strategy of Tension' in the Cold War Period," in Griffin and Scott, *9/11 and American Empire,* 99.
8. For the best surveys of conspiracy theory in U.S. history, see Hofstadter, *Paranoid Style*; Davis, *Slave Power Conspiracy* and *Fear of Conspiracy*; D. H. Bennett, *Party of Fear*; Goldberg, *Enemies Within*; Rogin, *Ronald Reagan, the Movie.*
9. Hofstadter, *Paranoid Style.*
10. Davis, *Fear of Conspiracy,* xiii.
11. For an interesting discussion of how Hoover effectively became the nation's internal security minister, see Frank Donner, "Hoover's Legacy," *Nation,* June 1, 1974.
12. On conspiracy theories as narratives, see Fenster, *Conspiracy Theories.* See also Jameson, "Cognitive Mapping"; Knight, *Conspiracy Culture.* On narrative, see H. White, *Content of the Form.*
13. Didion, *White Album,* 11.
14. Hagedorn, *Savage Peace,* 65–66.
15. For discussions of the "merchants of death" theories about World War I, see M. W. Coulter, *Senate Munitions Inquiry*; Wiltz, *In Search of Peace.* Some important refutations of Pearl Harbor conspiracy theories include Alvin D. Coox, "Repulsing the Pearl Harbor Revisionists: The State of Present Literature on the Debacle," *Military Affairs* 50, no. 1 (January 1985): 29–31; John Zimmerman, "Pearl Harbor Revisionism: Robert Stinnett's *Day of Deceit,*" *Intelligence and National Security* 17, no. 2 (Summer 2002): 127–46; Stephen Budiansky, "Closing the Book on Pearl Harbor," *Cryptologia* 24, no. 2 (April 2000): 119–30; Philip H. Jacobsen, "A Cryptologic Veteran's Analysis of 'Day of Deceit,'" *Cryptologia* 24, no. 2 (April 2000): 110–18. On communist spies and McCarthyism, see Sibley, *Red Spies in America*; Schrecker, *Many Are the Crimes*; Haynes and Klehr, *Venona.* The most complete refutation of JFK

conspiracy theories is Bugliosi, *Reclaiming History*. On Nixon's crimes, see Kutler, *Abuse of Power* and *The Wars of Watergate*. On conspiracy theories after Iran-contra, see Barkun, *Culture of Conspiracy*. Finally, there are many Web sites and books debunking 9/11 conspiracy theories, including Dunbar and Reagan, *Debunking 9/11 Myths*.

16. Ronald Inglehart, "Extremist Political Positions and Perceptions of Conspiracy: Even Paranoids Have Real Enemies," in Graumann and Moscovici, *Changing Conceptions*, 231–44. For more on who believes conspiracy theories, see Robins and Post, *Political Paranoia;* Pipes, *Conspiracy*; Showalter, *Hystories*.
17. M. Moore, *Dude*, 2.
18. Quoted in Michael Powell, "The Disbelievers," *Washington Post*, September 8, 2006.

For Analysis

1. Outline the scholarly "moves" that Olmstead uses, and compare these to the Scholarly Model on pp. 177–78. You might begin by writing notes in the margins about each paragraph's purpose. For example, the first two paragraphs attract the reader's attention and highlight the significance of her topic.
2. Examine how Olmstead uses endnotes. What kinds of additional information or support do these endnotes add to her argument that standard bibliographic citations (like MLA or APA style) do not?
3. Find two sources—one credible and one incredible—about a conspiracy theory of your choice. Why should one source be trusted more than the other?

For Writing

Watch the 9/11 conspiracy video *Loose Change* online. Write a 1,000-word rhetorical critique of Dylan Avery's arguments, concentrating on three to five key faults and gaps discussed in Chapter 9.

"Seeing Red? The Mind-Bending Power of Colour"

by Tom Chivers

Tom Chivers is a journalist who has worked as an assistant comment editor for *The Telegraph* and a senior writer for *Buzzfeed*. He frequently writes about science. This article was originally published in *The Telegraph* on February 27, 2015.

If you give the patient one pill, he perks up. If you give him another pill, he calms down. That might not surprise you. What might, though, is that it still works even when the pills contain no actual medicine.

Studies show that red pills are more effective stimulants than blue pills; blue pills are more effective as sleeping tablets than orange tablets. Green, white or blue pills aren't as effective as red ones as painkillers. But these were all placebos, administered in a series of experiments in the Sixties and Seventies, looking at how our perception of colour affects our minds and bodies. There was no painkiller, there was no stimulant.

The idea that colours affect our mood—red makes us angry, or sexually receptive; blue soothes us, or saddens us; that sort of thing–seems vaguely hippyish. Alternative medicine types push "chromotherapy", treating unwellness with colour; an odd amalgam of Victorian pseudoscience and cod-eastern mysticism. But now, the body of scientific research into colour is growing. And it all points to one thing: our perception of colour really does affect our minds, and our bodies. A 2004 study found that football teams wearing red were statistically more likely to win than teams in other colours. Another, in 2008, found that male volunteers shown photos of averagely attractive women on red and white backgrounds rated the women on red as more good-looking. Meanwhile, an experiment in the Seventies found that male prison inmates became physically weaker when they were housed in pink-painted cells.

And yet, while its effects on us may be profound, colour "doesn't really exist in the world", says Beau Lotto, a neuroscientist at University College London. Blue isn't a property of denim, or skies, or oceans, but of how our eyes interpret a particular set of wavelengths of electromagnetic radiation, which we call visible light. Red isn't a property of blood or cocktail dresses but how our eyes interpret another, longer set of wavelengths.

"Human vision is trichromatic," says Prof Andrew Stockman, a UCL colleague of Dr Lotto's. "Like a colour television." We have three different colour receptors, cones, in our eyes, each designed to pick up different wavelengths of light. These are red, green and blue. Most mammals, apart from a few of our fellow apes, have two, and so do most colour-blind people, meaning they can only detect green and blue wavelengths. If we had only one receptor, we'd see the world in something like black and white.

This is the product of billions of years of evolution. Long before our ancestors had anything you'd call an eye, back when they were single-celled organisms, they had some basic light sensitivity, and would have been able–to some degree–to detect differences between long-wavelength and short-wavelength light. This would have allowed them to tell when it was daylight (blue light) and sunset (red light). Later, as lifeforms grew more complex, we developed more sophisticated techniques for more sophisticated purposes.

"The whole point of colour vision is not to inspire poets, but to allow contrast detection," says Russell Foster, professor of circadian neuroscience at the University of Oxford. "You've got a much better chance of detecting an object against a background if you have colour vision." Birds are the masters at this, he says–they are tetrachromatic, having four colour detectors, and would see things that we see as a single red as an infinite, glorious wash of colours. (Mantis shrimp, a kind of predatory marine crustacean, have 12 detectors, but for some reason do not seem to be better at distinguishing colours than we lowly humans.)

Unlike birds, though, mammals are descended from small, timid creatures who scurried around avoiding dinosaurs–and, crucially, were nocturnal. Our ancestors had far less use for colour detection, which is much harder at night. It was only after the death of the dinosaurs 65 million years ago that our forebears ventured out into the daylight, and it is only 30 or 40 million years or so since a mutant ape developed a third colour receptor.

None the less, the wavelength of the light around us has affected us since the dawn of life, and it still does. Foster, who researches the effect of light on sleep, tells me that our circadian rhythms–our "biological clock"–are profoundly affected by not just the brightness of the light we're exposed to, but the colour of it. He was behind the discovery of a previously unknown cell in the optic nerve which acts as a sort of photon-counter, keeping track of how much light has hit it in the last few minutes. It is especially sensitive to blue light–specifically, the blue of a blue sky. If you're exposed to light of this colour, it will make you more alert. "Blue light keeps us awake far more effectively than red light," he says; "there are apps, now, that change your lighting before you go to bed, to get you ready for sleep."

But earlier, we saw that red made us perkier, and blue calmed us down. This is because, as Lotto says, context is everything; red can be friendly when it's associated with a ketchup bottle and baleful when associated with blood.

Lotto spends much of his time creating optical illusions to demonstrate how humans see and perceive colour, and the impact of context upon it. "I can take a grey patch, and cause you to see any colour in it," he says. "I can make you see blue or yellow, depending on what surrounds it. When I change your perception of it, what I'm changing is the meaning of the information, I'm not changing the physics of the information itself.

"If I make a patch appear as if it's under shadow, you'll see it as being lighter than if I make the same patch appear as if it's on a dark background. That's basically what your brain is constantly doing." The illusions are remarkable to look at: two patches of identical colour, brightness and shape will appear as utterly different colours to our eyes, because of simple tricks of perspective and shade which make one look as though it's under red light, or another under shadow. These illusions are unsettling to see, at least for me: they undermine my sense of being grounded in reality.

But we're not uniformly sensitive to these illusions; again, context matters. "How powerful people feel alters their perception of colour," says Lotto. "If I make you feel a bit more powerful, a little more in control, the strength of the illusions that I make decreases. If I put you in a state of powerlessness, the strength of illusions increases." It's because we're more sensitive to context when we feel out of control; we become less comfortable with uncertainty.

Similarly, he says, these illusions are more effective on people from eastern cultures, where social context is all-important. "The people around you are far more important in the east, whereas in the west we're far more individualistic."

It gets more complex: "context" can mean things as apparently unrelated as whether you're feeling morally compromised. A 2011 study published in the journal of the Association for Psychological Sciences found that people who had been asked to recall something unethical they'd done tended to judge the room they were in as darker than those who'd been asked to remember something ethical.

There's even some indication that the words we use to describe colour affect our ability to see it. Benjamin Whorf, a linguistic theorist, claimed that our language limits our perception: if our language lacks a word for something, we find it harder to think about that thing.

The Whorfian hypothesis has been largely discredited–after all, if we really couldn't think about things we didn't have a word for, we wouldn't need to come up with new words; English didn't have a word for "schadenfreude" until quite recently, but we understood the concept well enough. Neverthless, experiments have shown that societies such as the Tarahumara tribe in Northern Mexico, which lack different words for "blue" and "green", find it harder to find the odd one out in a group of greenish-blue squares. Meanwhile, the fact that we distinguish indigo and violet as separate colours is largely down to Newton, who named and split up the colours of the rainbow more subjectively than scientifically, leaving a large area between blue and green un-named.

The cultural contexts and meaning of colours has been picked up, of course, by marketers, as suggested by the title of a paper in the Journal of the Academy of Marketing Science, "Exciting red and competent blue: the importance of color in marketing". White is "purity, cleanness, simplicity, hygiene, clarity and peace"; black is "sophistication, glamour, status, elegance, richness and dignity". Purple is status, pink is femininity, and, of course, blue suggests competence while red is exciting. Using these colours in your brand or logo, apparently, will subtly instil those messages in potential customers' minds.

A lot of these highly specific claims are probably hogwash, as another paper, in the journal Color Research & Application, made clear in its own title: "Colour psychology and colour therapy: Caveat emptor". The evidence-based hypotheses are often hard to tease out from the mystical or made-up nonsense, writes its author, Zena O'Connor: "The information available is often presented in an authoritative manner exhorting the reader to believe a range of claims such as red is physically stimulating and arousing and blue is calming and healing. However, evidence is rarely cited and, when it is, it's often in reference to findings that are inappropriately generalised or out-of-date." But even after the dubious claims have been weeded out, colour clearly still has a profound impact on our mental life.

An obvious question is how much of this impact is innate, and how much is culturally learnt. For instance, the study into the psychological effects of pink, mentioned above, was carried out by Alexander Schauss in the Seventies. It showed that of 153 male prisoners put in cells painted pink, 98.7 per cent were weaker after being in the pink cells for only 15 minutes–presumably because of associations with the colour pink and femininity. But pink has only been associated with girls for 70 years or so; would the same result have been found in Victorian times? Probably not. But the red light/blue light distinction that Foster refers to must be written deep in our genes.

The allure of red certainly appears to cross cultural boundaries. A 2012 study conducted in Burkina Faso, in West Africa, where red has explicitly negative associations, still revealed it to be a sexual trigger. Paintings with red in fetch far higher prices than those without, and Brett Gorvy, chairman of contemporary art at Christie's international, has described it as the "most lucrative colour". Some scientists believe that we and other primates such as chimps and gorillas developed the ability to detect the colour red because of a common characteristic: bare-skinned faces. Suddenly, we could "read" the all-important expressions of anger, dominance and sexual readiness on the faces of those around us.

Since we know that "colour" is a product of how our eyes interpret electromagnetic radiation, we know that it's not an attempt to represent the world as it really is. Natural selection doesn't care whether you have a true representation of the universe. It only cares if you can find food and attract mates and avoid predators. "Your perception of colour either helped you behave usefully towards this thing, or it didn't," Lotto says. "Either it helped you decide whether to eat something, to mate with it, or to run away from it, or it didn't. And if it didn't, you died, and you got selected out through evolution."

All our perceptions, then, are grounded in our evolutionary history, which provides us with some of our underlying assumptions, and our personal, culture-infused life history, which provides us with the rest. Colour is simply a useful way that our brains have come up with for representing the world–and what we learn from colour vision applies to the rest of the brain's interaction with the world.

"And that, to me, is why colour vision is wonderful," says Lotto. "You begin looking there, and it opens up all these other questions, and reveals what the brain is trying to do."

For Analysis

1. This article is more like a research paper than an opinion essay. However, the author still develops a thesis and uses sources to build an argument. Where is the thesis located? How do you know this is the thesis? What other claims—either explicit or implied—do you detect in the article?
2. How well does the author integrate quotations and secondary sources into the article? What techniques does he use to incorporate sources, and why are these effective or not?
3. To expand your understanding of this topic, listen to Episode 13, "Colors," on Season 10 of *Radiolab*, a program distributed by National Public Radio and available online. As you listen, make note of subjects the episode covers that Chivers does and does not address. Compare claims he makes and research he cites with those discussed in the *Radiolab* episode. Then, discuss your findings as a class and evaluate the strengths and weaknesses of traditional text-based arguments versus auditory mediums like *Radiolab*.

For Writing

Select a topic that interests you; research the subject; and create a podcast, using *Radiolab*'s format, design, and content as inspiration. Develop a script to read, select soundbites to incorporate, interview other people, and—if you have the necessary technology—put everything together into a working podcast. Throughout the process, talk with others about the components of a successful podcast and reflect on the challenges and benefits of "writing" in this medium.

"Post Hoc Rides Again"
by Darrell Huff

Darrell Huff was an editor and freelance writer who authored more than a dozen books on topics ranging from home improvement to practical applications for mathematics. Although he was not educated as a statistician, Huff's book, *How to Lie with Statistics*, has been widely used and taught in statistics classes since its original publication in 1954.

There are two clocks which keep perfect time. When ***"a"*** *points to the hour* ***"b"*** *strikes. Did* ***"a"*** *cause* ***"b"*** *to strike?*

SOMEBODY once went to a good deal of trouble to find out if cigarette smokers make lower college grades than non-smokers. It turned out that they did. This pleased a good many people and they have been making much of it ever since. The road to good grades, it would appear, lies in giving up smoking; and, to carry the conclusion one reasonable step further, smoking makes dull minds.

This particular study was, I believe, properly done: sample big enough and honestly and carefully chosen, correlation having a high significance, and so on.

The fallacy is an ancient one which, however, has a powerful tendency to crop up in statistical material, where it is disguised by a welter of impressive figures. It is the one that says that if B follows A, then A has caused B. An unwarranted assumption is being made that since smoking and low grades go together, smoking causes low grades. Couldn't it just as well be the other way around? Perhaps low marks drive students not to drink but to tobacco. When it comes right down to it, this conclusion is about as likely as the other and just as well supported by the evidence. But it is not nearly so satisfactory to propagandists.

It seems a good deal more probable, however, that neither of these things has produced the other, but both are a product of some third factor. Can it be that the sociable sort of fellow who takes his books less than seriously is also likely to smoke more? Or is there a clue in the fact that somebody once established a correlation between extroversion and low grades—a closer relationship apparently than the one between grades and intelligence? Maybe extroverts smoke more than introverts. The point is that when there are many reasonable explanations you are hardly entitled to pick one that suits your taste and insist on it. But many people do.

To avoid falling for the *post hoc* fallacy and thus wind up believing many things that are not so, you need to put any statement of relationship through a sharp inspection. The correlation, that convincingly precise figure that seems to prove that something is because of something, can actually be any of several types.

One is the correlation produced by chance. You may be able to get together a set of figures to prove some unlikely thing in this way, but if you try again, your next set may not prove it at all. As with the manufacturer of the tooth paste that appeared to reduce decay, you simply throw away the results you don't want and publish widely those you do. Given a small sample, you are likely to find some substantial correlation between any pair of characteristics or events that you can think of.

A common kind of co-variation is one in which the relationship is real but it is not possible to be sure which of the variables is the cause and which the effect. In some of these instances cause and effect may change places from time to time or indeed both may be cause and effect at the same time. A correlation between income and ownership of stocks might be of that kind. The more money you make, the more stock you buy, and the more stock you buy, the more income you get; it is not accurate to say simply that one has produced the other.

Perhaps the trickiest of them all is the very common instance in which neither of the variables has any effect at all on the other, yet there is a real correlation. A good deal of dirty work has been done with this one. The poor grades among cigarette smokers is in this category, as are all too many medical statistics that are quoted without the qualification that although the relationship has been shown to be real, the cause-and-effect nature of it is only a matter of speculation. As an instance of the nonsense or spurious correlation that is a real statistical fact, someone has gleefully pointed to this: There is a close relationship between the salaries of Presbyterian ministers in Massachusetts and the price of rum in Havana.

Which is the cause and which the effect? In other words, are the ministers benefiting from the rum trade or supporting it? All right. That's so farfetched that it is ridiculous at a glance. But watch out for other applications of *post hoc* logic that differ from this one only in being more subtle. In the case of the ministers and the rum it is easy to see that both figures are growing because of the influence of a third factor: the historic and world-wide rise in the price level of practically everything.

And take the figures that show the suicide rate to be at its maximum in June. Do suicides produce June brides—or do June weddings precipitate suicides of the jilted? A somewhat more convincing (though equally unproved) explanation is that the fellow who licks his depression all through the winter with the thought that things will look rosier in the spring gives up when June comes and he still feels terrible.

Another thing to watch out for is a conclusion in which a correlation has been inferred to continue beyond the data with which it has been demonstrated. It is easy to show that the more it rains in an area, the taller the corn grows or even the greater the crop. Rain, it seems, is a blessing. But a season of very heavy rainfall may damage or even ruin the crop. The positive correlation holds up to a point and then quickly becomes a negative one. Above so-many inches, the more it rains the less corn you get.

We're going to pay a little attention to the evidence on the money value of education in a minute. But for now let's assume it has been proved that high-school graduates make more money than those who drop out, that each year of undergraduate work in college adds some more income. Watch out for the general conclusion that the more you go to school the more money you'll make. Note that this has not been shown to be true for the years beyond an undergraduate degree, and it may very well not apply to them either. People with Ph.D.s quite often become college teachers and so do not become members of the highest income groups.

A correlation of course shows a tendency which is not often the ideal relationship described as one-to-one. Tall boys weigh more than short boys on the average, so this is a positive correlation. But you can easily find a six-footer who weighs less than some five-footers, so the correlation is less than 1. A negative correlation is simply a statement that as one variable increases the other tends to decrease. In physics this becomes an inverse ratio: The further you get from a light bulb the less light there is on your book; as distance increases light intensity decreases. These physical relationships often have the kindness to produce perfect correlations, but figures from business or sociology or medicine seldom work out so neatly. Even if education generally increases incomes it may easily turn out to be the financial ruination of Joe over there. Keep in mind that a correlation may be real and based on real cause and effect—and still be almost worthless in determining action in any single case.

Reams of pages of figures have been collected to show the value in dollars of a college education, and stacks of pamphlets have been published to bring these figures—and conclusions more or less based on them—to the attention of potential students. I am not quarreling with the intention. I am in favor of education myself, particularly if it includes a course in elementary statistics. Now these figures have pretty conclusively demonstrated that people who have gone to college make more money than people who have not. The exceptions are numerous, of course, but the tendency is strong and clear.

The only thing wrong is that along with the figures and facts goes a totally unwarranted conclusion. This is the *post hoc* fallacy at its best.

It says that these figures show that if *you* (your son, your daughter) attend college you will probably earn more money than if you decide to spend the next four years in some other manner. This unwarranted conclusion has for its basis the equally unwarranted assumption that since college-trained folks make more money, they make it because they went to college. Actually we don't know but that these are the people who would have made more money even if they had not gone to college. There are a couple of things that indicate rather strongly that this is so. Colleges get a disproportionate number of two groups of kids: the bright and the rich. The bright might show good earning power without college knowledge. And as for the rich ones . . . well, money breeds money in several obvious ways. Few sons of rich men are found in low-income brackets whether they go to college or not.

The following passage is taken from an article in question-and-answer form that appeared in *This Week* magazine, a Sunday supplement of enormous circulation. Maybe you will find it amusing, as I do, that the same writer once produced a piece called "Popular Notions: True or False?"

Q: What effect does going to college have on your chances of remaining unmarried?
A: If you're a woman, it skyrockets your chances of becoming an old maid. But if you're a man, it has the opposite effect—it minimizes your chances of staying a bachelor.
Cornell University made a study of 1,500 typical middle-aged college graduates. Of the men, 93 per cent were married (compared to 83 per cent for the general population).
But of the middle-aged women graduates only 65 per cent were married. Spinsters were relatively three times as numerous among college graduates as among women of the general population.

When Susie Brown, age seventeen, reads this she learns that if she goes to college she will be less likely to get a man than if she doesn't.

That is what the article says, and there are statistics from a reputable source to go with it. They go with it, but they don't back it up; and note also that while the statistics are Cornell's the conclusions are not, although a hasty reader may come away with the idea that they are.

Here again a real correlation has been used to bolster up an unproved cause-and-effect relationship. Perhaps it all works the other way around and those women would have remained unmarried even if they had not gone to college. Possibly even more would have failed to marry. If these possibilities are no better than the one the writer insists upon, they are perhaps just as valid conclusions: that is, guesses.

Indeed there is one piece of evidence suggesting that a propensity for old-maidhood may lead to going to college. Dr. Kinsey seems to have found some correlation between sexuality and education, with traits perhaps being fixed at pre-college age. That makes it all the more questionable to say that going to college gets in the way of marrying.

Note to Susie Brown: It ain't necessarily so.

A medical article once pointed with great alarm to an increase in cancer among milk drinkers. Cancer, it seems, was becoming increasingly frequent in New England, Minnesota, Wisconsin, and Switzerland, where a lot of milk is produced and consumed, while remaining rare in Ceylon, where milk is scarce. For further evidence it was pointed out that cancer was less frequent in some Southern states where less milk was consumed. Also, it was pointed out, milk-drinking English women get some kinds of cancer eighteen times as frequently as Japanese women who seldom drink milk.

A little digging might uncover quite a number of ways to account for these figures, but one factor is enough by itself to show them up. Cancer is predominantly a disease that strikes in middle life or after. Switzerland and the states mentioned first are alike in having populations with relatively long spans of life. English women at the time the study was made were living an average of twelve years longer than Japanese women.

Professor Helen M. Walker has worked out an amusing illustration of the folly in assuming there must be cause and effect whenever two things vary together. In investigating the relationship between age and some physical characteristics of women, begin by measuring the angle of the feet in walking. You will find that the angle tends to be greater among older women. You might first consider whether this indicates that women grow older because they toe out, and you can see immediately that this is ridiculous. So it appears that age increases the angle between the feet, and most women must come to toe out more as they grow older.

Any such conclusion is probably false and certainly unwarranted. You could only reach it legitimately by studying the same women—or possibly equivalent groups—over a period of time. That would eliminate the factor responsible here. Which is that the older women grew up at a time when a young lady was taught to toe out in walking, while the members of the younger group were learning posture in a day when that was discouraged.

When you find somebody—usually an interested party—making a fuss about a correlation, look first of all to see if it is not one of this type, produced by the stream of events, the trend of the times. In our time it is easy to show a positive correlation between any pair of things like these: number of students in college, number of inmates in mental institutions, consumption of cigarettes, incidence of heart disease, use of X-ray machines, production of false teeth, salaries of California school teachers, profits of Nevada gambling halls. To call some one of these the cause of some other is manifestly silly. But it is done every day.

Permitting statistical treatment and the hypnotic presence of numbers and decimal points to befog causal relationships is little better than superstition. And it is often more seriously misleading. It is rather like the conviction among the people of the New Hebrides that body lice produce good health. Observation over the centuries had taught them that people in good health usually had lice and sick people very often did not. The observation itself was accurate and sound, as observations made informally over the years surprisingly often are. Not so much can be said for the conclusion to which these primitive people came from their evidence: Lice make a man healthy. Everybody should have them.

As we have already noted, scantier evidence than this—treated in the statistical mill until common sense could no longer penetrate to it—has made many a medical fortune and many a medical article in magazines, including professional ones. More sophisticated observers finally got things straightened out in the New Hebrides. As it turned out, almost everybody in those circles had lice most of the time. It was, you might say, the normal condition of man. When, however, anyone took a fever (quite possibly carried to him by those same lice) and his body became too hot for comfortable habitation, the lice left. There you have cause and effect altogether confusingly distorted, reversed, and intermingled.

For Analysis

1. How does this reading reinforce our discussion of fallacies in Chapter 9?
2. Research two or three of Huff's examples to find more evidence or verification that would support or refute his arguments.
3. What stylistic choices do you notice in Huff's writing? For example, how does he use less common punctuation (parentheses, dashes, colons, ellipses)? What kinds of conventional "rules for good writing" does he bend or break?

For Writing

This reading is, literally, the oldest one in this book. Although Huff's illustrations still work, many will seem dated to current readers. Write an updated, shorter (1,000 words) version of this chapter using contemporary examples and images. Consult Chapter 3 for guidance on how to effectively summarize and paraphrase the original text without quoting. Try to imitate Huff's simple, straightforward writing style.

SECTION 2
WHAT CHALLENGES DO COLLEGE STUDENTS FACE?

"Crass Frat Boys at Old Dominion"
by Conor Friedersdorf

Who is this guy? How old is he? What's his educational and professional background? What makes him qualified to write about this topic?

We have annotated the following article with some comments and questions to model the kinds of notations that apprentice scholars might make while reading any argument and especially when conducting a rhetorical analysis.

Conor Friedersdorf is a journalist who writes about politics and national affairs. He is also the founding editor of *The Best of Journalism* and a staff writer at *The Atlantic*, which published this commentary on August 25, 2015.

What's *The Atlantic*? Who are its typical readers?

The crudely suggestive banners hung to greet first-year students were in poor taste, but the condemnations lacked all sense of proportion.

This reads like a thesis. Is this the main point that the author will develop?

At Old Dominion University in Norfolk, Virginia, someone at an off-campus fraternity house hung crass, homemade banners from the balcony for incoming freshmen to see while being dropped off by their parents.

One banner said, "Rowdy and Fun, Hope Your Baby Girl Is Ready for a Good Time." Another said "Freshman Daughter Drop Off" and featured an arrow pointing to the front door of the house. A third sign said, "Go Ahead and Drop Off Mom Too."

He begins by acknowledging how inappropriate the banners were. He probably wants to make it clear from the beginning that he doesn't condone such crude behavior.

The banners were crude and distasteful. Even at 18, I wouldn't have hung them. If I were a professor there, I'd have told the kids that they have a First Amendment right to display the signs even as I tried to shame them into taking them down. If my kid put up those banners—not that I'd ever pay for a kid to live in a frat house—I'd tell him to take them down or never ask for my help with tuition again.

Interesting ways to establish credibility. First he acknowledges that he doesn't really support fraternities, and then he says how harshly he'd deal with the situation if it involved his own son. Doing so makes him seem more sincere/objective when he defends fraternities and their actions – or at least argues against such harsh attacks against them.

Even so, it staggers me that this is an international news story covered by scores of outlets. How did we reach a place where Local Frat Makes Crude Joke causes staffers at the BBC, CNN, *The Washington Post* and *USA Today* to spring into action?

Interesting question. So, is that his main controversy question – one of cause/consequence? Or is he going to examine how we should respond to the incident (question of policy/procedure)? What other controversy categories will he try to answer?

The answer begins with one interpretation of the banners. For some observers, they aren't just vulgar, rude, suggestive, bawdy, ribald, derogatory, or uncouth—they're an example of "rape culture." As Old Dominion's President John Broderick put it, "While we constantly educate students, faculty and staff about sexual assault and sexual harassment, this incident confirms our collective efforts are still failing to register with some." Nearly every press outlet that has covered

He summarizes one side's views on this issue. People in this camp believe that this incident is exemplary of "rape culture." What's "rape culture"? Is this an issue of definition?

the controversy connected it to ongoing efforts to reduce the number of rapes that occur on campus.

One Old Dominion student told *Jezebel*, "I feel very strongly about how the attitude towards sexual assault on campuses is met with a slap on the wrist . . . As a woman, it's frustrating to see the media bring awareness to the issue and then witness something related in your own community/school and see that nothing is changing."

The quotations from the student and President Broderick express one way of interpreting the incident (verifications).

What's *Jezebel*? Is this a credible source for supporting his argument? Would *Atlantic*'s readers be familiar with this publication and trust its credibility?

To other observers, those reactions make little sense.

Nice transition. This short paragraph functions as a pivot point for his essay.

As they see it, a college's sexual-assault problem is best gauged by the number of sexual assaults. They regard the banners as an obvious joke. And they insist that the humor is rooted in confronting parents, who like to guard the virginity of their daughters, with the trope that they go off to college and have sex with frat guys. In this telling, nothing about the trope implies a non-consensual encounter. And regardless of the joke's meaning, they believe it irrational to operate as if a sophomoric prank that seems like something a couple 19-year-olds cooked up in a few hours reveals their attitudes toward rape; the likelihood that they would rape someone; campus attitudes toward rape; or the success of campus anti-rape efforts.

Who is this "they" (or "other observers")? He can keep describing "their" perspective for a while, but soon I'll want him to provide a specific reference.

Then, he summarizes a different view of the issue. People in this camp interpret the incident as "an obvious joke."

What's a trope? I doubt many people know this term, which might indicate something about who reads *The Atlantic*.

"I'm usually in the position of defending extremely offensive speech on the grounds that it is protected by the First Amendment,"

Robby Soave wrote at *Reason*. "In this case, I struggle to grasp what was even so monstrous about the banners. *Hope your baby is ready for a good time, oh, mom too!* is certainly crude and in bad taste. But no specific person is being maligned, threatened, or disparaged. And some frat brothers are eager to have sex with girls—is this surprising?"

What's *Reason*? Is this a credible source for supporting his argument? Okay, so now he's providing a specific example of one of the "other observers" who support his perspective. But wait, he only includes this one example. . . .

He added that, "associating the banners with sexual assault, as Broderick did, is a considerable exaggeration. Sigma Nu members certainly didn't threaten anyone with sexual assault; putting up some mildly suggestive signs does not constitute an act of violence. The banners don't even clear the sexual harassment bar. They aren't severe, pervasive, objectively offensive, or directed at anyone in particular."

Where do I come down? It's lamentable that some women arrived on their college campus only to be greeted by signs treating them as sexual objects. These immature 19-year-olds displayed bad judgment, but so do the adults who are reacting as if they were stockpiling GHB. Pop culture is filled with material far more vulgar and offensive, including content that actually does transgress against the value placed on consent.

Here is where the author will present his viewpoint (argument).

By summarizing two opposing sides and then presenting his own view, the author shows that he understands the debate and what opposing sides believe. He demonstrates that he's listened to both sides, like a judge listening to both a prosecutor and defense attorney before making his decision. This makes him seem well informed. It also helps him demonstrate that both sides are too extreme in their responses, whereas his perspective is more levelheaded.

What's GHB?

Debates like this are polarizing because a false choice is often presented: defend the transgression that is generating outrage or join in condemning the perpetrators. But

This is an "either/or" fallacy or false binary.

there is a third way. It requires circumspection and a sense of proportion.

He is proposing a third interpretation that takes more of a middle ground. This makes the author seem reasonable and fair.

The banners do deserve criticism.

Again, style points for this pithy pivot paragraph.

Sigma Nu, the national fraternity, is within its rights to complain about the way this chapter is representing it; on Monday, it suspended the chapter pending the outcome of an investigation.

Should someone at Old Dominion explain to those kids the offensive assumptions implicit in their signs? Yes. Did they do something so awful that it warrants overnight CNN alerts, a BBC headline, and a university investigation into what happened?

No. Of course not.

Should the university president have made a statement? Sure. He could have said, "I've been getting inquiries about crude signs hung by some of our students from their off-campus house, as is their right under the First Amendment. I encourage those students to exercise their rights more thoughtfully in the future, to treat women respectfully, and to take this opportunity to learn from a youthful mistake. We've all made them. And I hope members of the media will recall instances when they showed poor judgment at 18, 19, or 20, as they cover this story."

Instead he showed no sense of proportion.

This is the problem that the author has with people's responses to the incident.

In a nation where the First Amendment guarantees the rights of Nazis to march through the streets of a Jewish community, the president of a public university declared of clearly protected speech: "Messages like the ones displayed yesterday by a few students on the balcony of their private residence are not and will not be tolerated."

And he asserted that one or two undergrads with bed sheets and black markers "undermine the countless efforts at Old Dominion University to prevent sexual assault." If that isn't hyperbole, he should try a different approach to preventing sexual assault.

Meanwhile, Sharon Grigsby writes in *The Dallas Morning News* that if you think the frat's banners were an obvious joke, as many students at the college reportedly concluded, "You've got to be kidding. Anyone who believes that is part of the problem." In fact, believing that they made a tasteless joke rather than an apology for rape culture does not make someone "part of the problem" of sexual assault.

Why not? I'd like to hear him defend this claim. I find myself agreeing with him, but I'd be more convinced if he elaborated more and explained exactly why Grigsby is off base.

Ultimately, this story lays bare a divide.

It is not a divide between people who care about reducing the rate of sexual assault and those who don't; rather, the divide concerns how best to achieve that common goal. Insofar as I can tell, one theory holds that what's best, in this case, is to hold up whoever made those banners as possible-rapist pariahs; to pursue disciplinary charges against them; to suspend their frat; and to condemn them as if they've consigned more women to rape by undermining their college's efforts to prevent it.

I have a different view.

It would be convenient for Old Dominion if harshly denouncing and punishing these boys would be taken as the prime measure of how seriously the school takes sexual assault.

I had to read this sentence a few times to understand it. Seems like he's making a good point, but I'd prefer not to have to work so hard to get it.

It's easy to grandstand against frat boys with crass signs.

But reducing sexual assaults requires sounder metrics of success. Controversies like this are a distraction; they distract from what's really required to make college campuses safer for women; and they alienate a portion of the public that tires of exaggerated outrage.

So, according to the author, this is the larger significance of the problem that he's identified. If authorities overreact and fixate on the wrong things, they won't be able to put their energies where they should to address the heart of the issue.

Focusing on the core problem of rape (rather than seizing on offensive comments from obscure undergrads as if they bear meaningful responsibility for that problem) also makes it easier to avoid getting trolled by provocateur 19-year-olds. Words they thoughtlessly scrawl on bed sheets do not belong at the center of our discourse.

Interesting. This section seems like his thesis statement, but it appears at the end of his essay. Is this how an evolving thesis is supposed to work?

For Analysis

1. How well does Friedersdorf treat both "sides" of this issue? Does he represent them fairly, or does he oversimplify any issues?
2. Friedersdorf advocates a "third way." How might advocating for a middle ground affect readers? How could this approach help build his credibility?
3. How effective is Friedersdorf's writing style? What features stand out, and how do these elements enhance or diminish his argument?

For Writing

Friedersdorf advocates "focusing on the core problem of rape," but he doesn't elaborate on what exactly this would entail. Write a 1,000-word proposal argument that describes specific policy changes or a course of action that you think would help reduce the number of sexual assaults on college campuses.

"The Coddling of the American Mind"

by Greg Lukianoff and Jonathan Haidt

Greg Lukianoff is the president and CEO of the Foundation for Individual Rights in Education and the author of *Unlearning Liberty: Campus Censorship and the End of American Debate.* **Jonathan Haidt** is a social psychologist, professor of ethical leadership, and author of *The Righteous Mind: Why Good People Are Divided by Politics and Religion.* This article was published by *The Atlantic* magazine in September 2015.

SOMETHING STRANGE IS happening at America's colleges and universities. A movement is arising, undirected and driven largely by students, to scrub campuses clean of words, ideas, and subjects that might cause discomfort or give offense. Last December, Jeannie Suk wrote in an online article for *The New Yorker* about law students asking her fellow professors at Harvard not to teach rape law—or, in one case, even use the word *violate* (as in "that violates the law") lest it cause students distress. In February, Laura Kipnis, a professor at Northwestern University, wrote an essay in *The Chronicle of Higher Education* describing a new campus politics of sexual paranoia—and was then subjected to a long investigation after students who were offended by the article and by a tweet she'd sent filed Title IX complaints against her. In June, a professor protecting himself with a pseudonym wrote an essay for Vox describing how gingerly he now has to teach. "I'm a Liberal Professor, and My Liberal Students Terrify Me," the headline said. A number of popular comedians, including Chris Rock, have stopped performing on college campuses (see Caitlin Flanagan's article in this month's issue). Jerry Seinfeld and Bill Maher have publicly condemned the oversensitivity of college students, saying too many of them can't take a joke.

Two terms have risen quickly from obscurity into common campus parlance. *Microaggressions* are small actions or word choices that seem on their face to have no malicious intent but that are thought of as a kind of violence nonetheless. For example, by some campus guidelines, it is a microaggression to ask an Asian American or Latino American "Where were you born?," because this implies that he or she is not a real American. *Trigger warnings* are alerts that professors are expected to issue if something in a course might cause a strong emotional response. For example, some students have called for warnings that Chinua Achebe's *Things Fall Apart* describes racial violence and that F. Scott Fitzgerald's *The Great Gatsby* portrays misogyny and physical abuse, so that students who have been previously victimized by racism or domestic violence can choose to avoid these works, which they believe might "trigger" a recurrence of past trauma.

Some recent campus actions border on the surreal. In April, at Brandeis University, the Asian American student association sought to raise awareness of microaggressions against Asians through an installation on the steps of an academic hall. The installation gave examples of microaggressions such as "Aren't you supposed to be good at math?" and "I'm colorblind! I don't see race." But a backlash arose among other Asian American students, who felt that the display itself was a microaggression. The association removed the installation, and its president wrote an e-mail to the entire student body apologizing to anyone who was "triggered or hurt by the content of the microaggressions."

This new climate is slowly being institutionalized, and is affecting what can be said in the classroom, even as a basis for discussion. During the 2014–15 school year, for instance, the deans and department chairs at the 10 University of California system schools were presented by administrators at faculty leader-training sessions with examples of microaggressions. The list of offensive statements included: "America is the land of opportunity" and "I believe the most qualified person should get the job."

The press has typically described these developments as a resurgence of political correctness. That's partly right, although there are important differences between what's happening now and what happened in the 1980s and '90s. That movement sought to restrict speech (specifically hate speech aimed at marginalized groups), but it also challenged the literary, philosophical, and historical canon, seeking to widen it by including more-diverse perspectives. The current movement is largely about emotional well-being. More than the last, it presumes an extraordinary fragility of the collegiate psyche, and therefore elevates the goal of protecting students from psychological harm. The ultimate aim, it seems, is to turn campuses into "safe spaces" where young adults are shielded from words and ideas that make some uncomfortable. And more than the last, this movement seeks to punish anyone who interferes with that aim, even accidentally. You might call this impulse *vindictive protectiveness*. It is creating a culture in which everyone must think twice before speaking up, lest they face charges of insensitivity, aggression, or worse.

We have been studying this development for a while now, with rising alarm. (Greg Lukianoff is a constitutional lawyer and the president and CEO of the Foundation for Individual Rights in Education, which defends free speech and academic freedom on campus, and has advocated for students and faculty involved in many of the incidents this article describes; Jonathan Haidt is a social psychologist who studies the American culture wars. The stories of how we each came to this subject can be read here.) The dangers that these trends pose to scholarship and to the quality of American universities are significant; we could write a whole essay detailing them. But in this essay we focus on a different question: What are the effects of this new protectiveness *on the students themselves*? Does it benefit the people it is supposed to help? What exactly are students learning when they spend four years or more in a community that polices unintentional slights, places warning labels on works of classic literature, and in many other ways conveys the sense that words can be forms of violence that require strict control by campus authorities, who are expected to act as both protectors and prosecutors?

There's a saying common in education circles: Don't teach students *what* to think; teach them *how* to think. The idea goes back at least as far as Socrates. Today, what we call the Socratic method is a way of teaching that fosters critical thinking, in part by encouraging students to question their own unexamined beliefs, as well as the received wisdom of those around them. Such questioning sometimes leads to discomfort, and even to anger, on the way to understanding.

But vindictive protectiveness teaches students to think in a very different way. It prepares them poorly for professional life, which often demands intellectual engagement with people and ideas one might find uncongenial or wrong. The harm may be more immediate, too. A campus culture devoted to policing speech and punishing speakers is likely to engender patterns of thought that are surprisingly similar to those long identified by cognitive behavioral therapists as causes of depression and anxiety. The new protectiveness may be teaching students to think pathologically.

How Did We Get Here?

It's difficult to know exactly why vindictive protectiveness has burst forth so powerfully in the past few years. The phenomenon may be related to recent changes in the interpretation of federal antidiscrimination statutes (about which more later). But the answer probably involves generational shifts as well. Childhood itself has changed greatly during the past generation. Many Baby Boomers and Gen Xers can remember riding their bicycles around their hometowns, unchaperoned by adults, by the time they were 8 or 9 years old. In the hours after school, kids were expected to occupy themselves, getting into minor scrapes and learning from their experiences. But "free range" childhood became less common in the 1980s. The surge in crime from the '60s through the early '90s made Baby Boomer parents more protective than their own parents had been. Stories of abducted children appeared more frequently in the news, and in 1984, images of them began showing up on milk cartons. In response, many parents pulled in the reins and worked harder to keep their children safe.

The flight to safety also happened at school. Dangerous play structures were removed from playgrounds; peanut butter was banned from student lunches. After the 1999 Columbine massacre in Colorado, many schools cracked down on bullying, implementing "zero tolerance" policies. In a variety of ways, children born after 1980—the Millennials—got a consistent message from adults: life is dangerous, but adults will do everything in their power to protect you from harm, not just from strangers but from one another as well.

These same children grew up in a culture that was (and still is) becoming more politically polarized. Republicans and Democrats have never particularly liked each other, but survey data going back to the 1970s show that on average, their mutual dislike used to be surprisingly mild. Negative feelings have grown steadily stronger, however, particularly since the early 2000s. Political scientists call this process "affective partisan polarization," and it is a very serious problem for any democracy. As each side increasingly demonizes the other, compromise becomes more difficult. A recent study shows that implicit or unconscious biases are now at least as strong across political parties as they are across races.

So it's not hard to imagine why students arriving on campus today might be more desirous of protection and more hostile toward ideological opponents than in generations past. This hostility, and the self-righteousness fueled by strong partisan emotions, can be expected to add force to any moral crusade. A principle of moral psychology is that "morality binds and blinds." Part of what we do when we make moral judgments is express allegiance to a team. But that can interfere with our ability to think critically. Acknowledging that the other side's viewpoint has any merit is risky—your teammates may see you as a traitor.

Social media makes it extraordinarily easy to join crusades, express solidarity and outrage, and shun traitors. Facebook was founded in 2004, and since 2006 it has allowed children as young as 13 to join. This means that the first wave of students who spent all their teen years using Facebook reached college in 2011, and graduated from college only this year.

These first true "social-media natives" may be different from members of previous generations in how they go about sharing their moral judgments and supporting one another in moral campaigns and conflicts. We find much to like about these trends; young people today are engaged with one another, with news stories, and with prosocial endeavors to a greater degree than when the dominant technology was television. But social media has also fundamentally shifted the balance of power in relationships between students and faculty; the latter increasingly fear what students might do to their reputations and careers by stirring up online mobs against them.

We do not mean to imply simple causation, but rates of mental illness in young adults have been rising, both on campus and off, in recent decades. Some portion of the increase is surely due to better diagnosis and greater willingness to seek help, but most experts seem to agree that some portion of the trend is real. Nearly all of the campus mental-health directors surveyed in 2013 by the American College Counseling Association reported that the number of students with severe psychological problems was rising at their schools. The rate of emotional distress reported by students themselves is also high, and rising. In a 2014 survey by the American College Health Association, 54 percent of college students surveyed said that they had "felt overwhelming anxiety" in the past 12 months, up from 49 percent in the same survey just five years earlier. Students seem to be reporting more emotional crises; many seem fragile, and this has surely changed the way university faculty and administrators interact with them. The question is whether some of those changes might be doing more harm than good.

The Thinking Cure

For millennia, philosophers have understood that we don't see life as it is; we see a version distorted by our hopes, fears, and other attachments. The Buddha said, "Our life is the creation of our mind." Marcus Aurelius said, "Life itself is but what you deem it." The quest for wisdom in many traditions begins with this insight. Early Buddhists and the Stoics, for example, developed practices for reducing attachments, thinking more clearly, and finding release from the emotional torments of normal mental life.

Cognitive behavioral therapy is a modern embodiment of this ancient wisdom. It is the most extensively studied nonpharmaceutical treatment of mental illness, and is used widely to treat depression, anxiety disorders, eating disorders, and addiction. It can even be of help to schizophrenics. No other form of psychotherapy has been shown to work for a broader range of problems. Studies have generally found that it is as effective as antidepressant drugs (such as Prozac) in the treatment of anxiety and depression. The therapy is relatively quick and easy to learn; after a few months of training, many patients can do it on their own. Unlike drugs, cognitive behavioral therapy keeps working long after treatment is stopped, because it teaches thinking skills that people can continue to use.

The goal is to minimize distorted thinking and see the world more accurately. You start by learning the names of the dozen or so most common cognitive distortions (such as overgeneralizing, discounting positives, and emotional reasoning; see the list at the bottom of this article). Each time you notice yourself falling prey to one of them, you name it, describe the facts of the situation, consider alternative interpretations, and then choose an interpretation of events more in line with those facts. Your emotions follow your new interpretation. In time, this process becomes automatic. When people improve their mental hygiene in this way—when they free themselves from the repetitive irrational thoughts that had previously filled so much of their consciousness—they become less depressed, anxious, and angry.

The parallel to formal education is clear: cognitive behavioral therapy teaches good critical-thinking skills, the sort that educators have striven for so long to impart. By almost any definition, critical thinking requires grounding one's beliefs in evidence rather than in emotion or desire, and learning how to search for and evaluate evidence that might contradict one's initial hypothesis. But does campus life today foster critical thinking? Or does it coax students to think in more-distorted ways?

Let's look at recent trends in higher education in light of the distortions that cognitive behavioral therapy identifies. We will draw the names and descriptions of these distortions from David D. Burns's popular book *Feeling Good*, as well as from the second edition of *Treatment Plans and Interventions for Depression and Anxiety Disorders*, by Robert L. Leahy, Stephen J. F. Holland, and Lata K. McGinn.

Higher Education's Embrace of "Emotional Reasoning"

Burns defines *emotional reasoning* as assuming "that your negative emotions necessarily reflect the way things really are: 'I feel it, therefore it must be true.'" Leahy, Holland, and McGinn define it as letting "your feelings guide your interpretation of reality." But, of course, subjective feelings are not always trustworthy guides; unrestrained, they can cause people to lash out at others who have done nothing wrong. Therapy often involves talking yourself down from the idea that each of your emotional responses represents something true or important.

Emotional reasoning dominates many campus debates and discussions. A claim that someone's words are "offensive" is not just an expression of one's own subjective feeling of offendedness. It is, rather, a public charge that the speaker has done something objectively wrong. It is a demand that the speaker apologize or be punished by some authority for committing an offense.

There have always been some people who believe they have a right not to be offended. Yet throughout American history—from the Victorian era to the free-speech activism of the 1960s and '70s—radicals have pushed boundaries and mocked prevailing sensibilities. Sometime in the 1980s, however, college campuses began to focus on preventing offensive speech, especially speech that might be hurtful to women or minority groups. The sentiment underpinning this goal was laudable, but it quickly produced some absurd results.

Among the most famous early examples was the so-called water-buffalo incident at the University of Pennsylvania. In 1993, the university charged an Israeli-born student with racial harassment after he yelled "Shut up, you water buffalo!" to a crowd of black sorority women that was making noise at night outside his dorm-room window. Many scholars and pundits at the time could not see how the term *water buffalo* (a rough translation of a Hebrew insult for a thoughtless or rowdy person) was a racial slur against African Americans, and as a result, the case became international news.

Claims of a right not to be offended have continued to arise since then, and universities have continued to privilege them. In a particularly egregious 2008 case, for instance, Indiana University–Purdue University at Indianapolis found a white student guilty of racial harassment for reading a book titled *Notre Dame vs. the Klan*. The book honored student opposition to the Ku Klux Klan when it marched on Notre Dame in 1924. Nonetheless, the picture of a Klan rally on the book's cover offended at least one of the student's co-workers (he was a janitor as well as a student), and that was enough for a guilty finding by the university's Affirmative Action Office.

These examples may seem extreme, but the reasoning behind them has become more commonplace on campus in recent years. Last year, at the University of St. Thomas, in Minnesota, an event called Hump Day, which would have allowed people to pet a camel, was abruptly canceled. Students had created a Facebook group where they protested the event for animal cruelty, for being a waste of money, and for being insensitive to people from the Middle East. The inspiration for the camel had almost certainly come from a popular TV commercial in which a camel saunters around an office on a Wednesday, celebrating "hump day"; it was devoid of any reference to Middle Eastern peoples. Nevertheless, the group organizing the event announced on its Facebook page that the event would be canceled because the "program

[was] dividing people and would make for an uncomfortable and possibly unsafe environment."

Because there is a broad ban in academic circles on "blaming the victim," it is generally considered unacceptable to question the reasonableness (let alone the sincerity) of someone's emotional state, particularly if those emotions are linked to one's group identity. The thin argument "I'm offended" becomes an unbeatable trump card. This leads to what Jonathan Rauch, a contributing editor at this magazine, calls the "offendedness sweepstakes," in which opposing parties use claims of offense as cudgels. In the process, the bar for what we consider unacceptable speech is lowered further and further.

Since 2013, new pressure from the federal government has reinforced this trend. Federal antidiscrimination statutes regulate on-campus harassment and unequal treatment based on sex, race, religion, and national origin. Until recently, the Department of Education's Office for Civil Rights acknowledged that speech must be "objectively offensive" before it could be deemed actionable as sexual harassment—it would have to pass the "reasonable person" test. To be prohibited, the office wrote in 2003, allegedly harassing speech would have to go "beyond the mere expression of views, words, symbols or thoughts that some person finds offensive."

But in 2013, the Departments of Justice and Education greatly broadened the definition of sexual harassment to include verbal conduct that is simply "unwelcome." Out of fear of federal investigations, universities are now applying that standard—defining unwelcome speech as harassment—not just to sex, but to race, religion, and veteran status as well. Everyone is supposed to rely upon his or her own subjective feelings to decide whether a comment by a professor or a fellow student is unwelcome, and therefore grounds for a harassment claim. Emotional reasoning is now accepted as evidence.

If our universities are teaching students that their emotions can be used effectively as weapons—or at least as evidence in administrative proceedings—then they are teaching students to nurture a kind of hypersensitivity that will lead them into countless drawn-out conflicts in college and beyond. Schools may be training students in thinking styles that will damage their careers and friendships, along with their mental health.

Fortune-Telling and Trigger Warnings

Burns defines *fortune-telling* as "anticipat[ing] that things will turn out badly" and feeling "convinced that your prediction is an already-established fact." Leahy, Holland, and McGinn define it as "predict[ing] the future negatively" or seeing potential danger in an everyday situation. The recent spread of demands for trigger warnings on reading assignments with provocative content is an example of fortune-telling.

The idea that words (or smells or any sensory input) can trigger searing memories of past trauma—and intense fear that it may be repeated—has been around at least since World War I, when psychiatrists began treating soldiers for what is now called post-traumatic stress disorder. But explicit trigger warnings are believed to have originated much more recently, on message boards in the early days of the Internet. Trigger warnings became particularly prevalent in self-help and feminist forums, where they allowed readers who had suffered from traumatic events like sexual assault to avoid graphic content that might trigger flashbacks or panic attacks. Search-engine trends indicate that the phrase broke into mainstream use online around 2011, spiked in 2014, and reached an all-time high in 2015. The use of trigger warnings on campus appears to have followed a similar trajectory; seemingly overnight, students at universities across the country have begun demanding that their professors issue warnings before covering material that might evoke a negative emotional response.

In 2013, a task force composed of administrators, students, recent alumni, and one faculty member at Oberlin College, in Ohio, released an online resource guide for faculty (subsequently retracted in the face of faculty pushback) that included a list of topics warranting trigger warnings. These topics included classism and privilege, among many others. The task force recommended that materials that might trigger negative reactions among students be avoided altogether unless they "contribute directly" to course goals, and suggested that works that were "too important to avoid" be made optional.

It's hard to imagine how novels illustrating classism and privilege could provoke or reactivate the kind of terror that is typically implicated in PTSD. Rather, trigger warnings are sometimes demanded for a long list of ideas and attitudes that some students find politically offensive, in the name of preventing other students from being harmed. This is an example of what psychologists call "motivated reasoning"—we spontaneously generate arguments for conclusions we want to support. Once *you* find something hateful, it is easy to argue that exposure to the hateful thing could traumatize some *other* people. You believe that you know how others will react, and that their reaction could be devastating. Preventing that devastation becomes a moral obligation for the whole community. Books for which students have called publicly for trigger warnings within the past couple of years include Virginia Woolf's *Mrs. Dalloway* (at Rutgers, for "suicidal inclinations") and Ovid's *Metamorphoses* (at Columbia, for sexual assault).

Jeannie Suk's *New Yorker* essay described the difficulties of teaching rape law in the age of trigger warnings. Some students, she wrote, have pressured their professors to avoid teaching the subject in order to protect themselves and their classmates from potential distress. Suk compares this to trying to teach "a medical student who is training to be a surgeon but who fears that he'll become distressed if he sees or handles blood."

However, there is a deeper problem with trigger warnings. According to the most-basic tenets of psychology, the very idea of helping people with anxiety disorders avoid the things they fear is misguided. A person who is trapped in an elevator during a power outage may panic and think she is going to die. That frightening experience can change neural connections in her amygdala, leading to an elevator phobia. If you want this woman to retain her fear for life, you should help her avoid elevators.

But if you want to help her return to normalcy, you should take your cues from Ivan Pavlov and guide her through a process known as exposure therapy. You might start by asking the woman to merely look at an elevator from a distance—standing in a building lobby, perhaps—until her apprehension begins to subside. If nothing bad happens while she's standing in the lobby—if the fear is not "reinforced"—then she will begin to learn a new association: elevators are not dangerous. (This reduction in fear during exposure is called habituation.) Then, on subsequent days, you might ask her to get closer, and on later days to push the call button, and eventually to step in and go up one floor. This is how the amygdala can get rewired again to associate a previously feared situation with safety or normalcy.

Students who call for trigger warnings may be correct that some of their peers are harboring memories of trauma that could be reactivated by course readings. But they are wrong to try to prevent such reactivations. Students with PTSD should of course get treatment, but they should not try to avoid normal life, with its many opportunities for habituation. Classroom discussions are safe places to be exposed to incidental reminders of trauma (such as the word *violate*). A discussion of violence is unlikely to be followed by actual violence, so it is a good way to help students change the associations that are causing them discomfort. And they'd better get their habituation done in college, because the world beyond college will be far less willing to accommodate requests for trigger warnings and opt-outs.

The expansive use of trigger warnings may also foster unhealthy mental habits in the vastly larger group of students who do not suffer from PTSD or other anxiety disorders. People acquire their fears not just from their own past experiences, but from social learning as well. If everyone around you acts as though something is dangerous—elevators, certain neighborhoods, novels depicting racism—then you are at risk of acquiring that fear too. The psychiatrist Sarah Roff pointed this out last year in an online article for *The Chronicle of Higher Education*. "One of my biggest concerns about trigger warnings," Roff wrote, "is that they will apply not just to those who have experienced trauma, but to all students, creating an atmosphere in which they are encouraged to believe that there is something dangerous or damaging about discussing difficult aspects of our history."

In an article published last year by *Inside Higher Ed*, seven humanities professors wrote that the trigger-warning movement was "already having a chilling effect on [their] teaching and pedagogy." They reported their colleagues' receiving "phone calls from deans and other administrators investigating student complaints that they have included 'triggering' material in their courses, with or without warnings." A trigger warning, they wrote, "serves as a guarantee that students will not experience unexpected discomfort and implies that if they do, a contract has been broken." When students come to *expect* trigger warnings for any material that makes them uncomfortable, the easiest way for faculty to stay out of trouble is to avoid material that might upset the most sensitive student in the class.

Magnification, Labeling, and Microaggressions

Burns defines *magnification* as "exaggerat[ing] the importance of things," and Leahy, Holland, and McGinn define *labeling* as "assign[ing] global negative traits to yourself and others." The recent collegiate trend of uncovering allegedly racist, sexist, classist, or otherwise discriminatory microaggressions doesn't *incidentally* teach students to focus on small or accidental slights. Its *purpose* is to get students to focus on them and then relabel the people who have made such remarks as aggressors.

The term *microaggression* originated in the 1970s and referred to subtle, often unconscious racist affronts. The definition has expanded in recent years to include anything that can be perceived as discriminatory on virtually any basis. For example, in 2013, a student group at

UCLA staged a sit-in during a class taught by Val Rust, an education professor. The group read a letter aloud expressing their concerns about the campus's hostility toward students of color. Although Rust was not explicitly named, the group quite clearly criticized his teaching as microaggressive. In the course of correcting his students' grammar and spelling, Rust had noted that a student had wrongly capitalized the first letter of the word *indigenous*. Lowercasing the capital *I* was an insult to the student and her ideology, the group claimed.

Even joking about microaggressions can be seen as an aggression, warranting punishment. Last fall, Omar Mahmood, a student at the University of Michigan, wrote a satirical column for a conservative student publication, *The Michigan Review*, poking fun at what he saw as a campus tendency to perceive microaggressions in just about anything. Mahmood was also employed at the campus newspaper, *The Michigan Daily*. *The Daily*'s editors said that the way Mahmood had "satirically mocked the experiences of fellow Daily contributors and minority communities on campus . . . created a conflict of interest." *The Daily* terminated Mahmood after he described the incident to two Web sites, The College Fix and The Daily Caller. A group of women later vandalized Mahmood's doorway with eggs, hot dogs, gum, and notes with messages such as "Everyone hates you, you violent prick." When speech comes to be seen as a form of violence, vindictive protectiveness can justify a hostile, and perhaps even violent, response.

In March, the student government at Ithaca College, in upstate New York, went so far as to propose the creation of an anonymous microaggression-reporting system. Student sponsors envisioned some form of disciplinary action against "oppressors" engaged in belittling speech. One of the sponsors of the program said that while "not . . . every instance will require trial or some kind of harsh punishment," she wanted the program to be "record-keeping but with impact."

Surely people make subtle or thinly veiled racist or sexist remarks on college campuses, and it is right for students to raise questions and initiate discussions about such cases. But the increased focus on microaggressions coupled with the endorsement of emotional reasoning is a formula for a constant state of outrage, even toward well-meaning speakers trying to engage in genuine discussion.

What are we doing to our students if we encourage them to develop extra-thin skin in the years just before they leave the cocoon of adult protection and enter the workforce? Would they not be better prepared to flourish if we taught them to question their own emotional reactions, and to give people the benefit of the doubt?

Teaching Students to Catastrophize and Have Zero Tolerance

Burns defines *catastrophizing* as a kind of magnification that turns "commonplace negative events into nightmarish monsters." Leahy, Holland, and McGinn define it as believing "that what has happened or will happen" is "so awful and unbearable that you won't be able to stand it." Requests for trigger warnings involve catastrophizing, but this way of thinking colors other areas of campus thought as well.

Catastrophizing rhetoric about physical danger is employed by campus administrators more commonly than you might think—sometimes, it seems, with cynical ends in mind. For instance, last year administrators at Bergen Community College, in New Jersey, suspended Francis Schmidt, a professor, after he posted a picture of his daughter on his Google+ account. The photo showed her in a yoga pose, wearing a T-shirt that read I WILL TAKE WHAT IS MINE WITH FIRE & BLOOD, a quote from the HBO show *Game of Thrones*. Schmidt had filed a grievance against the school about two months earlier after being passed over for a sabbatical. The quote was interpreted as a threat by a campus administrator, who received a notification after Schmidt posted the picture; it had been sent, automatically, to a whole group of contacts. According to Schmidt, a Bergen security official present at a subsequent meeting between administrators and Schmidt thought the word *fire* could refer to AK-47s.

Then there is the eight-year legal saga at Valdosta State University, in Georgia, where a student was expelled for protesting the construction of a parking garage by posting an allegedly "threatening" collage on Facebook. The collage described the proposed structure as a "memorial" parking garage—a joke referring to a claim by the university president that the garage would be part of his legacy. The president interpreted the collage as a threat against his life.

It should be no surprise that students are exhibiting similar sensitivity. At the University of Central Florida in 2013, for example, Hyung-il Jung, an accounting instructor, was suspended after a student reported that Jung had made a threatening comment during a review session. Jung explained to the *Orlando Sentinel* that the material he was reviewing was difficult, and he'd noticed the pained look on students' faces, so he made a joke. "It looks like you guys are being slowly suffocated by these questions," he recalled saying. "Am I on a killing spree or what?"

After the student reported Jung's comment, a group of nearly 20 others e-mailed the UCF administration explaining that the comment had clearly been made in jest. Nevertheless, UCF suspended Jung from all university duties and demanded that he obtain written certification from a mental-health professional that he was "not a threat to [himself] or to the university community" before he would be allowed to return to campus.

All of these actions teach a common lesson: smart people do, in fact, overreact to innocuous speech, make mountains out of molehills, and seek punishment for anyone whose words make anyone else feel uncomfortable.

Mental Filtering and Disinvitation Season

As Burns defines it, *mental filtering* is "pick[ing] out a negative detail in any situation and dwell[ing] on it exclusively, thus perceiving that the whole situation is negative." Leahy, Holland, and McGinn refer to this as "negative filtering," which they define as "focus[ing] almost exclusively on the negatives and seldom notic[ing] the positives." When applied to campus life, mental filtering allows for simple-minded demonization.

Students and faculty members in large numbers modeled this cognitive distortion during 2014's "disinvitation season." That's the time of year—usually early spring—when commencement speakers are announced and when students and professors demand that some of those speakers be disinvited because of things they have said or done. According to data compiled by the Foundation for Individual Rights in Education, since 2000, at least 240 campaigns have been launched at U.S. universities to prevent public figures from appearing at campus events; most of them have occurred since 2009.

Consider two of the most prominent disinvitation targets of 2014: former U.S. Secretary of State Condoleezza Rice and the International Monetary Fund's managing director, Christine Lagarde. Rice was the first black female secretary of state; Lagarde was the first woman to become finance minister of a G8 country and the first female head of the IMF. Both speakers could have been seen as highly successful role models for female students, and Rice for minority students as well. But the critics, in effect, discounted any possibility of something positive coming from those speeches.

Members of an academic community should of course be free to raise questions about Rice's role in the Iraq War or to look skeptically at the IMF's policies. But should dislike of *part* of a person's record disqualify her altogether from sharing her perspectives?

If campus culture conveys the idea that visitors must be pure, with résumés that never offend generally left-leaning campus sensibilities, then higher education will have taken a further step toward intellectual homogeneity and the creation of an environment in which students rarely encounter diverse viewpoints. And universities will have reinforced the belief that it's okay to filter out the positive. If students graduate believing that they can learn nothing from people they dislike or from those with whom they disagree, we will have done them a great intellectual disservice.

What Can We Do Now?

Attempts to shield students from words, ideas, and people that might cause them emotional discomfort are bad for the students. They are bad for the workplace, which will be mired in unending litigation if student expectations of safety are carried forward. And they are bad for American democracy, which is already paralyzed by worsening partisanship. When the ideas, values, and speech of the other side are seen not just as wrong but as willfully aggressive toward innocent victims, it is hard to imagine the kind of mutual respect, negotiation, and compromise that are needed to make politics a positive-sum game.

Rather than trying to protect students from words and ideas that they will inevitably encounter, colleges should do all they can to equip students to thrive in a world full of words and ideas that they cannot control. One of the great truths taught by Buddhism (and Stoicism, Hinduism, and many other traditions) is that you can never achieve happiness by making the world conform to your desires. But you can master your desires and habits of thought. This, of course, is the goal of cognitive behavioral therapy. With this in mind, here are some steps that might help reverse the tide of bad thinking on campus.

The biggest single step in the right direction does not involve faculty or university administrators, but rather the federal government, which should release universities from their fear of unreasonable investigation and sanctions by the Department of Education. Congress should define peer-on-peer harassment according to the Supreme Court's definition in the 1999 case *Davis v. Monroe County Board of Education*. The *Davis* standard holds that a single comment or thoughtless remark by a student does not equal harassment; harassment requires a pattern of objectively offensive behavior by one student that interferes with another student's access to education.

Establishing the *Davis* standard would help eliminate universities' impulse to police their students' speech so carefully.

Universities themselves should try to raise consciousness about the need to balance freedom of speech with the need to make all students feel welcome. Talking openly about such conflicting but important values is just the sort of challenging exercise that any diverse but tolerant community must learn to do. Restrictive speech codes should be abandoned.

Universities should also officially and strongly discourage trigger warnings. They should endorse the American Association of University Professors' report on these warnings, which notes, "The presumption that students need to be protected rather than challenged in a classroom is at once infantilizing and anti-intellectual." Professors should be free to use trigger warnings if they choose to do so, but by explicitly discouraging the practice, universities would help fortify the faculty against student requests for such warnings.

Finally, universities should rethink the skills and values they most want to impart to their incoming students. At present, many freshman-orientation programs try to raise student sensitivity to a nearly impossible level. Teaching students to avoid giving unintentional offense is a worthy goal, especially when the students come from many different cultural backgrounds. But students should also be taught how to live in a world full of potential offenses. Why not teach incoming students how to practice cognitive behavioral therapy? Given high and rising rates of mental illness, this simple step would be among the most humane and supportive things a university could do. The cost and time commitment could be kept low: a few group training sessions could be supplemented by Web sites or apps. But the outcome could pay dividends in many ways. For example, a shared vocabulary about reasoning, common distortions, and the appropriate use of evidence to draw conclusions would facilitate critical thinking and real debate. It would also tone down the perpetual state of outrage that seems to engulf some colleges these days, allowing students' minds to open more widely to new ideas and new people. A greater commitment to formal, public debate on campus—and to the assembly of a more politically diverse faculty—would further serve that goal.

Thomas Jefferson, upon founding the University of Virginia, said:

> This institution will be based on the illimitable freedom of the human mind. For here we are not afraid to follow truth wherever it may lead, nor to tolerate any error so long as reason is left free to combat it.

We believe that this is still—and will always be—the best attitude for American universities. Faculty, administrators, students, and the federal government all have a role to play in restoring universities to their historic mission.

Common Cognitive Distortions

A partial list from Robert L. Leahy, Stephen J. F. Holland, and Lata K. McGinn's Treatment Plans and Interventions for Depression and Anxiety Disorders *(2012).*

1. **Mind reading.** You assume that you know what people think without having sufficient evidence of their thoughts. "He thinks I'm a loser."
2. **Fortune-telling.** You predict the future negatively: things will get worse, or there is danger ahead. "I'll fail that exam," or "I won't get the job."
3. **Catastrophizing.**You believe that what has happened or will happen will be so awful and unbearable that you won't be able to stand it. "It would be terrible if I failed."
4. **Labeling.** You assign global negative traits to yourself and others. "I'm undesirable," or "He's a rotten person."
5. **Discounting positives.** You claim that the positive things you or others do are trivial. "That's what wives are supposed to do—so it doesn't count when she's nice to me," or "Those successes were easy, so they don't matter."

6. **Negative filtering.** You focus almost exclusively on the negatives and seldom notice the positives. "Look at all of the people who don't like me."
7. **Overgeneralizing.** You perceive a global pattern of negatives on the basis of a single incident. "This generally happens to me. I seem to fail at a lot of things."
8. **Dichotomous thinking.** You view events or people in all-or-nothing terms. "I get rejected by everyone," or "It was a complete waste of time."
9. **Blaming.** You focus on the other person as the source of your negative feelings, and you refuse to take responsibility for changing yourself. "She's to blame for the way I feel now," or "My parents caused all my problems."
10. **What if?** You keep asking a series of questions about "what if" something happens, and you fail to be satisfied with any of the answers. "Yeah, but what if I get anxious?," or "What if I can't catch my breath?"
11. **Emotional reasoning.** You let your feelings guide your interpretation of reality. "I feel depressed; therefore, my marriage is not working out."
12. **Inability to disconfirm.** You reject any evidence or arguments that might contradict your negative thoughts. For example, when you have the thought *I'm unlovable,* you reject as irrelevant any evidence that people like you. Consequently, your thought cannot be refuted. "That's not the real issue. There are deeper problems. There are other factors."

For Analysis

1. The authors assert that college is "a culture in which everyone must think twice before speaking up, lest they face charges of insensitivity, aggression, or worse" (317). Does this statement reflect your

college experience? Have you noticed trigger warnings and avoidance of microaggressions? How serious is this issue, in your opinion?

2. What evidence, verification, and illustrations are most persuasive in this article? What makes these supports so compelling? Can you think of additional sources of support for this argument? What about evidence that challenges this argument?
3. Compare the list of twelve common cognitive distortions at the end of the article to the fallacies we describe in Chapter 9. How are these cognitive distortions examples of breakdowns in reasoning?

For Writing

The authors claim, "The dangers that these trends pose to scholarship and to the quality of American universities are significant; we could write a whole essay detailing them" (317). Take up the authors' challenge by writing that essay. Research the dangers that Lukianoff and Haidt allude to and decide whether or not you agree that they are significant. Then, write a 1200-word argument that supports your viewpoint.

"Taking My Parents to College"

by Jennine Capó Crucet

Jennine Capó Crucet is a professor of English and ethnic studies and an award-winning author of a novel, *Make Your Home among Strangers*. Crucet has also written for *Guernica, Ploughshares, Epoch, The Rumpus, Prairie Schooner,* and *The New York Times*, which published this article on August 22, 2015.

IT was a simple question, but we couldn't find the answer in any of the paperwork the college had sent. How long was my family supposed to stay for orientation? This was 1999, so Google wasn't really a verb yet, and we were a low-income family (according to my new school) without regular Internet access.

I was a first-generation college student as well as the first in our family to be born in America—my parents were born in Cuba—and we didn't yet know that families were supposed to leave pretty much right after they unloaded your stuff from the car.

We all made the trip from Miami, my hometown, to what would be my new home at Cornell University. Shortly after arriving on campus, the five of us—my parents, my younger sister, my abuela and me—found ourselves listening to a dean end his welcome speech with the words: "Now, parents, please: Go!"

Almost everyone in the audience laughed, but not me, and not my parents. They turned to me and said, "What does he mean, *Go*?" I was just as confused as they were: We thought we *all* needed to be there for freshman orientation—the whole family, for the entirety of it. My dad had booked their hotel through the day after my classes officially began. They'd used all their vacation days from work and had been saving for months to get me to school and go through our orientation.

Every afternoon during that week, we had to go back to the only department store we could find, the now-defunct Ames, for some stupid thing we hadn't known was a necessity, something not in our budget: shower shoes, extra-long twin sheets, mesh laundry bags. Before the other families left, we carefully watched them—they knew what they were doing—and we made new shopping lists with our limited vocabulary: *Those things that lift up the bed*, we wrote. *That plastic thing to carry stuff to the bathroom.*

My family followed me around as I visited department offices during course registration. *Only four classes*? they asked, assuming I was mistakenly taking my first semester too easy. They walked with me to buildings I was supposed to be finding on my own. They waited outside those buildings so that we could all leave from there and go to lunch together.

The five of us wandered each day through the dining hall's doors. "You guys are still here!" the over-friendly person swiping ID cards said after day three. "They sure are!" I chirped back, learning via the cues of my hallmates that I was supposed to want my family gone. But it was an act: We sat together at meals—amid all the other students, already making friends—my mom placing a napkin and fork at each place, setting the table as we did at home.

I don't even remember the moment they drove away. I'm told it's one of those instances you never forget, that second when you realize you're finally on your own. But for me, it's not there—perhaps because, when you're the first in your family to go to college, you never truly feel like they've let you go.

They did eventually leave—of course they did—and a week into classes, I received the topics for what would be my first college paper, in an English course on the modern novel. I might as well have been my non-English-speaking grandmother trying to read and understand them: The language felt that foreign. I called my mom at work and in tears told her that I had to come home, that I'd made a terrible mistake.

She sighed into the phone and said: "Just read me the first question. We'll go through it a little at a time and figure it out."

I read her the topic slowly, pausing after each sentence, waiting for her to say something. The first topic was two paragraphs long. I remember it had the word *intersectionalities* in it. And the word *gendered*. And maybe the phrase *theoretical framework*. I waited for her response and for the ways it would encourage me, for her to tell me I could do this, that I would eventually be the first in my family to graduate from college.

"You're right," she said after a moment. "You're screwed."

Other parents—parents who have gone to college themselves—might have known at that point to encourage their kid to go to office hours, or to the writing center, or to ask for help. But my mom thought I was as alone as I feared.

"I have no idea what any of that means," she said. "I don't even know how it's a *question*."

While my college had done an excellent job recruiting me, I had no road map for what I was supposed to do once I made it to campus. I'd already embarrassed myself by doing things like asking my R.A. what time the dorm closed for the night. As far as I knew, there'd been no mandatory meeting geared toward first-generation students like me: Aside from a check-in with my financial aid officer when she explained what work-study was (I didn't know and worried it meant I had to join the army or something) and where she had me sign for my loans, I was mostly keeping to myself to hide the fact that I was a very special kind of lost. I folded the sheet with the paper topics in half and put it in my desk drawer.

"I don't know what you're gonna do," my mom almost laughed. "Maybe—have you looked in the dictionary?"

I started crying harder, my hand over the receiver.

"You still there?" she eventually asked, clearly hiding her own tears. I murmured *Mmmhmm*.

"Look, just stick it out up there until Christmas," she said. "We have no more vacation days this year. We can't take off any more time to go get you."

"O.K.," I swallowed. I started breathing in through my nose and out through my mouth, calming myself. "I can do that," I said.

My mom laughed for real this time and said, "Mamita, you don't really have a choice."

She didn't say this in a mean way. She was just telling me the truth. "This whole thing was your idea, remember?" she said. Then she told me she had to go, that she needed to get back to work.

SO I got back to work, too, and *Get back to work* became a sort of mantra for me. I tackled the paper with the same focus that had landed me, to everyone's surprise—even my own—at Cornell in the first place. I did O.K. on it, earning a "B-/C" (I never found out how a grade could have a slash in it, but now that I'm an English professor I understand what he was trying to say). The professor had covered the typed pages with comments and questions, and it was in his endnote that he listed the various campus resources available to me.

My mom didn't ask outright what grade I earned—she eventually stopped asking about assignments altogether—and I learned from my peers that grades were something that I didn't have to share with my parents the way I had in high school.

My grades were the first of many elements of my new life for which they had no context and which they wouldn't understand. With each semester, what I was doing became, for them, as indecipherable as that paper topic; they didn't even know what questions to ask. And that, for me, is the quintessential quality of the first-generation college student's experience. It's not even knowing what you don't know.

For Analysis

1. Crucet uses first-person narrative to describe her experience as a first-generation college student. How effective is her use of narrative? What makes it persuasive or not?

2. What are some implications of Crucet's argument?
3. Crucet's story is related to a number of important issues, many of which Crucet only subtly references. Use the controversy categories to identify underlying issues pertinent to Crucet's narrative.

For Writing

Write a 1,000-word narrative that describes your experience of navigating an important transition in your life. Help your readers see the significance of your experience.

"Let's Give Chivalry another Chance"
by Emily Esfahani Smith

> **Emily Esfahani Smith** writes about culture and relationships for *The New Criterion*, *The New York Times*, *The Wall Street Journal*, *Politico*, *Newsweek*, *The Daily Beast*, and *The Atlantic*, which published this article in 2012.

This past spring marked the 100th anniversary of the sinking of the Titanic. On April 14, 1912, as the ship was on its maiden journey from Southampton, UK, to New York City, it hit an iceberg in the North Atlantic. About three hours later, it sank. Three-quarters of the women on the ship survived; over three quarters of the men, by contrast, died. In Washington DC, there is a memorial to these men. The inscription on it reads: "To the brave men who perished in the wreck of the Titanic . . . They gave their lives that women and children might be saved."

About a year ago, a group of today's men were tested the way that the men on board the Titanic were. When the cruise ship Costa Concordia hit a rock and capsized off the coast of Isola del Giglio, Tuscany, last January, men pushed women and children out of the way to save themselves. One Australian woman on board reported at the time:

> The people that pushed their way on to the boat were then trying to tell them to shut the door, not to let any more people on the [life] boat after they had pushed their way on . . . We just couldn't believe it—especially the men, they were worse than the women.

This contrast is indicative of a larger trend—the decline of chivalry and the rise of boorish behavior among men. According to a 2010 Harris poll, 80 percent of Americans say that women are treated with less chivalry today than in the past. This is a problem that all women—especially feminists—should push back against.

After the women's liberation movement of the 1960s, which insisted on the equal treatment of women in all domains of life, feminists dismissed chivalry as sexist. They still do. A new study, published in the feminist journal *Psychology of Women Quarterly*, questions the entire enterprise of male chivalry, which, in an Orwellian flourish, it calls "benevolent sexism."

Chivalrous behavior is *benevolent* because it flatters women and leads to their preferential treatment. But it is *sexist* because it relies on the "gendered premise" that women are weak and in need of protection while men are strong. "Benevolent sexism," Kathleen Connelly and Martin Heesacker of the University of Florida write in the study, "is an ideology that perpetuates gender inequality." They advocate interventions to reduce its prevalence, even though, they found, chivalry is associated with greater life satisfaction and the sense that the world is fair, well-ordered, and a good place.

Charles Murray, the libertarian social scientist at the American Enterprise Institute, summed up the study with tongue-in-cheek, writing "the bad news is that gentlemanly behavior makes people happy." He goes on to ask, "When social scientists discover something that increases life satisfaction for both sexes, shouldn't they at least consider the possibility that they have come across something that is positive? Healthy? Something that might even conceivably be grounded in the nature of Homo sapiens?"

In an interview, Connelly tells me that despite Murray's points, the problem with chivalry is that it assumes "women are wonderful but weak." This assumption of female weakness puts women down, Connelly says.

Perhaps because of women's ambivalence about chivalry, men have grown confused about how to treat women. Will holding doors open for them or paying for the first date be interpreted as sexist? Does carrying their groceries imply they're weak? The breakdown in the old rules, which at one extreme has given rise to the hookup culture, has killed dating and is leaving a lot of well-meaning men and women at a loss.

Historically, the chivalry ideal and the practices that it gave rise to were never about putting women down, as Connelly and other feminists argue. Chivalry, as a social idea, was about respecting and aggrandizing women, and recognizing that their attention was worth seeking, competing for, and holding. If there is a victim of "benevolent sexism," it is not the career-oriented single college-aged feminist. Rather, it is unconstrained masculinity.

"We should have a clear notion of what chivalry is," argues Pier Massimo Forni, an award-winning professor of Italian literature and the founder of the Civility Institute at Johns Hopkins. "It was a form of preferential treatment that men once accorded to women generations ago, inspired by the sense that there was something special about women, that they deserve added respect, and that not doing so was uncouth, cowardly and essentially despicable."

Chivalry arose as a response to the violence and barbarism of the Middle Ages. It cautioned men to temper their aggression, deploying it only in appropriate circumstances—like to protect the physically weak and defenseless members of society. As the author and self-described "equity feminist" Christina Hoff Sommers tells me in an interview, "Masculinity with morality and civility is a very powerful force for good. But masculinity without these virtues is dangerous—even lethal."

Chivalry is grounded in a fundamental reality that defines the relationship between the sexes, she explains. Given that most men are physically stronger than most women, men can overpower women at any time to get what they want. Gentlemen developed symbolic practices to communicate to women that they would not inflict harm upon them and would even protect them against harm. The tacit assumption that men would risk their lives to protect women only underscores how valued women are—how elevated their status is—under the system of chivalry.

A story from the life of Samuel Proctor (d. 1997) comes to mind here. Proctor was the beloved pastor of Harlem's Abyssinian Baptist

Church. Apparently, he was in the elevator one day when a young woman came in. Proctor tipped his hat at her. She was offended and said, "What is that supposed to mean?"

The pastor's response was: "Madame, by tipping my hat I was telling you several things. That I would not harm you in any way. That if someone came into this elevator and threatened you, I would defend you. That if you fell ill, I would tend to you and if necessary carry you to safety. I was telling you that even though I am a man and physically stronger than you, I will treat you with both respect and solicitude. But frankly, Madame, it would have taken too much time to tell you all of that; so, instead, I just tipped my hat."

Some women are trying to bring back chivalry. Since 2009, for instance, a group of women at Arizona State University have devoted themselves to resuscitating gentlemanly behavior and chivalry on a campus whose social life is overwhelmingly defined by partying, frat life, and casual sex. Every spring for the past three years, these women have gathered for the "Gentlemen's Showcase" to honor men who have acted chivalrously by, for example, opening the door for a woman or digging a woman's car out of several feet of snow.

The event has spread to campuses nationwide. Its goal is "to encourage mutual respect between the sexes," Karin Agness tells me in an interview. Agness is the founder and president of the Network of Enlightened Women, the organization that hosts Gentlemen's Showcases at colleges each spring.

"The current framework is not generating healthy relationships," Blayne Bennett, the organizer of ASU's first Gentlemen's Showcase, has said. "I believe that chivalry provides the positive framework to maximize the overall happiness of men and women."

Women, she said, "want to be treated like ladies."

Bennett and her fellow chivalry advocates have the right idea. "If women give up on chivalry, it will be gone," Sommers tells me. "If boys can get away with being boorish, they will, happily. Women will pay the price."

If feminists want to level the playing field between men and women, they should find common cause with traditionalist women, like those at ASU, on the issue of chivalry. Both groups are concerned with how men treat women. They just differ in what that means: Feminists want men to treat women as equals; traditionalists want men to treat women like ladies. Are the two mutually exclusive?

Chivalry is about respect. It is about not harming or hurting others, especially those who are more vulnerable than you. It is about putting other people first and serving others often in a heroic or courageous manner. It is about being polite and courteous. In other words, chivalry in the age of post-feminism is another name we give to civility. When we give up on civility, understood in this way, we can never have relationships that are as meaningful as they could be.

If women today—feminists and non-feminists alike—encouraged both men and women to adopt the principles of civil and chivalrous conduct, then the standards of behavior for the two sexes would be the same, fostering the equality that feminists desire. Moreover, the relations between the sexes would be once again based on mutual respect, as the traditionalists want. Men and women may end up being civil and well-mannered in different ways, but at least they would be civil and well-mannered, an improvement on the current situation.

Through a tragic event that occurred last summer, our nation was jolted into recognizing chivalry's enduring power. During a screening of the Dark Knight, a deranged gunman opened fire in an Aurora, Colorado, theater, murdering twelve innocent people. Three men, all in their twenties, were in the audience that day with their girlfriends. When the shots rang out across the theater, these men threw themselves over their girlfriends, saving the women's lives. All three of the men died.

At the time, Hanna Rosin noted that what these men did was "deeper" than chivalry. It was heroic. I agree. But heroism and chivalry share a basic feature in common—the recognition, a transcendent one, that there is something greater than the self worth protecting, and that there is something greater than the self worth sacrificing your own needs, desires, and even life for. If we can all agree that the kind of culture we should aspire to live in is one in which men and women protect and honor each other in the ways that they can—and not one in which men are pushing past women and children to save their own lives—then that is progress that women everywhere should support.

For Analysis

1. Smith begins by citing a historical example—"the sinking of the Titanic"—that she compares to a recent shipping accident. What do you think of this comparison? Are the examples similar enough to draw direct comparisons? Do you think the difference between what happened on the Titanic versus the Costa Concordia accurately indicates "a larger trend—the decline of chivalry and the rise of boorish behavior among men"?
2. Smith creates a definition of chivalry by saying, "Chivalry is about respect. It is about not harming or hurting others, especially those who are more vulnerable than you. It is about putting other people first and serving others often in a heroic or courageous manner. It is about being polite and courteous. In other words, chivalry in the age of post-feminism is another name we give to civility." Look up the terms "chivalry" and "civility" in a dictionary and evaluate Smith's definition.
3. What objections might readers have to this argument? Why would these be valid counterarguments?

For Writing

Smith's argument relies on several terms, such as "sexist," "heroic," "benevolent," and "boorish." Choose one of these terms or another related one and write a 500-word definitional argument about the term as it relates to a dating practice or other relationship issue. Consult pp. 136–38 for help writing definitional arguments.

"Accents and Ebonics: When the Hood Goes to College"

by Taylor Callwood

Taylor Callwood is a student at James Madison University where she is studying Writing, Rhetoric & Technical Communication. This research report was published in the Spring 2014 edition of a campus journal called *Lexi@*.

Abstract

This paper examines how accents, with a focus on Ebonics, are related to how a person is treated, how literacy and accents are related, and the implications of such on a college campus. This paper discusses a survey of ten questions sent to 32 participants and their responses to being asked about Ebonics. The research in this paper suggests that accents are related to how a person is treated and how their intelligence level is perceived to be; however, it also suggests that colleges are more tolerant than the general population. This paper also explores different ways to overcome language prejudices, especially within children.

Keywords: Ebonics

One of the most recognized movie scenes of the 20th century is in the 1964 film, *My Fair Lady,* when Professor Henry Higgins attempted to teach Eliza Doolittle how to say, "The rain in Spain stays mainly in the plain," in "real English," without a Cockney accent. While the clip itself may be considered*slightly* outdated, the concept of language prejudice remains the same and just as prevalent in modern American society. For example, in 2010 the U.S. Drug Enforcement Administration sparked outrage in the general population when it created a new job for a translator of Ebonics, defined as a nonstandard form of American English characteristically spoken by African Americans in the United States (Ludden & McWhorter, 2010, p. 1; Princeton, n.p.). There were many debates over whether or not the DEA should have hired an Ebonics translator because in doing so, the DEA indirectly recognized Ebonics as an official language and not as the "bad English or broken English" that it was previously considered to be (Ludden & McWhorter, 2010, n.p.). Perry and Delpit (1998) attempted to validate this decision saying that Ebonics is as legitimate a language as French or Spanish. They argued that because teachers view Ebonics as a substandard form of English, and not as another language, the teachers help to form the stigma that children who speak Ebonics are stupid or lazy (n.p.).

The idea of language bias caught my attention in *My Fair Lady* and I began to think about my mother who grew up speaking Ebonics, but then studied at the Coast Guard Academy, University of Michigan and UCLA Berkeley. Each time she visited her home in West Philadelphia, her siblings would say that she talked "white." This piqued my interest because although my mother is an intelligent person, when she goes back to Philadelphia, she reverts to speaking Ebonics, changing the way she speaks to fit her surroundings. I wondered what her college counterparts thought when she spoke Ebonics rather than "white" at college because students living on a college campus tend to generally speak the same way. Between *My Fair Lady* and my mother, I realized I had two burning questions: are accents related to how a person is treated, and are perceptions of literacy and accents related? I believe that accents *are* related to how a person is treated even though literacy and accents share no correlation; however, in the academic world, thoughts alone are nothing without proof, and I set out to show the world that, even unknowingly, accents do affect the way a person is treated.

Although language prejudice has been studied extensively throughout the years, it has not been studied as thoroughly in a college atmosphere. Little focus has been placed on studying how college students, by nature, are more open-minded and accepting than older generations and uneducated people. I know that there is a language bias in the general population, but I wonder how prevalent it is on college campuses, and more specifically, how Ebonics plays a part in the language bias. Consequently, I placed my focus on college-aged students to get a feel for how they perceive Ebonics, and how Ebonics affects their perceptions of a speaker. In my study, I looked at 26 different college students from different colleges on the East Coast. It should be noted that for the sake of my study, Ebonics would be considered an accent as well as a dialect and not just a nonstandard form of American English characteristically spoken by African Americans in the United States.

Research Procedure

There was previous research available in order to answer the questions stated above to use as the basis for this paper; however, my research is specifically focused on how college students feel about language perception, not just how society feels. The research from this angle is minuscule. Thus this study targets college students ages 17–25 using a SurveyMonkey-created survey. The survey was done in the style of Ahn (2010) who devised a short survey about participants' general knowledge of accent perceptions and how it affected them. Ahn then interviewed subjects and played them tapes of different accents. My methodology is less personal, as the survey was conducted anonymously to increase participation. Ahn also focused on European and Asian accents, whereas this study focused on Ebonics.

The survey questions were developed in an attempt to get the most holistic view of how students feel about people who speak Ebonics. Although these questions may seem broad and unfocused, they were specifically chosen because they are unbiased and open-ended. They are directed at the participants to understand how they perceive Ebonics speakers.

Because the research focused specifically on the college population, the survey was only sent out to, and shared among, college students. After creating the survey, I used Facebook to send out a web link to all my friends currently attending college. I also had my brother at VCU and my sister at Wake Forest do the same. Our friends shared the link with their friends to help decrease the bias of only our friends participating.

There were some inherent limitations to this particular research method. The most glaring was that the survey was anonymous. Although this was done to encourage participation and honest answers, it was hard to guarantee the sanctity of the research because there was no way of keeping older, non-college students, from answering the survey. Since the survey was sent out over Facebook, I am assuming that I do not have to worry about a younger generation bias because I highly doubt that they would take the time to answer a survey like this. The second problem was the inability to force participation. Without enough responses, it would be almost impossible to collect and analyze enough data to make a legitimate argument. The last limitation was that the sample population was college students. College students are not the most patient people, nor do they have inordinate amounts of time to answer surveys. Because of this, the survey was limited to only ten short questions that would not take long to answer. This meant that all the detailed questions about Ebonics had to be curtailed and edited to broader, easier-to-answer questions so that the participants would feel more inclined to respond my survey. Despite the limitations, the survey was successful in answering the original questions about the relationship between Ebonics and how someone is treated.

By the time the survey closed, there were 32 participants. However, there were 6 surveys that were unusable due to inappropriate language or responses which called into question the credibility of the respondent.

Summary of the Findings

Out of the 26 usable surveys, ten participants (38%) said that they would negatively judge an Ebonics speaker, and would have no reservations about it. Eight (31%) said that they would not judge an

Ebonics speaker at all because they realize that accent is not an accurate reflection of character. Eight (31%) said that while they would initially judge an Ebonics speaker, they would not let that cloud their judgments because they recognize that first impressions can be wrong.

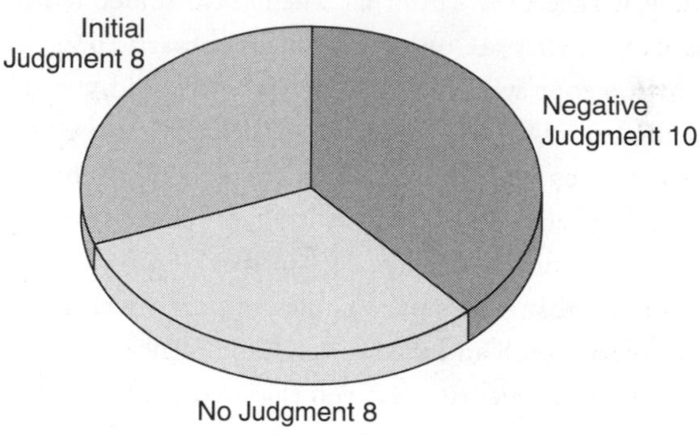

However, 20 participants (77%) said that if they heard someone speaking Ebonics, their initial impression would be that the speaker is less intelligent. Of these 20 participants, 12 (60%) made sure to clarify that this initial judgment was based solely on a first impression and noted they know that Ebonics does not necessarily reflect intelligence. One participant commented, "A final judgment of a person shouldn't be based on the way they speak." Other participants echoed this response. Many of the other responses stated that people speak Ebonics because they have "pride in their culture." Regardless, these participants still made a distinction between "proper English" and Ebonics. They seem to think that there is a time and a place for Ebonics.

Seven other participants (35%) were adamant that Ebonics and intelligence are positively correlated. Many were under the stereotypical opinion that Ebonics speakers are "lower socioeconomic African

Americans" who either "lack the ability to speak more properly, or they have no reason to" or "have a depleted vocabulary and lack education." As one participant stated "[Ebonics speakers] show a lackadaisical attitude toward the learning of the English language . . . I tend to believe the person is uneducated and has little, if any, desire to learn the language properly." Another participant reluctantly admitted that "Sadly, it's the basic truth that when I hear someone who speaks Ebonics I think they are unintelligent." One participant had never spoken to someone who speaks Ebonics but candidly said that she would probably "resort to the stereotypical view that they are uneducated" if she were to ever hear Ebonics. There was another participant who did not care about the speech by itself; the clothes were the deciding factor of his final judgment. When speaking to someone using Ebonics he said that if they use Ebonics, but dress well, it is a sign of confidence in one's self and accordingly, intelligence.

This prejudice is a curiosity given that many respondents change the way that they speak to fit in their surroundings. Eighteen (69%) of the participants admitted to doing so for various reasons, the most prevalent being that some speech is inappropriate to use around professors and figures of authority the way one does with friends. Unsurprisingly, the majority of the respondents who said that they change their speech to match their surroundings were more accepting of people who speak Ebonics, recognizing that it doesn't necessarily reflect on the speaker themselves, or their intelligence. Oddly, race and gender were insignificant factors in this survey though this may be due to the relatively low, workable turnout.

After analyzing the results, the expected difference between the participants who would negatively judge Ebonics speakers, and the ones who were more positive, were much smaller than expected. The results were mostly average, with few anomalies. Most participants would initially judge the speaker, and later change their opinion accordingly. The number of those in the middle were also expected to be significantly smaller because the findings were expected to be more consistent with Rakic (Friedrich-Schiller-Universität Jena, 2010) who found a significant correlation between accents and stereotypes. In 2010, Rakic conducted a study where participants were shown a photograph of German and Italian looking persons together with written statements about the individuals depicted. The participants were asked to match up the statement with the correct photograph. All the participants correctly matched the statement to the photograph. The participants were next asked to do the same exact thing while listening to a recording of the statements, some spoken with German accents, and others with Italian accents. In this part of the experiment, the participants placed more emphasis on the accent matching up to the picture rather than to the statement, showing that accents significantly shape people's perception more than written words or pictures. Rakic found that the majority of "participants orientated themselves nearly exclusively on the spoken accent while categorizing people" and that language is "a source of information in the ethnic categorization" (n.p.). This study showed that it is human nature to judge based on accent.

Although Rakic's study was done in the general population instead of being limited to college campuses, the results between my study and that of Rakic were still expected to be at least similar; however, the results did not exactly match up. It seems that accents, Ebonics in particular, are much more widely accepted, tolerated and less judged on college campuses than in the real world. The participants recognized the existence of the bias but chose not to act on them. This could be due to the general open-mindedness of college students and that college students are taught by their respective universities to be accepting of diversity. It could also be the fact that, within college campuses, African Americans who speak Ebonics, are also highly intelligent individuals who are able speak "proper English" when necessary, and other students recognize this.

Implications of this Study

On college campuses, students seem to be extremely open minded and accepting of Ebonics, although this study did not delve into the why. There are many theories about how to encourage the general public's acceptance of Ebonics, as it is on college campuses today.

In California, there is a school that formally recognizes Ebonics. Prescott Elementary School has implemented a Standard English Proficiency Program, which uses Ebonics to teach African-American and white students Standard English (Miner, 2012). The teachers in this program approach teaching Standard English as if they are teaching their students a second language, and "not fixing the home language you bring to school" (n.p.). The teachers believe that if "you don't respect the children's culture, you negate their very essence" (n.p.). They use theses philosophies as the basis for their program, which has proven to be successful because the students in this school grow up learning that accents are not the only part of a person.

However, my survey should not only encourage people to recognize their prejudice towards Ebonics, but also towards accents as a whole. The following are other ways that have been proposed to end accent prejudices. The Anti-Defamation League (ADL) (2010) recommends that parents begin the education of their children. They suggest that parents "teach [their] children respect and an appreciation for differences by providing opportunities for interaction with people of diverse groups," and "help children recognize instances of stereotyping, prejudice and discrimination" (n.p.). The theory means that if children are educated about language prejudice at a young age when they are less influenced by their peers, they will be more tolerant in the future.

In drama classrooms, where accents and voice inflections are especially important and stressed, Sabo (2012) addresses the teachers. She beseeches teachers to "not only present General American speech as just another accent students need to learn, but also emphasize that it has no intrinsic worth making it better than any other dialect" (p. 4).

She says that "[teachers] have an obligation to root out prejudice and challenge assumptions." These three examples are directed at teachers, parents and other figures of authority, who serve as role models and who are most able to make a difference in the future.

Now that we are aware that some people treat Ebonics speakers differently, we are able to act on it. Next time you hear someone speaking Ebonics, or speaking in any accent, before judging them, understand that just because they sound a certain way, does not mean that they *are* a certain way. Language prejudice is prevalent in our society, but it is up to us to overcome our initial judgments to see the person beyond. Perhaps in the future, no one will understand just how relevant that one prejudicial scene in *My Fair Lady* once was in everyone's daily lives.

References

Ahn, Jeahyeon. (2010). *The Effect of Accents on Cognitive Load and Achievement: The Relationship between Students' Accent Perception and Accented Voice Instructions in Students' Achievement.* Retrieved from http://etd.ohiolink.edu/view.cgi?acc_num=ohiou1282580640.

Anti-Defamation League. (2001). *What to Tell Your Child About Prejudice and Discrimination*. Retrieved from http://www.adl.org/ what_to_tell/print.asp.

Friedrich-Schiller-Universität Jena. (2010). Psychologists Show How Accent Shapes Our Perception of a Person. Science Daily. Retrieved from http://www.sciencedaily.com/releases /2010/12/101217145649.htm.

Ludden, J (Interviewer) & McWhorter, J (Interviewee). (2010). *Op-Ed: DEA Call For Ebonics Experts Smart Move* [Interview transcript]. Retrieved from NPR Website http://www.npr.org/templates/story / story.php?storyId=129682981.

Miner, B (Interviewer) & Secret, C (Interviewee). (2012). *An Interview with Oakland Teacher Carrie Secret.* Retrieved from http://www.rethinkingschools.org/publication/ebonics/ebsecret.shtml.

Perry, T., Delpit,L. (1998). *The Real Ebonics Debate: Power, Language, and the Education of African-American Children*. Retrieved from http://www.rethinkingschools.org/ publication/ ebonics/ ebintro. shtml.

Sabo, K. (2012). *Are You Teaching Prejudice?* Southern Theatre, 53 (3), p. 4.

For Analysis

1. What were Callwood's possible inspirations for writing? What might be the purpose of her research report?
2. Compare the components of Callwood's research report with the Scholarly Model described on pp. 177–78. How is Callwood's report similar to a scholarly research article? What is different?
3. What gaps do you notice in Callwood's research? What questions do you have about her research methods or findings?

For Writing

Replicate Callwood's study to see if you obtain similar or different results. When designing your study, decide whether you want to follow Callwood's research procedures closely or adapt the study to suit a different context. You can consult Callwood's survey in Appendix A in the online version of this article at http://commons.lib.jmu.edu/ lexia/vol2/iss1/5/.

"How to Live Wisely"
by Richard J. Light

Richard Light is a professor of teaching and learning at Harvard Graduate School of Education. He is actively involved in higher education policies and helps lead several efforts to address problems and controversies in higher education. His book *Making the Most of College: Students Speak Their Minds* was published in 2001. The following article was originally published on July 31, 2015 in *The New York Times*.

Imagine you are Dean for a Day. What is one actionable change you would implement to enhance the college experience on campus?

I have asked students this question for years. The answers can be eye-opening. A few years ago, the responses began to move away from "tweak the history course" or "change the ways labs are structured." A different commentary, about learning to live wisely, has emerged.

What does it mean to live a good life? What about a productive life? How about a happy life? How might I think about these ideas if the answers conflict with one another? And how do I use my time here at college to build on the answers to these tough questions?

A number of campuses have recently started to offer an opportunity for students to grapple with these questions. On my campus, Harvard, a small group of faculty members and deans created a noncredit seminar called "Reflecting on Your Life." The format is simple: three 90-minute discussion sessions for groups of 12 first-year students, led by faculty members, advisers or deans. Well over 100 students participate each year.

Here are five exercises that students find particularly engaging. Each is designed to help freshmen identify their goals and reflect systematically about various aspects of their personal lives, and to connect what they discover to what they actually do at college.

1. For the first exercise, we ask students to make a list of how they want to spend their time at college. What matters to you? This might be going to class, studying, spending time with close friends, perhaps volunteering in the off-campus community or reading books not on any course's required reading list. Then students make a list of how they actually spent their time, on average, each day over the past week and match the two lists.

Finally, we pose the question: How well do your commitments actually match your goals?

A few students find a strong overlap between the lists. The majority don't. They are stunned and dismayed to discover they are spending much of their precious time on activities they don't value highly. The challenge is how to align your time commitments to reflect your personal convictions.

2. Deciding on a major can be amazingly difficult. One student in our group was having a hard time choosing between government and science. How was she spending her spare time? She described being active in the Institute of Politics, running the Model U.N. and writing regularly for The Political Review. The discussion leader noted that she hadn't mentioned the word "lab" in her summary. "Labs?" replied the student, looking incredulous. "Why would I mention labs when talking about my spare time?" Half an hour after the session, the group leader got an email thanking him for posing the question.

3. I call this the Broad vs. Deep Exercise. If you could become extraordinarily good at one thing versus being pretty good at many things, which approach would you choose? We invite students to think about how to organize their college life to follow their chosen path in a purposeful way.

4. In the Core Values Exercise, students are presented with a sheet of paper with about 25 words on it. The words include "dignity," "love," "fame," "family," "excellence," "wealth" and "wisdom." They are told to circle the five words that best describe their core values. Now, we ask, how might you deal with a situation where your core values come into conflict with one another? Students find this question particularly difficult. One student brought up his own personal dilemma: He wants to be a surgeon, and he also wants to have a large family. So his core values included the words "useful" and "family." He said he worries a lot whether he could be a successful surgeon while also being a devoted father. Students couldn't stop talking about this example, as many saw themselves facing a similar challenge.

5. This exercise presents a parable of a happy fisherman living a simple life on a small island. The fellow goes fishing for a few hours every day. He catches a few fish, sells them to his friends, and enjoys spending the rest of the day with his wife and children, and napping. He couldn't imagine changing a thing in his relaxed and easy life.

A recent M.B.A. visits this island and quickly sees how this fisherman could become rich. He could catch more fish, start up a business, market the fish, open a cannery, maybe even issue an I.P.O. Ultimately he would become truly successful. He could donate some of his fish to hungry children worldwide and might even save lives.

"And then what?" asks the fisherman.

"Then you could spend lots of time with your family," replies the visitor. "Yet you would have made a difference in the world. You would have used your talents, and fed some poor children, instead of just lying around all day."

We ask students to apply this parable to their own lives. Is it more important to you to have little, accomplish little, yet be relaxed and happy and spend time with family? Or is it more important to you to work hard, use your talents, perhaps start a business, maybe even make the world a better place along the way?

Typically, this simple parable leads to substantial disagreement. These discussions encourage first-year undergraduates to think about what really matters to them, and what each of us feels we might owe, or not owe, to the broader community—ideas that our students can capitalize on throughout their time at college.

At the end of our sessions, I say to my group: "Tell me one thing you have changed your mind about this year," and many responses reflect a remarkable level of introspection. Three years later, when we check in with participants, nearly all report that the discussions had been valuable, a step toward turning college into the transformational experience it is meant to be.

For Analysis

1. Is this an argument? If so, what is the thesis? What controversy categories are addressed? If this isn't an argument, what genre is it? What's its purpose?
2. What assumptions does the author make? What beliefs or values must the audience share with Light in order to follow his advice?
3. Readers may challenge Light's claim that college should be a "transformational experience" if they think the purpose of college is to prepare students for job success. What other counterarguments might readers raise in response to this article?

For Writing

The author poses many compelling questions throughout the article. For instance, he asks, "What is one actionable change you would implement to enhance the college experience on campus?" and "What does it mean to live a good life?" Select one of the article's most significant questions and write a 1,000-word commentary in response.

"Get Your Stadiums out of Our Churches"
by Alan Levinovitz

Alan Levinovitz is a professor of Chinese philosophy and religion and the author of *The Gluten Lie: And Other Myths about What You Eat*. His articles also appear in *The Atlantic*, *Science 2.0*, and various scholarly journals. *Slate* published this article in December 2013.

James Madison University, my current employer, recently commissioned an "overall strategic plan" for its athletics program. Revealed to the public in an admirable gesture of institutional transparency, the plan claims that JMU is "well-positioned" for a transition to the highest level of college sports, the Football Bowl Subdivision.

Though administrators are open to the idea of moving on up, the James Madison faculty, myself included, is substantially less enthused. Why do the vast majority of us oppose the move?

First, we worry about the numbers. There is no question that FBS programs are risky investments and that they're correlated with disproportionately high levels of institutional athletics funding. (Statements to the contrary may reflect a conflict of interest, like when the company that produced your feasibility study is also retained to recruit your new head coach.) There's also widespread concern about endorsing a financial scheme dependent on unpaid labor for its solvency, labor that may one day be declared illegal. And yes, longtime professors who saw their salaries frozen for five years are viscerally upset by a plan that suggests hiking student fees to fund a major investment in our football program.

Yet the financial cost of college football is nothing compared with its cost to our integrity. Are some people such addicts that they will continue to rationalize the exploitation of workers on whose battered bodies their beloved entertainment industry is built? Does the rush of a win for the home team allow them to forget those teenagers who gamble on unlikely stardom and lose? Are they willing to stomach endemic sexism and the scourge of campus sexual assault?

So be it. But I will not stand by as the engineers and patrons of this system pervert my religion and desecrate its churches.

I see my job as both a career and a devotion. Max Weber, the founder of modern social science, referred to scholarship as "a vocation," evoking the traditional sense of a divine calling to serve in the priesthood. The earliest universities descended from religious schools, and it was only in the 19th century that Harvard, America's first university, changed its motto from "Truth for Christ and Church" to "Truth."

Though shorn of denominational religious rhetoric, that simple motto still represents the *mission* of higher education, the core of our academic faith. Professors puzzle over ancient languages, map the stars, and grade endless assignments not because "those who can't do, teach," but because we are devoted to truth and feel a duty to profess it. We think—we *know*—that our vocation has always been, and will continue to be, an essential element of any healthy society. In the words of another university motto: "Let knowledge grow from more to more; and so be human life enriched."

It is not my place to criticize the status of athletics in America. On that, our nation has already made a near unanimous decision. As Harvard philosopher Michael Sandel puts it in his book *What Money Can't Buy*: "From Yankee Stadium in New York to Candlestick Park in San Francisco, sports stadiums are the cathedrals of our civil religion, public spaces that gather people from different walks of life in rituals of loss and hope, profanity and prayer."

But these cathedrals should not be the crown jewels of college campuses, and athletes should not be our evangelists. It's true that academia and sports complement each other—Plato himself was an excellent wrestler, and Confucian students were expected to master archery and charioteering alongside writing and arithmetic. Yet Plato and Confucius would surely be appalled, as we should be, to hear that

University of California–Berkeley pays its Nobel laureate in physics one-tenth the salary of its football coach, or that some institutional athletics subsidies can reach 1.5 times the total library budget. The dubious profitability of athletics is beside the point: These figures represent and legitimize a profound disorder of values.

America, uniquely among nations, has normalized an absurd relationship between sports and higher education. Just imagine if a similar phenomenon were born of the Vatican's newly launched cricket team. The sentiment behind the team is laudable. Cardinal Gianfranco Ravasi hailed cricket as an "expression of inter-culturality" that could inspire "dialogue between peoples," and seminarian/cricketer Antony Fernando praised sports as a means of learning "to accept both victory and defeat."

But what if 10 years from now the Vatican's star cricketers are better known than saints, and more people recognize the coach's name than the Pope's? What if parishioners actually gave alms in proportion to the team's success? What if the St. Peter's Cricket Club stadium dwarfed St. Peter's Basilica? Catholicism, like our education system, would look like an unholy charade, its former worshippers slowly lost to services at the new cathedral of civic religion.

In the case of football stadiums, *coliseum* might be a better metaphor than *cathedral*. (UC–Berkeley's football stadium was actually modeled after the Roman Colosseum.) The Roman republic's gladiatorial matches were enormously popular, providing sponsors with publicity while satisfying the masses' desire for cheap entertainment. When the moral depravity of the games became undeniable, imperial edicts were passed to restrict them, but they were largely ineffective. The people could not go without their blood sport, and even Emperor Constantine turned a blind eye to his own laws.

The games finally ended thanks to the outrage of a monk. In 404 C.E., St. Telemachus had had enough. "After gazing upon the combat from the amphitheatre, he descended into the arena, and tried to separate the gladiators," writes Bishop Theodoret in his *History of the*

Church. "The sanguinary spectators, possessed by the demon who delights in the effusion of blood, were irritated at the interruption of their cruel sports, and stoned him who had occasioned the cessation. On being apprised of this circumstance, the admirable [Emperor Honorius] numbered him with the victorious martyrs, and abolished these iniquitous spectacles."

American college football has faced people like Telemachus, educators and administrators who resist the will (and deep pockets) of fanatics. In 1939, Robert Maynard Hutchins, then president of the University of Chicago, eliminated the school's football program. It was not a popular move. Harvard's athletic director mocked Hutchins' physique, and *Chicago Tribune* sports editor Arch Ward likened dropping football to Communism. Even Hutchins' fellow university presidents were skeptical. "There have been times when I wished that we might have colleges and universities without football," Purdue University president Edward C. Elliott told the *Tribune*. "This is perhaps a bit Utopian. Perhaps Chicago will prove that Utopia is possible. But Purdue is not Utopian and intends to continue to play football—and, we hope, good football."

Fifteen years later, Hutchins reflected on the significance of his decision in an article for *Sports Illustrated*. "No other country looks to its universities as a prime source of athletic entertainment," he wrote. "Anybody who has watched, as I have, 12 university presidents spend half a day solemnly discussing the Rose Bowl agreement, or anybody who has read portentous discussions of the 'decline' of Harvard, Yale, Stanford, or Chicago because of the recurring defeats of its football team must realize that we in America are in a different world."

Hutchins was aghast at his fellow presidents, who believed that "football had become the spiritual core of the modern campus." He was disgusted by a system that reduced boys "to perjurers, scalpers and football gigolos" and by colleges that "violate the rules they themselves have made," pandering to "alumni with endowment-available money."

"To anybody seriously interested in education intercollegiate football presents itself as an infernal nuisance," Hutchins declared. "If all the time, thought and effort that university presidents, professors and press agents have had to devote to this subject could have been spent on working out and explaining to the public a defensible program of higher education we should long since have solved every problem that confronts the colleges and universities of the U.S. Since there is no visible connection between big-time football and higher education, the tremendous importance attached to it by colleges and universities can only confuse the public about what these institutions are."

In the aftermath of the school's decision to drop football, Chicago had indeed proved that utopia was possible. It succeeded, Hutchins noted proudly, in demonstrating that "'normal' young Americans could get excited about the life of the mind."

Don't think for a moment that Chicago is some freakish exception. In 2009, Northeastern University dropped its football program, to the dismay of many alumni and students. What happened? "For Northeastern, life after football is good," reported the *Boston Globe* a year later. "There has been little or no blowback from alumni or students, as money once spent on football now serves other campus goals. In fact, the number of donors is up (from 19,559 to 21,797) as is the number of applicants (37,693 for 2,800 spots), and the stature of the university continues to rise."

At Boston University, which dropped its football program in 1997, the number of alumni donors is up this year, despite a nationwide downward trend in annual giving. Intramural sports participation has risen 55 percent. And then there's Spelman, and Hofstra, and UC–Santa Barbara, and, well, the list goes on.

Platitudes about potential loss of spirit aside, there's only one serious obstacle facing schools that are tempted to get rid of football: the lure of big money. Money makes universities do funny things. In exchange for a $6 million gift to the athletics program, Florida Atlantic University renamed its football stadium after controversy-wracked private prison corporation GEO Group, owned by alumnus, former board of trustees member, and enthusiastic booster George Zoley. (The naming rights deal eventually collapsed amid a torrent of bad publicity.)

As I contemplate the recently renovated $62 million stadium on my own campus (naming rights still available!), it strikes me that a traditional religion once compromised its morals to pay for fancy cathedrals. Originally a minor aspect of Catholicism, indulgences took off when they were monetized effectively. Despite limits placed by the Fourth Lateran Council in 1215, churches continued to bleed funds from the faithful in exchange for promises of salvation. The issue came to a head in 1517 when Pope Leo X sold indulgences to finance renovations of St. Peter's Basilica. Scandalized, Martin Luther nailed his 95 Theses to the door of All Saints' Church in Wittenberg and started the Protestant Reformation.

It is time for our own reformation. Students and parents: Choose schools based on the educational experiences they offer, not the ranking of their teams. Alumni: Donate because your school taught you something, not because it wins games. Faculty, administrators, and presidents: Don't let your fear of being martyred stop you from speaking out publicly against big-money college sports. If higher education in America wants to preserve its integrity, we have no choice but to demand together: *Get your stadiums out of our churches.*

For Analysis

1. Select one of Levinovitz's claims that isn't fully developed and find support to defend or refute the claim. For instance, he writes, "There is no question that FBS [Football Bowl Subdivision] programs are risky investments and that they're correlated with disproportionately high levels of institutional athletics funding" (363).

Collect sufficient evidence or verification to support or challenge this claim.

2. Levinovitz refers to many sources, which are hyperlinked in the online version of this article. Find and read three of these sources and summarize points that Levinovitz does not fully describe. Then, explain whether you agree with Levinovitz's interpretations of these sources.
3. What perspectives or issues does Levinovitz overlook? What other points would you add to this discussion?

For Writing

Write a rhetorical analysis and response to Levinovitz's argument. See the WHAT'S NEXT activity on p. 122 for detailed instructions on writing a rhetorical analysis.

"Effects of Gender and Type of Praise on Task Performance Among Undergraduates"

by Leah Lessard, Andrew Grossman, and Maggie L. Syme

Leah Lessard and **Andrew Grossman** were undergraduate psychology students at the University of San Diego when they completed this study. **Maggie L. Syme** is a gerontology professor who studies older adult sexuality. She is also a licensed psychologist with a background in counseling. This article was published in the Spring 2015 edition of *Psi Chi Journal of Psychological Research*.

ABSTRACT.

Research has suggested that receiving process praise (e.g., "You're working hard") increases children's academic performance and that person praise (e.g., "You're smart") can have detrimental effects. However, few studies have examined how these findings relate to young adults. This experimental study examined the effects of type of praise (person vs. process) and gender[1] on young adults' task performance. Forty-eight undergraduates were introduced to hidden-item puzzles by the experimenter, who completed the first set with them. Participants

Author Note. Leah Lessard and Andrew Grossman, Department of Psychological Sciences, University of San Diego, CA; Maggie L. Syme, Department of Psychology, San Diego State University, CA.

Correspondence concerning this manuscript should be addressed to Leah Lessard, Department of Psychological Sciences, University of San Diego, San Diego, CA 92110. E-mail: leahmlessard@sandiego.edu

[1]We acknowledge that the term *gender* refers to the social role of an individual and that the term *sex* refers to the biological characteristics of an individual. To stay consistent with the relevant developmental and learning literature, *gender* was used in the text when referring to men and women.

were then given 1 min to work on a similar task. Upon completion, they were given either person praise or process praise from the experimenter. After receiving the praise, participants completed a final set of 6 puzzles, which served as the dependent measure. The results indicated that participants who received process praise (M = 8.08, SD = 3.04) significantly outperformed those who received person praise (M = 6.54, SD = 1.56), $F(1, 44) = 5.00$, $p = .03$, $\eta^2 = .10$. However, there was no significant effect for gender and no interaction between type of praise and gender. These findings suggested that process praise may be an effective method of improving academic performance in undergraduate students. Implications for classroom practice and the need for further research that considers longitudinal designs and larger sample sizes are discussed.

Despite the fact that the United States is considered to be a world power, when compared globally, American students rank 25th in math and 14th in reading (Jones, 2010). Clearly, even in our achievement-based society, our students are not up to par. As adults and educators, it is our responsibility to provide the best possible education for children and do all that we can to set them up for academic success. However, many commonly used practices may actually deter students from reaching their potential by affecting their motivation and mindset for learning. Teaching strategies intended to enhance learning can cause students to develop maladaptive self-theories about the nature of intelligence, ultimately hindering the learning process and contributing to gender and racial achievement gaps (Aronson & Steele, 2005).

Why do some students quit at the slightest confrontation with difficulty, when others persevere despite all odds against their success? Students who give up easily may have extrinsic motivation, meaning they are driven by external forces or controls (Henderlong & Lepper, 2002). On the other hand, students who work through challenges may possess intrinsic motivation, which can be defined as engagement due to inner gratification. These students are motivated to master educational tasks for the value of learning itself, rather than for a high grade, accolades, or some other extrinsic reward. Intrinsic motivation has been shown to have many positive outcomes including persistence, creativity, and academic achievement (Henderlong & Lepper, 2002).

Epistemological beliefs of intelligence have similarly been shown to influence academic achievement (Mueller & Dweck, 1998). Specifically, if an individual has an entity view of intelligence (i.e., fixed mindset), they believe that intelligence is an unchanging characteristic and are more likely to think effort plays little to no role in outcome. Students with fixed mindsets are more likely to develop a fear of failure (Kamins & Dweck, 1999; Mueller & Dweck, 1998), resulting in the avoidance of intellectual tasks, (Elliott & Dweck, 1988) and giving up in the face of difficulty (Dweck, 1999). The rationale is that effort is unnecessary if individuals are smart because everything should come easy, and if individuals are not smart, hard work cannot compensate for this deficiency.

On the other hand, students who believe that intelligence is adjustable have an incremental view of intelligence (i.e., growth mindset). Students with this growth mindset believe that intelligence is the result of hard work and the use of appropriate strategies. Rather than giving up in the face of failure or challenge, those with a growth mindset interpret setbacks as inevitable for learning to take place. Because they are not worried that exertion of effort is a reflection of lack of intelligence, they are not afraid to work hard, resulting in a superior performance compared to their fixed mindset peers (Dweck, 2007). To illustrate, Blackwell, Trzesniewski, and Dweck (2007) found that, even after 2 years, students with an incremental view of intelligence academically outperformed students with an entity view of intelligence.

It is clear that intrinsic motivation and the development of an incremental view of intelligence are critical to achievement, but where do these conceptions come from? One factor that is controllable and has been shown to be influential is the type of praise that students receive (Hattie, 2003; Hattie & Timperley, 2007). Verbal praise is often administered as a way to reinforce the performance or behavior of students. Although there may be positive intentions, some types of praise can have debilitating effects for the recipient, specifically depending on what the praise is directed toward. For example, person praise focuses on the individuals themselves, similar to an affirmation of self-worth such as, "Wow, you're so smart." Because it applauds the individual by applying a label or an unchangeable characteristic, person praise promotes an entity view of intelligence (Pomerantz & Kempner, 2013). Students are being rewarded, through praise, for their performance based on their ability. On the other hand, process praise focuses on the actions taken by the individual, especially their effort and problem solving strategies such as, "Great job! You're working really hard." Process praise reinforces the association between success and effort (or behavior) rather than a fixed ability, which cultivates a more adaptive, incremental view of intelligence.

Significant research has linked person praise with a fixed mindset and process praise with a growth mindset. Mueller and Dweck (1998) randomly assigned fifth graders to receive either person or process praise while they solved a set of progressive matrices. The researchers found that those who were given person praise had worse task performance, made more low-ability attributions, reported less task enjoyment, and exhibited less task persistence than children who were given process praise. Additionally, the children given person praise were more focused on performance goals and described intelligence as a fixed trait. This is in contrast to the children given process praise, who were more focused on learning goals and described intelligence as a fluid concept.

Type of praise not only affects immediate behaviors, beliefs, and emotions, but it has also been shown to have long-term consequences. Specifically, it affects how individuals deal with future difficulties and their willingness to apply effort to challenges that may come their way (Cimpian, Arce, Markman, & Dweck, 2007; Corpus & Lepper, 2007; Dweck, 1999; Henderlong & Lepper, 2002; Pomerantz & Kempner, 2013). For example, Kamins and Dweck (1999) showed that person praise is more likely to promote helpless responses to subsequent failures than process praise.

It is important to note that type of praise is not a clear-cut predictor of performance. The individual giving the praise, the recipient's beliefs, and other contextual factors also need to be taken into account and can play a significant role in the strength of the effect (Maclellan, 2005). Brummelman and colleagues (2014) found that adults are more inclined to give person praise to children whom they perceive to have low self-esteem and give process praise to children whom they perceive to have high self-esteem. The gender of the individual receiving the praise might also be an important characteristic. Research exploring the effect of gender, however, is somewhat conflicting. Koestner, Zuckerman, and Koestner (1989) found that the performance of fifth- and sixth-grade boys was enhanced on a hidden-figure task when they were given person praise, whereas the performance of their female peers was enhanced by process praise. In their meta-analysis, Henderlong and Lepper (2002) reported the results of Henderlong's unpublished doctoral dissertation work with upper-elementary students, indicating that process praise enhanced intrinsic motivation in all children, whereas person praise decreased intrinsic motivation in girls and did not significantly affect boys. Thus, the way in which gender interacts with praise to affect motivation and performance remains in question.

The majority of the research conducted on the effects of praise has focused on school-aged children, and little is known about whether the influences remain consistent in young adulthood. The few studies that have involved the undergraduate population have suggested that a similar effect exists. However the findings remain inconsistent. Hancock (2000) examined the impact of praise on the amount of time college students spent on homework. The results showed that those who were given verbal praise by their professors spent significantly more time on their homework than those that did not receive any praise. The students who received praise also outperformed their peers on the final exam. Nevertheless, the study did not differentiate between types of praise. Haimovitz and Corpus (2011) found that, among undergraduate students, process praise increased intrinsic motivation and perceived competence, whereas person praise decreased overall academic motivation. Koestner, Zuckerman, and Koestner (1987) asked undergraduate students to complete a set of hidden-item puzzles after receiving person praise, process praise, or no praise by the experimenters. The results showed that participants who received process praise spent significantly more time playing with hidden-item puzzles during a solitary free-choice period than those who received person praise or no praise at all. These studies suggested that praise, specifically process praise, may be an effective strategy for enhancing performance in undergraduates.

The present study expanded upon past findings to explore how gender and type of praise (person vs. process) affected young adults' performance on a hidden-item puzzle task. To isolate the effect of praise on task performance and avoid the potential confounds of prior exposure and ability, the hidden-item puzzle task was chosen as the dependent measure. As a characteristic effort task, trying harder should improve performance on hidden-item puzzles (Baumeister, Hutton, & Cairns, 1990).

By investigating the role of gender, we hoped to shed more light on the gender gap in achievement and learn about contextual factors involved in praise. Consistent with the literature regarding the effect of type of praise on children, we hypothesized significantly higher task performance following process praise as compared to person praise. We expected to observe no gender difference in task performance, a finding that has been substantiated by past research (Butler & Nisan, 1986; Pintrich & de Groot, 1990). Finally, we also predicted an interaction between type of praise and gender, such that process praise would be significantly more effective for women than men. The results have important implications for the classroom environment and suggest pedagogical techniques to improve students' learning.

Methods

Participants

This study involved 48 undergraduate students from a small private university in southern California. There were 24 (50%) women and 24 (50%) men enrolled in the study. Their ages ranged from 18 to 25 ($M = 20.96, SD = 1.44$). Most students were White ($n = 34$, 70.8%) and upper-middle class ($n = 19$, 39.6%), but a range of race/ethnicities and socioeconomic backgrounds were represented (34 White, 4 Asian, 4 Hispanic or Latino, 3 Black, 2 multi racial, 1 Middle Eastern). The sample of students included a range of student achievement levels and academic majors. Participants were recruited either from the introductory psychology participant pool or through informal advertisement of the study in on-campus dormitories. Six (12.5%) were from the introductory psychology pool, and received course credit for their participation. Otherwise, no incentives were offered to participants.

Measures

Demographic questionnaire. Participants were asked to self-report their birth date, the current date, their gender, race/ethnicity, annual household income, grade, major, and GPA on a questionnaire developed by the researchers.

Nina puzzles. Several related studies have used Nina puzzles as a measure of intrinsic motivation and task performance of undergraduates (e.g., Harackiewicz, 1979; Koestner et al., 1987). The puzzles are a compilation of 10 cartoon style hidden-item drawings by artist Al Hirschfeld. In each of the drawings, the word *Nina* is hidden anywhere from 2 to 40 times. To measure task performance, for each of the pictures, the participants are asked to circle the word *Nina* as many times as they can find it. A high number of *Nina's* circled is indicative of higher performance.

Design

The present study employed an experimental, between-subjects design to examine the effect of different types of praise and participant gender on task performance. To eliminate the potential confound that type of praise may have different effects when elicited by the opposite gender, we gender-matched the experimenter and participant, such that a female experimenter tested a female participant, and vice versa. This design was also conducted by Baumeister et al. (1990). Participants were randomly assigned within gender to receive either person praise or process praise by a gender-matched experimenter. Person praise was operationalized as, "Great! You are really good at these!" Process praise was operationalized as, "Great! You are really working hard!" The outcome variable of task performance was operationalized as the score on the Nina puzzles. Gender was self-reported by participants on the demographics questionnaire.

Procedure

All procedures in this study were approved by the Institutional Review Board of the University of San Diego. To ensure gender congruency, a female experimenter met individually with female participants, and a male experimenter met individually with male participants. The experimenters were peers of the participants and were aware of the study's hypotheses.

First, participants were asked to give informed consent and then filled out a demographics questionnaire. The experimenter then introduced the Nina puzzle task and assisted the participant in solving two practice Nina puzzles to ensure understanding. The participant was then given two additional puzzles and asked to find and circle as many *Nina* words as possible over the course of 1 min. After the minute passed, in the *person praise* condition, the experimenter stated, "Great! You are really good at these!" In the *process praise* condition, the experimenter stated, "Great! You are working really hard!" For both conditions, the feedback was in reference to the participants' performance solving the Nina puzzles thus far. Finally, for the dependent measure, the experimenter gave the participant a set of six Nina puzzles to solve, instructing him or her to find and circle as many Nina words as possible in 3 min. Once this was complete, the experimenter debriefed the participant as to the actual purpose of the study. The total number of *Nina's* circled by the participant across the six puzzles was subsequently counted by the experimenter, representing the outcome variable of interest.

Results

A 2 × 2 Analysis of Variance was conducted to test the effects of two different types of praise and gender on task performance in undergraduate students. It was hypothesized that students given process praise would perform significantly better than students given person praise. We predicted no significant gender differences on task performance. Additionally, it was hypothesized that task performance of those in the different praise conditions would differ by gender.

The results confirmed the first hypothesis, yielding a main effect for type of praise, such that the average number of *Nina's* found across the final set of puzzles was significantly higher for participants who received process praise (M = 8.08, SD = 3.04) than for those who received person praise (M = 6.54, SD = 1.56), $F(1, 44) = 5.00$, $p = .03$, $\eta^2 = .10$. Effect size of these differences indicated that 10% of the difference in the number of Nina's the participants found was due to the type of praise they received. The second hypothesis related to gender effects was similarly confirmed because no significant difference in task performance between genders was found, $F(1,44) = 2.66$, $p = .11$, $\eta^2 = .06$.

In addition to the main effects of type of praise and gender, this study also examined the interaction between type of praise and gender.

It was hypothesized that both genders would perform similarly when receiving person praise, but that women would perform significantly better than men when receiving process praise. The means and standard deviations for task performance as a function of type of praise and gender are presented in Table 1. The interaction effect was found to be not significant, $F(1, 44) = 0.30, p = .59, \eta^2 = .01$, indicating that type of praise had a similar effect on men and women.

Discussion

In the present study, we explored the effect of person and process praise, as well as gender, on task performance in young adults. We hypothesized that individuals who received process praise would perform significantly better on the Nina puzzle task than those who had received person praise. Our research findings were consistent with this hypothesis. The results also confirmed our expectation of no differences between men and women on task performance. We also predicted that gender differences would contribute to the effect of praise. However, the data collected failed to support this hypothesis.

In the broadest sense, our results were consistent with Hancock (2000), suggesting that praise does influence the performance of young adults. However, our findings extended this work, suggesting that there is more to this concept of positive reinforcement with the effect of praise being significantly dependent upon the type of praise given.

Consistent with the many studies conducted with children (Corpus & Lepper, 2007; Kamins & Dweck, 1999; Mueller & Dweck, 1998), the superior effects of process praise, compared to person praise, appeared to continue along the developmental trajectory into young adulthood. Similarly, Haimovitz and Corpus (2011) found that, when studying undergraduates, process praise increased intrinsic motivation and perceived competence, whereas person praise decreased students' motivation. These results, along with our own findings, supported the basic tenets of Dweck and colleagues' theory of attribution, motivation, and achievement (Blackwell et al., 2007; Dweck, 2007; Henderlong & Lepper, 2002; Kamins & Dweck, 1999; Mueller & Dweck, 1998; Pomerantz & Kempner, 2013).

Undergraduate students in this study receiving process praise might have attributed their successes to the controllable factor that they were praised for, effort. It is likely that they acted in accordance with this belief by responding to challenge by increasing effort, resulting in superior task performance. In contrast, students receiving person praise might have attributed their successes or failures to a fixed variable or unchangeable trait. This might have resulted in less motivation to work hard because the person praised participants believed the outcome was out of their hands (Weiner, 2010).

The lack of interaction between type of praise and gender in our results conflicted with past findings that task performance and intrinsic motivation is significantly more enhanced for women after receiving process praise than for men (Koestner et al., 1987; 1989). In their work with undergraduates, Haimovitz and Corpus (2011) reported a marginally significant interaction of gender and type of praise in terms of intrinsic motivation, suggesting that process praise was especially beneficial for women. Our failure to replicate similar results may be explained by our small sample size or other dependent variables such as time spent on the task, which might be more sensitive to gender differences. We suggest that future research conduct a power analysis to explore whether a larger sample size might reveal a clearer pattern and clarify this discrepancy.

In the real world, individuals often receive praise from the opposite gender. Thus, more ecologically valid classroom research is needed to explore whether gender congruency between the individual offering the praise and the recipient of the praise influences the effect of type of praise. Further research should examine how contextual features such as the gender, age, and familiarity of the individual offering praise impact the effect of type of praise. If contextual features are found to mediate the effect of praise type, then this would have important implications for feedback procedures in the classroom.

The results of our study have been limited by the fact that the participants may not be representative of the larger population of undergraduate students. Although this study utilized an experimental design with random assignment, the participants were recruited from a very specific population (e.g., most were White, upper middle class students), representing little demographic diversity. Therefore, our findings can only be generalized to a similarly limited population. Future research should explore the possibility of a larger and more diverse sample of participants, which may display stronger trends with conclusions that can be more confidently applied across settings. Additionally, it is important to address the dependent measure used. Although hidden-item puzzle tasks, particularly *Nina's,* have been used in the past as an indicator of task performance (Baumeister et al., 1990), a more comprehensive measure, clearly indicative of academic performance is recommended as a way to capture the variable of interest.

Table 1 MEANS AND STANDARD DEVIATIONS FOR TASK PERFORMANCE

GENDER	PRAISE TYPE	*M (SD)*
Female	Person	6.92 (1.78)
	Process	8.83 (3.13)
Male	Person	6.17 (1.27)
	Process	7.33 (2.87)

Because the experimenters were not naive to the study's hypotheses, it is possible that the process praise was delivered more enthusiastically or believably than the person praise. However, to control for this as much as possible, and to avoid any potentially influential spontaneous conversation, the experimenters followed a script. Future research should involve blind experimenters to reduce bias.

Perhaps the most significant limitation was the single session intervention. Although our procedure did reveal that just a few minor words have the power to influence participants' performance, we measured the effect immediately after the feedback was provided. Would students who were praised for their effort outperform their counterparts who were praised for their skill over a long-term period? How does this effect hold up across domains (e.g., classroom, homework)? Knowing whether performance is affected by type of praise, and also how strongly this effect pervades educational outcomes, would be valuable for research on achievement motivation and contribute to educators' ability to provide the most optimal learning environment for students.

Despite these significant limitations, this study provided important insight into a population that has been, for the most part, omitted from the large body of research on the effects of praise. Because our results were generally consistent with the findings on children, it is likely that the praise young adults receive everyday is shaping their performance in a variety of areas. Specifically, process praise contributes to a mastery learning orientation (Kamins & Dweck, 1999; Pomerantz & Kempner, 2013), whereas person praise not only harms long-term academic performance, but is also associated with shame, lower self-esteem, and lower intrinsic motivation (Brummelman et al., 2014; Heyman, 2008). If these malleable factors play such a significant role in achievement, then educators do students a disservice by offering them feedback based on fixed characteristics, or those that could be perceived as fixed. Rather, our findings suggested that an effective way to maximize performance would be to extend process praise to students immediately before they begin a task. Ultimately, educators should be mindful of the underlying messages they are communicating when offering praise to their students.

References

Aronson, J., & Steele, C. M. (2005). Stereotypes and the fragility of academic competence, motivation, and self-concept. In A. J. Elliot & C. S. Dweck (Eds.), *Handbook of competence and motivation* (pp. 436–456). New York, NY: Guilford Press.

Baumeister, R. F., Hutton, D. G., & Cairns, K. J. (1990). Negative effects of praise on skilled performance. *Basic and Applied Social Psychology, 11,* 131–148. doi:10.1207/s15324834basp1102_2

Blackwell, L. S., Trzesniewski, K. H., & Dweck, C. S. (2007). Implicit theories of intelligence predict achievement across an adolescent transition: A longitudinal study and an intervention. *Child Development, 78,* 246–263. doi:10.1111/j.1467-8624.2007.00995.x

Brummelman, E., Thomaes, S., Overbeek, G., Orobio de Castro, B., van den Hout, M. A., & Bushman, B. J. (2014). On feeding those hungry for praise: Person praise backfires in children with low self-esteem. *Journal of Experimental Psychology: General, 143,* 9–14. doi:10.1037/a0031917

Butler, R., & Nisan, M. (1986). Effects of no feedback, task-related comments, and grades on intrinsic motivation and performance. *Journal of Educational Psychology, 78,* 210–216. doi:10.1037/0022-0663.78.3.210

Cimpian, A., Arce, H. C., Markman, E. M., & Dweck, C. S. (2007). Subtle linguistic cues affect children's motivation. *Psychological Science, 18,* 314–316. doi:10.1111/j.1467-9280.2007.01896.x

Corpus, J. H., & Lepper, M. R. (2007). The effects of person versus performance praise on children's motivation: Gender and age as moderating factors. *Educational Psychology, 27,* 487–508. Retrieved from http://www.reed.edu/motivation/docs/Corpus_Lepper_07.pdf

Dweck, C. S. (1999). Caution—Praise can be dangerous. *American Educator, 23,* 4–9. Retrieved from https://www.aft.org/pdfs/americaneducator/spring1999/PraiseSpring99.pdf

Dweck, C. S. (2007). The perils and promises of praise. *Educational Leadership, 65,* 34–39. Retrieved from http://www.ascd.org/publications/educational-leadership/oct07/vol65/num02/The-Perils-and-Promises-of-Praise.aspx

Elliott, E. S., & Dweck, C. S. (1988). Goals: An approach to motivation and achievement. *Journal of Personality and Social Psychology, 54,* 5–12. doi:10.1037/0022-3514.54.1.5

Haimovitz, K., & Corpus, J. H. (2011). Effects of person versus process praise on student motivation: Stability and change in emerging adulthood. *Educational Psychology, 31,* 595–609. doi:10.1080/01443410.2011.585950

Hancock, D. R. (2000). Impact of verbal praise on college students' time spent on homework. *Journal of Educational Research, 93,* 384–389. doi:10.1080/00220670009598733

Harackiewicz, J. M. (1979). The effects of reward contingency and performance feedback on intrinsic motivation. *Journal of Personality and Social Psychology, 37,* 1352–1363. doi:10.1037/0022-3514.37.8.1352

Hattie, J. (2003, October). *Teachers make a difference: What is the research evidence?* Paper presented at the Australian Council for Educational Research Conference, Melbourne, Australia.

Hattie, J., & Timperley, H. (2007). The power of feedback. *Review of Educational Research, 77,* 81–112. doi:10.3102/003465430298487

Henderlong, J., & Lepper, M. R. (2002). The effects of praise on children's intrinsic motivation: A review and synthesis. *Psychological Bulletin, 128,* 774–795. doi:10.1037/0033-2909.128.5.774

Heyman, G. D. (2008). Talking about success: Implications for achievement motivation. *Journal of Applied Developmental Psychology, 29,* 361–370. Retrieved from http://www.ncbi.nlm.nih.gov/pmc/articles/PMC2605085/

Jones, B. (2010, December 7). In ranking, U.S. students trail global leaders. *USA Today.* Retrieved from http://www.usatoday.com/news/education/2010-12-07-us-students-international-ranking_N.htm

Kamins, M. L., & Dweck, C. S. (1999). Person versus process praise and criticism: Implications for contingent self-worth and coping. *Developmental Psychology, 35,* 835–847. doi:10.1037/0012-1649.35.3.835

Koestner, R., Zuckerman, M., & Koestner, J. (1987). Praise, involvement, and intrinsic motivation. *Journal of Personality and Social Psychology, 53,* 383–390. doi:10.1037/0022-3514.53.2.383

Koestner, R., Zuckerman, M., & Koestner, J. (1989). Attributional focus of praise and children's intrinsic motivation: The moderating role of gender. *Personality and Social Psychology Bulletin, 15,* 61–72. doi:10.1177/0146167289151006

Maclellan, E. (2005). Academic achievement: The role of praise in motivating students. *Active Learning in Higher Education, 6,* 194–206. doi:10.1177/1469787405057750

Mueller, C. M., & Dweck, C. S. (1998). Praise for intelligence can undermine children's motivation and performance. *Journal of Personality and Social Psychology, 75,* 33–52. doi:10.1037/0022-3514.75.1.33

Pintrich, P. R., & de Groot, E. V. (1990). Motivational and self-regulated learning components of classroom academic performance. *Journal Of Educational Psychology, 82,* 33–40. doi:10.1037/0022-0663.82.1.33

Pomerantz, E. M., & Kempner, S. G. (2013). Mothers' daily person and process praise: Implications for children's theory of intelligence and motivation. *Developmental Psychology, 49,* 2040–2046. doi:10.1037/a0031840

Weiner, B. (2010). The development of an attribution-based theory of motivation: A history of ideas. *Educational Psychologist, 45,* 28–36. doi:10.1080/00461520903433596

For Analysis

1. Construct a reverse outline of this article. How does this reading compare to the Research Article template described in Appendix B?
2. Which claims do the authors support with verifications (outside sources)?
3. How do the authors *qualify* their conclusions? Do those qualifications make their research more or less credible?

For Writing

The writers suggest several possibilities for future research. Select one of their suggestions or identify another focus and develop a research proposal.

To begin, work in small groups to brainstorm a list of research questions you would like to investigate related to this topic. Then, list possible research methods and procedures (such as surveys, observations, interviews) that you could use to answer your research questions. After this initial brainstorming, write a 500-word proposal that persuades your professor that your proposed study is significant and possible. To support your proposal, explain your research questions and methods and incorporate outside sources.

SECTION 3
WHAT'S THE POINT OF GOOD WRITING?

"9 Qualities of Good Writing"
by Ann Handley

Ann Handley has worked as a journalist, editor, and digital marketing consultant. She writes regularly for *Entrepreneur Magazine*, and she coauthored the book *Content Rules: How to Create Killer Blogs, Podcasts, Videos, Ebooks, Webinars (and More) that Engage Customers and Ignite Your Business*. She posted this 2013 blog post about "good writing" on her professional website.

There are two kinds of people: Those who think they can write, and those who think they can't. And, very often, both are wrong.

The truth is, most of us fall somewhere in the middle. We are all capable of producing good writing. Or, at least, *better* writing.

Why does good writing matter? Isn't the best content marketing very often something short, snappy, and non-text? Like Skype's Born Friends video, Lowe's Vines, or Chipotle's haunting video commentary?

Sometimes, yes. But here I'm not just talking about content in a marketing context. I'm talking about content, *period*.

Text is the backbone of the Web, and it's often the backbone of any content you watch or listen to, as well. That Born Friends video started with a story and a script.

> **Words matter. Your words (what you say) and style (how you say it) are your most cherished (and undervalued) assets.**

Yet, so often, they are overlooked. Think of it this way: If a visitor came to your website without its branding in place (logo, tagline, and so on), would he or she recognize it as yours? Are you telling your story there from your unique perspective, with a voice and style that's clearly all you?

Here, in no particular order, is what I've learned about the necessary qualities of good writing (or content, in our digital vernacular), based on my own 25 years' working as a writer and editor. . . and even longer career as a reader.

1. Good writing anticipates reader questions. Good writing serves the reader, not the writer. It isn't indulgent. "The reader doesn't turn the page because of a hunger to applaud," said longtime writing teacher Don Murray. Rather, good writing anticipates what questions readers will have as they read a piece, and (before they ask them) it answers them.

That means most good writers are natural skeptics, especially regarding their own work. They relentlessly think of things from their reader's point of view: *What experience is this creating for the reader? What questions might they have?*

(I did this above, when, before listing the qualities of good writing, I thought, "Why does good writing even matter to you? Why should any of us care?")

George Orwell said the "scrupulous writer" will ask himself at least four questions in every sentence: "*What am I trying to say? What words will express it? What image or idiom will make it clearer? Is this image fresh enough to have an effect?* And he or she will probably ask himself two more: *Could I put it more shortly? Have I said anything that is avoidably ugly?*" (Hat tip to The Economist style guide for that one.)

Here's where marketing can really help add value in a business context, by the way, because "simple" means "making it easy for the customer." It means being the advocate for them. As Georgy Cohen writes, "The marketer should be identifying (and ruthlessly refining) the core messages and the top goals, then working with the web professionals to create a website supporting them."

2. Good writing is grounded in data. Data puts your content in context and gives you credibility. Ground your content in facts: Data, research, fact-checking and curating. Your ideas and opinions and spin might be part of that story—or they might not be, depending on what you are trying to convey. But content that's rooted in something true—not just your own opinions—is more credible.

Said another way: Data before declaration. If you are going to tell me what you think, give me a solid reason why you think it.

3. Good writing is like good teaching. Good writing strives to explain, to make things a little bit clearer, to make sense of our world. . . even if it's just a product description.

"A writer always tries. . . to be part of the solution, to understand a little about life and to pass this on," says Anne Lamott in *Bird by Bird*.

4. Good writing tells a full story. Good writing roots out opposing viewpoints. As Joe Chernov says, "There's a name for something with a single point of view: It's called a press release." Incorporate multiple perspectives when the issue lends itself to that. At the very least, don't ignore the fact that other points of view might exist; to do so makes your reader not trust you.

So make sure he or she knows you're watching out for them. To quote Hemingway: "The most essential gift for a good writer is a built-in, shockproof, shit detector."

5. Good writing comes on the rewrite. That implies that there *is* a rewrite, of course. And there should be.

Writing is hard work, and producing a shitty first draft is often depressing. But the important thing is to get something down to start chipping into something that resembles a coherent narrative.

As Don Murray said, "The draft needs fixing, but first it needs writing." Or Mark Twain: "Writing is easy. All you have to do is cross out the wrong words."

6. Good writing is like math. I mean this in two ways: First, good writing has logic and structure. It feels solid to the reader: The writer is in control and has taken on the heavy burden of shaping a lumpy jumble of thoughts into something clear and accessible.

It might not follow a formula, exactly. But there's a kind of architecture to it. Good writing has more logic to it than you might think.

Second, good writing is inherently teachable—just as trigonometry or algebra or balancing a balance sheet is a skill any of us can master. Journalism professor Matt Waite writes in his essay, *How I Faced My Fears and Learned to Be Good at Math*: "The difference between good at math and bad at math is hard work. It's trying. It's trying hard. It's trying harder than you've ever tried before. That's it."

I think the same is true about writing. Ta-Nehisi Coates, a senior editor at *The Atlantic*, spent a year teaching writing to MIT students. He later wrote, "I felt that the rigor of math had better prepared these kids for the rigor of writing. One of my students insisted that whereas in math you could practice and get better, in writing you either 'had it' or you didn't. I told her that writing was more like math then she suspected."

7. Good writing is simple, but not simplistic. Business—like life—can be complicated. Products can be involved or concepts may seem impenetrable. But good content deconstructs the complex to make it easily understood: It sheds the corporate Frankenspeak and conveys things in human, accessible terms. A bit of wisdom from my journalism days: *No one will ever complain that you've made things too simple to understand.*

"Simple" does not equal "dumbed-down." Another gem from my journalism professors: *Assume the reader knows nothing. But don't assume the reader is stupid.*

If you think your business-to-business concept is too complex to be conveyed simply, take a look at the very first line of *The Economist's style guide*: "The first requirement of *The Economist* is that it should be readily understandable. Clarity of writing usually follows clarity of thought. So think what you want to say, then say it as simply as possible."

8. Good writing doesn't get hung up on what's been said before. Rather, it elects to simply say it better. Here's where style be a differentiator—in literature and on your website.

Mark Twain described how a good writer treats sentences: "At times he may indulge himself with a long one, but he will make sure there are no folds in it, no vaguenesses, no parenthetical interruptions of its view as a whole; when he has done with it, it won't be a sea-serpent with half of its arches under the water; it will be a torch-light procession." He also might've said: "Write with clarity and don't be indulgent." But he didn't.

That doesn't mean you need to be a literary genius, of course. It only means you have to hone your own unique perspective and voice.

9. A word about writers: Good writers aren't smug. Most of the really good writers I know still feel a little sheepish calling themselves a "writer," because that's a term freighted with thick tomes of excellence. But like many achievements in life—being called a success, or a good parent—the label seems more meaningful when it's bestowed upon you by others.

"Most of the time I feel stupid, insensitive, mediocre, talentless and vulnerable—like I'm about to cry any second—and wrong. I've found that when that happens, it usually means I'm writing pretty well, pretty deeply, pretty rawly." —Andre Dubus III (*House of Sand and Fog*)

BONUS: Good writing has a good editor. Writers get the byline and any glory. But behind the scenes, a good editor adds a lot to process.

Remember what I said above about there being two kinds of people? Those who think they can write, and those who think they can't? And very often, both being wrong? A good editor teases the best out of so-called writers and non-writers alike.

The best writing—like the best parts of life, perhaps—is collaborative.

And by the way, is it odd that I'm seeding what's essentially business advice with insight from artists? And if so, why is that odd?

Because in a world where we have an opportunity and responsibility to tell our stories online, we need to find not just the right words... but the very best ones.

For Analysis

1. How does Handley introduce her sources? Is the information she provides sufficient to establish their credibility?
2. Which of her "rules" do you think apply to scholarly writing? Which would not? Why?
3. Compare three of Handley's rules with the guidance we provide in this book. How does our advice reinforce or contradict hers?

For Writing

How well does Handley follow her own advice for "good writing"? Write a one-page analysis that includes specific examples of how she obeys or breaks her own rules.

"Will We Use Commas in the Future?"

by Matthew J.X. Malady

Matthew J.X. Malady is a columnist for *Slate* magazine who also writes for *The AWL* and holds degrees in journalism and law. Malady has served as an editor for the *Columbia Law School Magazine*, *AVENUE* magazine, and *Strong* magazine. He has also written for *The New Yorker*, *The New Republic*, *The New York Times*, and other publications. This article from *Slate* was published on January 28, 2014.

There's no denying that commas are helpful little flecks of punctuation. They allow us to separate written clauses and do good work when especially numerous or complicated groups of things exist in a single sentence. But do we really *need* them?

That's a trickier question.

In some ways commas are like ketchup and mustard. We're glad those things exist. They surely make our french fries and hamburgers taste better. But we'd all survive without them. Some assert that the same is true of commas. Linguist and Columbia University professor John McWhorter suggests we "could take [the commas out of] a great deal of modern American texts and you would probably suffer so little loss of clarity that there could even be a case made for not using commas at all."

That may sound crazy to folks who bristle at Oxford comma problems or enjoy pointing out that life without commas could result in lots of sentences like "let's eat grandma." But support for McWhorter's contention isn't tough to unearth. We needn't look any further than our beloved cellphones and computer screens. We're dropping commas more than ever because so much of our daily writing now consists of quick text messages and hastily typed emails. We're also engaging in frequent IM discussions and drafting lots of sub-140-character tweets. Commas don't thrive in those environs.

Here's one recent example from social media: Last week Gmail crapped out for about 50 minutes. So people took to Twitter for the purpose of gabbing about it. And many folks in my feed did so without using commas. One *New Yorker* writer went with: "**ok gmail is down we can just use twitter what could go wrong / back to work.**" An editor at *BuzzFeed* tweeted "**whoa whoa guys I can't respond to all zero gmails at once.**" Writer and biographer Rachel Syme joked about causing the problem: "**I rubbed my genie lamp and wished for one of those Freedom programs that keeps you from email but I wished TOO BIG sorry guys sorry.**" And writer Jen Doll capped off the Gfail afternoon with this: "**I guess all those losers outside skiing or like at the movies or whatever missed out on this exciting adventure we just had.**"

Similar comma-less dispatches crop up often in the text-messaging context. University of Michigan English professor and language historian Anne Curzan says that the decreasing use of commas in texts and tweets may be tied to efforts at making communications more stylistically fun and more similar to spoken conversation. She's talked with her students about how they are repurposing punctuation in their day-to-day communications with friends. They tell her the period is being reimagined to signify seriousness or **anger**. And the ellipsis can be used to convey skepticism or sometimes unhappiness about something. But she says the comma doesn't seem to be getting repurposed in texts. It's being purged.

Curzan suspects that's because commas have come to be associated with a more proper and polished approach to writing that doesn't intuitively jibe with forums that aspire to be highly conversational. She says if you use commas in your text messages "in some ways what it signals is that you're being more formal."

It also could signal that you're an old fogey. And it may get you made fun of by your kids. Consider these recent tweets that concern comma usage:

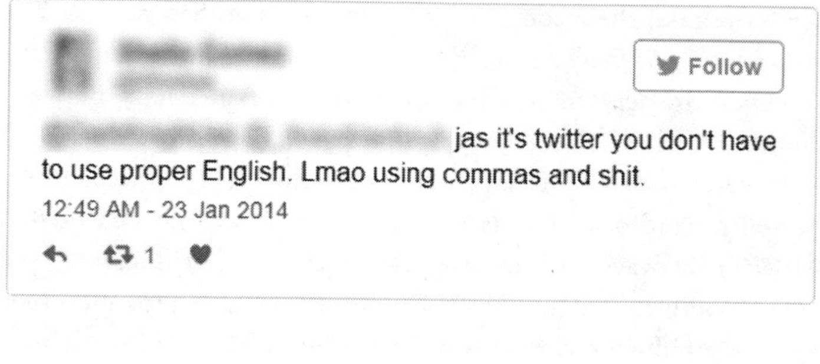

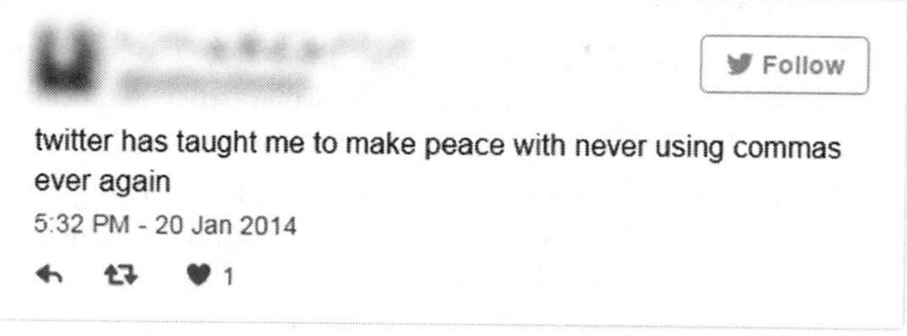

Swearing off commas altogether might be welcomed by the millions who don't feel confident in their usage of the frequently perplexing mark. Commas are tough to master and easy to mess up. There is no universally accepted set of rules for their use. Even the most seemingly straightforward comma guidelines are burdened by exceptions and inconsistencies and caveats. So we often find ourselves devising our own subjective justifications for where to place them.

McWhorter offers the Oxford comma as an example: "Nobody has any reason for [using a comma after the penultimate item in a series] that is scientifically sensible and logical in the sense that we know how hydrogen and oxygen combine to form water.* So these things are just fashions and conventions. They change over time." Curzan adds that whether someone is using commas properly in specific instances is "going to depend on what style guide you use."

Many take their comma cues from William Strunk Jr.'s ***The Elements of Style***. That nearly 100-year-old publication instructs sentence drafters to "enclose parenthetic expressions between commas" and to "place a comma before *and* or *but* introducing an independent clause." It says writers should use a semicolon or a period instead of a comma in that case if there's no *and* or *but*. McWhorter waves off any suggestion that such things are "the rules." He points out that William Strunk "also probably wore spats. He probably also wore a detachable collar. We wouldn't do any of those things now."

McWhorter and Curzan both suggest that the lack of definitive comma guidelines results in a punctuation mark that is especially malleable and prone to use modifications. (There is no similar confusion about when to place a question mark or a period.) And it's not surprising that we're seeing commas being dropped more frequently in the social media and online context during an era when so much of our day-to-day writing attempts to mimic speech or exude a conversational tone. But what might this mean for more formal written pieces? Is it inevitable that 10 or 20 years from now we'll be reading *New York Times* articles that don't include any commas? Will college professors soon be grading compositions devoid of commas because students can't effectively distinguish between the 400 texts they send each day and the essays they need to submit for class?

Signs point to *no*.

Younger students may experience greater difficulty in **separating informal writing from the more formal**. But as we get older we become better equipped to develop and maintain those boundaries. Neither Curzan nor McWhorter have noticed their current students dropping commas from formal writing assignments more often than those in the past. And a recently published study examining texting's impact on college-level writing concluded that "university students recognise the different requirements of different recipients and modalities when considering textism use and that **students are able to**

avoid textism use in exams despite media reports to the contrary." (*Textism* is their word for the language of texting.)

That finding makes perfect sense to McWhorter. He says that Americans have become accustomed to an English language that doesn't vary widely by region or over time. So we may expect that people will struggle to use two different forms of the same language. "There's this sense that if there's something colloquial and spontaneous and non-standard the proper question to ask is what's going to happen to the standard [form]." He adds that we shouldn't be surprised when someone who sends hundreds of texts each day is able to "write a paper about Walt Whitman that weekend and knows where to put their commas." And that dual approach to comma usage may be "exactly the way it's going to stay." In other words: One realm doesn't have to engulf the other just because they are different.

But some of the most talented and engaging young writers are pushing those boundaries on purpose. Here are a few sentences that appear near the end of a brutally honest and introspective *Brooklyn Magazine* essay that Edith Zimmerman recently wrote about lifestyle changes: "Although I really want to tell you about this white noise machine I just got!!!!!!!!!!! No but it seriously has changed my life!!! hahahah I don't even know if I'm joking or not!!! **I mean I am but also it really has changed my life.**" Writer Mary H.K. Choi recently published a piece in the *Awl* on SoulCycle that was drafted to be highly conversational. It is evocative of the sort of thing one might read on Facebook. Choi uses commas in places. But it's immediately clear when reading the essay that there's something atypical about its form and style. She writes at one point: **"It's gross but I don't care because I need it and I love it (ha ha so gross)."** Then later in the piece: "The main things to remember is hand placement on the handlebars and each class includes a series of push ups on the bars but they're the wussiest of all wuss-ass push-ups since it's a tiny movement."

Those sentences do not represent Choi forgetting she's not on social media. The piece is different and conversational and fun. It may not be to everyone's taste. And it's unlikely that you'd find something like it in ***Slate***. But I wouldn't say it's confusing. And you don't really miss the commas.

Three of 13 commenters on the piece nonetheless went off on Choi. One asked if the writer was 12. Another wrote: "Did a very long facebook post somehow get published as an article. PROTIP when you write like this you sound ridiculous. Ha ha. Sorreee. Happy New Year!"

The criticisms seem more tied to style preferences than concerns about a lack of clarity. But they lead to an interesting question: What if that style became the norm in all writing environments and we got rid of commas altogether? Curzan notes that the result would not be without its associated challenges: "We know there would be problems. Lists need commas. Lots of clauses in a row benefit from commas." That is undeniably true. But she adds that we're pretty creative and capable when it comes to dealing with such language issues. It's possible that we'd simply come up with some other way to avoid confusion in those cases. Problem solved. Sort of.

Getting rid of commas wouldn't sit well with those who prefer traditional methods of doing things and aesthetic consistency over time. It wouldn't be your cup of tea if you hate socks that don't match or noticed before right now that this piece has yet to include a single comma.

"Let's say everybody wore their socks mismatched," posits McWhorter. "Well, you know, it wouldn't look great, to the extent that we look at anybody's feet anyway. But it would be very hard to say that it was creating any kind of problem. Now, of course, a certain smarty-pants kind of person could come up with some situation where somebody's mismatched socks really did create some sort of social misunderstanding. And it would be just that one thing. Really, the world would keep spinning. And I think it's the same thing with commas."

For Analysis

1. Does Malady use more evidence or verification to support his argument? What are some examples of these supports?
2. Malady suggests that punctuation usage, like fashion, changes over time. Do you think punctuation should change over time? What are the implications of such changes?
3. In what ways, if any, do your informal writing practices (texting, social media posts) influence your formal writing practices (like school or work assignments)? Have you noticed ways that your peers' informal writing affects their formal writing?

For Writing

Malady discloses that his article doesn't contain a single comma (beyond those that appear in quotations). Select two paragraphs and revise several sentences to add commas. Then, share your paragraphs with a peer and discuss the following: What specific changes did you make when adding commas? How did the style change by adding commas? Which version of the paragraphs do you prefer, and why?

"Through Glasses Half Full"

by Kurt Schick

Kurt Schick is a professor of writing, rhetoric and technical communication at James Madison University, where he also administers the tutoring centers. Schick has authored articles on teaching and tutoring writing, and he co-edited a teachers' reference book, *A Guide to Composition Pedagogies*. This 2008 article from *The Writing Lab Newsletter* encourages tutors to consider using more generous feedback techniques.

The liveliest writing center listserv discussion in recent memory began with a somewhat innocent posting of a student's "grammar goof" for the amusement of list readers. Astonishingly, the email elicited more than seventy responses. Most contributors added bloopers they'd seen or committed themselves; a few debated whether or not we should mock student writing. Though mostly lighthearted and sometimes comical, what struck me most about the conversation, labeled by the listserv thread's title as "best bad grammar mistakes," was its sheer volume. Why devote so much attention to stylistic or mechanical deficits? Why gaze at student writing through half-empty glasses?

Later that same week, students in our tutor education course displayed similar behavior during a simulated, in-class writing consultation. Acting together, nine students tutored an instructor who'd brought everyone copies of a sample draft. True to "best practices," our neophyte tutors asked their "student" to read her draft aloud as they followed along. Yet despite several weeks spent discussing higher order rhetorical concerns and producing-better-writers-not-(so-much)-better-writing, the tutors-in-training couldn't set down their pens to just listen and read. They couldn't resist the corrective habits passed down to them from their teachers and their teachers' teachers. Happily, the session ended well—students provided plenty of wonderful help regarding substantive issues such as focus and coherence. But I kept wondering:

How much better could they have listened without first nitpicking? What unintended messages might their busy pens send to a student-writer while she nervously reads aloud?

Neither my students nor my colleagues on the listserv were just plain wrong. Writers can obviously learn from having good readers identify weaknesses in their work. Certainly, most of us have done so. But that's only part of how we learned, and perhaps not the best approach for most of the folks who visit our writing centers: developing, often anxious, often struggling student-writers. Instead of deficit-based evaluation that devalues student writing, I propose that we consider alternative means of *ascribing* value through a practice of *valuation* that builds on strengths instead of trying to fix every little deficiency (Note 1).

Old-fashioned classroom *evaluation* enabled teachers to quickly process stacks of student writing by focusing mostly on easily marked defects. Good performance equaled compliance to pre-established rules: correct grammar, spelling and punctuation; clearly stated thesis and topic sentences; proper citations; and so forth. Copious red ink taught many of us, even if subconsciously or against our will, to equate good writing with a checklist of "do nots" that teachers scrupulously enforced and students sheepishly obeyed.

Of course, we're not those old fashioned teachers. As enlightened modern writing consultants, we've broken this cycle of abuse because folks like Donald Murray, Peter Elbow, and Steven North helped re-program our brains to embrace the writing process and the glorious, necessary, inevitable messiness of drafts-in-progress. Still, grammar gaffe discussions linger on, and my tutors still cannot locate the safeties on their error-seeking ink-missiles. We've even developed clever coping mechanisms to hide (or hide from) our affliction. *Don't touch student papers. Don't write on them. Don't hijack them. Lock away your marking missiles. Protect the children!* It's as if we need to save our students from ourselves. (Notice, too, that these negative imperatives fail to teach us what we're supposed to do instead.)

Before we begin to enact more positive practices of valuation, we probably each need to admit that we have a problem: *Hello, my name is Kurt, and I habitually wince at unintended sentence fragments, rogue commas, and essays that begin, "Since the dawn of human civilization. . . ." Some such blunders I really hate, even though I realize how irrational it is to care so much about issues that really don't significantly impede communication. I'm Kurt, and I'm a recovering STYLIST. I sometimes see student writing through half-empty glasses.*

Compulsive deficit-driven evaluation results from *stylism*: ossified bias against violations of written decorum that mostly don't hamper meaning but still bother most folks whose formative writing processes were permanently stained by red ink. (The term "stylism" derives from "style" in its broadest sense, as the sum effect of how a writer conforms to or deviates from conventional rules and expectations. Style, in this sense, can be seen at the level of a sentence or an essay.) Stylism is conservative, even reactionary—slow to change, based in rules already "written," though often not explicitly disclosed. As habituated dogma, stylism can be as irrational and potentially damaging, metaphorically speaking, to budding writers as other discriminatory *-isms* can be to their victims. Stylism jades how we see developing writers and diminishes our expectations for what we might achieve together. Worst of all, like any recalcitrant orientation, stylism is especially insidious because we often don't admit or even realize when we do it.

Just as stylism afflicts us, it infects those students we tutor. A student who recently visited our writing center provides a typical case study. Ashley brought a draft essay for her composition class that had already been through in-class peer review. She asked for help interpreting and implementing her peers' comments, most of which were surface-level quibbles that affected meaning only in minor ways. Ashley said she needed to "fix" those problems first, implying that if she could only mend those deficits, then and only then would her paper be acceptable. *Hello, my name is Ashley, and now they've got ME addicted to correction fluid.*

Like many student writers, Ashley equated "grammar mistakes" with everything from actual grammar errors to problems with syntax, spelling, punctuation, citation, and stylistic *faux pas*. What she wanted from me, then, was a stylism fix—the rush of a quick and easy high (grade), whether or not the effect lasted past her current assignment. Had I given her the quick fix she wanted, I would only have strung her out and reinforced her diminished view of what a good writer she might become.

Since this was Ashley's first visit to the center, I tried to enlarge her idea of what good writing and a good writing process might look like by advocating the kinds of help we could provide, from support with mechanics such as grammar and punctuation to larger issues of structure and coherence, along with assorted revision strategies that we might try, from reading aloud to reverse outlining. By doing this, I hoped to entice her to consider the choices available to her in fuller, more creative terms than a quick fix. Then I asked her how she'd like to proceed, how she thought we ought to spend our time together. Though reluctant to give up on repairing what was wrong (or what her stylist colleagues had found wrong), Ashley agreed to try a more valuative approach: re-building her essay from strengths by first working to improve the structure and coherence of what she already thought was working well.

After she explained the main points of her paper, we read through the essay together. Immediately, I noticed that her introduction—really, her entire first page—seemed weak in content and in style in contrast to the rest of her essay. But I bit my stylist tongue (remember, I'm still recovering) and continued into her body paragraphs, which were more substantive, more cogent, and even more eloquent. Together, we read and built upon those ideas, paragraphs, and sentences, refining and reorganizing, adapting them more deliberately for her intended audience. By the end, she had created—in the remnants of her draft, in her notes, and in her mind—a stronger version that, she began to notice, no longer needed that mediocre first page anymore.

What was weak simply melted away in the process of building on strengths. Of course, I admit that Ashley seems like a terrific student—maybe not *yet* a terrific writer, but someone who's willing, with encouragement, to take risks to learn, not just for the grade. Others who come to our center leave frustrated when we defer their quick fix, or when they leave with a "messier" draft than what they brought. But, oh, what progress Ashley made in a single session, drinking from, and looking through, glasses half-full! What time and effort might we have wasted by dwelling only on what was "wrong"?

The key to Ashley's successful experience was how we began. We deliberately and explicitly decided to free ourselves from stylism's grasp. We resisted our urge to give in to error, to react to our preexisting biases. As recovering correction addicts, Ashley and I needed to negotiate and commit to a plan to keep us both on track, to avoid backsliding so we could concentrate on the larger, more productive issues that really mattered. Correcting errors, we realized, would only have been an easy way out.

Writers who only worry about what's going wrong will likely never become good writers, or at least their growth will likely be much slower, less efficient, and more painful. Building on strengths can be at least as productive, and typically more efficient, than mending weaknesses. Of course, I'm not the first person to come up with a valuative approach to teaching writing. Among others, Peter Elbow proposed a similar method as the "believing game" in *Writing without Teachers*. Admittedly, his ideas first sounded to me as idealistic as my explanation above may sound to you ("What was weak simply melted away. . ."). But instead of hedging my claims, I'll inflate them. I advocate that we use valuation to reframe our perceptions of, and interactions across, an even broader range of learning activities.

In a faculty writing group this semester, a reticent colleague waited until the end of our first peer review session before saying, "Well, now that I know that you're nice, that everyone here wants to value each other's work rather than tear it down, I'm ready to offer my draft to the group." She's not alone. Since I began working with faculty writers, I've been amazed at the ugly scars colleagues across campus bear from brutal editorial lashings received from dissertation readers or journal editors. I'm pleased that our faculty groups can sooth some of those wounds and help scholars re-engage in collaborative writing. But our kinder, gentler writers' groups do more than build confidence. The results are not only affective but also practical; building on the strengths of each other's work has been amazingly productive. One writer, who offered a draft that at first (evaluative) glance seemed to go in a few directions at once, discovered with our valuative help that she actually had two potentially terrific publications already half-done, rather than a single, less coherent manuscript. Another writer, hearing horror stories of his colleagues' editorial rejections responded, "Those aren't failures. Lots of rejections mean you're being productive. You're writing and submitting manuscripts. Many of us can't even get anything together to send out."

Valuation transforms problems into opportunities. Instead of hindering students by slapping their wrists, we might instead reframe our biases in a positive light. For example, we might say: *It's not so much that passive verbs harm readers, really, but punchier active verbs can propel them along through your prose. It's not so much that clichés taste like cardboard; rather, original metaphors and analogies can enable writers to make complex arguments very efficiently, and sometimes even allow us to create new understandings. And complicated citation systems really weren't invented just to frustrate students, but instead to enable scholarly collaboration across time and space.* When we try harder to explain and convince student-writers of the value of these sometimes strange, socially constructed preferences, we increase their chances to integrate these conventions more successfully into their own writing.

We must also remember not to write rules in stone. Absolutes and universals should always make us nervous—as when we hear teachers (or fellow tutors) say things like "*Never* use" first person, or contractions, or clichés, or split infinitives (all of which I've used plenty in this essay)—especially if they fail to provide justification or alternatives as I have tried to do above. As socially contingent preferences, standards for good writing necessarily vary according to the rhetorical particulars of audience, occasion, and purpose. This variation is especially important in writing centers where, on a daily basis, we must value whatever apples, oranges, or kumquats diverse students bring to us from diverse courses, assignments, and disciplines. We need valuation most, perhaps, when dealing with genres and styles from disciplines we know least. Isn't our job to help students discover the distinctive criteria of their disciplinary discourse, or the particulars of each class assignment? Further, we must remember the potentially lasting effects of transforming rules into harmful biases. It's unfair and irrational to equate a few mechanical errors or stylistic *faux pas* with laziness, ignorance, or stupidity. Shouldn't we judge more by content and character?

In practice, valuation works through all stages of the composing process. During invention, we might help students see possibilities in latent questions or lingering experiences they might otherwise discount. In arrangement, we can help writers see fresh order and coherence in a chaotic outline or draft by challenging them to re-sequence their ideas or tease out connections to strengthen transitions. And with sentence-level style, we can encourage students to play with diction, syntax, and figurative expression in ways that provide them with glimpses of their own eloquence. In the final edit, valuation doesn't ignore what's "wrong" but instead asks, *What's an even better way to say that?*

Whereas traditional evaluation makes readers overly comfortable critics, valuation prompts us to imagine possibilities, to allow student-writers to surprise us, and even to enable them to revise what we tutors think good writing ought to be. When we help students see writing as a tool for independent thinking, we invite them to question whatever beliefs they inherited and, alternatively, to suspend disbelief in new alternatives. Similarly, valuation provides a reconstructive path beyond our own worldview, beyond what Jim Corder calls our own "arrogance, ignorance, and dogma" (29). Only by creative estimation and experimentation can we discover and measure alternatives together.

In our struggle to resist the corrective habits of our teachers and our teachers' teachers, we must remember that in the writing center we serve as tutors, as writing consultants. Arguably, classroom teachers need evaluation, mainly because they must assign grades to student essays. Happily enough, we are obliged not to evaluate writing but rather to educate writers (Note 2).

Notes

1. John Dewey defined valuation as a type of imaginative or "creative" judgment that is "concerned with estimating values not in existence and with bringing them into existence" ("Valuation and Experimental Knowledge" 332). I first applied his theories to teaching in a longer, denser article titled "Valuating Academic Writing."
2. I'm indebted to many colleagues for their contributions, including Janet Auten, Beth Browning, Amy Drewes, John Erdos, Ginny Ficker, Dolores Flamiano, Karen McDonnell, Margie Mika, Patti Ro, Cheryl Talley, Mark Thomas, Alicia Wendt, Ashley Wilson, Jim Zimmerman, and Gary Tate.

Works Cited

Corder, Jim W. "Argument as Emergence, Rhetoric as Love." *Rhetoric Review* 4.1 (Sep. 1985): 16–32.

Dewey, John. "Valuation and Experimental Knowledge." *Philosophical Review* 31.4 (Jul. 1922): 325–51.

Elbow, Peter. *Writing without Teachers*. New York: Oxford UP, 1973.

Schick, Kurt. "Valuating Academic Writing." *Teaching Writing: Landmarks and Horizons*. Eds. Rob & Christina McDonald. S. Illinois UP, 2002. 228–49.

For Analysis

1. What inspirations prompted Schick's argument?
2. Schick uses several stylistic techniques to make his writing come alive. Which ones do you notice and appreciate most? Why do these work?
3. Schick supports his argument with several illustrations and examples. Create a reverse outline that lists the article's main points and supports. Then, evaluate the strength of these supports in terms of relevance and sufficiency.

For Writing

Schick describes several implications of his argument for writing tutors. Extend his argument by thinking about the implications for using "valuation" in the classroom. Write a 600- to 800-word proposal for teachers to adopt a framework of valuation. Explain specific benefits of this approach, describe what this principle would look like in practice, and discuss how it would affect your growth as a writer. Use your personal experience as evidence.

"The Art of the Police Report"
by Ellen Collett

Ellen Collett currently works in law enforcement and crime analysis. Her writing has been featured in publications such as *LOST Magazine*, *Utne Reader*, and *The Writer's Chronicle*, which is the source of the following 2011 article about stylistic differences in police writing.

Monday through Friday, I'm enthralled by a man I've never met. His name is Martinez and he's a cop with the Los Angeles Police Department.

Martinez works in crime suppression in South Central L.A. He and his partner, Brown, patrol the streets and respond to scenes-of-crimes. Every incident they investigate generates a written account.

I know Martinez only through his incident reports, as a five-digit number on a sheet of paper. In our precinct's Crime Analysis Division, I read and code hundreds of these reports each day. They are written by every serving officer on roster, and by design most of them sound exactly alike.

Surprisingly, writing is the one constant in a cop's daily life. Whether he's assigned to vice or patrol, working bunco or undercover, every day he'll write. Most precincts have specially designated writing rooms, where the average cop hates spending time—worse than on shoot-outs, stakeouts, and court appearances put together. As with everything in the department, strict rules govern report writing, and as with any dangerous undertaking, the department will train you to do it properly. The most despised class at the police academy is the one that teaches writing. A cadet can't be sworn as a police officer without passing it.

The incident report he'll learn to write is the factual narrative account of a crime—of a rape, robbery, murder, criminal threat, lewd act, vandalism, burglary, sexual molestation, kidnapping, or assault. Every event a cop responds to generates a report.

Crime reports are written in neutral diction, and in the dispassionate uni-voice that's testament to the academy's ability to standardize writing. They feel generated rather than authored, the work of a single law enforcement consciousness rather than a specific human being.

So how can I identify Martinez from a single sentence? Why do his reports make me feel pity, terror, or despair? Make me want to put a bullet in someone's brain—preferably a wife beater's or a pedophile's, but occasionally my own? How does he use words on paper to hammer at my heart? Like all great cops, Sergeant Martinez is a sneaky fucker. He's also a master of inflection and narrative voice.

An incident report tells only what happened: where, when, and to whom. It offers multiple perspectives of the same event from often contradictory points of view of cop, victim, suspect, and witnesses. Even when these accounts agree, no two people see things identically or invest their attention in the same details. Each person's agenda is inherently personal.

An incident report lists the inventory of all physical evidence collected and booked. Anything from shell casings and rape-kit underwear to a three-legged dog in a custody dispute.

In structure, an incident report is a strict chronological narrative. It begins with a Source of Activity section, which tees up the story. It's where the narrator introduces himself and offers his credentials for telling this tale: "On 4-6-10 at approx. 1922 hours, my partner Ofcr. Brown (badge #13312) and I (Ofcr. Martinez badge #14231) were in full uniform traveling westbound on Gage Avenue when we received the radio call of an LUAC in progress at 82nd St./Central Ave."

In the investigation section that follows, the narrator tells briefly what his investigation revealed. He lists the actions taken by himself and his partner, and the facts of the case as discovered. The strict emphasis is on verifiable information.

If versions of the event differ from his, these are recorded as witness statements. These can be summaries, but quotes are often included. The narrative voice at the center of an incident report is always emotionally neutral. He's the ultimate reliable narrator. His sole job is to convince us that everything he tells us is the absolute truth. It all begins with diction.

Cadets are taught to write with care and deliberation, to choose each word for maximum accuracy. Precision, not firepower, is the goal; you don't use a semiautomatic at close range when you're packing a Smith & Wesson. Good cop diction means checking each word in a sentence to verify that it can mean only one thing. The officer must avoid words that carry associations, subtext, or bias.

Officers are encouraged to use action verbs in preference to *is* and *has*. *Is* and *has* speak abstractions—existence and possession, respectively—and where they go, descriptors follow. Action verbs, on the other hand, move us through time and space. "The Subject removed a hammer from the kitchen drawer and struck the Victim three times in the head and neck" is a good sentence. It tells what physically happened without embellishment.

Avoid modifiers, says the academy. Adverbs—words ending in *ly*—are slippery and subjective; they shade reality and opine. Any adverb can be eliminated by choosing a better verb. "The Suspect snatched the Victim's chain and fled" is a sentence without speculation. To know the manner in which the snatching or fleeing transpired would be interpretive.

The academy dislikes adjectives unless they pertain to direction, color, or amount. These are "empirical adjectives." Because they speak to precision of detail, they resist interpretation. "The black Escalade fired 12 shots into the dwelling on 865 Inglewood Avenue" can mean only one thing.

Parenthetically, the two exceptions to the "no adjectives" rule are the words *bloody* and *suspicious*, invoked to justify officer initiative in field investigations. If a suspect "fled while holding his waistband in a *suspicious* manner," it's presumptive of a concealed weapon. If an officer investigates a neighbor complaint and the victim "opened the door wearing *bloody* clothing," there's a pretext to enter and reconnoiter the premises.

These guidelines about diction and story efficiency serve a deeper purpose, which is the legitimizing of the narrative "voice." The police narrator uses neutral language and uninflected storytelling to assure us of his credibility and to win the reader's trust. He never judges.

The perpetrator in a crime report is always the "Suspect," even when 15 witnesses, half of them preachers, see him exit his car and shoot his cousin at point-blank range in a church parking lot. Until a jury reviews the evidence and pronounces, under the law, no crime took place. The police narrator is careful not to imply that he thinks otherwise.

The police narrator further proves his lack of bias by presenting everyone's version of the same event, giving equal space to the "truth" as reported by victim, suspect, and witness. While he might state that DeWayne "aka Baby Insane" Johnson of the Rolling '60s Crips shot and killed J'Marcus "aka L'il Monster" Faye of Florencia Trece, he'll include Baby's explanation that he was merely examining the gun with an eye toward purchase when that muthafucker up and went off. The narrator's job isn't to judge but to relay facts to the best of his ability, and let the reader decide the truth of it.

Words committed to paper have an agenda. The purpose of a police report is to be cited in court as proof of who did what to whom. Its ultimate agenda is justice. It seeks to protect the weak and punish the guilty. Because the stakes are high—freedom, death, or life without parole—it's written with special care. Above all else, it aims to be truthful. At the same time, to do its job, it needs to be convincing. The story it tells should persuade 12 people in a jury box of something.

On the face of it, these two goals—truthful and persuasive—seem uncomfortably at odds. Shouldn't facts alone persuade? Should truth need composing? And assuming that it's possible to write toward this goal—to be truthful and persuasive at once—shouldn't all fiction writers want to learn how?

Which brings us back to that sneaky fucker, Martinez. Martinez writes incident reports that technically follow the academy's guidelines. He avoids modifiers and descriptors. He traces the physical action of an event without opining or speculating. He offers accounts that contradict his own findings. He's succinct and factual. He tells the literal and empirical truth. He writes in the dispassionate narrative uni-voice that conveys objectivity and distance. So why is Martinez instantly discernable on the page from a hundred other cops?

Despite the neutrality of his diction, Martinez's choices are idiosyncratic. Everything he sees reveals him. And syntactically, though he bends every rule to the breaking point, you can't bust him.

At a Lewd Acts on Child crime scene, Martinez's partner, Brown, writes, "The Victim sustained multiple injuries." Martinez would tell us, "The baby was bleeding from three orifices." There's a world of difference here. Brown gives us a victim; Martinez gives us a baby. Brown offers a fact; Martinez paints a picture.

Brown's statement moves us forward; Martinez makes us stop dead and envision the horrific crime that caused such injuries. Both statements are neutral on the surface, but the specificity of Martinez's language makes the reader see and feel.

At the same crime scene, Brown says, "We placed the Suspect in a felony prone position and took him into custody without incident." Martinez would write, "We cuffed the father." Martinez's version reminds us of the unnatural aspect of the crime, that a father (presumably) committed it. He edges near the academy no-fly zone with *father* in place of *suspect*, but gets away with it because the sentence describes police action—the cuffing—rather than any actions of the suspect. Also, nobody disputes the fact that the suspect *is* the father; it's the type of father he is that's at issue.

At the same crime scene, Martinez might note that there's "no food in the apartment." This is an empirical fact, so technically admissible. It doesn't speak to the specific crime of Lewd Acts on Child, but it does subtly add to the moral charges against the parents. Martinez inflects the barren apartment and makes it speak. Details bring scenes to life. Sometimes the image can tell everything.

In the witness section of the report, Brown might say, "Victim's mother gave no statement." Martinez would tell us, "Mother refused to cooperate." This carries a totally different emphasis and meaning. Martinez doesn't speculate if she's protecting her husband at the expense of her child. He doesn't need to. What kind of mother refuses to speak when her baby is bleeding from three orifices?

Examine these two versions of the same incident, side by side. They admit the same facts. They're both truthful. But one—Martinez's—is also persuasive. Why? It's subtly inflected in every line to signal its agenda. Though it labors under the constraints of the report format, it uses emphasis and diction to suggest how we interpret what it tells us. It may look impartial, but it's aimed like a weapon.

From a strict moral perspective or the police academy vantage point, Martinez's incident reports are flawed. They're failures of objective reportage. Though everything in them is literally true, they're technically "suspicious"; if Martinez saw a baby-raper, he's making damn sure we do too.

From a reader's perspective, Martinez's incident reports are deeply satisfying. They engage us emotionally; they vest us in the events he describes, and in the teller. They're narratives that hint at larger truths—about Martinez himself and the South Central universe he polices. They reverberate beyond the time it takes to read them. They offer a way to understand the world.

My Sergeant Martinez may be writing reports, but he's also using the alchemy of inflection to turn them into stories—narratives that believe themselves and make us believe them, too.

Martinez succeeds—or fails, if you're his supervisors—because of his commitment to what his stories mean. He continues to protect and serve because inflection isn't illegal, and you won't catch him. It's not a story, it's "just the facts, ma'am."

Like Martinez, a good story always has an agenda.

Like Martinez, a good story is a sneaky fucker.

For Analysis

1. How does technical writing, such as police reports, compare with scholarly writing? List the main features of the police report, and compare these to characteristics of scholarly writing.
2. Collett compares examples from two officers' reports to show how subtle word changes can sketch different pictures. Look more closely at these examples: Why are Martinez's descriptions more persuasive?
3. Collett makes two claims that seem contradictory. The first claim explains how individual perspective is subjective, that "no two people see things identically or invest their attention in the same details." In the second claim, she describes a more objective perspective: "the narrative voice at the center of an incident report is always emotionally neutral. He's the ultimate reliable narrator." How can writing be both subjective and objective?

For Writing

Revise one page of a draft that you are writing to adhere to the police academy's writing rules. Incorporate precise words, use active verbs that reflect observable action, avoid adverbs and adjectives, and eliminate biased language.

"Zombie Nouns"
by Helen Sword

Helen Sword writes books and articles about literature, teaching, and writing. She also created the WritersDiet Test, an online tool that analyzes sentence style to help writers create leaner prose. In this 2012 *New York Times* commentary, Sword critiques the overuse of nominalizations.

Take an adjective (*implacable*) or a verb (*calibrate*) or even another noun (*crony*) and add a suffix like *ity*, *tion* or *ism*. You've created a new noun: *implacability*, *calibration*, *cronyism*. Sounds impressive, right?

Nouns formed from other parts of speech are called nominalizations. Academics love them; so do lawyers, bureaucrats and business writers. I call them "zombie nouns" because they cannibalize active verbs, suck the lifeblood from adjectives and substitute abstract entities for human beings:

> The *proliferation* of *nominalizations* in a discursive *formation* may be an *indication* of a *tendency* toward *pomposity* and *abstraction*.

The sentence above contains no fewer than seven nominalizations, each formed from a verb or an adjective. Yet it fails to tell us *who* is doing *what*. When we eliminate or reanimate most of the zombie nouns (*tendency* becomes *tend*, *abstraction* becomes *abstract*) and add a human subject and some active verbs, the sentence springs back to life:

> Writers who overload their sentences with nominalizations tend to sound pompous and abstract.

Only one zombie noun—the key word *nominalizations*—has been allowed to remain standing.

At their best, nominalizations help us express complex ideas: *perception*, *intelligence*, *epistemology*. At their worst, they impede clear communication. I have seen academic colleagues become so enchanted by zombie nouns like *heteronormativity* and *interpellation* that they forget how ordinary people speak. Their students, in turn, absorb the dangerous message that people who use big words are smarter—or at least appear to be—than those who don't.

In fact, the more abstract your subject matter, the more your readers will appreciate stories, anecdotes, examples and other handholds to help them stay on track. In her book "Darwin's Plots," the literary historian Gillian Beer supplements abstract nouns like *evidence*, *relationships* and *beliefs* with vivid verbs (*rebuff*, *overturn*, *exhilarate*) and concrete nouns that appeal to sensory experience (*earth*, *sun*, *eyes*):

> Most major scientific theories rebuff common sense. They call on evidence beyond the reach of our senses and overturn the observable world. They disturb assumed relationships and shift what has been substantial into metaphor. The earth now only seems immovable. Such major theories tax, affront, and exhilarate those who first encounter them, although in fifty years or so they will be taken for granted, part of the apparently common-sense set of beliefs which instructs us that the earth revolves around the sun whatever our eyes may suggest.

Her subject matter—scientific theories—could hardly be more cerebral, yet her language remains firmly anchored in the physical world.

Contrast Beer's vigorous prose with the following passage from a social sciences book:

> The partial participation of newcomers is by no means "disconnected" from the practice of interest. Furthermore, it is also a dynamic concept. In this sense, peripherality, when it is enabled, suggests an opening, a way of gaining access to sources for understanding through growing involvement. The ambiguity inherent in peripheral participation must then be connected to issues of

> legitimacy, of the social organization of and control over resources, if it is to gain its full analytical potential.

Why does reading this paragraph feel like trudging through deep mud? The secret lies at its grammatical core: *Participation is. . . . It is. . . . Peripherality suggests. . . . Ambiguity must be connected.* Every single sentence has a zombie noun or a pronoun as its subject, coupled with an uninspiring verb. Who are the people? Where is the action? What story is being told?

To get a feeling for how zombie nouns work, release a few of them into a sentence and watch them sap all of its life. George Orwell played this game in his essay "Politics and the English Language," contrasting a well-known verse from Ecclesiastes with his own satirical translation:

> I returned and saw under the sun, that the race is not to the swift, nor the battle to the strong, neither yet bread to the wise, nor yet riches to men of understanding, nor yet favour to men of skill; but time and chance happeneth to them all.

Here it is in modern English:

> Objective considerations of contemporary phenomena compel the conclusion that success or failure in competitive activities exhibits no tendency to be commensurate with innate capacity, but that a considerable element of the unpredictable must invariably be taken into account.

The Bible passage speaks to our senses and emotions with concrete nouns (*sun, bread*), descriptions of people (*the swift, the wise, men of understanding, men of skill*) and punchy abstract nouns (*race, battle, riches, time, chance*). Orwell's "modern English" version, by contrast, is teeming with nominalizations (*considerations, conclusion, activities, tendency, capacity, unpredictable*) and other vague abstractions (*phenomena, success, failure, element*). The zombies have taken over, and the humans have fled the village.

Zombie nouns do their worst damage when they gather in jargon-generating packs and infect every noun, verb and adjective in sight: *globe* becomes *global* becomes *globalize* becomes *globalization*. The grandfather of all nominalizations, *antidisestablishmentarianism*, potentially contains at least two verbs, three adjectives and six other nouns.

A paragraph heavily populated by nominalizations will send your readers straight to sleep. Wake them up with vigorous, verb-driven sentences that are concrete, clearly structured and blissfully zombie-free.

For Analysis

1. Sword writes about a seemingly trivial issue (overwhelming sentences with nouns). Where does she demonstrate the implications of this subject? What are they?
2. Track how Sword uses the zombie motif throughout the article, and then discuss with a peer whether you think such an extended metaphor works or if it's overkill.
3. Sword uses textual examples as evidence to demonstrate the lifeless effect of nominalizations. How persuasive is this evidence? Do you think Sword's opinion article would be more compelling if she had included other kinds of support, like verification? Where could she have included additional support?

For Writing

Upload a few pages from an essay that you are currently drafting or have recently written to Sword's online WritersDiet Test. After receiving your "diagnosis," edit your essay to make it leaner. Then, write a paragraph that describes what you learned about your writing style and the specific changes you made to tighten up your sentences.

"N/A 101, Prof. Blank, A Month/Some Day/The Year, A Love Story"

by Alan Linic

Alan Linic published this article in the 2011 edition of *Gardy Loo*, a literary and arts magazine that publishes student writing at James Madison University. Linic writes a satirical critique of academic assignments, including footnotes in which he translates passages from his "authentic" style into academic prose.

So I've been writing academic papers for like eight years now. As a matter of fact, thanks to me selecting English as a major, academic papers might as well have been my on-again, off-again girlfriend since sophomore year. By adding up the page lengths of all the documents in my folders, I can comfortably estimate that I've written over 300 pages since my enrollment in college. The thing is, my experience with all of the papers I've written has been consistent whether I enjoyed the topics/theses/whatever or not. I always find myself doing three things: adjusting the way I write to make myself sound sophisticated and intellectual, adding piles of superfluous "proof" to hit page requirements and enhance arguments, and assuming some kind of pseudo-objective divine point of view. The question I've been asking myself lately isn't "why?" so much as "what the fuck for?"

Besides the fact that it would hurt my grade to use slang/contractions/MY REAL HONEST-TO-GOD-FEELINGS, I got nothing.[1] My professors have led me to believe that the way I communicate an idea is more important than what I'm actually trying to say, and that appearing smart is better than presenting something real. I even have to pretend I don't exist (even going so far as to remove the first person from my work entirely, like my shit descended from the sky or sprung up out of the ground). My name is right there on the byline, so why am I pretending to be an omnipresent authority on whatever I'm writing about? It seems to me that distancing myself from the ownership of my own words is more hurtful to my credibility than helpful. Can you imagine if people in everyday life debated or spoke without the first person all the time?[2] In the academic world, the statement "such-and-such calls to mind so-and-so, suggesting this-or-that" is prized over "such-and-such reminded me of so-and-so, which suggested to me this-or-that." Every instinct I have tells me that it's bad to make sweeping generalizations like "this passage suggests this particular thing for sure to everyone all the time." My subjective approach to an issue or text or topic should be celebrated. By presenting my opinions and thoughts I'm not telling anybody what to think—I'm telling them what I think. Ergo, being personal allows the reader to better form their own opinion. I mean, I don't understand who made the rule that being "academic" necessarily means not being yourself. The most important thing as far as I'm concerned is approaching something intellectually and communicating your ideas about it in a way that is easily accessible to a reader. This business of presenting my thoughts in the most boring, impersonal way possible makes no sense to me. Basically what I'm saying is that the first person rules. Can you imagine if this paper wasn't written in the first person?[3] It would present the same basic evidence, but my God would it be boring. Shit, I wouldn't even want to read it.[4]

And another thing—it makes no sense that "big" papers have to be a certain length. If you can prove a point in three lines, why stretch those three out to a page? A concise argument is always better than a really wordy one, as far as I'm concerned. Every critical essay I've ever read is like a billion pages long, single-spaced, and they all have stupidly long introductions that talk about all kinds of useless shit before we get to the part where they say what the paper is actually about. That's why I hate quoting and citing sources in academic papers—there's so much fluff involved. I've got to quote some other guy's contrived, intellectualized words out of context, then I have to cite them, then I have to explain them, and then I have to tie the explanation into my argument. Speaking of outside sources, the only good way to use them is to paraphrase.[5] My reasoning for this is two-fold, and I'm going to organize those two points in NON-PARAGRAPH FORM[6] to make it easier on the eye:

Why Paraphrasing Is The Best Way To Incorporate Sources

1. I have never, ever, ever checked to verify quotes, sources, or page numbers for any of the papers I've read in my life. That's because I trust the person writing the paper; I assume that if they're incorporating outside sources they've got no reason to lie about them. If this sort of trust (or laziness, depending on your view) is held by most people, then why quote directly at all? It will save the time of having to explicate the words of somebody else and the need of quotes to justify even the simplest of claims, like that Little Red Riding Hood's cloak is, in fact, red.[7]

2. I would never want to make a reader plod through four sentences where I could have just used one good sentence instead. So instead of using a quote that has to be dismantled and justified, I can just paraphrase to keep my momentum going while crediting someone else for their ideas. I feel like citations are parenthetical to encourage a focus on what I'm trying to say, not what I'm saying somebody else said. I don't really know what to do with concluding paragraphs either. It ties back into my dislike of fluff; as far as I understand it, I use the archetypal concluding paragraph to really knock my shit out of the park. But I do so by restating things I've already said, but in brand new ways.[8] That strikes me as a colossal waste of time. What, I bust my ass churning out the ten pages that are required of me, and then I've got to recondense my argument into a one-two punch to end it? As far as I'm concerned, when my argument is done it's done, and that should be the end of it.

Notes

1. [Academic Paper Translation:] Other than the notion that the use of slang, contractions and a more subjective approach to textual analysis would result in the penalization of one's grade, there is no readily available evidence to suggest why writers observe normative essay or paper conventions.
2. "That a caramel macchiato is the tastiest and most cost-effective purchase to be made at Starbucks is a justifiable opinion; one need only look at the blend of flavors, the use of caramel as a sweetening agent, and its ability to be equally enjoyed hot or iced for suggestions of such a claim being true."
   "So you do want a caramel macchiato then?"
   "...Yes, please."
3. [Possible non-first person opening for this paper:] The typical approach to essay writing as it is taught by American public schools calls for a thesis-based, objectively-written paper organized into paragraphs by topic. Although this format is the most acceptable to academic institutions throughout the nation, careful examination suggests that writing papers from a more subjective and personal place could provide just as much insight and analysis while preserving the personality and creativity of the works' authors. One might consider works by Ralph Waldo Emerson and other Transcendentalist writers for evidence of such a claim... (etc.)
4. I'm not saying we should all cuss in everything all the time. It really does make people sound uneducated, for whatever reason. But if it fits, then what the fuck, right?
5. I didn't use the first person here, but this is my opinion. If you agree, fine. If you don't, bite me. I'm not claiming any universal truths anywhere in this paper, except that because my paper doesn't claim any universal truths, it is superior to all papers that do.
6. "Omg wtf. Can he do that?"
7. [Acadmic paper translation:] ... for instance, that the character of Little Red Riding Hood typically dons a red cloak before embarking on her journey; this titular implication is made real by direct references such as "this good woman had a little red riding hood...[that] suited the girl so extremely well that everybody called her Little Red Riding Hood" (1) from Charels Perrault's translation.

8. Or by rewording my previous arguments, or by presenting my ideas in unique constructions, or by telling you the same shit over but shorter and different, etc.

For Analysis

1. When writing for class assignments, to what extent do you think you have to pretend to be someone you're not? What potential costs and benefits might there be for doing so?
2. How do Linic's ideas about using sources correspond to those we present in Chapter 3?
3. Does Linic really knock his conclusion "out of the park" (424), as he suggests writers should do? What else might he have done to conclude his essay?

For Writing

Write a response to Linic's arguments. Begin by highlighting his main claims, then select a few to argue for or against using support from this book and your own experiences. Suggested length: as long as it takes to persuade your professor.

SECTION 4
WHAT MAKES US HAPPY?

"Pursuing the Science of Happiness"
by Andrew Guest

Andrew Guest is a professor of social and behavioral sciences at the University of Portland. His research focuses on sports and child development. Published in the journal *Oregon Humanities* in 2010, this article synthesizes Guest's and other scholars' research on the "science of happiness."

"I just want to be happy." It sounds like such a simple, noble goal. When I overhear it in discussions by the generally earnest and well-meaning college students I teach, my first reaction is to think that worries about rampant materialism among today's youth are vastly overstated. But my second, more considered reaction is to wonder what they mean. Being happy, I want to tell them, is much more complicated than it sounds.

That considered reaction, that hesitation about a most American ideal—the inalienable right to "the pursuit of happiness"—is born primarily from my work as an academic psychologist. But the reason I do that work in Oregon is born of my own pursuit of happiness: Portland seemed like a place I could be happy. It may be a little out of the way for academia, but it's got a good quality of life—the trees are green, the coffee is rich, the ethos is a certain type of friendly. After six years here I sometimes think that has worked out. Sometimes.

I have, of course, had many happy moments in Oregon. The clichés have proven true: I've enjoyed beautiful mountain vistas, engaged with good friends and loving family, savored a fine meal accompanied by a hearty microbrew, felt part of conversations that might somehow contribute to a better community. Portland has even been good for idiosyncratic things, such as my soccer addiction: when the Timbers slice another slab off the victory log, it makes me happy. But am I a happier person?

My answer to that question is inevitably biased by some of my research experiences. About a decade ago I spent the end of my graduate school years searching for happiness in unlikely places, including Angolan refugee camps. Ostensibly I was doing a dissertation in developmental psychology and focusing on the distinct cultural roles of play, games, and sports for children in marginalized communities. But implicitly, in the guise of social science, I was trying to figure out what it means to be happy—I was fascinated by the relationships between human psychology and the circumstances of our lives.

At the time, Angola was a paragon of bad circumstances; it was rated by the United Nations Children's Fund as the "worst place in the world to be a child" thanks to a twenty-seven-year civil war, decimated health care and education systems, and massive income inequality. The camps were hardscrabble patches of ruby red dirt and quasi-permanent mud-brick homes, teeming with families bereft of tangible opportunities. And yet, when I asked the refugee youths in formal surveys about their psychological well-being, more than three quarters reported being generally happy. This is not meant to romanticize poverty, because the people I worked with were decidedly *un*happy with their objectively dismal material realities. They wanted real schools, decent shelter, and opportunities for their parents and their future. They deserved a life expectancy beyond fifty years and the power to choose what they would do with their lives. But they did not necessarily internalize those problems; on a day-to-day basis they played with their friends, laughed with their siblings, and lived their lives. They found ways to feel happy.

Ironically, at that point in my life I was not sure how I would rate my own happiness. I was a lonely graduate student pining over a distant, ill-fated relationship and wracked with anxiety about whether I had any future in academia. I'm usually not an early riser, but during my six months in Angola I regularly woke at 4:00 in a lukewarm sweat only to stare for hours at the gritty white mesh of my mosquito net, listening to the spasmodic traffic in Luanda's old town. I genuinely appreciated the experience, and I felt deeply engaged with the research and the community, but I couldn't wait to leave. I wanted to settle in a place like Oregon to teach classes full of earnest and well-meaning college students eager to discuss the psychology of happiness. And fortunately, for the sake of that discussion, no matter how hard it is to live the science, a large and growing body of research has offered me a few things to say.

The modern science of happiness often goes by the name "positive psychology" and presents itself as an evolution away from psychology's historical focus on dysfunction—a focus seeded by Freud and fed by a desire to help the mentally ill. As University of Pennsylvania psychology professor Martin Seligman, the generally acknowledged founder of positive psychology, framed it in a 2004 conversation with the Edge Foundation, "In the same way I can claim unblushingly that psychology and psychiatry have decreased the tonnage of suffering in the world, my aim is that psychology and maybe psychiatry will increase the tonnage of happiness in the world."

The core belief of positive psychology as a field is that science will lead the way. In the last decade new peer-reviewed scientific journals of happiness studies and positive psychology have appeared, which mostly dispense with the anecdotes and intuitions of self-help gurus. Institutions such as the august University of Pennsylvania have started offering degrees in applied positive psychology, and organizations such as the Templeton Foundation have invested millions of dollars in grants, conferences, and awards.

Amidst this flurry of modern science, however, lies a classical challenge: there is no widespread agreement about how to define happiness. In fact, some contemporary psychologists go back to ancient Greek philosophic debates about *hedonia* and *eudaimonia*. In the

2001 *Annual Review of Psychology*, for example, Richard Ryan and Edward Deci contrasted contemporary scholarship taking "the hedonic approach," which focuses more on measuring subjective feelings of pleasure, with "the eudaimonic approach," which emphasizes the satisfactions of a meaningful life and self-realization.

Each approach tells us something about the human experience of happiness, but each has its limitations. The hedonic approach, for example, risks seeming superficial, while the eudaimonic approach risks unfair value judgments. From a research perspective, how can I decide whether someone's life is meaningful? In most cases researchers get around the thorny problem of judging meaningful happiness by keeping their measures as general as possible. The most common measures of what scholars call "subjective well-being" or "subjective happiness" essentially just ask people to define it for themselves, responding on a scale of 1 to 7 to prompts such as, "In general, I consider myself not a very happy person" (1) to "In general, I consider myself a very happy person" (7). A researcher can then aggregate results and suggest variables that do and do not correlate with happiness.

What those results rarely report is that most people in most places subjectively perceive themselves to be reasonably happy. For example, in her book *The How of Happiness*, University of California psychology professor Sonja Lyubomirsky mentions in passing, amidst various prescriptions for becoming happier, that the average adult scores around 5.6 on her 7-point scale; college students score lower—only around 5 out of 7.

What's more, our subjective perceptions of happiness don't tend to change much over time—even when our lives change dramatically. In one oft-cited 1978 study, for example, researchers from Northwestern University interviewed people at two extremes: people who had won the lottery and people who had been paralyzed in accidents. The point of the study was that, when asked, people in those groups agreed that the initial events had made a great difference in their lives: winning the lottery was joyful, becoming paralyzed was agonizing. But after six months or a year, the events seemed to make little difference. The lottery winners had settled into new stresses and burdens; they took less pleasure in the mundane realities of daily life. The people who had been paralyzed gradually found new satisfactions, challenges, and opportunities. They were nostalgic about the past, but also optimistic about the future. People in both groups adapted.

Combining the results of that study with findings from more recent research, Harvard psychologist Daniel Gilbert, in a 2004 TED conference talk, went so far as to say, "If it happened over three months ago, with a few exceptions, it has no impact on our happiness." This phenomenon has been much discussed and is occasionally controversial among psychologists, even garnering its own scientific-sounding name "hedonic adaptation," or sometimes, the "hedonic treadmill." The idea is that the more steps we take in our pursuit of happiness, the more we stay in the same place. There is, for example, an old newspaper poll finding that when you ask people making less than $30,000 per year how much income it would take to fulfill their dreams, they say $50,000. But when you ask people making just over $100,000 the same question, they say it would take $250,000. The technical terms for these ever-adjusting dreams are "relative deprivation" or "reference anxiety." The more human term is "jealousy." The end result is the same: we adapt.

Is this good news or bad news? Probably a bit of both. Our psychological ability to adapt means we can often cope better than we might expect with many of life's inevitable challenges, but it also means that our successes are more temporal than we might hope. When my team loses, it is never as devastating as I worry it might be, but when they win the joy is almost always fleeting.

In my mind, however, the most profound implication is what hedonic adaptation means for the pursuit of happiness over a lifetime. If I want to know how happy the students in my classes will be in twenty or thirty years, I could try to collect a lot of data: What will they do for a living? Will they fall in love? Have kids? Live in a vibrant community? Suffer tragedy? Make a lot of money? Have a fulfilling spiritual life? Make an artistic contribution? Cheer for the winning team? Get soft, wet kisses from a puppy? I could try to learn about all that, but I don't need to. If I'm trying to make a statistical prediction of their future happiness, all I need to know is how happy they are now.

Researchers studying happiness sometimes talk about this phenomenon as a genetic "set point" for happiness, or perhaps a deeply rooted psychological dynamic—an emotional predisposition around which we vary from time to time, but to which we usually return. The idea of living in Oregon may have once made me happy, but based on my own predispositions, I might as well be back in Illinois or (shiver) Ohio.

Fortunately, however, the story is not quite that simple: the set point is, if anything, a set range within which there is much room for negotiation. As such, positive psychologists such as Sonja Lyubomirsky assert that although something around half of our happiness is determined by hardwired dispositions, another forty percent is shaped by voluntary activities. Of course, that means a mere ten percent is down to the circumstances of our lives. In fact, in my reading, the science of happiness has as much to say about what is *not* likely to make us happy as what is.

Take money, for example. The voluminous (and sometimes controversial) research on wealth suggests that having more money correlates with happiness only up to a point. Being very poor creates hardships that can affect well-being, and having enough money to satisfy basic needs is important. But beyond a certain point (which seems to vary according to relative standards in different communities and cultures), more money seems to have little to do with happiness. In fact, according to statistics reported by Nobel prize-winning economist Daniel Kahneman and his colleagues, more than 80 percent of Americans at all income levels report being either "pretty happy" or "very happy."

What about other circumstances idealized by the popular imagination as being keys to happiness: Youth? Beauty? Intelligence? No.

Nope. Not really. There are certain social advantages to being young, beautiful, or smart, but happiness does not seem to be one of them. In fact, compelling evidence suggests that our psychological well-being is highest in old age because we've dropped the pretense of wanting to be more attractive or intelligent than we are. Older adults tend to be more accepting of themselves and, in some cases, that can override even the challenging physical health problems of aging.

One other provocative example of a life circumstance that seems to have little relationship to happiness is having children. In the popular imagination, children are often the joy of their parents' lives, but the evidence suggests otherwise. In a phenomenon some scholars call the "parenting paradox," no matter how you measure it—looking at overall well-being, day-to-day emotional states, broader life satisfaction—people with children are no happier than people without children (unless, some research suggests, the childless people wanted to have children but couldn't). Children bring joys, but they also bring burdens and anxieties. The fact that we are convinced children will make us happy may just be another peculiar trick of human nature. As Daniel Gilbert explained to *Harvard Magazine*, "Imagine a species that figured out that children don't make you happy. . . .We have a word for that species: extinct. There is a conspiracy between genes and culture to keep us in the dark about the real sources of happiness."

Most of the modern science exploring the source of real happiness seems to come back to a formulation that Freud famously (and perhaps apocryphally) proposed a century ago: love and work. Love, in its broadest definition as healthy social relationships and meaningful interpersonal engagements, seems to matter. Social isolation is one of the best predictors of depression and other mental health problems. Being married and having friends, however, is one of the best predictors of well-being. There are many nuances to how love can play out in our lives, but at the most general level, being connected to people matters.

Work, in the sense of engaging with meaningful projects that offer reasonable degrees of challenge and a sense of purpose, also seems important. Work does not have to be a remunerative job—it can be family responsibilities, community volunteering, artistic projects, and the like. But at its best it allows us to cultivate our strengths and contribute to something larger than ourselves.

Other statistical correlates of happiness often seem to integrate a healthy balance of these broad categories. There is, for example, convincing evidence that religious people are happier than the nonreligious, but this may be because religion often involves interpersonal connections within a community and a larger sense of purpose for our lives. It may also be the case that religion does not so much make people happy as happy people tend to be attracted to religion— teasing out the causal nature of these relationships is always as much an art as it is a science.

The presence of fulfilling love and meaningful work may also be conducive to the types of voluntary activities that positive psychologists like to prescribe for those looking to increase their levels of happiness. Practices such as showing gratitude to others, intentionally savoring small daily pleasures, and spending time in activities that use our personal strengths seem to have a significant impact on how we subjectively feel about ourselves and our lives.

So does this kind of descriptive science give us a road map to happiness? Should I just tell my students to stay connected to the people they love, worry a little less about money, find work that offers them a sense of purpose, think twice before having kids, go to church, and give thanks for their blessings? Maybe I should—but I can't. It may just go back to that classical challenge of defining happiness, but I don't think I sat in Angola pining to settle down in a place like Oregon because I wanted to boost my "subjective well-being." I moved here because I thought it would make for a good quality of life. And what constitutes good quality in our minds may not be the same thing as happiness.

In fact, the positive psychology movement has begun to generate a vocal cadre of detractors to accompany its many acolytes. Books such as *Against Happiness* by English professor Eric Wilson offer different critiques, but fundamentally agree that framing happiness as an ultimate goal seems shallow. Here even my college students tend to agree. If I offer them a hypothetical choice between a constant, slightly positive emotional state—permanent moderate happiness—or the chance to experience a range of emotions with higher highs and lower lows averaging out to less gross happiness, most (though not all) make what classic economics would consider the irrational choice: they are willing to sacrifice some happiness for the full range of human experience.

Yet, even if we could have it all, even if we recognize happiness as dependent upon seemingly valorous statistical correlates such as healthy relationships, purposeful work, and making meaningful contributions to a community, there is room for critique. In fact, social critics including Barbara Ehrenreich, in *Bright Sided: How Positive Thinking Is Undermining America*, and Chris Hedges, in *Empire of Illusion*, argue that positive psychology and the modern pursuit of happiness are ultimately related to some of the deepest problems of modern society. Do you think gaping economic inequalities, unjust wars, and ferocious un/underemployment are problems? Don't worry, be happy.

I appreciate the critics' perspectives and worry that adopting the baser tenets of positive psychology can blind us individually to broader social problems, but I also can't help but think that criticizing the pursuit of happiness is an oversimplification. Indeed, I sometimes remind my students that the founding documents of our country pointedly do not suggest that happiness itself is an inalienable right—only its *pursuit*. So perhaps the pursuit is the thing. Perhaps in their vast wisdom the founders offered us the primary lesson of happiness: that it is a process rather than an outcome.

So when I overhear my students saying they "just want to be happy," I like to imagine that the new science of positive psychology can help them. As University of Virginia psychology professor

Jonathan Haidt points out in *The Happiness Hypothesis*, the research on happiness ultimately distills into the wise words of Shakespeare: "There is nothing either good or bad, but thinking makes it so." And for me, I've come to realize, there are ways in which thinking itself makes me happy.

In perhaps a final irony of my research experience, I often reminisce happily about that angst-ridden experience in Angola. I recall long days of equatorial sun glistening off the distant Atlantic Ocean, crafting amateur Portuguese into conversations with Angolans who challenged me, with their strength amidst adversity, to separate psychological well-being from structural well-being. And I think about long days in Oregon classrooms with the Willamette River flowing in the distance, hoping for chances to convey those experiences to students in ways that might challenge them to reconsider what it means to "just be happy." Happiness, I want to tell them, is more complicated than it sounds—but it is also much more interesting.

For Analysis

1. Why do you think a social scientist would publish his work in a journal like *Oregon Humanities*? How does Guest adapt his style for this particular audience?
2. Which controversy categories does Guest address? Which do you think his readers would find most significant?
3. How does Guest establish the credibility of his sources?

For Writing

Using the TRY THIS guidelines on p. 51, write a 500-word summary of this article. Compare your summary to one your classmate wrote, and then condense your summary to 250 words.

"A Wandering Mind Is an Unhappy Mind"
by Matthew A. Killingsworth and Daniel T. Gilbert

Matthew A. Killingsworth is a research fellow at the University of California, Berkeley. As a doctoral student in psychology, he developed a smartphone app to study happiness (http://www.trackyourhappiness.org/). Killingsworth coauthored this article with his Harvard professor, **Daniel T. Gilbert**, who has published extensively on emotions, beliefs, and perceptions. Gilbert has also hosted or appeared in documentaries on PBS, NatGeo, CNN, and elsewhere. This brief article, which examines the correlation between our thoughts and emotions, appeared in 2010 in *Science*, a prestigious journal of the American Association for the Advancement of Science.

Unlike other animals, human beings spend a lot of time thinking about what is not going on around them, contemplating events that happened in the past, might happen in the future, or will never happen at all. Indeed, "stimulus-independent thought" or "mind wandering" appears to be the brain's default mode of operation (*1–3*). Although this ability is a remarkable evolutionary achievement that allows people to learn, reason, and plan, it may have an emotional cost. Many philosophical and religious traditions teach that happiness is to be found by living in the moment, and practitioners are trained to resist mind wandering and "to be here now." These traditions suggest that a wandering mind is an unhappy mind. Are they right?

Laboratory experiments have revealed a great deal about the cognitive and neural bases of mind wandering (*3–7*), but little about its emotional consequences in everyday life. The most reliable method for investigating real-world emotion is experience sampling, which involves contacting people as they engage in their everyday activities and asking them to report their thoughts, feelings, and actions at that moment. Unfortunately, collecting real-time reports from large numbers of people as they go about their daily lives is so cumbersome and expensive that experience sampling has rarely been used to investigate the relationship between mind wandering and happiness and has always been limited to very small samples (*8*, *9*).

We solved this problem by developing a Web application for the iPhone (Apple Incorporated, Cupertino, California), which we used to create an unusually large database of real-time reports of thoughts, feelings, and actions of a broad range of people as they went about their daily activities. The application contacts participants through their iPhones at random moments during their waking hours, presents them with questions, and records their answers to a database at www.trackyourhappiness.org. The database currently contains nearly a quarter of a million samples from about 5000 people from 83 different countries who range in age from 18 to 88 and who collectively represent every one of 86 major occupational categories.

To find out how often people's minds wander, what topics they wander to, and how those wanderings affect their happiness, we analyzed samples from 2250 adults (58.8% male, 73.9% residing in the United States, mean age of 34 years) who were randomly assigned to answer a happiness question ("How are you feeling right now?") answered on a continuous sliding scale from very bad (0) to very good (100), an activity question ("What are you doing right now?") answered by endorsing one or more of 22 activities adapted from the day reconstruction method (*10*, *11*), and a mind-wandering question ("Are you thinking about something other than what you're currently doing?") answered with one of four options: no; yes, something pleasant; yes, something neutral; or yes, something unpleasant. Our analyses revealed three facts.

First, people's minds wandered frequently, regardless of what they were doing. Mind wandering occurred in 46.9% of the samples and in at least 30% of the samples taken during every activity except making love. The frequency of mind wandering in our real-world sample was considerably higher than is typically seen in laboratory experiments. Surprisingly, the nature of people's activities had only a modest impact on whether their minds wandered and had almost no impact on the pleasantness of the topics to which their minds wandered (*12*).

Second, multilevel regression revealed that people were less happy when their minds were wandering than when they were not [slope (b) = −8.79, $P < 0.001$], and this was true during all activities, including the least enjoyable. Although people's minds were more likely to wander to pleasant topics (42.5% of samples) than to unpleasant topics (26.5% of samples) or neutral topics (31% of samples), people were no happier when thinking about pleasant topics than about their current activity ($b = -0.52$, not significant) and were considerably unhappier when thinking about neutral topics ($b = -7.2$, $P < 0.001$) or unpleasant topics ($b = -23.9$, $P < 0.001$) than about their current activity (**Fig. 4.1**, bottom). Although negative moods are known to cause mind wandering (*13*), time-lag analyses strongly suggested that mind wandering in our sample was generally the cause, and not merely the consequence, of unhappiness (*12*).

Third, what people were thinking was a better predictor of their happiness than was what they were doing. The nature of people's activities explained 4.6% of the within-person variance in happiness and 3.2% of the between-person variance in happiness, but mind wandering explained 10.8% of within-person variance in happiness and 17.7% of between-person variance in happiness. The variance explained by mind wandering was largely independent of the variance explained by the nature of activities, suggesting that the two were independent influences on happiness.

In conclusion, a human mind is a wandering mind, and a wandering mind is an unhappy mind. The ability to think about what is not happening is a cognitive achievement that comes at an emotional cost.

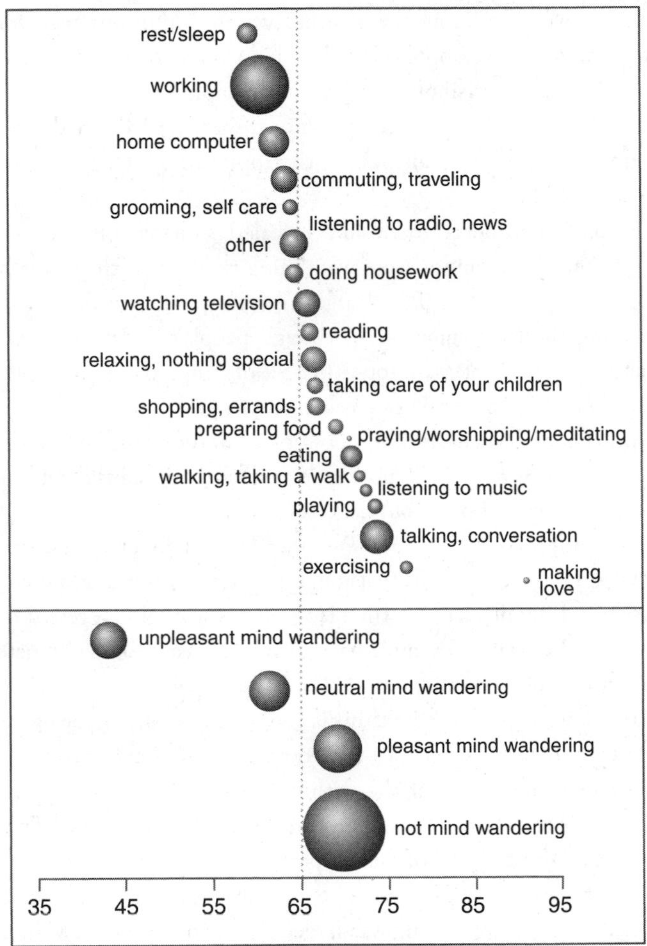

Figure 4.1

Mean happiness reported during each activity (top) and while mind wandering to unpleasant topics, neutral topics, pleasant topics or not mind wandering (bottom). Dashed line indicates mean of happiness across all samples. Bubble area indicates the frequency of occurrence. The largest bubble ("not mind wandering") corresponds to 53.1% of the samples, and the smallest bubble ("praying/worshipping/meditating") corresponds to 0.1% of the samples.

References and Notes

1. M. E. Raichle *et al.*, A default mode of brain function. Proc. Natl. Acad. Sci. U.S.A. 98, 676 (2001).
2. K. Christoff, A. M. Gordon, J. Smallwood, R. Smith, J. W. Schooler, Experience sampling during fMRI reveals default network and executive system contributions to mind wandering. Proc. Natl. Acad. Sci. U.S.A.106, 8719 (2009).
3. R. L. Buckner, J. R. Andrews-Hanna, D. L. Schacter, The brain's default network: Anatomy, function, and relevance to disease. Ann. N. Y. Acad. Sci. 1124, 1 (2008).
4. J. Smallwood, J. W. Schooler, The restless mind. Psychol. Bull. 132, 946 (2006).
5. M. F. Mason *et al.*, Wandering minds: The default network and stimulus-independent thought. Science 315,393 (2007).
6. J. Smallwood, E. Beach, J. W. Schooler, T. C. Handy, Going AWOL in the brain: Mind wandering reduces cortical analysis of external events. J. Cogn. Neurosci. 20, 458 (2008).
7. R. L. Buckner, D. C. Carroll, Self-projection and the brain. Trends Cogn. Sci. 11, 49 (2007).
8. J. C. McVay, M. J. Kane, T. R. Kwapil, Tracking the train of thought from the laboratory into everyday life: An experience-sampling study of mind wandering across controlled and ecological contexts. Psychon. Bull. Rev. 16, 857 (2009).
9. M. J. Kane *et al.*, For whom the mind wanders, and when: An experience-sampling study of working memory and executive control in daily life. Psychol. Sci. 18, 614 (2007).
10. D. Kahneman, A. B. Krueger, D. A. Schkade, N. Schwarz, A. A. Stone, A survey method for characterizing daily life experience: The day reconstruction method. Science 306, 1776 (2004).
11. A. B. Krueger, D. A. Schkade, The reliability of subjective well-being measures. J. Public Econ. 92, 1833(2008).
12. Materials and methods are available as supporting material on *Science* Online.
13. J. Smallwood, A. Fitzgerald, L. K. Miles, L. H. Phillips, Shifting moods, wandering minds: Negative moods lead the mind to wander. Emotion 9, 271 (2009).

14. We thank V. Pitiyanuvath for engineering www.trackyourhappiness.org and R. Hackman, A. Jenkins, W. Mendes, A. Oswald, and T. Wilson for helpful comments.

For Analysis

1. Identify this article's inspiration, thesis, support, rationales, and implications. For additional guidance, review the Guided Analysis of a Scholarly Argument (pp. 106–114).
2. Compare this article with Killingsworth's video TED Talk, using the WHAT'S NEXT (Question 2) on p. 121.
3. Read the online supplementary material at http://www.sciencemag.org/content/suppl/2010/11/09/330.6006.932.DC1/Killingsworth.SOM.pdf. What kinds of additional support do these materials provide? Does this information make their argument more persuasive for you as a reader? Would it persuade a different audience?

For Writing

Trace the scholarly "genealogy" of this article using the WHAT'S NEXT activity on p. 68.

"What Happy People Do Differently"

by Robert Biswas-Diener and Todd B. Kashdan

Robert Biswas-Diener is a psychologist, writer, and instructor at Portland State University. **Todd B. Kashdan** is a professor at George Mason University who has published extensively on anxiety and emotional well-being. Their article appeared in *Psychology Today* in 2013.

For psychologists who frequently fly cross-country, how we describe our career to seatmates—mentioning for example, that we are psychologists—determines whether we get five hours of airborne intrigue or inside access to a decaying marriage or more detail than you can imagine about an inability to resist maple-glazed Krispy Kremes. Even wearing oversized headphones often fails to dissuade the passenger hell-bent on telling her story of childhood abandonment (which is why it is handy for research psychologists to simply say we study "judgments"). For those of us who risk the truth and admit that we study happiness, there's one practically guaranteed response: *What can I do to be happy?*

The secret of happiness is a concern of growing importance in the modern era, as increased financial security has given many the time to focus on self-growth. No longer hunter-gatherers concerned with where to find the next kill, we worry instead about how to live our best lives. Happiness books have become a cottage industry; personal-development trainings are a bigger business than ever.

The pursuit of happiness is not uniquely American either—in a study of more than 10,000 participants from 48 countries, psychologists Ed Diener of the University of Illinois at Urbana-Champaign and Shigehiro Oishi of the University of Virginia discovered that people from every corner of the globe rated happiness as being more important than other highly desirable personal outcomes, such as having meaning in life, becoming rich, and getting into heaven.

The fever for happiness is spurred on, in part, by a growing body of research suggesting that happiness does not just feel good but is good for you—it's been linked to all sorts of benefits, from higher earnings and better immune-system functioning to boosts in creativity.

Most people accept that true happiness is more than a jumble of intensely positive feelings—it's probably better described as a sense of "peace" or "contentedness." Regardless of how it's defined, happiness is partly emotional—and therefore tethered to the truth that each individual's feelings have a natural set point, like a thermostat, which genetic baggage and personality play a role in establishing. Yes, positive events give you a boost, but before long you swing back toward your natural set point.

True happiness lasts longer than a burst of dopamine, however, so it's important to think of it as something more than just emotion. Your sense of happiness also includes cognitive reflections, such as when you give a mental thumbs-up or thumbs-down to your best friend's sense of humor, the shape of your nose, or the quality of your marriage. Only a bit of this sense has to do with how you feel; the rest is the product of mental arithmetic, when you compute your expectations, your ideals, your acceptance of what you can't change—and countless other factors. That is, happiness is a state of mind, and as such, can be intentional and strategic.

Regardless of your emotional set point, your everyday habits and choices—from the way you operate in a friendship to how you reflect on your life decisions—can push the needle on your well-being. Recent scholarship documenting the unique habits of those who are happiest in life even provides something of an instruction manual for emulating them. It turns out that activities that lead us to feel uncertainty, discomfort, and even a dash of guilt are associated with some of the most memorable and enjoyable experiences of people's lives. Happy people, it seems, engage in a wide range of counterintuitive habits that seem, well, downright *un*happy.

The Real Rewards of Risk

When Anxiety is an Optimal State

It's a Friday night and you're planning on meeting friends for dinner. If you want to ensure that you'll go home full, you grab pizza or burgers. If you instead pick a cuisine you've never tried before (Ethiopian—sure, why not?) you run the risk that you won't like your injera and wat that much—but you might also uncover a surprising delight.

Truly happy people seem to have an intuitive grasp of the fact that sustained happiness is not just about doing things that you like. It also requires growth and adventuring beyond the boundaries of your comfort zone. Happy people, are, simply put, curious. In a 2007 study, Todd Kashdan and Colorado State psychologist Michael Steger found that when participants monitored their own daily activities, as well as how they felt, over the course of 21 days, those who frequently felt curious on a given day also experienced the most satisfaction with their life—and engaged in the highest number of happiness-inducing activities, such as expressing gratitude to a colleague or volunteering to help others.

Yet curiosity—that pulsing, eager state of not knowing—is fundamentally an anxious state. When, for instance, psychologist Paul Silvia showed research participants a variety of paintings, calming images by Claude Monet and Claude Lorrain evoked happy feelings, whereas the mysterious, unsettling works by Egon Schiele and Francisco Goya evoked curiosity.

Curiosity, it seems, is largely about exploration—often at the price of momentary happiness. Curious people generally accept the notion that while being uncomfortable and vulnerable is not an easy path, it is the most direct route to becoming stronger and wiser. In fact, a closer look at the study by Kashdan and Steger suggests that curious people invest in activities that cause them discomfort as a springboard to higher psychological peaks.

Of course, there are plenty of instances in life where the best way to increase your satisfaction is to simply do what you know feels good, whether it's putting your favorite song on the jukebox or making plans to see your best friend. But from time to time, it's worth seeking out an experience that is novel, complicated, uncertain, or even upsetting—whether that means finally taking the leap and doing karaoke for the first time or hosting a screening of your college friend's art-house film. The happiest people opt for both so that they can benefit, at various times, from each.

A Blind Eye to Life's Vicissitudes

The Benefit of Seeing the Forest but not the Trees

A standard criticism of happy people is that they're not realistic—they sail through life blissfully unaware of the world's ills and problems. Satisfied people are less likely to be analytical and detail-oriented. A study led by University of New South Wales psychologist Joseph Forgas found that dispositionally happy people—those who have a general leaning toward the positive—are less skeptical than others. They tend to be uncritically open toward strangers and thus can be particularly gullible to lies and deceit. Think of the happy granny who is overcharged at the car dealership by the smiling salesperson compared with more discerning, slightly less upbeat consumers.

Certainly having an eye for the finer points can be helpful when navigating the complicated social world of colleagues, acquaintances, and dates—and it's something the less sunny among us bring to bear. In fact, Virginia Commonwealth University psychologist Paul Andrews has argued that depression is actually adaptive. Depressed people, the logic goes, are more likely than others to reflect on and process their experiences—and thereby gain insight into themselves or the human condition—albeit at an emotional price. A little attention to detail helps with a more realistic evaluation of the social world.

Yet too much attention to detail can interfere with basic day-to-day functioning, as evidenced by research from Queen's University psychologist Kate Harkness, who found that people in a depressed mood were more likely to notice minute changes in facial expressions. Meanwhile, happy people tend to overlook such second-to-second alterations—a flash of annoyance, a sarcastic grin. You probably recognize this phenomenon from interactions you've had with your partner. While in a bad mood we tend to notice the tiniest shifts and often can't seem to disengage from a fight ("I saw you roll your eyes at me! Why did you do that!?!"), whereas when we're in a good mood, we tend to brush off tiny sleights ("You tease me, but I know you love being around me"). The happiest people have a natural emotional protection against getting sucked in by the intense gravitational pull of little details.

Similarly, the happiest people possess a devil-may-care attitude about performance. In a review of the research literature by Oishi and his colleagues, the happiest people—those who scored a 9 or 10 out of 10 on measures of life satisfaction—tended to perform less well than moderately happy people in accomplishments such as grades, class attendance, or work salaries. In short, they were less conscientious about their performance; to them, sacrificing some degree of achievement seems to be a small price to pay for not having to sweat the small stuff.

This is not to say that we should take a laissez-faire attitude to all our responsibilities; paying attention to detail is helpful. But too much focus on minutiae can be exhausting and paralyzing. The happiest among us (cheerfully) accept that striving for perfection—and a perfectly smooth interaction with everyone at all times—is a loser's bet.

The Unjealous Friend

We're Buoyed by Others' Good Fortune

You've heard it a million times: The definition of a good friend is one who's there to lend a hand in times of need. In a recent Gallup World Poll, the biggest predictor of happiness at work was whether or not a person had a best friend they could call on for support. It makes sense, then, that we often assume that a good friend is the one who takes us out for beer and sympathy after we get passed up for a promotion—or that we're being one when we pick up our buddy at the bar after his post-layoff binge leaves him too drunk to drive.

Indeed, such support softens the blow of difficult life circumstances by helping the sufferer move past them. Still, new research reveals a less intuitive idea about friendship: The happiest people are the ones who are present when things go right for others—and whose own wins are regularly celebrated by their friends as well.

Support for this idea comes from psychologist Shelly Gable, of the University of California, Santa Barbara, and her colleagues, whose research revealed that when romantic partners fail to make a big deal out of each other's success, the couple is more likely to break up. On the flipside, when partners celebrate each other's accomplishments, they're more likely to be satisfied and committed to their relationship, enjoying greater love and happiness.

Outside of your primary relationship, however, why would capitalizing on others' success make you happier? Why should you support your born-lucky buddy by listening to him detail yet another sexual conquest when you're spending far too many Friday nights reading zombie comic books? For one thing, he really does need you. The process of discussing a positive experience with a responsive listener actually changes the memory of the event—so after telling you about it, your friend will remember that night with the model as even more positive than it was, and the encounter will be easier for him to recall a few years down the line when he's been dumped. But equally important, you'll get to "piggyback" on your friend's positivity. Just as we feel happier when we spend money on gifts or charitable contributions rather than on ourselves, we feel happier after spending valuable time listening to the accomplishments of friends.

In life, it seems, there are an abundance of Florence Nightingales waiting to show their heroism. What's precious and scarce are those people who can truly share in others' joy and gains without envy. So while it might be kind to send flowers to your friend when she's in the hospital for surgery, you'll both derive more satisfaction out of the bouquet you send her when she finishes medical school or gets engaged.

A Time for Every Feeling

The Upside of Negative Emotions

The most psychologically healthy people might inherently grasp the importance of letting some things roll off their backs, yet that doesn't mean that they deny their own feelings or routinely sweep problems under the rug. Rather, they have an innate understanding that emotions serve as feedback—an internal radar system providing information about what's happening (and about to happen) in our social world.

Happy, flourishing people don't hide from negative emotions. They acknowledge that life is full of disappointments and confront them head on, often using feelings of anger effectively to stick up for themselves or those of guilt as motivation to change their own behavior. This nimble mental shifting between pleasure and pain, the ability to modify behavior to match a situation's demands, is known as psychological flexibility.

For example, instead of letting quietly simmering jealousy over your girlfriend's new buddy erode your satisfaction with your relationship, accept your feelings as a signal, which allows you to employ other strategies of reacting that are likely to offer greater dividends. These include compassion (recognizing that your girlfriend has unmet needs to be validated) and mindful listening (being curious about what interests her).

The ability to shift mental states as circumstances demand turns out to be a fundamental aspect of well-being. Columbia University psychologist George Bonanno found, for instance, that in the aftermath of 9/11, the most flexible people living in New York City during the attacks—those who were angry at times but could also conceal their emotions when necessary—bounced back more quickly and enjoyed greater psychological and physical health than their less adaptable counterparts.

Opportunities for flexible responding are everywhere: A newlywed who has just learned that she is infertile may hide her sense of hopelessness from her mother but come clean to her best friend; people who have experienced a trauma might express their anger around others who share similar sentiments but conceal it from friends who abide by an attitude of forgiveness. The ability to tolerate the discomfort that comes from switching mind-sets depending on whom we're with and what we're doing allows us to get optimal results in every situation.

Similar to training for a triathlon, learning the skill of emotional discomfort is a task best taken on in increasing increments. For example, instead of immediately distracting yourself with an episode of *The Walking Dead* or pouring yourself a whiskey the next time you have a heated disagreement with your teenage son, try simply tolerating the emotion for a few minutes. Over time, your ability to withstand day-to-day negative emotions will expand.

The Well-Being Balancing Act

Pleasure and Purpose Work Together

Even the most ardent strivers will agree that a life of purpose that is devoid of pleasures is, frankly, no fun. Happy people know that allowing yourself to enjoy easy momentary indulgences that are personally rewarding—taking a long, leisurely bath, vegging out with your daughter's copy of *The Hunger Games*, or occasionally skipping your Saturday workout in favor of catching the soccer match on TV—is a crucial aspect of living a satisfying life. Still, if you're primarily focused on activities that feel good in the moment, you may miss out on the benefits of developing a clear purpose. Purpose is what drives us to take risks and make changes—even in the face of hardship and when sacrificing short-term happiness.

Working to uncover how happy people balance pleasure and purpose, Colorado State's Steger and his colleagues have shown that the act of trying to comprehend and navigate our world generally causes us to deviate from happiness. After all, this mission is fraught with tension, uncertainty, complexity, short bursts of intrigue and excitement, and conflicts between the desire to feel good and the desire to make progress toward what we care about most. Yet overall, people who are the happiest tend to be superior at sacrificing short-term pleasures when there is a good opportunity to make progress toward what they aspire to become in life.

If you want to envision a happy person's stance, imagine one foot rooted in the present with mindful appreciation of what one has—and the other foot reaching toward the future for yet-to-be-uncovered sources of meaning. Indeed, research by neuroscientist Richard Davidson of the University of Wisconsin at Madison has revealed that making advances toward achievement of our goals not only causes us to feel more engaged, it actually helps us tolerate any negative feelings that arise during the journey.

Nobody would pretend that finding purpose is easy or that it can be done in a simple exercise, but thinking about which activities you found most rewarding and meaningful in the past week, what you're good at and often recognized for, what experiences you'd be unwilling to give up, and which ones you crave more time for can help. Also, notice whether your answers reflect something you feel that you ought to say as opposed to what you truly love. For example, being a parent doesn't necessarily mean that spending time with your children is the most energizing, meaningful part of your life—and it's important to accept that. Lying to yourself is one of the biggest barriers to creating purpose. The happiest people have a knack for being honest about what does and does not energize them—and in addition to building in time for sensory pleasures each day, they are able to integrate the activities they most care about into a life of purpose and satisfaction.

There's More to Life Than Being Happy

Nobel Laureate Albert Schweitzer once quipped that "happiness is nothing more than good health and a bad memory." Despite the apparent luster of achieving a predominantly positive state of mind, critics argue that the pursuit of happiness is a misguided goal—it's fleeting, superficial, and hedonistic.

Research backs up some of these claims. Studies by psychologist Ed Diener show that people actually pay an emotional price for intensely positive events because later ones—even moderately pleasant ones—seem less shiny by contrast. (Sure, getting a raise feels terrific, but it might mean you fail to fully appreciate your son's performance in the school play that afternoon.)

Perhaps more damning is a series of studies led by University of California, Berkeley psychologist Iris Mauss, which revealed that people who place a premium on being happy report feeling more lonely. Yes, being happy might be healthy—but craving happiness is a slippery slope.

As well-being researchers, we don't deny the importance of happiness—but we've also concluded that a well-lived life is more than just one in which you feel "up." The good life is best construed as a matrix that includes happiness, occasional sadness, a sense of purpose, playfulness, and psychological flexibility, as well autonomy, mastery, and belonging.

While some people will rank high in happiness and social belonging, others will find they've attained a sense of mastery and achievement. This approach appreciates that not only do people differ in their happiness matrices—but they can shift in their own respective matrices from moment to moment.

For instance, your sense of autonomy might spike dramatically when, as a college freshman, you shift from living under your parents' rules to the freedom of dorm life—and then plummet a decade later when you become a parent and must sacrifice even the ability to choose your hours of sleep. Yet it would be a mistake to assume that coeds have greater well-being than new parents. Rather, each group is experiencing a unique flavor.

Parsing the good life into a matrix is more than linguistic trickery; shifting toward a mixed-bag view of well-being opens more paths to achieving a personally desirable life. Enjoying success in even one area of the matrix can be a cause for celebration.

Happiness by the Numbers

.62

Distance from home, in miles, at which point people's tweets begin declining in expressed happiness (about the distance expected for a short work commute).

40

The percentage of our capacity for happiness that is within our power to change, according to University of California, Riverside researcher Sonja Lyubomirsky.

85

Number of residents out of every 100 who report feeling positive emotions in Panama and Paraguay, the most positive countries in the world.

20

The percentage of the U.S. population wealthy enough that their feelings of happiness are not affected by fluctuations in Americans' income equality.

For Analysis

1. Biswas-Diener and Kashdan cite several studies to support their claims. Find three of these sources using your library's reference databases. Practice writing a scholarly citation for each source.
2. The authors use some illustrations, or hypothetical examples, that might not be relevant for traditional college-aged students. What illustrations would work better for a younger audience?
3. Do you think this genre might be more persuasive than a more clinical or scholarly argument? Why, and for whom?

For Writing

This article presents five main ideas about how happiness works. Translate these ideas into a 1,000-word how-to guide for college students seeking to be happier. Use specific, compelling illustrations that will be relevant for your audience.

"For the Love of Money"
by Sam Polk

Sam Polk formerly worked as a hedge-fund trader but now co-runs Groceryships, a nonprofit organization that helps "poor families struggling with obesity and food addiction." Polk also writes articles and op-eds and speaks for various organizations. This 2014 *New York Times* commentary examines "wealth addiction."

IN my last year on Wall Street my bonus was $3.6 million—and I was angry because it wasn't big enough. I was 30 years old, had no children to raise, no debts to pay, no philanthropic goal in mind. I wanted more money for exactly the same reason an alcoholic needs another drink: I was addicted.

Eight years earlier, I'd walked onto the trading floor at Credit Suisse First Boston to begin my summer internship. I already knew I wanted to be rich, but when I started out I had a different idea about what wealth meant. I'd come to Wall Street after reading in the book "Liar's Poker" how Michael Lewis earned a $225,000 bonus after just two years of work on a trading floor. That seemed like a fortune. Every January and February, I think about that time, because these are the months when bonuses are decided and distributed, when fortunes are made.

I'd learned about the importance of being rich from my dad. He was a modern-day Willy Loman, a salesman with huge dreams that never seemed to materialize. "Imagine what life will be like," he'd say, "when I make a million dollars." While he dreamed of selling a screenplay, in reality he sold kitchen cabinets. And not that well. We sometimes lived paycheck to paycheck off my mom's nurse-practitioner salary.

Dad believed money would solve all his problems. At 22, so did I. When I walked onto that trading floor for the first time and saw the glowing flat-screen TVs, high-tech computer monitors and phone turrets with enough dials, knobs and buttons to make it seem like the cockpit of a fighter plane, I knew exactly what I wanted to do with the rest of my life. It looked as if the traders were playing a video game inside a spaceship; if you won this video game, you became what I most wanted to be—rich.

IT was a miracle I'd made it to Wall Street at all. While I was competitive and ambitious—a wrestler at Columbia University—I was also a daily drinker and pot smoker and a regular user of cocaine, Ritalin and ecstasy. I had a propensity for self-destruction that had resulted in my getting suspended from Columbia for burglary, arrested twice and fired from an Internet company for fistfighting. I learned about rage from my dad, too. I can still see his red, contorted face as he charged toward me. I'd lied my way into the C.S.F.B. internship by omitting my transgressions from my résumé and was determined not to blow what seemed a final chance. The only thing as important to me as that internship was my girlfriend, a starter on the Columbia volleyball team. But even though I was in love with her, when I got drunk I'd sometimes end up with other women.

Three weeks into my internship she wisely dumped me. I don't like who you've become, she said. I couldn't blame her, but I was so devastated that I couldn't get out of bed. In desperation, I called a counselor whom I had reluctantly seen a few times before and asked for help.

She helped me see that I was using alcohol and drugs to blunt the powerlessness I felt as a kid and suggested I give them up. That began some of the hardest months of my life. Without the alcohol and drugs in my system, I felt like my chest had been cracked open, exposing my heart to air. The counselor said that my abuse of drugs and alcohol was a symptom of an underlying problem—a "spiritual malady," she called it. C.S.F.B. didn't offer me a full-time job, and I returned, distraught, to Columbia for senior year.

After graduation, I got a job at Bank of America, by the grace of a managing director willing to take a chance on a kid who had called him every day for three weeks. With a year of sobriety under my belt, I was sharp, cleareyed and hard-working. At the end of my first year I was thrilled to receive a $40,000 bonus. For the first time in my life, I didn't have to check my balance before I withdrew money. But a week later, a trader who was only four years my senior got hired away by C.S.F.B. for $900,000. After my initial envious shock—his haul was 22 times the size of my bonus—I grew excited at how much money was available.

Over the next few years I worked like a maniac and began to move up the Wall Street ladder. I became a bond and credit default swap trader, one of the more lucrative roles in the business. Just four years after I started at Bank of America, Citibank offered me a "1.75 by 2" which means $1.75 million per year for two years, and I used it to get a promotion. I started dating a pretty blonde and rented a loft apartment on Bond Street for $6,000 a month.

I felt so important. At 25, I could go to any restaurant in Manhattan—Per Se, Le Bernardin—just by picking up the phone and calling one of my brokers, who ingratiate themselves to traders by entertaining with unlimited expense accounts. I could be second row at the Knicks-Lakers game just by hinting to a broker I might be interested in going. The satisfaction wasn't just about the money. It was about the power. Because of how smart and successful I was, it was someone else's job to make me happy.

Still, I was nagged by envy. On a trading desk everyone sits together, from interns to managing directors. When the guy next to you makes $10 million, $1 million or $2 million doesn't look so sweet. Nonetheless, I was thrilled with my progress.

My counselor didn't share my elation. She said I might be using money the same way I'd used drugs and alcohol—to make myself feel powerful—and that maybe it would benefit me to stop focusing on accumulating more and instead focus on healing my inner wound. "Inner wound"? I thought that was going a little far and went to work for a hedge fund.

Now, working elbow to elbow with billionaires, I was a giant fireball of greed. I'd think about how my colleagues could buy Micronesia if they wanted to, or become mayor of New York City. They didn't just have money; they had power—power beyond getting a table at Le Bernardin. Senators came to their offices. They were royalty.

I wanted a billion dollars. It's staggering to think that in the course of five years, I'd gone from being thrilled at my first bonus—$40,000—to being disappointed when, my second year at the hedge fund, I was paid "only" $1.5 million.

But in the end, it was actually my absurdly wealthy bosses who helped me see the limitations of unlimited wealth. I was in a meeting with one of them, and a few other traders, and they were talking about the new hedge-fund regulations. Most everyone on Wall Street thought they were a bad idea. "But isn't it better for the system as a whole?" I asked. The room went quiet, and my boss shot me a withering look. I remember his saying, "I don't have the brain capacity to think about the system as a whole. All I'm concerned with is how this affects our company."

I felt as if I'd been punched in the gut. He was afraid of losing money, despite all that he had.

From that moment on, I started to see Wall Street with new eyes. I noticed the vitriol that traders directed at the government for limiting bonuses after the crash. I heard the fury in their voices at the mention of higher taxes. These traders despised anything or anyone that threatened their bonuses. Ever see what a drug addict is like when he's used up his junk? He'll do anything—walk 20 miles in the snow, rob a grandma—to get a fix. Wall Street was like that. In the months before bonuses were handed out, the trading floor started to feel like a neighborhood in "The Wire" when the heroin runs out.

I'd always looked enviously at the people who earned more than I did; now, for the first time, I was embarrassed for them, and for me. I made in a single year more than my mom made her whole life. I knew that wasn't fair; that wasn't right. Yes, I was sharp, good with numbers. I had marketable talents. But in the end I didn't really do anything. I was a derivatives trader, and it occurred to me the world would hardly change at all if credit derivatives ceased to exist. Not so nurse practitioners. What had seemed normal now seemed deeply distorted.

I had recently finished Taylor Branch's three-volume series on the Rev. Dr. Martin Luther King Jr. and the civil rights movement, and the image of the Freedom Riders stepping out of their bus into an infuriated mob had seared itself into my mind. I'd told myself that if I'd been alive in the '60s, I would have been on that bus.

But I was lying to myself. There were plenty of injustices out there — rampant poverty, swelling prison populations, a sexual-assault epidemic, an obesity crisis. Not only was I not helping to fix any problems in the world, but I was profiting from them. During the market crash in 2008, I'd made a ton of money by shorting the derivatives of risky companies. As the world crumbled, I profited. I'd seen the crash coming, but instead of trying to help the people it would hurt the most—people who didn't have a million dollars in the bank—I'd made money off it. I don't like who you've become, my girlfriend had said years earlier. She was right then, and she was still right. Only now, I didn't like who I'd become either.

Wealth addiction was described by the late sociologist and playwright Philip Slater in a 1980 book, but addiction researchers have paid the concept little attention. Like alcoholics driving drunk, wealth addiction imperils everyone. Wealth addicts are, more than anybody, specifically responsible for the ever widening rift that is tearing apart our once great country. Wealth addicts are responsible for the vast and toxic disparity between the rich and the poor and the annihilation of the middle class. Only a wealth addict would feel justified in receiving $14 million in compensation—including an $8.5 million bonus—as the McDonald's C.E.O., Don Thompson, did in 2012, while his company then published a brochure for its work force on how to survive on their low wages. Only a wealth addict would earn hundreds of millions as a hedge-fund manager, and then lobby to maintain a tax loophole that gave him a lower tax rate than his secretary.

DESPITE my realizations, it was incredibly difficult to leave. I was terrified of running out of money and of forgoing future bonuses. More than anything, I was afraid that five or 10 years down the road, I'd feel like an idiot for walking away from my one chance to be really important. What made it harder was that people thought I was crazy for thinking about leaving. In 2010, in a final paroxysm of my withering addiction, I demanded $8 million instead of $3.6 million. My bosses said they'd raise my bonus if I agreed to stay several more years. Instead, I walked away.

The first year was really hard. I went through what I can only describe as withdrawal—waking up at nights panicked about running out of money, scouring the headlines to see which of my old co-workers had gotten promoted. Over time it got easier—I started to realize that I had enough money, and if I needed to make more, I could. But my wealth addiction still hasn't gone completely away. Sometimes I still buy lottery tickets.

In the three years since I left, I've married, spoken in jails and juvenile detention centers about getting sober, taught a writing class to girls in the foster system, and started a nonprofit called Groceryships to help poor families struggling with obesity and food addiction. I am much happier. I feel as if I'm making a real contribution. And as time passes, the distortion lessens. I see Wall Street's mantra—"We're smarter and work harder than everyone else, so we deserve all this money"—for what it is: the rationalization of addicts. From a distance I can see what I couldn't see then—that Wall Street is a toxic culture that encourages the grandiosity of people who are desperately trying to feel powerful.

I was lucky. My experience with drugs and alcohol allowed me to recognize my pursuit of wealth as an addiction. The years of work I did with my counselor helped me heal the parts of myself that felt damaged and inadequate, so that I had enough of a core sense of self to walk away.

Dozens of different types of 12-step support groups—including Clutterers Anonymous and On-Line Gamers Anonymous—exist to help addicts of various types, yet there is no Wealth Addicts Anonymous. Why not? Because our culture supports and even lauds the addiction. Look at the magazine covers in any newsstand, plastered with the faces of celebrities and C.E.O.'s; the superrich are our cultural gods. I hope we all confront our part in enabling wealth addicts to exert so much influence over our country.

I generally think that if one is rich and believes they have "enough," they are not a wealth addict. On Wall Street, in my experience, that sense of "enough" is rare. The money guy doing a job he complains about for yet another year so he can add $2 million to his $20 million bank account seems like an addict.

I recently got an email from a hedge-fund trader who said that though he was making millions every year, he felt trapped and empty, but couldn't summon the courage to leave. I believe there are others out there. Maybe we can form a group and confront our addiction together. And if you identify with what I've written, but are reticent to leave, then take a small step in the right direction. Let's create a fund, where everyone agrees to put, say, 25 percent of their annual bonuses into it, and we'll use that to help some of the people who actually need the money that we've been so rabidly chasing. Together, maybe we can make a real contribution to the world.

For Analysis

1. How compelling is Polk's narrative? What specifically makes his story interesting? What techniques does he use to narrate his experience?
2. Polk doesn't incorporate much verification to corroborate his experience. Does this weaken his argument? If he had supported his

argument with verification, what kinds of sources could he include? Where should he have added verification?

3. Polk ends by listing a few solutions to the problem. How satisfied are you with these suggestions? Do they sound sufficient, realistic, and effective?

For Writing

In the online version of this article, several readers comment that Polk exaggerates his claims and overgeneralizes his experience. Read some of these comments and find other accounts of life on Wall Street to determine how accurate Polk's story is. Then, write a 600- to 800-word essay that synthesizes these views and develops an argument about the health of Wall Street professionals.

Excerpt from "An Interview on 'The Paradox of Choice' with Barry Schwartz"

by Elizabeth Cosgriff

Barry Schwartz is a psychologist and professor at Swarthmore College. He has written several books, including *The Paradox of Choice,* which prompted this interview by **Elizabeth Cosgriff**, published in the journal *Open Spaces: Views from the Northwest.* Cosgriff has worked as an attorney, legal editor, magazine editor, and writer.

Americans today are faced with a bewildering, not to say overwhelming, variety of choices in many areas of our lives. Food, electronics, entertainment, utilities, college courses, retirement plans, medical care, job choices, religious observance, love interests,—even decisions about how we identify ourselves, and, with the advent of cosmetic surgery, about how we want to look—all confront us with an unprecedented number of options. Although we have traditionally, and correctly, viewed having choices as essential to our well-being by improving the quality of our lives and enabling us to control our destinies, Professor Schwartz argues that we have reached the point where we have too much of a good thing. Americans' love of freedom, self-determination, and variety has a downside.

Making decisions is difficult, and the more choices we have, the more difficult it becomes. We come to feel overloaded by the number of options, unable to cope. Too many choices also increase our regret for all the options we didn't choose, and make us more disappointed with ourselves if our decisions turn out badly. Additionally, the time we devote to making decisions decreases the time we have to spend on other aspects of life, such as forming close relationships. Professor Schwartz prescribes some attitudinal adjustments that he says will help us deal with this overload, including "choosing when to choose," being satisfied with "good enough," and controlling our expectations. This is an unusual message for our society, but the enthusiastic reception of *The Paradox of Choice* indicates that it resonates with a number of people.

Barry Schwartz Interview

E Why did you write *The Paradox of Choice*?

B That's a simple question with a complicated answer. For 25 years I have been working on the ideology that the magic of the market is the solution to all problems. But what occurred to me was: why would anyone think that the market is such a wonderful device for achieving happiness? And more and more it seemed to me the central thing that people liked so much about it is the freedom of choice it provides. It's not the most efficient, but it lets everybody get what they want, and what could be more important than that? So I started asking whether this freedom of choice was just an unequivocal, unalloyed good, and then a paper came out about five years ago [by Drs. Sheena Iyengar and Mark Lepper] that reported on this study where they showed that when you give people lots of choices of jam to try they are very attracted, but they don't buy.

For about 40 years psychologists had studied the benefits of choice, comparing, say, two options to only one, and people were always happier when they had two rather than one. It never occurred to anyone to ask about three, or four, or five, but it turns out that if the options get large enough the good news turns to bad news. So that's what got me to focus specifically on choice and what it might be about choice that could produce negative rather than positive psychological consequences.

So my colleague and I devised a scale that measures people's orientation to making choices, whether they want the best or just good enough, and did some research on that. Meanwhile other research consistently showed that there's some number after which adding options makes it less likely people will choose anything.

E Do you have a specific number for that?
B No, there's no right number of choices. Two different things are going on: One of them is, the greater the number of options, the more likely you are to find something that suits your desires, so that's what's good about it. But probably a point is reached at which additional options don't add much. Because one of the eight is good enough. And when you add more options, you don't produce much more additional benefit in being able to select what you want, and all of the negative effects—difficulty choosing, regret, missed opportunity—add up, and you start to pay a price. This one guy did a study with pens, where people got to choose a pen from 2, 4, 6, 8, 10, 12, 14, 16, 18, or 20, and what he found was that optimum satisfaction with the choice seemed to occur between 8 and 12. So that's a ballpark number for ballpoint pens, but for dishes on a restaurant menu, the number could be different.

E In the area of consumer goods, given that it is market-driven, is there any end in sight?
B Yes, actually. This may be optimistic on my part, but in the 2 1/2 years since *The Paradox of Choice* came out, I must have given talks at 30 or 40 commercial industry-type organizations, and every time I've given a talk almost everyone in the room agrees that I have identified a problem; they can see in their own lives and in what they sell. So the task then becomes, "How do we fix this? What do we do about it?" And that suggests to me that there will be entrants into the marketplace that actually try to make life easier for consumers rather than torturing them with lots of options. The model was customization: there should be a version of X for everyone, no matter how weird your taste is. Now there will be more and more sensitivity to making the decision easier for people. Which means more structuring of the

possibilities so we don't have to look at all hundred of them; we can look at five. You can answer one question: "Do you want a fuel-efficient car or a powerful car? Then you answer another question: "Do you want an American car or a foreign car?" So you're always making binary decisions or decisions between two or three things, and not between the hundred. In that way you make the choice problem less acute. So I'm optimistic that people who do take initiative in that direction will start stealing business from places that don't, and over time, even in something like the marketplace, there will be a movement away from what we now experience toward something that's a little less insane.

E Do you know of any actual examples of this?
B I know of a few places where they're committed to doing this. The problem, of course, is that there are many slips between what I say, what they hear, and what they do. So what it will end up turning out to look like may not be what I would have designed. A very large consumer electronics chain is taken with the ideas, and thinks that it really needs to re-brand itself as the place that has the solution to your problem, rather than as the place that has everything under the sun. There's a large retailer of office supplies that is similarly committed now to reducing the number of options in paper clips, printer paper, etc.

E That's fascinating. Such a paradigm shift.
B It is a complete paradigm shift. The standard model of retailing is not to let anyone walk out of the store empty-handed, and that means you have to have something for everybody. And what people didn't appreciate is that, yes, if you don't have something for everybody some people will leave with nothing, but meanwhile, people who leave with something leave with greater satisfaction than they would if you made it so hard for them. There are some clear examples of this working. There's a supermarket chain called Trader Joe's—it's the fastest-growing supermarket in the United States. One reason, I

think, is that they have very limited selection. The big box store Costco is the store that people leave happiest. And they too, unlike Wal-Mart, have very limited selection. They only have two or three kinds of toilet paper. Plus you have to buy a package of 4,000 rolls! But people walk out of there happy, because they're getting good prices; they haven't gone to the fifteenth level of hell to go shopping; and so they find the experience positive. I don't think it occurred to people prior *The Paradox of Choice* that one of the reasons Costco makes people happy and the reason Trader Joe's is so successful is that limited variety. And with those as models, we might well see limited choice start to spread to others.

I've given talks to web and technology developers, and what they hear is that the task for the future of technology is designing intelligent filters for search engines—Google on steroids. So that no matter how many things are out there in the world you can look at them through a filter that only shows you the four or five you ought to care about. So it's as if there only are four or five. The other ones will just be invisible. They've already done the job of making every imaginable piece of information accessible. Now the trick is to help you manage all of that information, including hiding a lot of it. If that actually comes to pass, at least for online retailers it will solve the problem.

E One thing you said that I found very interesting was that on a personal level people aren't necessarily good at making choices. You said one of the problems with having too many options is that it leads you to make choices that don't really reflect your highest values. Do you have any more examples of that?

B Yes, one is in the case of choosing romantic partners, where, when you meet a lot of people you end up choosing on the basis of the easiest to assess criteria, which is physical attractiveness, which you know is not what you care most about. Another is in choosing investment options. When there is a large number of alternatives of stock funds, people who know that it's foolish to choose none of them, or to choose not to invest, still manage to choose none of the stock funds, but put their money into a money market fund, which pays three-quarters of one percent interest, so it's certainly the worst investment you can make if you're 30 years old and putting money away for your retirement, but it's better than doing nothing.

The general point—and it hasn't been well studied yet—is that if it's a complicated decision you might be able to make it well if there aren't too many options—Complicated meaning that there are many dimensions to the choice. But if there aren't many options you can maybe give a full assessment of all of the options, considering all of the criteria. If it's a simple decision, then it doesn't maybe matter how many options there are. You can just apply your standard, whatever it is, to everything. If all you care about is fuel efficiency, you can rank all of the cars in the world by that one thing. And the more cars there are, the better, because the more likelihood you'll find that one car that gets 80 miles to the gallon, and you just pick the most efficient one, no problem. But if there are many dimensions that matter and many options that matter it now becomes a task that exceeds our capacity. And either you reduce the choice set, which people tend not to do, or you reduce the features that you evaluate, which is what people tend to do, though they don't necessarily realize that they're doing it. So they'll make a decision that's the best they can do under the circumstances, but really not the best they can do, and not a reflection of the things they care most about. So they'll end up regretting the decision in the light of the next day.

E Do you think people in their 20s and 30s are having more problems than earlier generations in making some of these major life decisions—are putting off choosing a career, a mate—some of those really big decisions?

B The answer to that in my own personal experience is unequivocally yes. Whether there is systematic research data indicating that my impression is correct I don't know. But I find that kids have an incredibly hard time making important life decisions and the more talented they are the worse it is. Because if you're very talented and have cultivated many of those talents you are both interested in a lot of things and good at a lot of things. And that means you're going to have to say good-bye to things that you're good at and that you like, when you finally decide what your grown-up life's going to look like. I think it's totally debilitating, and people graduate from college and start what they think is going to be a year but often extends into the indefinite future trying to figure out what to do. And this is a reflection of all the choice that is available to people not in the domain of goods, but of lifestyle. "What kind of person am I going to be, where am I going to live, anything is possible. This is one of the benefits of freedom and affluence, I should take advantage of all that." But then the time comes to choose and people don't know how to choose.

E Do you think it's worse now?

B I think it's worse now than it's been since I've been teaching. It's a nice steady progression; it just keeps getting worse. Everyone just takes it for granted that they're going to make a living. The question is, which job? Where? A depression would change all of that and makes the question: Am I going to be able to pay my bills and support my family? You take the first thing that comes along. It's even possible that people would be more satisfied with the work they do, even though they've been almost coerced into doing, it than they are now, when they're always looking over their shoulders and thinking about whether this other career path would have been more satisfying.

E Looking at how we make decisions, it seems that in our political discourse things have gotten so polarized that people tend only to go to news sources that have the viewpoint they already believe in, and talk to persons of similar viewpoints.

B This is another consequence of choice that I think is a civic disaster. We have choice in media in a way that we didn't before, and what's good about that is clear—you get to listen to just the kind of music you like, and just the kind of political commentary you like. What's bad about it is that people are no longer forced to encounter an idea they disagree with. And what that means is that where on earth are people ever going to change their minds about anything? Wherever are they going to find common ground with their opponents so that they can get to some agreement at a higher level? It's not going to happen; there's no need for it to happen. When everyone was watching the network news, conservatives and liberals alike get hit in the face with things that neither of them was happy about. And either a new understanding and a new set of aspirations come out of that, or they remain unhappy—sometimes there are problems that can't be fixed. But now that just doesn't happen. And I think this is very bad news, and it creates a poorly informed public, and it creates polarization.

E There are interesting trends going on. Because there is a consolidation of media outlets in the hands of fewer owners. Yet on the other hand, you have this explosion of Internet blogs and websites.

B There's no question that there's massive concentration of ownership of traditional media. The only reason people are not completely distressed by this is they think the new technology provides an outlet that's much broader than ever existed before. There are no barriers to entry. You don't need three million dollars to set up a station; all you need is a web cam and the world can hear you. The problem is, when there are only a few web logs, people might notice them. When there are several million of them, there might just as well be none, and some research has been done that shows that as the number of these non-traditional outlets increases, people become more and more likely to go to the computer versions of mainstream outlets. So you will go to USAtoday.com, instead of some other source of news that you've not heard of. And where there are a million of these sources of news, USA Today gets a bigger share, because you use that as a way of filtering: "Which of these thousand web logs should I go to? Well, I'll go to one I've heard of; they must be more reliable, they've had a presence in the world of journalism for a long time." You get further concentration on this web outlet of traditional media. So it ends up that they're all out there, these million blogs, but the only people who read them are the parents of the people who write them.

E Why are there class differences in how people perceive choice?
B One possibility is that for people in the upper classes, choice is mostly a good thing, that is to say, the consequences of choosing. You get to make good choices among good alternatives. And so there's no down side, no loss of security, in choosing, and there's a huge upside. Among the working class the choices they get faced with are often choices among mediocre or worse alternatives so there's nothing great in being able to choose. And meanwhile the price they pay for having all of this choice is that their security, which is precarious, is compromised. Because there is a price for choice. No one is guaranteeing you what you need to survive. The choices are out there and if you make mistakes, you may fall through the bottom. Given that choice is among not really attractive alternatives, it's not a price worth paying. The other thing is that the aspirations of educated classes in this country are all about self-expression and self-individuation and self-actualization. That is the highest good, to be able to cultivate and to display my uniqueness. For the working class, uniqueness is not a good thing, necessarily. They're more interested in fitting in to a community with whom they have common values. So self-expression is just not what they think life is about. It's about being true to the things you think are important, and taking care of the people who are close to you. And they want freedom to do that—that's why they want the government off their necks, so they can live according to the values that they aspire to. But they're happy, not sad, if the person living next to them shares the same values and wants the same things. It affirms their values, and uniqueness is just a non-issue.

I also think that this distinction between different senses of what freedom means goes a long way towards explaining this great big red state/blue state divide, or at least red voter/blue voter. Because this notion of self-expression, that's what captures this educated elite that tends to be Democratic. And the red state commitment to values and religious institutions, I think deep down what that's revealing is this freedom is about being able to live life the right way, and not about being able to express yourself.

For Analysis

1. What was the inspiration for Schwartz's investigation?
2. What are the practical implications of Schwartz's findings for writers? For example: How might the "paradox of choice" help you design better arguments? What document design features can give readers a comfortable range of choices?
3. Watch Schwartz's online TED Talk, "The Paradox of Choice." What kinds of support from the video might have made this interview more compelling?

For Writing

Based on his "own personal experience," Schwartz claims that decision-making has become more difficult for young people than for older generations. Work with another student in class to design a brief interview that you could use to corroborate or refute this claim. Create questions that would prompt the most objective responses possible (specific examples rather than just opinions). Limit your questions to what you think someone could answer in fifteen minutes. Then, interview two younger and two older people (two interviews per student), transcribe their responses, and write a brief conclusion about what you discover (250 words or less). Consult Appendix A for guidelines on collaborating effectively.

"Suicide on Campus and the Pressure of Perfection"

by Julie Scelfo

Julie Scelfo is a journalist who has written for *Newsweek*; *Salon; O, The Oprah Magazine; Epicurious; Time Out New York;* and other magazines. She frequently writes about health, relationships, and food. *The New York Times* published this article about college suicide in July 2015.

Kathryn DeWitt conquered high school like a gold-medal decathlete. She ran track, represented her school at a statewide girls' leadership program and took eight Advanced Placement tests, including one for which she independently prepared, forgoing the class.

Expectations were high. Every day at 5 p.m. test scores and updated grades were posted online. Her mother would be the first to comment should her grade go down. "I would get home from track and she would say, 'I see your grade dropped.' I would say, 'Mom, I think it's a mistake.' And she would say, 'That's what I thought.'" (The reason turned out to be typing errors. Ms. DeWitt graduated with straight A's.)

In her first two weeks on the University of Pennsylvania campus, she hustled. She joined a coed fraternity, signed up to tutor elementary school students and joined the same Christian group her parents had joined at their alma mater, Stanford.

But having gained admittance off the wait list and surrounded by people with seemingly greater drive and ability, she had her first taste of self-doubt. "One friend was a world-class figure skater. Another was a winner of the Intel science competition. Everyone around me was so spectacular and so amazing and I wanted to be just as amazing as they are."

Classmates seemed to have it all together. Every morning, the administration sent out an email blast highlighting faculty and student accomplishments. Some women attended class wearing full makeup. Ms. DeWitt had acne. They talked about their fantastic internships. She was still focused on the week's homework. Friends' lives, as told through selfies, showed them having more fun, making more friends and going to better parties. Even the meals they posted to Instagram looked more delicious.

Her confidence took another hit when she glanced at the cellphone screen of a male student sitting next to her who was texting that he would "rather jump out of a plane" than talk to his seatmate.

When, on Jan. 17, 2014, Madison Holleran, another Penn freshman, jumped off the top of a parking garage and killed herself, Ms. DeWitt was stunned. She had never met Ms. Holleran, but she knew the student was popular, attractive and talented. In a blog post soon afterward, Ms. DeWitt would write: "What the hell, girl?! I was supposed to be the one who went first! You had so much to live for!"

Despite her cheery countenance and assiduous completion of assignments, Ms. DeWitt had already bought razor blades and written a stack of goodbye letters to loved ones.

Ms. Holleran was the third of six Penn students to commit suicide in a 13-month stretch, and the school is far from the only one to experience a so-called suicide cluster. This school year, Tulane lost four students and Appalachian State at least three—the disappearance in September of a freshman, Anna M. Smith, led to an 11-day search before she was found in the North Carolina woods, hanging from a tree. Cornell faced six suicides in the 2009-10 academic year. In 2003-4, five New York University students leapt to their deaths.

Nationally, the suicide rate among 15- to 24-year-olds has increased modestly but steadily since 2007: from 9.6 deaths per 100,000 to 11.1, in 2013 (the latest year available from the Centers for Disease Control and Prevention). But a survey of college counseling centers has found that more than half their clients have severe psychological problems, an increase of 13 percent in just two years. Anxiety and depression, in that order, are now the most common mental health diagnoses among college students, according to the Center for Collegiate Mental Health at Penn State.

Soon after Ms. Holleran's death, Penn formed a task force to examine mental health on campus. Its final report, issued earlier this year, encouraged the school to step up outreach efforts, expand counseling center hours, and designate a phone line so that anyone with concerns could find resources more easily. It also recognized a potentially life-threatening aspect of campus culture: Penn Face. An apothegm long used by students to describe the practice of acting happy and self-assured even when sad or stressed, Penn Face is so widely employed that it has showed up in skits performed during freshman orientation.

While the appellation is unique to Penn, the behavior is not. In 2003, Duke jolted academe with a report describing how its female students felt pressure to be "effortlessly perfect": smart, accomplished, fit, beautiful and popular, all without visible effort. At Stanford, it's called the Duck Syndrome. A duck appears to glide calmly across the water, while beneath the surface it frantically, relentlessly paddles.

"Nobody wants to be the one who is struggling while everyone else is doing great," said Kahaari Kenyatta, a Penn senior who once worked as an orientation counselor. "Despite whatever's going on—if you're stressed, a bit depressed, if you're overwhelmed—you want to put up this positive front."

Citing a "perception that one has to be perfect in every academic, cocurricular and social endeavor," the task force report described how students feel enormous pressure that "can manifest as demoralization, alienation or conditions like anxiety or depression."

William Alexander, director of Penn's counseling and psychological services, has watched a shift in how some young adults cope with challenges. "A small setback used to mean disappointment, or having that feeling of needing to try harder next time," he said. Now? "For some students, a mistake has incredible meaning."

Meeta Kumar, who has been counseling at Penn for 16 years, has noticed the same change. Getting a B can cause some students to fall apart, she said. "What you and I would call disappointments in life, to them feel like big failures."

As the elder child of a civil engineer and preschool teacher in San Mateo, Calif., Ms. DeWitt, now 20, has understood since kindergarten that she was expected to attend an elite college. While she says her parents are not overbearing, she relishes their praise for performing well. "Hearing my parents talk about me in a positive way, or hearing other parents talk about their kids doing well in academics or extracurriculars, that's where I got some of the expectations for myself," she said. "It was like self-fulfillment: I'd feel fulfilled and happy when other people were happy with what I'm doing, or expectations they have are met."

Penn had felt like a long shot but was her top choice. When she was admitted off the wait list in June 2013, she made a pact with herself not to squander the precious opportunity. Over that summer, she studied the course catalog, and decided that declaring a major early would help her plan more efficiently. She chose math, envisioning a teaching career. "I'm a person who lives by a schedule," she said. "I have a plan for maybe the next two years, next three years, maybe five years."

And so she had made a plan for making her life turn out the way she thought it was supposed to. "I had the idea that I was going to find this nice Christian boyfriend at college and settle down and live the life my parents had led," she said.

But there was the issue of her sexuality. Several times in high school she had found herself attracted to other girls, but believing her parents and church did not fully accept homosexuality, she had pushed aside those feelings. Her resolve was strengthened when her father sat her down for a heartfelt speech about how proud he was of her getting into Penn and of the direction her life was going. "Tears rolling down his face, he said, 'Kathryn, the reason I'm living is to pass you off to your husband.' "

Now, upon noticing a cute girl in her dorm, she had a terrifying realization: "I couldn't deny it anymore."

Every day, she grew more despondent. She awoke daily at 7:30 a.m. and often attended club meetings until as late as 10 p.m. She worked 10 hours a week as part of her financial aid package, and studied furiously, especially for her multivariable calculus class. Would she never measure up? Was she doing enough? Was she taking full advantage of all the opportunities?

Then came a crushing blow: a score in the low 60s on her calculus midterm. The class was graded on a curve, but surely she would fail it, she thought, dooming her plan to major in math and to teach.

"I had a picture of my future, and as that future deteriorated," she said, "I stopped imagining another future." The pain of being less than what she thought she ought to be was unbearable. The only way out, she reasoned with the twisted logic of depression, was death.

She researched whether the university returned tuition to parents of students who die by suicide, and began cutting herself to "prepare" for the pain.

The existential question "Why am I here?" is usually followed by the equally confounding "How am I doing?" In 1954, the social psychologist Leon Festinger put forward the social comparison theory, which posits that we try to determine our worth based on how we stack up against others.

In the era of social media, such comparisons take place on a screen with carefully curated depictions that don't provide the full picture. Mobile devices escalate the comparisons from occasional to nearly constant.

Gregory T. Eells, director of counseling and psychological services at Cornell University, believes social media is a huge contributor to the misperception among students that peers aren't also struggling. When students remark during a counseling session that everyone else on campus looks happy, he tells them: "I walk around and think, 'That one's gone to the hospital. That person has an eating disorder. That student just went on antidepressants.' As a therapist, I know that nobody is as happy or as grown-up as they seem on the outside."

Madison Holleran's suicide provided what might be the ultimate contrast between a shiny Instagram feed and interior darkness. Ms. Holleran posted images that show her smiling, dappled in sunshine or kicking back at a party. But according to her older sister, Ashley, Madison judged her social life as inferior to what she saw in the online posts of her high school friends. An hour before she killed herself, she posted a dreamy final photo of white holiday lights twinkling in the trees of Rittenhouse Square.

Where the faulty comparisons become dangerous is when a student already carries feelings of shame, according to Dr. Anthony L. Rostain, a pediatric psychiatrist on Penn's faculty who was co-chairman of the task force on student psychological health and welfare. "Shame is the sense one has of being defective or, said another way, not good enough," Dr. Rostain said. "It isn't that one isn't doing well. It's that 'I am no good.'" Instead of thinking "I failed at something, these students think, 'I am a failure.'"

America's culture of hyperachievement among the affluent has been under scrutiny for at least the last decade, but recent suicide clusters, including the deaths of three high school students and one recent graduate in Palo Alto, Calif., have renewed the debate. "In the Name of College! What Are We Doing to Our Children?" blared a Huffington Post headline in March. Around the same time, the New York Times columnist Frank Bruni published "Where You Go Is Not Who You'll Be: An Antidote to the College Admissions Mania," which he was inspired to write after years of observing the insanity surrounding the process—not only among students but also their parents. Numerous other alarms have been sounded over helicopter parenting, and how it robs children of opportunities to develop independence and resiliency, thereby crippling them emotionally later in life. These cultural dynamics of perfectionism and overindulgence have now combined to create adolescents who are ultra-focused on success but don't know how to fail.

Beginning in 2002, when she became dean of freshmen at Stanford, Julie Lythcott-Haims watched the collision of these two social forces up close. In meetings with students, she would ask what she considered simple questions and they would become paralyzed, unable to express their desires and often discovering midconversation that they were on a path that they didn't even like.

"They could say what they'd accomplished, but they couldn't necessarily say who they were," said Ms. Lythcott-Haims. She was also troubled by the growing number of parents who not only stayed in near-constant cellphone contact with their offspring but also showed up to help them enroll in classes, contacted professors and met with advisers (illustrating the progression from helicopter to lawn mower parents, who go beyond hovering to clear obstacles out of their child's way). But what she found most disconcerting was that students, instead of being embarrassed, felt grateful. Penn researchers studying friendship have found that students' best friends aren't classmates or romantic partners, but parents.

Children "deserve to be strengthened, not strangled, by the fierceness of a parent's love," Ms. Lythcott-Haims wrote in a 2005 op-ed piece for The Chicago Tribune. If by adulthood they cannot fend for themselves, she asked, "shouldn't we worry?"

Eventually she came to view her students' lack of self-awareness, inability to make choices and difficulty coping with setbacks as a form of "existential impotence," a direct result of a well-meaning but misguided approach to parenting that focuses too heavily on external measures of character. In June, Ms. Lythcott-Haims, who left Stanford in 2012, published a book on the subject, "How to Raise an Adult: Break Free of the Overparenting Trap and Prepare Your Kid for Success."

These observations echo those made by the psychologist Alice Miller in her seminal book for therapists, "The Drama of the Gifted Child: The Search for the True Self." In the book, published in 1979 and translated into 30 languages, Ms. Miller documents how some especially intelligent and sensitive children can become so attuned to parents' expectations that they do whatever it takes to fulfill those expectations—at the expense of their own feelings and needs. This can lead to emotional emptiness and isolation. "In what is described as depression and experienced as emptiness, futility, fear of impoverishment, and loneliness," she wrote, "can usually be recognized as the tragic loss of the self in childhood."

Ms. DeWitt had said goodbye and provided explanations to close friends and relatives on pink rose-adorned paper, stacked up neatly on her desk. Her roommate noticed that she had stopped eating after Madison Holleran's suicide, expressed concern and invited conversation. During an hourlong discussion, Ms. DeWitt disclosed how she had been contemplating suicide, but she pretended those feelings had gone away. To make sure her denial was convincing, she tossed the letters in the recycling bin.

But when the roommate returned hours later, she discovered that the letters had been taken out of the trash, and she told a resident adviser, who contacted the house dean. The dean insisted that Ms. DeWitt go for counseling. She did, and was immediately hospitalized.

After lots of counseling, a leave of absence and an internship at the headquarters of Active Minds, a nonprofit youth mental health advocacy group in Washington, D.C., Ms. DeWitt returned to campus in January.

Elite colleges often make it difficult for students to take time off, and readmission is not always guaranteed, something frequently cited as a deterrent to getting help (Yale eased its policy in April after a student's suicide note expressed anguish over readmission). Other elite schools are likewise examining the issue. When Ms. DeWitt's mother came to visit her in the hospital, one of the first things she brought up was the readmittance process.

Both of Ms. DeWitt's parents confirmed the contents of this article but declined to provide comments beyond expressing their love and support and saying, in a jointly written email, "Her courage and resilience have been a real blessing and example to us. We want to give Kathryn the opportunity to tell her own story."

Ms. DeWitt has tried to forge a new path for herself that is kinder and more forgiving. Rather than stay involved with the Christian group favored by her parents, she joined the progressive-minded Christian Association and the Queer Christian Fellowship, where she feels comfortable talking about her newly found identity as a lesbian. She was among the first students to write openly about her emotional state for Pennsive, a blog started to create "a safe space for Penn students to better understand and openly discuss issues regarding mental health."

Other efforts at Penn include the formation of a peer counseling program, to start in the fall, and the posting of "ugly selfies" to Instagram and Facebook, a perfectionism-backlash movement that took place for a few weeks earlier this year. Nationally, researchers from 10 universities have joined forces to study resiliency, and the Jed and Clinton Health Matters Campus Program has enlisted 90 schools to help develop mental health and wellness programs. Active Minds, which was founded at Penn in 2001, now has more than 400 chapters, including ones at community colleges and high schools. Ms. DeWitt is the Penn chapter's webmaster.

These days, Ms. DeWitt's lime-green watch covers up a scar where she had cut herself. But she is less concerned about covering up her true self. She has confessed her sexual feelings to her parents. They are working on acceptance. "My mom is there," Ms. DeWitt said. "My dad is still working on it." Having made it through her first year—the 60-something on her calculus midterm, graded on a curve, ended up netting her an A minus—she has become a lot more relaxed about her grades, her life and her future. "I'm probably going to major in psychology," she said. Her career plans are up in the air, an uncertainty that would have been intolerable to her former self.

"I need some experience before I make the decision. It's nice to have the freedom not to know."

For Analysis

1. This article raises issues related to hyperachievement, social media, helicopter parenting, and sexuality, among other topics. What do you think is the heart of the issue?
2. Scelfo devotes much of her article to recounting one woman's experience. Does this case study adequately support the claim that a serious problem exists? How does Scelfo demonstrate that DeWitt is not the only one who struggles with destructive perfectionism?
3. Consider some implications for Scelfo's argument. Assuming readers agree with her argument, what should they do? Make a list of possible actions for various stakeholders to take.

For Writing

Conduct a survey and a series of interviews at your college or university to assess whether perfectionism, suicide, anxiety, and depression are serious concerns among students at your institution. Then, write a report that describes your findings and discusses recommendations for addressing these problems.

"Hey Internet, Please Quit With the Happiness Articles"
by Katy Waldman

Katy Waldman writes articles on entertainment, literature, and language for *Slate*. She is also an award-winning poet. In this commentary from February 2014, she uses humor to critique the "happiness lobby." Boldface phrases are hyperlinked references in the original online version of this article.

The Internet happiness lobby is really stressing me out. In the course of researching something completely unrelated, I've blundered into a cotton-candy whorl of insipidly blithe articles on how to paste a permanent smile on my face. There's **this circular argument** about the benefits of optimism (being upbeat makes you—wait for it—upbeat); **this** on how exercise is "the single most proven way to get happier"; and **this** about techniques for tackling envy and reclaiming positivity. The new issue of *Marie Claire* claims that **drinking ayahuasca will reveal hard truths** about your imbalance of masculine and feminine energies, whooshing you to well-being on a wave of cosmic tough love. Forbes has ranked the **10 beamiest states.** On Facebook, cheery notices inform me that various friends have signed up for **#100HappyDays**, a new project that exhorts you to post a picture of something mood-lifting every day for 100 days. "Why would I do that?" asks the website, all yellow sunshine and playfulness, before rattling off its list of implausible answers: "be in a better mood," "become more optimistic," "receive more compliments," "realize how lucky [you] are," "fall in love."

None of these articles has any chance of actually making anyone happy, of course. The envy one is annoying because it prescribes vague, unpracticable cures like learning that praise and love are not finite. (I *know* that. But I still get envious.) The ayahuasca one is annoying because lots of people don't have $200 to spend on a single cup of enlightenment sludge—and some still cling to the fond belief that they can find joy without hallucinating a spirit animal. The piece on optimism is annoying because it describes in great detail all the ways our sanguinity is misplaced:

> Yet data clearly shows that most people overestimate their prospects for professional achievement; expect their children to be extraordinarily gifted; miscalculate their likely life span (sometimes by twenty years or more); expect to be healthier than the average person and more successful than their peers; hugely underestimate their likelihood of divorce, cancer, and unemployment; and are confident overall that their future lives will be better than those their parents put up with.

And then, the writer proceeds to tell us why the ebullience she's just smashed to smithereens was so great while it lasted.

> Hope keeps our minds at ease, lowers stress, and improves physical health . . . optimists are healthier and live longer . . . Expecting our future to be good reduces stress and anxiety . . . it keeps us moving forward . . . and helps motivate us to pursue our goals.

Maybe her goal was to give the most solipsistic pep talk ever. But, in fact, that contradiction—the call to happiness that leaves you sadder than you were before—seems baked into most of these pieces. By now we know (or think we know) that **only 12 percent of our happiness lies within our control**. The rest is genetics and recent events. Stories that insist on the importance of contentment are like those frustrating magic maps in fairy tales that only show you the route if you already know where you're going.

Last September, Andy Ward wrote a piece for *Medium* entitled "**Stop Telling Me to Be Happy**." He argued that browbeating people into finding their inner felicity doesn't work—just as showering them in impossibly vague, expensive, or otherwise unfollowable tips doesn't work. The essay opens with a funny dream sequence in which a sick guy begs a pharmacist for help, and the pharmacist whispers, "Just don't be sick." "If that were the cure to depression," Ward asks, "wouldn't Zoloft be out of business?"

I can think of a few more reasons why the happiness lobby needs to simmer down. Sadness can be cathartic. Occasional heartache helps you appreciate the good, and it can show you, as you slog through it, your own strength. Plus, all that sunbeam worshipping has a normative effect: It may deepen the shadows around depressed people and discourage them from seeking help. Not least, from a narrative perspective, happiness is boring. Who really wants to read about your perfect and fulfilling life, purged of envy, glowing with positivity, rinsed in endorphins from your awesome daily exercise regime? (I *am,* however, interested in the intense emotional dislocation and estrangement from your humanity that must come with suppressing every negative feeling. Looking at you, **Unikitty**.)

I understand why the Web overflows with happiness articles. All around us online, people are manicuring and curating and polishing their lives. They post images of their cute kids and mod renovations to Facebook; **upload vacation pics to Instagram**; hop arm-in-arm into rollicking **Twitter canoes**. We get jealous. Comparing our insides to everyone else's glimmering surfaces, we decide that we suck. Then the websites swoop in to grab our clicks by promising to heal our jealousy/sadness/boredom. They will instruct us in the art of well-being! But the lessons don't take, which bums us out, so we dive back into a new trough of self-improvement articles, and on and on it goes.

To me, this cycle resembles nothing so much as the ancient dance of lady magazines and beauty products. The media surrounds women with airbrushed knockouts, gives them inferiority complexes, and then offers them creams and dyes to fill the gap. Likewise, the Internet culture of "I'm having the best time ever at my beach house, here are pictures" is great at breeding feelings of inadequacy, which in turn create a need for *Lifehacker* articles telling us how to live richly.

Happiness is the new size zero. No **journal that helps you count your blessings with charts** or tutorial in how to "**stop giving a F@$% what people think**" is going to get you into those jeans.

For Analysis

1. In the online version of this article, Waldman embeds links to several articles that she finds annoying. Find Waldman's article online and read a few of her hyperlinked references, and then determine whether you agree with Waldman's evaluation. What makes these articles potentially unsuccessful? Why might audiences find them effective?
2. How well does Waldman support her claim that "the happiness lobby needs to simmer down"? Does she provide evidence or verification? Does she need to?
3. How well does Waldman incorporate humor? Does it help or hurt her argument? Where could she incorporate a more serious tone to strengthen her case?

For Writing

Write a humorous piece about something that you find annoying. Create a memorable tone by incorporating techniques such as sarcasm, satire, analogy, and interesting word choices.

"The All-or-Nothing Marriage"

by Eli J. Finkel

> **Eli J. Finkel** is a professor of social psychology, management, and organizations at Northwestern University. He has published numerous scholarly articles on romantic attraction, interpersonal conflict, and self-control, as well as op-eds for *The New York Times*, like this one that was published on Valentine's Day of 2014.

ARE marriages today better or worse than they used to be?

This vexing question is usually answered in one of two ways. According to the marital decline camp, marriage has weakened: Higher divorce rates reflect a lack of commitment and a decline of moral character that have harmed adults, children and society in general. But according to the marital resilience camp, though marriage has experienced disruptive changes like higher divorce rates, such developments are a sign that the institution has evolved to better respect individual autonomy, particularly for women. The true harm, by these lights, would have been for marriage to remain as confining as it was half a century ago.

As a psychological researcher who studies human relationships, I would like to offer a third view. Over the past year I immersed myself in the scholarly literature on marriage: not just the psychological studies but also work from sociologists, economists and historians. Perhaps the most striking thing I learned is that the answer to whether today's marriages are better or worse is "both": The *average* marriage today is weaker than the average marriage of yore, in terms of both satisfaction and divorce rate, but the *best* marriages today are much stronger, in terms of both satisfaction and personal well-being, than the best marriages of yore.

Consider, for example, that while the divorce rate has settled since the early 1980s at around 45 percent, even those marriages that have remained intact have generally become less satisfying. At the same time, consider the findings of a recent analysis, led by the University of Missouri researcher Christine M. Proulx, of 14 longitudinal studies between 1979 and 2002 that concerned marital quality and personal well-being. In addition to showing that marital quality uniformly predicts better personal well-being (unsurprisingly, happier marriages make happier people), the analysis revealed that this effect has become much stronger over time. The gap between the benefits of good and mediocre marriages has increased.

How and why did this divergence occur? In answering this question, I worked with the psychologists Chin Ming Hui, Kathleen L. Carswell and Grace M. Larson to develop a new theory of marriage, which we will publish later this year in a pair of articles in the journal Psychological Inquiry. Our central claim is that Americans today have elevated their expectations of marriage and can in fact achieve an unprecedentedly high level of marital quality—but only if they are able to invest a great deal of time and energy in their partnership. If they are not able to do so, their marriage will likely fall short of these new expectations. Indeed, it will fall further short of people's expectations than at any time in the past.

Marriage, then, has increasingly become an "all or nothing" proposition. This conclusion not only challenges the conventional opposition between marital decline and marital resilience; but it also has implications for policy makers looking to bolster the institution of marriage—and for individual Americans seeking to strengthen their own relationships.

To understand marriage today, it is important to see how we got to where we are. Throughout America's history, its populace has experienced three distinct models of marriage, as scholars like the sociologist Andrew J. Cherlin and the historian Stephanie Coontz have chronicled. In the era of the *institutional marriage*, from the nation's founding until around 1850, the prevalence of individual farming households meant that the main requirements Americans had for their marriage revolved around things like food production, shelter and protection from violence. To be sure, Americans were pleased if they experienced an emotional connection with their spouse, but such affinities were perquisites of a well-functioning marriage rather than its central purpose.

In the era of the *companionate marriage,* from roughly 1850 until 1965, American marriage increasingly centered around intimate needs such as to love, to be loved and to experience a fulfilling sex life. This era overlapped with the shift from rural to urban life. Men increasingly engaged in wage labor outside of the home, which amplified the extent to which the two sexes occupied distinct social spheres. As the nation became wealthier and its social institutions became stronger, Americans had the luxury of looking to marriage primarily for love and companionship.

Since around 1965, we have been living in the era of the *self-expressive marriage*. Americans now look to marriage increasingly for self-discovery, self-esteem and personal growth. Fueled by the countercultural currents of the 1960s, they have come to view marriage less as an essential institution and more as an elective means of achieving personal fulfillment. "You make me want to be a better man," from the 1997 movie "As Good as It Gets," could serve as this era's marriage ideal. In the words of the sociologist Robert N. Bellah, love has become, in good part, "the mutual exploration of infinitely rich, complex and exciting selves."

As a psychologist, I could not help noticing that this history of marriage echoes the classic "hierarchy of needs" outlined in the 1940s by the psychologist Abraham Maslow. According to Maslow, human needs fit into a five-level hierarchy: The lowest need is that of physiological well-being—including the need to eat and drink—followed by the need for safety, then for belonging and love, then for esteem and finally for self-actualization. The emergence of each need characteristically depends on the prior satisfaction of a more basic need. A person unable to satisfy the need for food, for example, is wholly concerned with meeting that need; only once it is met can he focus on satisfying the need above it (safety), and so on.

My colleagues and I contend that an analogous process has occurred in our expectations about marriage. Those expectations were set at the low levels of Maslow's hierarchy during the institutional era, at medium levels during the companionate era and at high levels during the self-expressive era.

This historical ascent is, on its own, neither good nor bad. But it has major implications for marital well-being: Though satisfying higher-level needs yields greater happiness, serenity and depth of inner life, people must invest substantially more time and energy in the quality of their relationship when seeking to meet those higher-level needs through their marriage. To be sure, it was no small feat, circa 1800, to produce enough food or keep a house warm, but the effort required to do so did not require deep insight into, and prolonged involvement with, each other's core essence.

As the expectations of marriage have ascended Maslow's hierarchy, the potential psychological payoffs have increased—but achieving those results has become more demanding.

Here lie both the great successes and great disappointments of modern marriage. Those individuals who can invest enough time and energy in their partnership are seeing unprecedented benefits. The sociologists Jeffrey Dew and W. Bradford Wilcox have demonstrated that spouses who spent "time alone with each other, talking, or sharing an activity" at least once per week were 3.5 times more likely to be very happy in their marriage than spouses who did so less frequently. The sociologist Paul R. Amato and colleagues have shown that spouses with a larger percentage of shared friends spent more time together and had better marriages.

But on average Americans are investing less in their marriages—to the detriment of those relationships. Professor Dew has shown that relative to Americans in 1975, Americans in 2003 spent much less time alone with their spouses. Among spouses without children, weekly spousal time declined to 26 hours per week from 35 hours, and much of this decline resulted from an increase in hours spent at work.

Among spouses with children at home, spousal time declined to 9 hours per week from 13, and much of this decline resulted from an increase in time-intensive parenting.

Though this is not a specifically socioeconomic phenomenon, it does have a socioeconomic dimension. One of the most disturbing facts about American marriage today is that while divorce increased at similar rates for the wealthy and the poor in the 1960s and '70s, those rates diverged sharply starting around 1980. According to the sociologist Steven P. Martin, among Americans who married between 1975 and 1979, the 10-year divorce rate was 28 percent among people without a high school education and 18 percent among people with at least a college degree: a 10 percentage point difference. But among Americans who married between 1990 and 1994, the parallel divorce rates were 46 percent and 16 percent: an astonishing 30 percentage point difference.

The problem is not that poor people fail to appreciate the importance of marriage, nor is it that poor and wealthy Americans differ in which factors they believe are important in a good marriage. The problem is that the same trends that have exacerbated inequality since 1980—unemployment, juggling multiple jobs and so on—have also made it increasingly difficult for less wealthy Americans to invest the time and other resources needed to sustain a strong marital bond.

What can be done? Government actions that reduce inequality and family-friendly work policies like on-site child care are likely to help strengthen marriage. But they are not the only options, particularly for individual couples.

First and foremost, couples can choose to invest more time and energy in their marriage, perhaps by altering how they use whatever shared leisure time is available. But if couples lack the time and energy, they might consider adjusting their expectations, perhaps by focusing on cultivating an affectionate bond without trying to facilitate each other's self-actualization.

The bad news is that insofar as socioeconomic circumstances or individual choices undermine the investment of time and energy in our relationships, our marriages are likely to fall short of our era's expectations. The good news is that our marriages can flourish today like never before. They just can't do it on their own.

For Analysis

1. The article begins with a question, similar to a research question that forms the basis of a thesis. What might be some of the inspirations for this question? What might have motivated Finkel to write this article?
2. Finkel mentions several research studies that inform his argument. Find and read one of these studies to evaluate how substantial the support is. How do you interpret the researchers' results? What other implications can you draw from the scholars' findings?
3. Finkel ends by addressing the controversy category of policy (that is, what we should do about this problem). How satisfied are you with his suggestions? What else needs to happen?

For Writing

Interview at least two married friends or family members about their successes and obstacles in marriage. Then, write a "how to" article, based in your findings, that gives advice for sustaining a successful marriage.

SECTION 5
HOW DO WE PURSUE JUSTICE?

"The Caging of America"
by Adam Gopnik

> **Adam Gopnik** is an essayist, fiction writer, reporter, book reviewer, humorist, and art critic who has written for *The New Yorker* since 1986. In this 2012 article, Gopnik examines the causes and implications of growing incarceration rates.

A prison is a trap for catching time. Good reporting appears often about the inner life of the American prison, but the catch is that American prison life is mostly undramatic—the reported stories fail to grab us, because, for the most part, nothing *happens*. One day in the life of Ivan Denisovich is all you need to know about Ivan Denisovich, because the idea that anyone could live for a minute in such circumstances seems impossible; one day in the life of an American prison means much less, because the force of it is that one day typically stretches out for decades. It isn't the horror of the time at hand but the unimaginable sameness of the time ahead that makes prisons unendurable for their inmates. The inmates on death row in Texas are called men in "timeless time," because they alone aren't serving time: they aren't waiting out five years or a decade or a lifetime. The basic reality of American prisons is not that of the lock and key but that of the lock and clock.

That's why no one who has been inside a prison, if only for a day, can ever forget the feeling. Time stops. A note of attenuated panic, of watchful paranoia—anxiety and boredom and fear mixed into a kind of enveloping fog, covering the guards as much as the guarded.

"Sometimes I think this whole world is one big prison yard, / Some of us are prisoners, some of us are guards," Dylan sings, and while it isn't strictly true—just ask the prisoners—it contains a truth: the guards are doing time, too. As a smart man once wrote after being locked up, the thing about jail is that there are bars on the windows and they won't let you out. This simple truth governs all the others. What prisoners try to convey to the free is how the presence of time as something being done to you, instead of something you do things with, alters the mind at every moment. For American prisoners, huge numbers of whom are serving sentences much longer than those given for similar crimes anywhere else in the civilized world—Texas alone has sentenced more than four hundred teen-agers to life imprisonment—time becomes in every sense this thing you serve.

For most privileged, professional people, the experience of confinement is a mere brush, encountered after a kid's arrest, say. For a great many poor people in America, particularly poor black men, prison is a destination that braids through an ordinary life, much as high school and college do for rich white ones. More than half of all black men without a high-school diploma go to prison at some time in their lives. Mass incarceration on a scale almost unexampled in human history is a fundamental fact of our country today—perhaps *the* fundamental fact, as slavery was the fundamental fact of 1850. In truth, there are more black men in the grip of the criminal-justice system—in prison, on probation, or on parole—than were in slavery then. Over all, there are now more people under "correctional supervision" in America—more than six million—than were in the Gulag Archipelago under Stalin at its height. That city of the confined and the controlled, Lockuptown, is now the second largest in the United States.

The accelerating rate of incarceration over the past few decades is just as startling as the number of people jailed: in 1980, there were about two hundred and twenty people incarcerated for every hundred thousand Americans; by 2010, the number had more than tripled, to seven hundred and thirty-one. No other country even approaches that. In the past two decades, the money that states spend on prisons has risen at six times the rate of spending on higher education. Ours is, bottom to top, a "carceral state," in the flat verdict of Conrad Black, the former conservative press lord and newly minted reformer, who right now finds himself imprisoned in Florida, thereby adding a new twist to an old joke: A conservative is a liberal who's been mugged; a liberal is a conservative who's been indicted; and a passionate prison reformer is a conservative who's in one.

The scale and the brutality of our prisons are the moral scandal of American life. Every day, at least fifty thousand men—a full house at Yankee Stadium—wake in solitary confinement, often in "supermax" prisons or prison wings, in which men are locked in small cells, where they see no one, cannot freely read and write, and are allowed out just once a day for an hour's solo "exercise." (Lock yourself in your bathroom and then imagine you have to stay there for the next ten years, and you will have some sense of the experience.) Prison rape is so endemic—more than seventy thousand prisoners are raped each year—that it is routinely held out as a threat, part of the punishment to be expected. The subject is standard fodder for comedy, and an uncoöperative suspect being threatened with rape in prison is now represented, every night on television, as an ordinary and rather lovable bit of policing. The normalization of prison rape—like eighteenth-century japery about watching men struggle as they die on the gallows—will surely strike our descendants as chillingly sadistic, incomprehensible on the part of people who thought themselves civilized. Though we avoid looking directly at prisons, they seep obliquely into our fashions and manners. Wealthy white teen-agers in baggy jeans and laceless shoes and multiple tattoos show, unconsciously, the reality of incarceration that acts as a hidden foundation for the country.

How did we get here? How is it that our civilization, which rejects hanging and flogging and disembowelling, came to believe that caging vast numbers of people for decades is an acceptably humane sanction? There's a fairly large recent scholarly literature on the history and sociology of crime and punishment, and it tends to trace the American zeal for punishment back to the nineteenth century, apportioning blame in two directions. There's an essentially Northern explanation, focussing on the inheritance of the notorious Eastern State Penitentiary, in Philadelphia, and its "reformist" tradition; and a Southern explanation, which sees the prison system as essentially a slave plantation continued by other means. Robert Perkinson, the author of the Southern revisionist tract "Texas Tough: The Rise of America's Prison Empire," traces two ancestral lines, "from the North, the birthplace of rehabilitative penology, to the South, the fountainhead of subjugationist discipline." In other words, there's the scientific taste for reducing men to numbers and the slave owners' urge to reduce blacks to brutes.

William J. Stuntz, a professor at Harvard Law School who died shortly before his masterwork, "The Collapse of American Criminal Justice," was published, last fall, is the most forceful advocate for the view that the scandal of our prisons derives from the Enlightenment-era, "procedural" nature of American justice. He runs through the immediate causes of the incarceration epidemic: the growth of post-Rockefeller drug laws, which punished minor drug offenses with major prison time; "zero tolerance" policing, which added to the group; mandatory-sentencing laws, which prevented judges from exercising judgment. But his search for the ultimate cause leads deeper, all the way to the Bill of Rights. In a society where Constitution worship is still a requisite on right and left alike, Stuntz startlingly suggests that the Bill of Rights is a terrible document with which to start a justice system—much inferior to the exactly contemporary French Declaration of the Rights of Man, which Jefferson, he points out, may have helped shape while his protégé Madison was writing ours.

The trouble with the Bill of Rights, he argues, is that it emphasizes process and procedure rather than principles. The Declaration of the Rights of Man says, Be just! The Bill of Rights says, Be fair! Instead of announcing general principles—no one should be accused of something that wasn't a crime when he did it; cruel punishments are always wrong; the goal of justice is, above all, that justice be done—it talks procedurally. You can't search someone without a reason; you can't accuse him without allowing him to see the evidence; and so on. This emphasis, Stuntz thinks, has led to the current mess, where accused criminals get laboriously articulated protection against procedural errors and no protection at all against outrageous and obvious violations of simple justice. You can get off if the cops looked in the wrong car with the wrong warrant when they found your joint, but you have no recourse if owning the joint gets you locked up for life. You may be spared the death penalty if you can show a problem with your appointed defender, but it is much harder if there is merely enormous accumulated evidence that you weren't guilty in the first place and the jury got it wrong. Even clauses that Americans are taught to revere are, Stuntz maintains, unworthy of reverence: the ban on "cruel and unusual punishment" was designed to *protect* cruel punishments—flogging and branding—that were not at that time unusual.

The obsession with due process and the cult of brutal prisons, the argument goes, share an essential impersonality. The more professionalized and procedural a system is, the more insulated we become from its real effects on real people. That's why America is famous both for its process-driven judicial system ("The bastard got off on a technicality," the cop-show detective fumes) and for the harshness and inhumanity of its prisons. Though all industrialized societies started sending more people to prison and fewer to the gallows in the eighteenth century, it was in Enlightenment-inspired America that the taste for long-term, profoundly depersonalized punishment became most aggravated. The inhumanity of American prisons was as much a theme for Dickens, visiting America in 1842, as the cynicism of American lawyers. His shock when he saw the Eastern State Penitentiary, in Philadelphia—a "model" prison, at the time the most expensive public building ever constructed in the country, where every prisoner was kept in silent, separate confinement—still resonates:

> I believe that very few men are capable of estimating the immense amount of torture and agony which this dreadful punishment, prolonged for years, inflicts upon the sufferers. . . . I hold this slow and daily tampering with the mysteries of the brain, to be immeasurably worse than any torture of the body: and because its ghastly signs and tokens are not so palpable to the eye and sense of touch as scars upon the flesh; because its wounds are not upon the surface, and it extorts few cries that human ears can hear; therefore I the more denounce it, as a secret punishment which slumbering humanity is not roused up to stay.

Not roused up to stay—that was the point. Once the procedure ends, the penalty begins, and, as long as the cruelty is routine, our civil responsibility toward the punished is over. We lock men up and forget about their existence. For Dickens, even the corrupt but communal debtors' prisons of old London were better than *this*. "Don't take it personally!"—that remains the slogan above the gate to the American prison Inferno. Nor is this merely a historian's vision. Conrad Black, at the high end, has a scary and persuasive picture of how his counsel, the judge, and the prosecutors all merrily congratulated each other on their combined professional excellence just before sending him off to the hoosegow for several years. If a millionaire feels that way, imagine how the ordinary culprit must feel.

In place of abstraction, Stuntz argues for the saving grace of humane discretion. Basically, he thinks, we should go into court with an understanding of what a crime is and what justice is like, and then let common sense and compassion and specific circumstance take over. There's a lovely scene in "The Castle," the Australian movie about a family fighting eminent-domain eviction, where its hapless lawyer, asked in court to point to the specific part of the Australian constitution that the eviction violates, says desperately, "It's . . . just the *vibe* of the thing." For Stuntz, justice ought to be just the vibe of the thing—not one procedural error caught or one fact worked around. The criminal law should once again be more like the common law, with judges and juries not merely finding fact but making law on the basis of universal principles of fairness, circumstance, and seriousness, and crafting penalties to the exigencies of the crime.

The other argument—the Southern argument—is that this story puts too bright a face on the truth. The reality of American prisons, this argument runs, has nothing to do with the knots of procedural justice or the perversions of Enlightenment-era ideals. Prisons today operate less in the rehabilitative mode of the Northern reformers "than in a retributive mode that has long been practiced and promoted in the South," Perkinson, an American-studies professor, writes. "American prisons trace their lineage not only back to Pennsylvania penitentiaries but to Texas slave plantations." White supremacy is the real principle, this thesis holds, and racial domination the real end. In response to the apparent triumphs of the sixties, mass imprisonment became a way of reimposing Jim Crow. Blacks are now incarcerated seven times as often as whites. "The system of mass incarceration works to trap African Americans in a virtual (and literal) cage," the legal scholar Michelle Alexander writes. Young black men pass quickly from a period of police harassment into a period of "formal control" (i.e., actual imprisonment) and then are doomed for life to a system of "invisible control." Prevented from voting, legally discriminated against for the rest of their lives, most will cycle back through the prison system. The system, in this view, is not really broken; it is doing what it was designed to do. Alexander's grim conclusion: "If mass incarceration is considered as a system of social control—specifically, racial control—then the system is a fantastic success."

Northern impersonality and Southern revenge converge on a common American theme: a growing number of American prisons are now contracted out as for-profit businesses to for-profit companies. The companies are paid by the state, and their profit depends on spending as little as possible on the prisoners and the prisons. It's hard to imagine any greater disconnect between public good and private profit: the interest of private prisons lies not in the obvious social good of having the minimum necessary number of inmates but in having as many as possible, housed as cheaply as possible. No more chilling document exists in recent American life than the 2005 annual report of the biggest of these firms, the Corrections Corporation of America. Here the company (which spends millions lobbying legislators) is obliged to caution its investors about the risk that somehow, somewhere, someone might turn off the spigot of convicted men:

> Our growth is generally dependent upon our ability to obtain new contracts to develop and manage new correctional and detention facilities. . . . The demand for our facilities and services could be adversely affected by the relaxation of enforcement efforts, leniency in conviction and sentencing practices or through the decriminalization of certain activities that are currently proscribed by our criminal laws. For instance, any changes with respect to drugs and controlled substances or illegal immigration could affect the number of persons arrested, convicted, and sentenced, thereby potentially reducing demand for correctional facilities to house them.

Brecht could hardly have imagined such a document: a capitalist enterprise that feeds on the misery of man trying as hard as it can to be sure that nothing is done to decrease that misery.

Yet a spectre haunts all these accounts, North and South, whether process gone mad or penal colony writ large. It is that the epidemic of imprisonment seems to track the dramatic decline in crime over the same period. The more bad guys there are in prison, it appears, the less crime there has been in the streets. The real background to the prison boom, which shows up only sporadically in the prison literature, is the crime wave that preceded and overlapped it.

For those too young to recall the big-city crime wave of the sixties and seventies, it may seem like mere bogeyman history. For those whose entire childhood and adolescence were set against it, it is the crucial trauma in recent American life and explains much else that happened in the same period. It was the condition of the Upper West Side of Manhattan under liberal rule, far more than what had happened to Eastern Europe under socialism, that made neo-con polemics look persuasive. There really was, as Stuntz himself says, a liberal consensus on crime ("Wherever the line is between a merciful justice system and one that abandons all serious effort at crime control, the nation had crossed it"), and it really did have bad effects.

Yet if, in 1980, someone had predicted that by 2012 New York City would have a crime rate so low that violent crime would have largely disappeared as a subject of conversation, he would have seemed not so much hopeful as crazy. Thirty years ago, crime was supposed to be a permanent feature of the city, produced by an alienated underclass of super-predators; now it isn't. Something good happened to change it, and you might have supposed that the change would be an opportunity for celebration and optimism. Instead, we mostly content ourselves with grudging and sardonic references to the silly side of gentrification, along with a few all-purpose explanations, like broken-window policing. This is a general human truth: things that work interest us less than things that don't.

So what *is* the relation between mass incarceration and the decrease in crime? Certainly, in the nineteen-seventies and eighties, many experts became persuaded that there was no way to make bad people better; all you could do was warehouse them, for longer or shorter periods. The best research seemed to show, depressingly, that nothing works—that rehabilitation was a ruse. Then, in 1983, inmates at the maximum-security federal prison in Marion, Illinois, murdered two guards. Inmates had been (very occasionally) killing guards for a long time, but the timing of the murders, and the fact that they took place in a climate already prepared to believe that even ordinary humanity was wasted on the criminal classes, meant that the entire prison was put on permanent lockdown. A century and a half after absolute solitary first appeared in American prisons, it was reintroduced. Those terrible numbers began to grow.

And then, a decade later, crime started falling: across the country by a standard measure of about forty per cent; in New York City by as much as eighty per cent. By 2010, the crime rate in New York had seen its greatest decline since the Second World War; in 2002, there were fewer murders in Manhattan than there had been in any year since 1900. In social science, a cause sought is usually a muddle found; in life as we experience it, a crisis resolved is causality established. If a pill cures a headache, we do not ask too often if the headache might have gone away by itself.

All this ought to make the publication of Franklin E. Zimring's new book, "The City That Became Safe," a very big event. Zimring, a criminologist at Berkeley Law, has spent years crunching the numbers of what happened in New York in the context of what happened in the rest of America. One thing he teaches us is how little we know. The forty per cent drop across the continent—indeed, there was a decline throughout the Western world—took place for reasons that are as mysterious in suburban Ottawa as they are in the South Bronx. Zimring shows that the usual explanations—including demographic shifts—simply can't account for what must be accounted for. This makes the international decline look slightly eerie: blackbirds drop from the sky, plagues slacken and end, and there seems no absolute reason that societies leap from one state to another over time. Trends and fashions and fads and pure contingencies happen in other parts of our social existence; it may be that there are fashions and cycles in criminal behavior, too, for reasons that are just as arbitrary.

But the additional forty per cent drop in crime that seems peculiar to New York finally succumbs to Zimring's analysis. The change didn't come from resolving the deep pathologies that the right fixated on—from jailing super predators, driving down the number of unwed mothers, altering welfare culture. Nor were there cures for the underlying causes pointed to by the left: injustice, discrimination, poverty.

Nor were there any "Presto!" effects arising from secret patterns of increased abortions or the like. The city didn't get much richer; it didn't get much poorer. There was no significant change in the ethnic makeup or the average wealth or educational levels of New Yorkers as violent crime more or less vanished. "Broken windows" or "turnstile jumping" policing, that is, cracking down on small visible offenses in order to create an atmosphere that refused to license crime, seems to have had a negligible effect; there was, Zimring writes, a great difference between the slogans and the substance of the time. (Arrests for "visible" nonviolent crime—e.g., street prostitution and public gambling—mostly went *down* through the period.)

Instead, small acts of social engineering, designed simply to stop crimes from happening, helped stop crime. In the nineties, the N.Y.P.D. began to control crime not by fighting minor crimes in safe places but by putting lots of cops in places where lots of crimes happened—"hot-spot policing." The cops also began an aggressive, controversial program of "stop and frisk"—"designed to catch the sharks, not the dolphins," as Jack Maple, one of its originators, described it—that involved what's called pejoratively "profiling." This was not so much racial, since in any given neighborhood all the suspects were likely to be of the same race or color, as social, involving the thousand small clues that policemen recognized already. Minority communities, Zimring emphasizes, paid a disproportionate price in kids stopped and frisked, and detained, but they also earned a disproportionate gain in crime reduced. "The poor pay more and get more" is Zimring's way of putting it. He believes that a "light" program of stop-and-frisk could be less alienating and just as effective, and that by bringing down urban crime stop-and-frisk had the net effect of greatly reducing the number of poor minority kids in prison for long stretches.

Zimring insists, plausibly, that he is offering a radical and optimistic rewriting of theories of what crime is and where criminals are, not least because it disconnects crime and minorities. "In 1961, twenty six percent of New York City's population was minority African American or

Hispanic. Now, half of New York's population is—and what that does in an enormously hopeful way is to destroy the rude assumptions of supply side criminology," he says. By "supply side criminology," he means the conservative theory of crime that claimed that social circumstances produced a certain net amount of crime waiting to be expressed; if you stopped it here, it broke out there. The only way to stop crime was to lock up all the potential criminals. In truth, criminal activity seems like most other human choices—a question of contingent occasions and opportunity. Crime is not the consequence of a set number of criminals; criminals are the consequence of a set number of opportunities to commit crimes. Close down the open drug market in Washington Square, and it does not automatically migrate to Tompkins Square Park. It just stops, or the dealers go indoors, where dealing goes on but violent crime does not.

And, in a virtuous cycle, the decreased prevalence of crime fuels a decrease in the prevalence of crime. When your friends are no longer doing street robberies, you're less likely to do them. Zimring said, in a recent interview, "Remember, nobody ever made a living mugging. There's no minimum wage in violent crime." In a sense, he argues, it's recreational, part of a life style: "Crime is a routine behavior; it's a thing people do when they get used to doing it." And therein lies its essential fragility. Crime ends as a result of "cyclical forces operating on situational and contingent things rather than from finding deeply motivated essential linkages." Conservatives don't like this view because it shows that being tough doesn't help; liberals don't like it because apparently being nice doesn't help, either. Curbing crime does not depend on reversing social pathologies or alleviating social grievances; it depends on erecting small, annoying barriers to entry.

One fact stands out. While the rest of the country, over the same twenty-year period, saw the growth in incarceration that led to our current astonishing numbers, New York, despite the Rockefeller drug laws, saw a marked decrease in its number of inmates. "New York City, in the midst of a dramatic reduction in crime, is locking up a much smaller number of people, and particularly of young people, than it was at the height of the crime wave," Zimring observes. Whatever happened to make street crime fall, it had nothing to do with putting more men in prison. The logic is self-evident if we just transfer it to the realm of white-collar crime: we easily accept that there is no net sum of white-collar crime waiting to happen, no inscrutable generation of super-predators produced by Dewar's-guzzling dads and scaly M.B.A. profs; if you stop an embezzlement scheme here on Third Avenue, another doesn't naturally start in the next office building. White-collar crime happens through an intersection of pathology and opportunity; getting the S.E.C. busy ending the opportunity is a good way to limit the range of the pathology.

Social trends deeper and less visible to us may appear as future historians analyze what went on. Something other than policing may explain things—just as the coming of cheap credit cards and state lotteries probably did as much to weaken the Mafia's Five Families in New York, who had depended on loan sharking and numbers running, as the F.B.I. could. It is at least possible, for instance, that the coming of the mobile phone helped drive drug dealing indoors, in ways that helped drive down crime. It may be that the real value of hot spot and stop-and-frisk was that it provided a single game plan that the police believed in; as military history reveals, a bad plan is often better than no plan, especially if the people on the other side think it's a good plan. But one thing is sure: social epidemics, of crime or of punishment, can be cured more quickly than we might hope with simpler and more superficial mechanisms than we imagine. Throwing a Band-Aid over a bad wound is actually a decent strategy, if the Band-Aid helps the wound to heal itself.

Which leads, further, to one piece of radical common sense: since prison plays at best a small role in stopping even violent crime, very few people, rich or poor, should be in prison for a nonviolent crime. Neither the streets nor the society is made safer by having marijuana users or peddlers locked up, let alone with the horrific sentences now dispensed so easily. For that matter, no social good is served by having the embezzler or the Ponzi schemer locked in a cage for the rest of his life, rather than having him bankrupt and doing community service in the South Bronx for the next decade or two. Would we actually have more fraud and looting of shareholder value if the perpetrators knew that they would lose their bank accounts and their reputation, and have to do community service seven days a week for five years? It seems likely that anyone for whom those sanctions aren't sufficient is someone for whom no sanctions are ever going to be sufficient. Zimring's research shows clearly that, if crime drops on the street, criminals coming out of prison stop committing crimes. What matters is the incidence of crime in the world, and the continuity of a culture of crime, not some "lesson learned" in prison.

At the same time, the ugly side of stop-and-frisk can be alleviated. To catch sharks and not dolphins, Zimring's work suggests, we need to adjust the size of the holes in the nets—to make crimes that are the occasion for stop-and-frisks *real* crimes, not crimes like marijuana possession. When the New York City police stopped and frisked kids, the main goal was not to jail them for having pot but to get their fingerprints, so that they could be identified if they committed a more serious crime. But all over America the opposite happens: marijuana possession becomes the serious crime. The cost is so enormous, though, in lives ruined and money spent, that the obvious thing to do is not to enforce the law less but to change it now. Dr. Johnson said once that manners make law, and that when manners alter, the law must, too. It's obvious that marijuana is now an almost universally accepted drug in America: it is not only used casually (which has been true for decades) but also talked about casually on television and in the movies (which has not). One need only watch any stoner movie to see that the perceived risks of smoking dope are not that you'll get arrested but that you'll get in trouble with a rival frat or look like an idiot to women. The decriminalization of marijuana would help end the epidemic of imprisonment.

The rate of incarceration in most other rich, free countries, whatever the differences in their histories, is remarkably steady. In countries with Napoleonic justice or common law or some mixture of the two, in countries with adversarial systems and in those with magisterial ones, whether the country once had brutal plantation-style penal colonies, as France did, or was once itself a brutal plantation-style penal colony, like Australia, the natural rate of incarceration seems to hover right around a hundred men per hundred thousand people. (That doesn't mean it doesn't get lower in rich, homogeneous countries—just that it never gets much higher in countries otherwise like our own.) It seems that one man in every thousand once in a while does a truly bad thing. All other things being equal, the point of a justice system should be to identify that thousandth guy, find a way to keep him from harming other people, and give everyone else a break.

Epidemics seldom end with miracle cures. Most of the time in the history of medicine, the best way to end disease was to build a better sewer and get people to wash their hands. "Merely chipping away at the problem around the edges" is usually the very best thing to do with a problem; keep chipping away patiently and, eventually, you get to its heart. To read the literature on crime before it dropped is to see the same kind of dystopian despair we find in the new literature of punishment: we'd have to end poverty, or eradicate the ghettos, or declare war on the broken family, or the like, in order to end the crime wave. The truth is, a series of small actions and events ended up eliminating a problem that seemed to hang over everything. There was no miracle cure, just the intercession of a thousand smaller sanities. Ending sentencing for drug misdemeanors, decriminalizing marijuana, leaving judges free to use common sense (and, where possible, getting judges who are judges rather than politicians)—many small acts are possible that will help end the epidemic of imprisonment as they helped end the plague of crime.

"Oh, I have taken too little care of this!" King Lear cries out on the heath in his moment of vision. "Take physic, pomp; expose thyself to feel what wretches feel." "This" changes; in Shakespeare's time, it was flat-out peasant poverty that starved some and drove others as mad as poor Tom. In Dickens's and Hugo's time, it was the industrial revolution that drove kids to mines. But every society has a poor storm that wretches suffer in, and the attitude is always the same: either that the wretches, already dehumanized by their suffering, deserve no pity or that the oppressed, overwhelmed by injustice, will have to wait for a better world. At every moment, the injustice seems inseparable from the community's life, and in every case the arguments for keeping the system in place were that you would have to revolutionize the entire social order to change it—which then became the argument for revolutionizing the entire social order. In every case, humanity and common sense made the insoluble problem just get up and go away. Prisons are our this. We need take more care.

For Analysis

1. Writing about prisons might seem like choosing a "stock argument"—an overdone, clichéd topic. How does Gopnik breathe new life into this issue and engage readers in his argument?
2. Review the stylistic techniques we describe in Chapter 10 and then analyze Gopnik's style. What rhetorical devices does he use? What makes these stylistic choices effective—or not?
3. Create a reverse outline (a technique we describe on p. 50) of this argument to fully understand its various components. Pay particular attention to places where the thesis shifts.

For Writing

Gopnik addresses few objections to his viewpoints. Choose an issue from the article that interests you, such as prison rehabilitation, marijuana legalization, or crime reduction, and find two or three sources that present alternative arguments. In about 750 words, synthesize the different perspectives and draw your own conclusions about the issue.

"With Liberty and Justice for Some"

by Emanuel Grant

Emanuel Grant wrote this argument in his first-year writing class at James Madison University. His essay examines the tension between liberty and distribution of wealth, proposing a "maximum wage" for corporate executives.

As Americans, we are in love with the concept of justice. Freedom and fairness are as integral to our identity as hot apple pie and cookouts on a summer's day. I feel downright lucky to be here—in a land of opportunity where the hardworking are rewarded. In my readings of the works of the greats of economic commentary (Milton Friedman, Steven Levitt, and Stephen Dubner to name a few), it has become quite clear that our nation's success is formally attributed to our warm embrace of democratic and capitalistic ideals. We are described as the world's wealthiest country in terms of GDP (Gross Domestic Product), yet what does that wealth mean? Who owns it?

In terms of financial wealth—described by UCSC professor G. William Domhoff as "total net worth minus the value of one's home"—in 2007, 42.7% of our nation's wealth is owned by the top 1% of our population and another 50.3% is owned by the next 19% in the economic ladder. With some simple number crunching, a shocking, unnerving statistic unfolds: the wealthiest 20% in our society own a whopping 93% of our nation's wealth. That leaves a paltry 7% of wealth to the bottom 80% of Americans. Maybe these discrepancies are a good thing. Maybe they prove that if you work hard in life, you're going to be living large. To me, however, these statistics spin a tale much different than that of the American dream. They bastardize any notions of equality, justice, and social responsibility that I once identified as truly American. Though no economic system is perfect, it seems the structure of the one present leaves the poor grasping for straws as the rich enjoy the fruits of their labor.

Unless you are in this top 1% bracket (in which case go ahead and burn my paper now; you won't find comfort here) or *at least* within the remaining 19% of wage earners, you should be furious! Why should a select few Americans live in the lap of luxury while the others are forced to live paycheck to paycheck? I'm no socialist nut; I agree that people should be rewarded for their hard efforts. But, there must be a way to narrow the gap, to spread the wealth a little more. 7% of our nation's wealth for 80% of its people just doesn't *sound* right. With this in mind, I plan to target the highest echelons of our society and find an alternative to the farce of economic justice that pervades our economic system.

A fun little riddle before we delve deeper: try naming one thing NBA, National Rugby League (NSWRL) and MLB players all have in common. If you can't think of an answer besides that they all are athletic and have ridiculous amounts of money, you're probably not alone. In the sports world, the commonality is known as a salary cap—there's a literal limit that a league sets on how much LeBron can make for a year of excellence on the court; in the real world, the same phenomenon has been called a wage ceiling or a maximum wage—a government set standard on how much an earner can take home. I believe the introduction of maximum wage policies is a solution for the income inequality we see in our nation. Yes, I said it; cue the USSR anthem and call up the retired McCarthyites to put me away for good. I think there's a maximum amount of money you should be legally allowed to make. Try your best to palate my words. Remain skeptical; don't trust me yet. But, I beg you to keep an open mind. Remember, I am no politician; I'm not trying to trick you with some underhanded rhetoric. I have a bona fide, genuine concern for the majority of Americans (i.e. the 80%) who are fighting an uphill battle in their "pursuit of happiness," and I will use the principles of Macroeconomics to fortify my argument and fight for you—the little guy.

Though I am arguing for ceilings on wage, I bet you didn't know that the government already built a structural roof on your earnings.

You just happen to be standing on it. It's called a minimum wage. We all accept it. Whether you're serving up burgers at your local McDonald's or ripping up ticket stubs at the premier of Tarantino's next violent thriller, the government has already stepped in and said that there's a minimum amount you are allowed to earn for that job. While we generally accept this ideal, there are formidable consequences on the economy at large. These consequences make up the roof of which I previously spoke. To see these consequences, we first need to see how wages are decided.

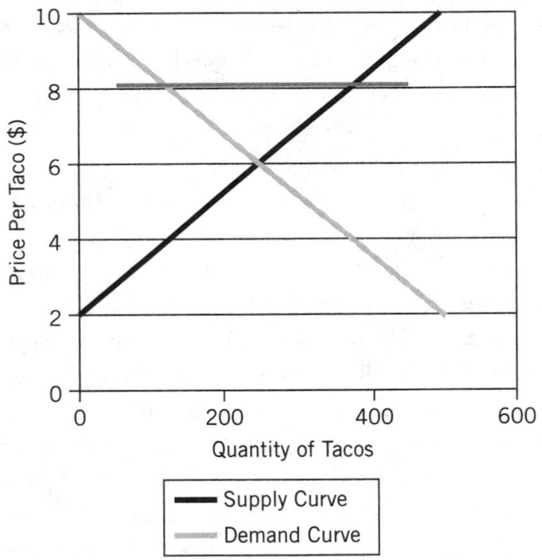

Figure 1

Bill's Taco Stand

British economist Alfred Marshall was the first person to depict a complete picture for the determinant of price–what the market decides as a fair amount for a good or service—in his creation of the laws of Supply and Demand (Frank and Bernanke 65). Put simply, there is a market for *anything*. On one side, there's a group of producers that creates a product (the supply) and wants to get as much money as possible for it. On the other, there's a group of consumers that want a product for as low as a price as possible (the demand). These motives are opposing; where the forces meet is the point at which a price is determined. Take a look at Figure 1 for a fictional example of how much our friend Bill will get for his tacos sold at his taco stand. The light gray line denotes the demand. At eight dollars, Bill would like to sell 400 tacos, but his customers are only willing to buy 100 at that price. If he refused to sell below that price, there would be an excess supply of 300 tacos (400 – 100)—the difference between the points of intersection of the horizontal line between the Supply and Demand curves. In a free market, this process goes back and forth until the lines intersect, at what is called an equilibrium price, where Bill's production of tacos meets his demand.

These same principles carry over to labor markets. The only thing that really changes is the label on the axes. What was once the price of a good or service is now the wage of a worker. What was once quantity now becomes employment, the number of jobs available. Again, there is a supply side and a demand side. In this case, employers are the supply while people looking for work make up the demand. A true free market economy would use this model to determine wage, and an equilibrium price (wage in this example) would be reached—this is how much a worker would be paid. However, this supposedly ideal scenario does not reflect reality; the government in an effort to help the lower class has instituted a minimum wage. Reflected in Figure 2, a serious problem emerges. Though the government may have altruistic motives, the minimum wage intrinsically expands unemployment. Companies can't afford to pay workers more than that equilibrium price a free market economy would set for wage, so what they do is simply higher less workers—this time, an excess supply of job seekers (and, thus, more unemployment) ensues.

Suffering an influx of unemployment, a minimum wage economy operates inefficiently; this economy is not utilizing its resource of labor to its full potential, since people that could otherwise be working are not (Frank and Bernanke 177). Regardless, it still seems necessary and just for workers to have some sort of minimum so that we don't have Americans bringing home just a couple of dollars a day, no matter how menial the labor. It becomes a necessary evil. America is not the only country that faces this dilemma. In Australia, there has been heated debate on this same issue. As previous chairman of the Australian Fair Pay Commission, Ian Harper posits that it is equally inefficient to pursue the abolishment of a minimum wage as it is to keep it, for it would evaporate the "safety net" on wage that these laws create (4). In his opinion, all that is necessary is the maintenance of some sort of minimum, anywhere below the equilibrium levels. I would challenge Mr. Harper to think outside the box; the solution

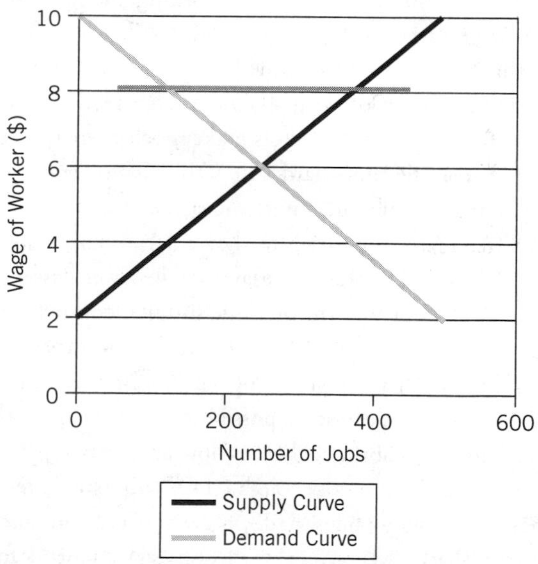

Figure 2

Labor Markets

that we both seek—one "economically efficient" as well as socially acceptable for wage redistributions—may lie in the additional adoption of a maximum wage, the exact opposite policy (5).

The target market for the implementation of this kind of law is American CEOs. They make the most. If the wealth distribution in America got you a little frustrated, go ahead and grab yourself a couple aspirins to calm down that heart of yours before we continue; the magnitude of CEO salaries might just put you in a stretcher. Venkat Venkatasubramanian in a longitudinal analysis of wage distributions for Purdue University magnifies the following statistic in his research: while in the 70s CEOs made about 50 times as much as minimum wage workers, as of 2007 they now make on average 866 (that's right; *eight-hundred-and-sixty-six*) times as much (766). To put that into perspective, for every eight dollars a person makes in an hour, a CEO makes close to 7,000 dollars. If you're working an eight hour day, a minimum wage earner brings home about 64 dollars, while a CEO working that same amount of time brings home 56,000 dollars—more than that worker would make in two years working full time. These are just averages, many CEOs make much more than that. Do CEOs really work 866 times harder than their lowest employees? Emphatically, I answer "of course not!" Sure they have highly stressful jobs, but a free market approach to their salaries makes up a double standard (767). Why do we set wage laws for the lower classes that have proved to increase unemployment while simultaneously ignoring the opposite side of the spectrum? Let's turn the minimum wage graph on its head and show what a wage ceiling will do for our economy; look now to Figure 3. As we can see, a possible benefit occurs in the divergence away from equilibrium; there is now an excess supply of CEO job openings available but not enough CEOs willing to take the wage.

In an interview with James Madison University Economics professor Dr. Vipul Bhatt, I went over this theoretical framework for a maximum wage. Though he lauded the model in theory for what I was setting out to solve, he coerced me away from what I now see as

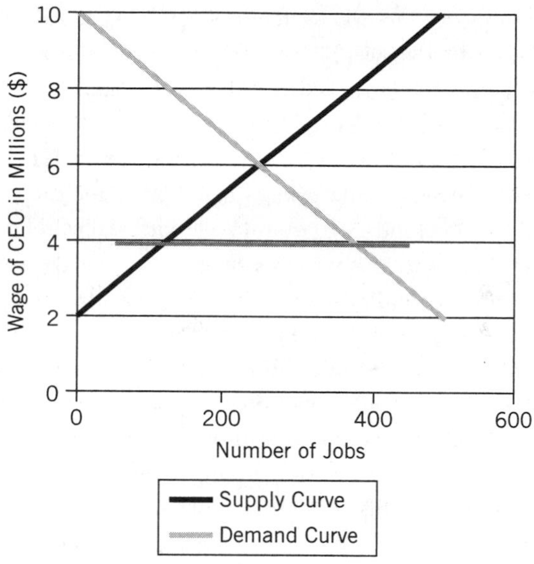

Figure 3

Proposed CEO Labor Market

naivety and explained what would happen in reality. "There will be a shortage of CEOs in your model," he said. Even if the government did put a cap on CEO wages, "they will always find a way to get money outside of their salary in the form of bonuses and stock options." On top of this, if they are not getting paid in full, their performance will decrease and more poor decisions will be made, and government "does not want to interfere with performance." Fine. But if a maximum wage isn't realistic, then what is?

As we can see, a chasm exists between economic theory and its practice. As Dr. Maureen Ramsay of the University of Leeds expressed in her "A Modest Proposal: The Case for a Maximum Wage," "it seems implausible that it is necessary to make some individuals hundreds of time richer than others in order to retain incentives" (207). But, we somehow continue to operate under that principle. If a flat out ceiling won't work, what else is there? I kept my nose to the grindstone, and the answer hit me in the face while reading Venkat's work: the greater the fairness of a company, the greater the entropy (capability for work) in that company (777). While he posited the idea of pay scales, why not simply tie the salary of the CEO to a set ratio of that earned by the lowest paid worker for the company, fusing the ideals behind a maximum wage with real world practicality (776)? Two enormously successful companies have been built upon such a principle. Praised in *Time Magazine*, Ben & Jerry's ice cream and Whole Foods supermarkets, from their inceptions, tied the top of management to the bottom tier of workers (Fonda 63). Though Ben & Jerry's had to abandon the practice in the mid-90s to hire a new CEO, Whole Foods still operates on a maximum of a 14:1 ratio (63). Their CEO is only taking home 14 times more than the person that's bagging the groceries they sell (sounds much better than 866 times, right?). With this idea in practice, the bosses are still rewarded handsomely for their efforts, but the bottom tier workers do not feel alienated from their executives—growth in salary is still possible. You can have your cake and eat it too. As an added bonus, this practice would inherently boost productivity across the spectrum once implemented; anyone who works in the company, no matter what their rank, has the extra incentive to do their best at all times because any increase in the profitability of the company is shared directly with the worker. The *incentive* to do well serves as a catalyst for both the growth of the company and of personal salary.

Increased incentives for workers, no matter how important, lead to economic growth (Bhatt). While the flat salary caps remain regrettably implausible, the adoption of ratio driven salaries for corporate America has unlimited potential. I'll set a bar, middle of the road, in comparison to today's standards. If we required CEOs to be paid a maximum of 100 times what their lowest workers are getting, that's still a difference in a factor of 766 times what it is today. Think how much more wealth could be shared! Unfortunately, the biggest problem the implementation of a ratio-wage policy faces is founded in the culture of American greed that got us here in the first place: the wretched bedfellow of the free market. However, if our nation is the wealthiest on this planet, why should only a select few enjoy it? Possibly, there may be a need for a call for change—a change in the distribution of wealth in our society. The wealth of our nation should be our greatest benefit as Americans, holistically. That wealth cannot and should not be contained all within the grasp of an elite echelon of the top wage earners. I'm not here to spark a Marxist revolution in America, but I very well want to level the playing field—and expand social justice with economic policy, reframing what it means to be an American and to be free. At the end of the day, if both you and your boss can stand to benefit, what is there to lose?

Works cited

Bhatt, Vipul. Personal Interview. 3 Nov. 2010.

Domhoff, G. William. "Who Rules America: Wealth, Income, and Power." *Power in America*. UC Santa Cruz, n.d. Web. 8 Nov. 2010.

Fonda, Daren, et al. "The Rumble Over Executive Pay." *Time* 163.22 (2004): 62–64. *Academic Search Complete*. Web. 8 Nov. 2010.

Frank, Robert H., and Ben Bernanke. *Principles of Macroeconomics*. 4th ed. Boston: McGraw-Hill Irwin, 2009. Print.

Harper, Ian. "Why Would an Economic Liberal Set Minimum Wages?" *Policy* 25.4 (2009): 3–7. *Academic Search Complete*. Web. 8 Nov. 2010.

Ramsay, Maureen. "A Modest Proposal: The Case for a Maximum Wage." *Contemporary Politics* 11.4 (2005): 201–215. *Academic Search Complete*. Web. 8 Nov. 2010.

Venkatasubramanian, Venkat. "What is Fair Pay for Executives? An Information Theoretic Analysis of Wage Distributions." *Entropy* 11.4 (2009): 766–781. *Academic Search Complete*. Web. 8 Nov. 2010.

For Analysis

1. Use the TRY THIS activity on p. 165 to examine how Grant's thesis evolves throughout his essay.
2. How effectively does Grant use sources to verify his argument?
3. Imagine Grant as a fellow student in the class you're now taking. Use the section on Providing Helpful Feedback (pp. 535–40) to generate some constructive responses for a peer review of his article.

For Writing

1. Summarize Grant's essay in 300 words or less. See pp. 49–50 for guidance.
2. Practice the Believing and Doubting Game and write a blog post, as described in the TRY THIS on p. 119.

"Why Should Married Women Change Their Names? Let Men Change Theirs"

by Jill Filipovic

Jill Filipovic edits the *Feministe* blog and writes regularly for *Salon*, *Al Jazeera America*, and *The Guardian*, which published this article in 2013. Filipovic argues that women should not take their husbands' last names.

Your name is your identity. The reasons women give for changing their names after marrying don't make much sense.

Excuse me while I play the cranky feminist for a minute, but I'm disheartened every time I sign into Facebook and see a list of female names I don't recognize. You got married, congratulations! But why, in 2013, does getting married mean giving up the most basic marker of your identity? And if family unity is so important, why don't men ever change their names?

On one level, I get it: people are really hard on married women who don't change their names. Ten percent of the American public still thinks that keeping your name means you aren't dedicated to your marriage. And a full 50% of Americans think you should be legally required to take your husband's name. Somewhere upwards of 90% of women do change their names when they get married. I understand, given the social judgment of a sexist culture, why some women would decide that a name change is the path of least resistance.

But that's not what you usually hear. Instead, the defense of the name change is something like, "We want our family to share a name" or "His last name was better" or "My last name was just my dad's anyway"—all reasons that make no sense. If your last name is really your dad's, then no one, including your dad, has a last name that's actually theirs.

It may be the case that in your marriage, he did have a better last name. But if that's really a gender-neutral reason for a name change, you'd think that men with unfortunate last names would change theirs as often as women do. Given that men almost never change their names upon marriage, either there's something weird going on where it just so happens that women got all of the bad last names, or "I changed my name because his is better" is just a convenient and ultimately unconvincing excuse.

Not that I'm unsympathetic to the women out there who have difficult or unfortunate last names. My last name is "Filipovic." People can't spell it or pronounce it, which is a liability when your job includes writing articles under your difficult-to-spell last name, and occasionally doing television or radio hits where the host cannot figure out what to call you. It's weird, and it's "ethnic," and it makes me way too easily Google-able. But Jill Filipovic is my name and my identity. Jill Smith is a different person.

That is fundamentally why I oppose changing your name (and why I look forward to the wider legalization of same-sex marriage, which in addition to just being good and right, will challenge the idea that there are naturally different roles for men and women within the marital unit). Identities matter, and the words we put on things are part of how we make them real. There's a power in naming that feminists and social justice activists have long highlighted. Putting a word to the most obvious social dynamics is the first step toward ending inequality. Words like "sexism" and "racism" make clear that different treatment based on sex or race is something other than the natural state of things; the invention of the term "Ms" shed light on the fact that men simply existed in the world while women were identified based on their marital status.

Your name is your identity. The term for you is what situates you in the world. The cultural assumption that women will change their names upon marriage—the assumption that we'll even think about it, and be in a position where we make a "choice" of whether to keep our names or take our husbands'—cannot be without consequence. Part of how our brains function and make sense of a vast and confusing universe is by naming and categorizing. When women see our names as temporary or not really ours, and when we understand that part of being a woman is subsuming your own identity into our husband's, that impacts our perception of ourselves and our role in the world. It lessens the belief that our existence is valuable unto itself, and that as individuals we are already whole. It disassociates us from ourselves, and feeds into a female understanding of self as relational—we are not simply who we are, we are defined by our role as someone's wife or mother or daughter or sister.

Men rarely define themselves relationally. And men don't tend to change their names, or even let the thought cross their mind. Men, too, seem to realize that changing one's name has personal and professional consequences. In the internet age, all the work you did under your previous name isn't going to show up in a Google search. A name change means a new driver's license, passport, professional documentation, the works. It means someone trying to track you down—a former client, an old classmate, a co-worker from a few years back with an opportunity you may be interested in—is going to have a tough time finding you. It means lost opportunities personally and professionally.

Of course, there's also power in a name change. Changing your name if, for example, you change your gender presentation makes sense—a new, more authentic name to match the new, more authentic you. But outside of the gender transition context, marriage has long meant a woman giving up her identity, and along with it, her basic rights. Under coverture laws, a woman's legal existence was merged with her husband's: "husband and wife are one," and the one was the husband. Married women had no right to own property or enter into legal contracts. It's only very recently that married women could get their own credit cards. Marital rape remained legal in many states through the 1980s. The idea that a woman retains her own separate identity from her husband, and that a husband doesn't have virtually unlimited power over a woman he marries, is a very new one.

Fortunately, feminists succeeded in shifting the law and the culture of marriage. Today marriages are typically based on love instead of economics. Even conservative couples who still believe a husband should be the head of the household have more egalitarian marriages than previous generations, and are less likely than their parents or grandparents to see things like domestic violence as a private matter or a normal part family life.

Unfortunately, despite all of these gains, the marital name change remains. Even the small number of women who do keep their names after marriage tend to give their children the husband's name. At best there's hyphenation. That's a fair solution, but after many centuries of servitude and inequality, allow me to suggest some gender push-back: Give the kids the woman's last name.

Allow me to suggest an even stronger push: If it's important to you that your family all share a last name, make it the wife's. Yes, men, that means taking your wife's name. Or do what this guy did and invent a new name with your wife. And women, if the man you're set to marry extols the virtues of sharing a family name but won't consider taking yours? Perhaps ask yourself if you should be marrying someone who thinks your identity is fundamentally inferior to his own.

The suggestion that men change their names may sound unfair given everything I just wrote about the value of your name and identity, and the psychological impact of growing up in a world where your own name for yourself is impermanent. But men don't grow up with that sense of psychological impermanence. They don't grow up under the shadow of several thousand years of gender-based discrimination. So if you'd rather your family all shared a name, it actually makes much more sense to make it the woman's. Or we can embrace a modern vision of family where individuals form social and legal bonds out of love and loyalty, instead of defining family as a group coalesced under one male figurehead and a singular name.

At the very least, everyone keeping their own name will make Facebook less confusing.

For Analysis

1. Like most good online writing, Filipovic embeds hyperlinks as citations to support her arguments. Find this article online and read the linked references associated with these two claims: "people are really hard on married women who don't change their names"; and "do what this guy did and invent a new name with your wife." What does reading these additional sources add to Filipovic's argument? Why would she need these references to support her claims?
2. How does Filipovic's essay compare with the template for proposal arguments presented in Appendix B?
3. Do you find Filipovic's arguments persuasive? If so, why? If not, what would it take to change your mind?

For Writing

Write an 800- to 1,000-word blog post that responds to Filipovic's arguments or addresses a related topic. Include several hyperlinked references.

"New Home School Law a Threat"
by Katie Brown

Katie Brown is a resident of New Market, Virginia. Her commentary, which advocates for parents' rights to homeschool their children, was published by a local newspaper, *The Daily News-Record*, on January 31, 2014.

Whether you are religious, religious liberty should matter to you. Why? If your neighbor's freedoms are taken from them, what's to protect your freedoms and rights? A government that doesn't respect the rights and beliefs of one group is not bound to respect those of another group. Religious freedom has been called the first of rights and the freedom on which all other rights rest. It was a key freedom upon which our nation was founded, one that led many immigrants to seek shelter in America at its birth and today.

Del. Tom Rust, R-Fairfax, is seeking to "clarify" the religious exemption law for Virginia homeschoolers. In his proposed resolution, HR92, he seeks to "study" the law and wishes to "ensure these children are getting an adequate education." Homeschoolers have proven that they are giving their children an adequate education. Children homeschooled under the religious exemption score 33 percentile points above other students. Many students taught under this law are grown and living normal, successful lives.

Particularly troubling is his concern about standardizing the way school boards determine whether the family applying for the exemption is religious "enough." The implication seems to be that the law should be more restrictive or that the government should be responsible for determining whether these families are "religious." How is it "separation of church and state" to have the government defining what constitutes religion or deeming whether someone is religious enough to merit a religious exemption?

In Germany, where homeschooling has been illegal since 1918, two families, the Wunderlichs and the Romeikes, want to be allowed to homeschool. Police forcibly seized the Wunderlichs' children and social workers and kept them in government custody for three weeks. The children were returned to their parents on the condition that they would be enrolled in public school, despite having scored high on both social and academic tests.

When the family tried to emigrate to France where homeschooling is legal, German judge, Marcus Malkmus, ruled that they were not allowed to leave the county, and if they left without permission, the German government would prosecute them as criminals. The judge's reasoning should be frightening to any freedom-loving American. Malkmus acknowledged that the children were well-adjusted, well-cared for and doing well academically, but worried that the children would grow up "without having learned to be integrated" or to have a "sense of practicing tolerance." The father of the children said, "We are happy for them to be connected to society. We just prefer to homeschool them because we believe it is better for them. . . . Judge Malkmus has erected another Berlin Wall apparently designed to prevent all parents who might leave to homeschool from leaving Germany." This is how Germany ensures its people are "tolerant."

The Romeikes fled Germany in 2008 after facing exorbitant fines, forcible removal of their children, and possible imprisonment for homeschooling their children. They were granted asylum in the United States in 2010. In 2012, the Obama administration overturned their asylum and is seeking to return them to Germany. Said Michael Farris, chairman of Home School Legal Defense, said, "No one can understand why the White House is showing so much leniency to millions of immigrants who have come here illegally . . . but is so determined to deport this one family." Why is the Obama administration siding with Germany?

If we do not protect our neighbors' freedoms, the rights we hold dear may be next to go. Virginia has a long history of protecting religious freedom; let's keep it that way by asking Del. Rust to withdraw his unnecessary resolution. As a threat to religious freedom, it should concern everyone.

For Analysis

1. Why do you think Brown chose to write a newspaper commentary? What do you imagine she wanted to accomplish?
2. What "moves" did she make that correspond to those made in scholarly arguments?
3. Brown describes a homeschooling situation in Germany to support her argument. How persuasive do you think this example is for her readers, and why?

For Writing

Brown's inspiration was the proposal of Virginia House of Delegates Joint Resolution 92. Find and read the Resolution online, then write a 250-word evaluation of how fairly and accurately Brown represents this source.

"The Gender Wage Gap Lie"
by Hanna Rosin

Hannah Rosin co-founded the women's website, *DoubleX*. She authored the book *The End of Men: And the Rise of Women*, and she writes regularly for *The Atlantic* and *Slate*, where this article appeared in 2013. Rosin argues that the US gender pay gap is often exaggerated.

How many times have you heard that "women are paid 77 cents on the dollar for doing the same work as men"? Barack Obama said it during his last campaign. Women's groups say it every April 9, which is Equal Pay Day. In preparation for Labor Day, a group protesting outside Macy's this week repeated it, too, holding up signs and sending out press releases saying "women make $.77 to every dollar men make on the job." I've heard the line enough times that I feel the need to set the record straight: It's not true.

The official Bureau of Labor Department statistics show that the median earnings of full-time female workers is 77 percent of the median earnings of full-time male workers. But that is very different than "77 cents on the dollar for doing the same work as men." The latter gives the impression that a man and a woman standing next to each other doing the same job for the same number of hours get paid different salaries. That's not at all the case. "Full time" officially means 35 hours, but men work more hours than women. That's the first problem: We could be comparing men working 40 hours to women working 35.

How to get a more accurate measure? First, instead of comparing annual wages, start by comparing average weekly wages. This is considered a slightly more accurate measure because it eliminates variables like time off during the year or annual bonuses (and yes, men get higher bonuses, but let's shelve that for a moment in our quest for a pure wage gap number). By this measure, women earn 81 percent of what men earn, although it varies widely by race. African-American women, for example, earn 94 percent of what African-American men earn in a typical week. Then, when you restrict the comparison to men and women working 40 hours a week, the gap narrows to 87 percent.

But we're still not close to measuring women "doing the same work as men." For that, we'd have to adjust for many other factors that go into determining salary. Economists Francine Blau and Lawrence Kahn did that in a recent paper, "The Gender Pay Gap." They first accounted for education and experience. That didn't shift the gap very much, because women generally have at least as much and usually more education than men, and since the 1980s they have been gaining the experience. The fact that men are more likely to be in unions and have their salaries protected accounts for about 4 percent of the gap. The big differences are in occupation and industry. Women congregate in different professions than men do, and the largely male professions tend to be higher-paying. If you account for those differences, and then compare a woman and a man doing the same job, the pay gap narrows to 91 percent. So, you could accurately say in that Obama ad that, "women get paid 91 cents on the dollar for doing the same work as men."

The point here is not that there is no wage inequality. But by focusing our outrage into a tidy, misleading statistic we've missed the actual challenges. It would in fact be much simpler if the problem were rank sexism and all you had to do was enlighten the nation's bosses or throw the Equal Pay Act at them. But the 91 percent statistic suggests a much more complicated set of problems. Is it that women are choosing lower-paying professions or that our country values women's professions less? And why do women work fewer hours? Is this all discrimination or, as economist Claudia Goldin likes to say, also a result of "rational choices" women make about how they want to conduct their lives.

Goldin and Lawrence Katz have done about as close to an apples-to-apples comparison of men's and women's wages as exists. (They talk about it here in a Freakonomics discussion.) They tracked male and female MBAs graduating from the University of Chicago from 1990 to 2006. First they controlled for previous job experience,

GPA, chosen profession, business-school course and job title. Right out of school, they found only a tiny differential in salary between men and women, which might be because of a little bit of lingering discrimination or because women are worse at negotiating starting salaries. But 10 to 15 years later, the gap widens to 40 percent, almost all of which is due to career interruptions and fewer hours. The gap is even wider for women business school graduates who marry very high earners. (Note: Never marry a rich man).

If this midcareer gap is due to discrimination, it's much deeper than "male boss looks at female hire and decides she is worth less, and then pats her male colleague on the back and slips him a bonus." It's the deeper, more systemic discrimination of inadequate family-leave policies and childcare options, of women defaulting to being the caretakers. Or of women deciding that are suited to be nurses and teachers but not doctors. And in that more complicated discussion, you have to leave room at least for the option of choice—that women just don't want to work the same way men do.

For Analysis

1. Rosin's main argument addresses a controversy of fact. What kinds of support does she use to support her claims? How effective are these supports?
2. Rosin is known for advocating for women's issues. Why does she want to "set the record straight" on the gender wage gap?
3. What does Rosin want readers to do about the wage gap?

For Writing

Read at least four other credible sources that examine the existence and causes of the gender pay gap. In 1,000 words, synthesize what these sources say to answer the question "What's the Real Gender Pay Gap?"

"Executive Summary: Injustice on Our Plates: Immigrant Women in the U.S. Food Industry"

by Mary Bauer and Mónica Ramírez

> **Mary Bauer** is the executive director of the Legal Aid Justice Center and former legal director of the Southern Poverty Law Center (SPLC), a civil rights organization that fights injustice and hate crimes. **Mónica Ramírez** is an attorney, author, and advocate for farmworkers and immigrant women. She is also the co-editor of *Representing Farmworker Women Who Have Been Sexually Harassed: A Best Practices Manual.* The SPLC published this Executive Summary as part of a longer report in 2010.

They're the backbone of our food supply.

Their hands sliced the chicken breast we had for lunch. Their sweat brought the fresh tomato to our plates. Their backs bent to pick the lettuce in our salads.

They are America's undocumented workers. Every single day, virtually all of us rely on their labor. At least six in 10 of our country's farmworkers are undocumented immigrants—probably many more. On farms across America, they help produce billions of dollars worth of grapes, tomatoes, strawberries, melons, beans and other grocery store staples.

Despite their contribution to our economy, these immigrants live at the margins of U.S. society—subsisting on poverty wages, enduring humiliation and exploitation in the workplace, and living in constant fear that their families will be shattered if they are detected.

Because of their status, they remain in the shadows, their voices silent. They are unable to speak out about the indignities they suffer and the crimes committed against them. As one 59-year-old Mexican woman says: "No one sees the people in the field. We're ignored."

This report is based on extensive interviews conducted with 150 immigrant women from Mexico, Guatemala and other Latin-American countries. They live and work in Florida, California, North Carolina, New York, Iowa, Arkansas and other states. All have worked in the fields or in the factories that produce our food. They are among the 4 million undocumented women living in the U.S.

They are the linchpin of the immigrant family. And they are surely the most vulnerable of all workers in America—seen by their employers as easily exploitable and, at the end of the day, disposable.

Their stories are remarkably similar. Virtually all say they came to the United States to escape devastating poverty and to try, like waves of immigrants before them, to lay a foundation for their children's future. They tell harrowing stories of survival in the desert they crossed to get here. They tell of being cheated out of hard-earned wages by unscrupulous employers. They tell of working in dangerous conditions without adequate safety precautions. And they tell of enduring near-constant sexual harassment in the fields and factories.

The laws that protect these workers are grossly inadequate. More importantly, the workers' ability to enforce what protections they *do* have is generally nonexistent.

When the debate over immigration policy once again reaches Congress—the only venue where it can be resolved—it's important to understand the motivation that drives these women across our borders, their role in our economy and our communities, and the exploitation they face.

They are economic refugees—pushed from their home countries by abject poverty, hunger and desperation. They're pulled north by the alluring images in their heads of a bountiful country overflowing with opportunity—a meritocracy where one need only work hard to have enough food to eat and to provide decent clothes and shelter. They don't come here expecting a handout.

Some find their American dream is little more than a mirage. Others, finding a modicum of success, are able to put their children on an upward path and help sustain their relatives back home. Many come to the U.S. for what they believe will be a temporary stay but find their plans to return home complicated by community ties, their desire to give their children the opportunity the U.S. offers and tighter border controls.

These women live at the bottom of a world where titans of finance send capital across borders at the speed of light and transnational corporations move factories—and jobs—around the globe like a chess match to take advantage of the lowest labor costs. It's a world where trade and foreign policies established in Washington and other faraway places can mean a job or no job to people who have no say in the matter. Though the world's economy has never before been so interwoven, it's still a world where *people*, the workers who run the factories and whose labor helps enrich those at the top, are supposed to stay within the lines.

America is now at war with the immigrant hands that feed us. Communities and states across the country are enacting a patchwork of highly restrictive laws that will only drive undocumented immigrants further underground and make them even more exploitable by the businesses that employ them and the criminals who prey on them. Immigrant women face the additional danger of sexual assault and rape, crimes they often are afraid to report to police because it could lead to deportation.

Not only is this war costing taxpayers many billions, it is eroding wage and workplace protections for U.S. workers as well, especially for low-skilled workers, as businesses find they can exploit immigrant labor with virtual impunity.

U.S. immigration policy has not kept pace with these challenges. Border security has been greatly enhanced. But the reality is that about 11 million people are now living and working in the U.S. without documentation. Millions of them are raising U.S.-born children. Deporting all of these immigrants, according to one recent study, would leave a $2.6 trillion hole in the U.S. economy over the next decade. That does not include the billions of dollars that would be required to enforce such a policy. And it does not take into account the massive human rights violations that would inevitably occur.

Fifty years ago this Thanksgiving, CBS broadcast "Harvest of Shame," an Edward R. Murrow documentary that chronicled the plight of migrant farmworkers. Murrow closed the program with this commentary: "The migrants have no lobby. Only an enlightened, aroused and perhaps angered public opinion can do anything about the migrants. The people you have seen have the strength to harvest your fruit and vegetables. They do not have the strength to influence legislation."

Not much has changed.

Congress must address this crisis in a comprehensive way—a way that recognizes the contributions of these immigrants to our country and our fundamental values of fairness and dignity. Our recommendations for doing so appear at the conclusion of this report.

For Analysis

1. This report is an "executive summary." Read about this genre online and develop a list of conventions that executive summaries typically follow.
2. The authors include many claims and supports in the executive summary that they do not cite. Choose 5-7 claims or supports (such as facts or information) that the authors state in the executive summary but do not cite. Then, look for places in the larger report where these claims and supports are described in more detail. What sources do the authors reference? You can find this report online by searching for "Injustice on Our Plates" on the Southern Poverty Law Center's website.
3. What are some counterarguments that audiences might raise in response to this report? How could the authors respond to these objections?

For Writing

At the end of the full report, "Injustice on Our Plates" (published online), the authors list a number of recommendations. Select one of their recommendations and conduct some library research to develop a more robust plan of action. Then, write a letter to a specific stakeholder who can enact change. Describe, explain, and justify actions that this stakeholder should take, based on your research findings. You might also include infographics that display your findings.

Appendix A

How to Benefit from Peer Review and Collaboration

THE ABILITY TO give and receive effective feedback is among the most valuable skills you can learn in life. You probably have a friend or relative who gives great advice, a person whom you and others trust, who listens carefully and provides help when needed. Employers and coworkers also value a person who can identify exactly what is and isn't working and give useful suggestions for improvement. Such sharp critical thinking skills can benefit everyone and make you a sought-after colleague. Peer review is an excellent way to develop and practice these skills.

However, your experiences with peer review may be mixed. Think back on times when you've given or received feedback on writing. What worked, what didn't, and why? Compare those occasions with a time when you received excellent advice about something important other than writing. How was that advice given? What made the experience valuable for you? Now, consider what would be needed for peer review to be effective and for students to take it seriously.

The Advantages of Peer Review

In the following sections, we'll describe the benefits of peer review to you as a writer, a reader, and a collaborator; and we'll give you some suggestions for insightful questions and comments to offer during peer review.

How to Benefit as a Reader

Becoming a strong, critical reader takes careful practice, and peer review can help you cultivate keen analytical skills that you can put to use right away in other classes. In college, you'll be expected to critically review (that is, read and analyze) a considerable amount of scholarly writing. Peer review gives you a chance to do that with essays that are typically more accessible than the professional scholarly writing you'll also encounter. Use peer review to strengthen your reading skills.

How to Benefit as a Writer

Peer review lets you investigate other writers' styles, strategies, and pitfalls. You see approaches you might want to borrow and ones you definitely want to avoid. For example, reading your peer's vivid conclusion might inspire you to try a similar technique. Reading other students' work can also show you different ways to interpret an assignment, and such insight can give you a fuller understanding of the task at hand. If your peers' interpretations conflict, it's a great opportunity to identify potential questions, to talk with your instructor about her expectations, and to clarify the best ways to tackle the assignment.

The most difficult part of writing is imagining how an audience will interpret and respond to your writing. Participating in peer review gives you a glimpse into this perspective by showing you the effect of your writing on readers. Without that perspective, you can only guess whether your ideas are working.

Experienced writers take advantage of every available opportunity to have someone—either their real audience or someone who can play substitute—read and respond to their work in progress. To publish their writing, scholars submit their manuscripts to editors for feedback. Every once in a while, a scholarly journal will accept an article for publication with little revision, but much more often, editors respond with substantial feedback on how to improve the draft and a recommendation to "revise and resubmit." A demanding reader helps you better imagine your audience and then revise your essay to meet their needs.

An Unforeseen Benefit: Practice Collaborating

Practicing peer review will also strengthen your collaboration skills. You'll get to practice the interpersonal skills and social gestures essential for teamwork. For instance, when helping another writer find a better way to communicate a controversial idea or organize an elaborate proposal, you might have to soften your criticism with polite suggestions. Or you might have to help a writer avoid feeling embarrassed about a silly mistake or find a tactful way of saying that his thesis seems clichéd. Such honest communication is not easy. Tactfulness requires sophisticated conversation skills that must be learned through practice. Collaborating on writing is also tricky because you can't just rewrite portions of the paper for the writer. Instead, you have to help a writer help himself, meaning you give assistance but cannot write the paper for him. Examples include asking stimulating questions, highlighting problem areas for the writer to solve, or giving several options and allowing him to choose.

Providing Helpful Feedback

Right about now, you might be wondering, "How can I be expected to provide high-quality response if I'm not an expert writer who has read or written much scholarly writing?"

Indeed, many students find themselves saying things such as "Nice job," or "I don't have much to add," or maybe "I think there's something fishy here but I'm not sure what," simply because they don't know what else to say. We understand that many students have had bad experiences with peer review and that you may feel unprepared to give assistance, so we're offering you a model of questioning and commenting that can facilitate productive peer review. These questions are ones that you can ask each other and ask *yourself*, whenever you are writing.

Keep in mind that peer review shouldn't look the same during every stage of the writing process. In fact, you'll probably want to adapt the review process, just like the writing process and the reading process, depending on what you're trying to accomplish.

Prewriting Feedback

During the discovery (or prewriting) stage of the writing process, it's helpful to have a conversation with your peers: talk about your ideas, pose and answer questions, serve as "devil's advocates" for each other, and identify possible plans for your papers. In this stage, you'll want to ask each other questions such as:

- What interests you most about this assignment? What's your inspiration?
- How does this assignment connect to concepts you're studying in other classes, your personal experience, or other ideas you've thought about?
- What makes your topic controversial?
- Why would this topic matter to your reader? What are the implications?
- Who would care most about this topic? Who are other stakeholders?

Feedback on Drafts

Once you have a first draft, your instructor might ask you to review each other's drafts ahead of time and come to class prepared with questions and comments. Before you give your draft to someone for review, try to develop some specific questions or concerns for your reviewers to address. (See the sample note that the student wrote to his reviewer on page 555). Identifying specific issues will help reviewers customize their feedback to meet your needs as they read.

You might also spend time in class reading your drafts aloud and sharing feedback. A very successful technique that doesn't require much expertise but yields great results is for the writer to read her paper aloud, pausing every paragraph or two for the listener to summarize. This checks clarity, helps the writer better imagine her audience, and gives the reader practice summarizing. Reading your writing aloud or hearing someone else read it may be unnerving at first, but it can be a tremendously helpful way to detect confusing sentences, grammatical errors, or just an awkward tone. We hope you'll keep an open mind about such a useful exercise and be willing to try new strategies throughout the writing process.

When reviewing a draft, a smart place to start is simply to share your perspective as the reader. Writers need to know how their ideas are coming across, whether their points make sense, where their argument falls apart, and what the reader is confused about. Often the best thing you can do is to serve as an "ignorant" reader. You can point out questions that writers didn't consider, identify gaps in their reasoning, challenge their assumptions, and help them see where a reader might stumble. Essentially, you can give them a peek inside the mind of their audience so that they realize why readers might cringe over an insensitive comment, laugh at a lame example, or think of something they overlooked.

You might have noticed that we haven't yet said anything about helping with grammar. You might be tempted to pick the proverbial low-hanging fruit of misspellings, punctuation problems, and grammar errors, but remember, these are later order concerns that you'll want to save for editing. **Early on in the process, try to concentrate on global or higher order concerns that will help the writer revise.**

In fact, one of the best things you can do for a writer, rather than nitpick or criticize, is to talk about what you *appreciate* about a paper, what you think is really working well. Again, dig deeper than saying things like "nice job." Tell the writer *why* you think something works well for her intended audience and purpose, and suggest ways for her to build on that success.

Responding as a reader helps to adjust your expectations, both as a writer and as a reviewer, for how useful peer review will be. As an ignorant but curious reader, you really can't say something wrong or do harm (unless you're being downright mean, of course). You are the reader, and the writer needs to hear what you think and how you experience the text. To see examples of reader response comments, consult the peer review sample in Appendix C.

Responding with Questions

It's particularly useful to ask writers stimulating questions that help them discover what is and isn't working in a draft.

What is your purpose? Ask the writer what he is trying to achieve, and tell him what you perceive as his main points (You can say something like "I think what you're getting at is ______________________. Is that what you're trying to say, or am I missing something?"). This summary can help the writer see whether his message is coming across as intended.

Who is your intended audience? Talk to the writer about the audience he has in mind and why this audience is a good fit. Think about the background of these potential readers—their values, their experience, their knowledge—and talk about how they might respond to the writer's message. You can ask the writer why he thinks his writing style, analysis, examples, and so forth will work for this particular audience. Often, a writer forgets to think about his audience's perspective, so you can help him imagine that reader.

What questions do you have for me about the ideas presented? Tell the writer how you understand his arguments, saying something such as "So, what I hear you saying is . . ." or "Overall, I'm left with the impression that ______________________. Is that right?"

Discuss any questions you have about the overall message, share your opinion on the issues presented, suggest other examples that might fit, and help the writer think more carefully about his ideas.

Is the organization working? Ask the writer why he organized his points in this way, and identify any places where you became confused, sidetracked, or lost. To help the writer transition between his ideas more smoothly, you can ask "What is the connection between these two points? How are they related? What do they have in common?"

What is significant about this issue? Ask the writer why his argument matters, why his readers should care. Sometimes, writers assume that the importance of an issue is obvious, but readers wonder, *so what?* You can help a writer identify the significance of his position by raising questions such as "What are the broader implications of this idea?" or "Why do readers need to think about this topic?" or "What other concepts does this controversy relate to?"

Responding with Helpful Comments

All in all, you want to facilitate a *conversation* with the writer, not just search for grammatical errors. Remember, during this stage, your purpose is to critique and to help, not to edit. Be careful, though, not to overwhelm writers by giving them too much feedback. Instead, focus and prioritize your comments. Here are additional examples of helpful comments that offer a reader's perspective:

- "This section of the paper confused me because . . . It is not clear what you mean by . . ."
- "This argument may have more impact if you first start with your own experience, and then incorporate research and statistics."
- "I completely agree with your argument. The issues you raised related to ________________________ are important because . . ."
- "I see what you're saying about ________________________, but what kinds of evidence do you have to support that claim?"

- "I'm having a hard time seeing the significance of what you're saying. Can you tell me more about why this is important?"

Feedback during Editing

The kind of response that's needed while drafting and revising is usually quite different from what writers need when editing. Reader response is a good place to start and will remain useful throughout the writing process, but it keeps the reviewer in the driver's seat. As you develop as a writer—and especially as you gain more control with and become more deliberate about adapting your writing process—take the wheel by asking your reader for particular kinds of response. During the editing stage, you can ask your reviewers questions such as:

- How does the writing "sound"? Is the tone appropriate?
- Are there any sentences that are confusing, awkward, or otherwise unclear?
- Are there any word choices that are vague, confusing, or overly technical?
- Where can the writing be more concise? Where can I reduce unnecessary wordiness?
- Where should I combine or divide sentences?
- Where can I add more personality, through humor or vividness or other stylistic devices?
- Where do you see mistakes, such as missing commas, subject-verb agreement problems, or misspellings?

Accepting and Rejecting Advice

As we've said, the right kind of feedback can help you develop your writing expertise. But responding to criticism is not easy. Sometimes you will hear conflicting advice from different readers. At other times, you will disagree with a reader's suggestions. In both cases, you have to make decisions about how to revise. When deciding how to implement changes based on feedback, you should keep in mind that **scholarly writing is public writing**. Unlike writing that you may do simply to express your feelings or to record experiences for yourself, scholarly writing prioritizes the readers' needs, reactions, and preferences over your own. As they say in retail, "The customer is always right." If several reviewers give you similar feedback, then they're probably right—even if you disagree. Keep in mind that it's more important for your readers to understand and be moved by your message than it is for you to keep a potentially unclear sentence, example, or style that you love.

Different cultures place different values on complex, ambiguous expression—the kind you might find in poetry or fiction. Unless you're writing literature, scholars and professionals in the US typically expect writers to express themselves clearly so readers can expend less effort to interpret intended meaning. In some other cultures, writers expect readers to do much more work: to draw subtle linkages, to fill in gaps, to think of examples, to know the source of famous quotations, and so forth. But, in Western writing, you'll typically have to do these things for your readers. This is why you need to add explanations or explicitly state your meaning when readers miss the point, even if the meaning seems obvious to you.

However, that isn't to say that you should just blindly take every piece of advice you're given. In cases of conflicting or questionable suggestions, for example, you should consider the source. Think carefully about the reliability and skill level of the reader and the impact or cost of making recommended changes. You might even want to get a second opinion from a trained writing tutor or your instructor. The most important thing is to be thoughtful and strategic about revision—just as you should be during every stage of the writing process, knowing that good writing is all about good choices.

Collaborating Effectively

Collaboration skills have become essential in nearly every workplace. As a scholarly apprentice, you can learn effective strategies for group brainstorming by participating actively in class discussions or by visiting with your instructor during office hours. By using the techniques for peer review that we've discussed, you can also learn how scholars give and receive feedback on drafts.

Perhaps the most daunting kind of collaboration involves writing with others. At its best, group writing can help you create projects that you could not possibly write by yourself. But if you've ever done group work before, you probably know how frustrating it can be when things go wrong.

Here are some strategies to ensure a more successful and less stressful experience when writing with others:

1. **Plan ahead.** As soon as you get your assignment, meet with your group to develop a detailed, written plan for how you want to accomplish the project. Think carefully about how you will organize your time to give adequate attention to discovery, drafting, revision, and editing. Create a timeline with milestones to mark your progress, and allow extra time in case something goes wrong, like a group member getting sick.
2. **Decide on roles for your group members.** Most groups either write together, delegate tasks, or use some combination of methods. If it's convenient for members of the group to meet, either physically or online, then writing together can be a good technique, especially during the planning stage when many heads can be smarter than one. Drafting and revising can be accomplished together by using online tools, such as wikispaces or shared online documents. Many writers find it easier to take turns when drafting together to avoid tripping over each other in the same document. If you can find a time and place to meet together with a big screen or projector, group editing can be lively and help to achieve a consistent style.

Another common technique is delegated collaboration, which assigns different tasks to team members, usually based on their expertise and interests. One approach is to break the project into chunks; members each investigate and draft a portion that interests them the most.

Alternatively, you can assign someone who's good at research to take a leadership role for that portion of the assignment and let those who are best at drafting and editing lead those efforts. You should also consider assigning a project leader to manage communications and deadlines and generally keep everyone on track.

Delegated collaboration can be more efficient than writing together, but this technique sometimes misses the opportunity for *synergy*—when collaborators create something better than the sum of their efforts. (This book, for example, is immeasurably better because we wrote most of it together.)

However you decide to collaborate, it's a good idea to begin by discussing goals for what each participant wants to get out of the experience: A good grade? Better understanding of course content? More experience with leadership, editing, or organizing a group project? Fun? Not everyone approaches assignments the same way, and you can help boost motivation and trust by trying to help each other achieve your goals—even when they're different for everyone on the team.

3. **Establish rules and expectations for your group.** Most collaboration horror stories result from disagreements among members or group members acting inappropriately. Collaboration is complicated. You cannot completely avoid problems, but you can minimize their negative effects by agreeing up front to some rules and expectations for how you will work together. Here's a checklist of questions to consider before you begin writing:

    - How will the group make decisions when circumstances change (as they inevitably will)?

- How will the group handle missed deadlines or substandard work?
- How will you deal with a group member who doesn't pull her weight?
- How will the group respond to a member who's too bossy?

Another issue that's worth settling in advance is project evaluation. Many students cringe at the idea that their grade might be affected by other students' performance. If this is a problem for your group, ask your instructor if he wants—or will accept—separate evaluations for each member of the group. If so, then you could devise a system to document each member's contributions. Settle on criteria in advance (for example, level of effort, quality of work, collaboration performance). When the project is complete, everyone should complete a self-evaluation and peer evaluations for each group member. Realize, though, that it's difficult to weigh collaborative contributions accurately and that everyone will inevitably contribute at different levels.

Any time and effort that you devote to thinking about "what ifs" before you start writing will help you to avoid problems later. We recommend writing down your group's answers to the questions above, along with any others you can think of, in a shared document. You can begin the group conversation by asking each other: What strategies have you used in the past to make group projects work well? What problems or difficulties did you have?

Appendix B

Templates for Organizing Arguments

Research Article

The research article, also known as a scholarly paper, is somewhat different from the research papers you may have done before, when you used library sources or the Internet to learn about a topic. You'll write some of those papers in college, too, especially as an apprentice, but as you develop as a scholar you may begin to conduct research like scholars do, to enlighten the community of scholars. You might, for example, research a medieval poet or battle that no one else has studied before. Or you may investigate a very specific environmental or genetic cause of Parkinson's disease. In either case, you will likely report the results of your research to other scholars in a recognizable genre containing the following elements, along with a title page:

1. **Abstract**, which summarizes the investigation so that readers can quickly preview the article. When reviewing previous research, scholars often sift through stacks of sources by scanning article abstracts.
2. **Introduction**, which engages the reader, establishes the significance of the research (why it's needed), and states the problem or research question.
3. **Research (or "literature") review**, which synthesizes what other scholars have already said about the topic so that readers understand the subject's history and its theoretical foundation. Along

with the introduction, the research review establishes the *so what?* for the research question.

4. **Methods**, which explains the process used to answer a research question or to study a problem (for example, methods used to collect and analyze data). Typically, authors aim to provide enough information so that readers see their methods as valid and reliable.
5. **Results**, which reports and tabulates the data and results gathered through investigation. This section often uses figures and charts to report data. (Sometimes scholars report large quantities of data in a separate *Appendix* at the end of an article.)
6. **Analysis/Discussion**, which presents and makes sense of the findings. Although not necessarily the longest, this section is usually the most meaty—full of analysis, interpretations, and applications—and therefore often the most important part of the research paper. When readers trust the methods and results, they often skim ahead to the analysis and discussion—like peeking ahead to find out how the story ends.
7. **Conclusion**, which synthesizes the discussion, identifies the larger significance and implications of the findings, and/or raises questions for further research.
8. **Bibliography**, which gives credit to other authors and directs readers to other relevant sources. Sometimes called a References or Works Cited page, this section identifies the sources that informed and validated the author's work.

The research article is an appropriate structure for most research papers, especially for papers that showcase *primary source* data (collected through experiments, interviews, surveys, etc.). This format also works well for assignments that ask for portions of a research paper but don't require the whole kit and caboodle. The general structure of the research article can be adapted to fit different assignments and rhetorical situations.

A Research (or "Literature") Review

This genre typically contains four main sections: Introduction, Research Review, Conclusion, and Bibliography. Professors assign research reviews when they want students to summarize, analyze, and synthesize prominent research on a topic. Research reviews help scholars understand and analyze what others have already said about a subject and then identify a research area, topic, or question that has not been fully explored.

A Research Proposal

This genre typically contains an Introduction, Research Review, Methods, and Bibliography. Scholars write research proposals to pitch research projects that they have designed. They describe the experiments or research plans they would conduct to collect data and answer a research question. Often, the purpose of the proposal is to secure funding, support, or approval for a project, so scholars give readers an overview of their plans. A research proposal is a specific kind of *proposal argument* that offers or presents plans to solve an unanswered question or problem.

Proposal Argument

1. **Problem**
    a. Describe the problem.
    b. Explain why it deserves our attention.
2. **Potential solution(s)**
    a. Present one or multiple solutions, along with the costs and benefits of each.
    b. Remember that doing nothing about the problem is also an option.

3. **Justification**
    a. Explain how and why your proposed solution will work.
    b. Describe why the advantages will outweigh the costs or drawbacks.
    c. Convince readers that your solution is better than alternative fixes.
    d. Reference previous similar solutions that suggest similar positive outcomes.

Appendix C

Sample Rhetorical Analysis

To demonstrate a typical rhetorical analysis assignment, we've included the professor's instructions, a sample draft with marginal peer review comments, a note from the writer to the peer reviewer, and comments from the peer reviewer about the draft.

Professor's Assignment Guidelines: Write a rhetorical analysis of Conor Friedersdorf's article "Crass Frat Boys at Old Dominion" from the August 25, 2015 online issue of *The Atlantic*. Aim for about 1,000 words.

In your analysis, describe the argument's rhetorical situation and evaluate the author's choices. Your goal is to describe *how* Friedersdorf makes his argument. Since you can't analyze all of the rhetorical elements (author, audience, purpose, inspiration, support, rationales, genre, style, controversy categories, and implications), develop a thesis that focuses on a few significant elements of the argument.

After you compose a draft of your essay, write a note to your peer reviewer that identifies what kind of feedback you would like to receive on your draft.

[Student's Name]
[Professor's Name]
[Course]
[Date]

Verbal Assault or Fraternity Pranks?

> I like that your title introduces your topic, catches the reader's attention, and hints at the main idea of Friedersdorf's article. I'm glad that you didn't just title this "Rhetorical Analysis," but you may want to indicate somewhere in the title or introduction that that's what you're doing.

Stories about campus sexual harassment and assault seem to be everywhere these days in the news and social media. In the August 24, 2015 issue of *The Atlantic* magazine, Conor Friedersdorf argues for a more reasonable response to sexually charged incidents. Referring to a recent event at Old Dominion University (ODU) where members of a fraternity displayed banners with offensive statements aimed at freshmen females, Friedersdorf summarizes the extreme reactions from the University administration and the public to assert that people are responding to such incidents in unhelpful ways. Friedersdorf's argument is effective because the topic is timely and significant, he develops good credibility, his writing style is engaging, and his message is reasonable and thoughtful.

> Good attempt to summarize the article in such a short space. However, this is a lot to pack into one sentence. Maybe break this into two sentences to make it easier to digest?
>
> Also, would readers consider "freshmen" to be a sexist term? Is there an alternative?

A quick review of article titles on *The Atlantic*'s website indicates that the magazine covers a variety of current events involving business, technology, education, politics, culture, and health. Friedersdorf uses the incident at ODU to make a larger point about the problems we face in combatting sexual violence on college campuses. Connecting his commentary to recent events that people care about makes his overall argument seems more relevant. This move also lends a sense of urgency to his case. He takes the opportunity to join a conversation that is already going on, which is evident by the amount of passionate comments that follow the article online.

> This paragraph seems to mostly be about context, but it also touches on the audience, genre, and the author's purpose. That's a lot to do in one paragraph. Would it be better to separate these elements and examine them in more detail?
>
> Also, you haven't really explained everything enough. For example, your first sentence lists the kinds of topics that *The Atlantic* publishes. That seems like support for a claim that you haven't yet written.

Although Friedersdorf taps into a controversial, "hot" topic that many people are currently discussing, he makes his perspective sound reasonable, levelheaded, and informed. By highlighting the extreme responses that people in opposing camps are taking, Friedersdorf underscores the harm of such polarized reactions based in either/or reasoning. The argument's organization reinforces his message. He presents each side from the extreme and then offers his perspective, which he signals in a one-sentence paragraph: "I have a different view" (p. 313). This is effective because his argument emphasizes a "third way" (p. 311) or a middle ground that sounds much more sensible and moderate. By arguing for a more reasonable response, he projects a trustworthy and rationale credibility. Also, by summarizing two opposing sides and then presenting his own view, the author shows that he understands the debate and what opposing sides believe. He demonstrates that he has listened carefully to both sides, like a judge listening to both a prosecutor and defense attorney before making his decision. This makes him

> In this sequence of sentences, I like how you offer an observation (support), then interpretation (make a claim about what it means). Seems almost scientific.

seem well informed and judicious. One move that really builds his credibility is when he makes clear upfront that he does not condone or support the young men's actions or the banners' messages. Clarifying this position up front is important because he does not want to alienate readers who are offended by the fraternity's banners. He also does not want to align himself with the fraternity's actions, which would hurt his credibility.

> Again, there seems to be a lot going on in this paragraph. You've got some great ideas, but I think your main point could be clearer. This paragraph seems pretty long, too. Maybe you could break it into two paragraphs?

Friedersdorf's writing style is engaging, conversational, and straight to the point. Throughout the essay, he avoids using dense or overly formal language that would make the essay difficult and boring to read. Instead, he uses the first person, short sentences, and interesting diction and metaphors, such as phrases like "spring into action" (p. 308), "a sophomoric prank that seems like something a couple 19-year-olds cooked up in a few hours" (p. 309), and "so do the adults who are reacting as if they were stockpiling GHB" (p. 310). These engaging metaphors and lively phrasing make the writing style a pleasure to read. His one- to two-sentence paragraphs also assert his message strongly and memorably. By balancing longer paragraphs with one-liners like "No. Of course not" (p. 311) and "Ultimately, this story lays bare a divide" (p. 312), Friedersdorf makes his points quite clear. He has to be careful, though, not to overuse

> Okay, so here you make the main topic of the paragraph very clear, and you're on your way to making a good claim about that topic. I anticipate that you'll be discussing whether you think style was effective for his audience and purpose, right?

this technique because it may irritate some readers. Even more potentially annoying is his use of frequent questions and answers. He frequently asks a question and then answers it, such as in the following examples: "Should someone at Old Dominion explain to those kids the offensive assumptions implicit in their signs? Yes" (p. 311) and "Should the university president have made a statement? Sure" (p. 311). These short questions and answers have a conversational feel that may work for some readers, but others could claim he overdoes it. The danger of employing such a conversational style is he may sound overly informal and risk sounding insincere, lighthearted, or flippant about the issue.

> Who are these readers, specifically? Who is his intended audience?
>
> Is there something about these stylistic moves that might be especially effective for his purpose?

Overall, his argument makes sense and it gets at the heart of the issue. By summarizing the two common reactions as either "defend the transgression that is generating outrage or join in condemning the perpetrators" (p. 310), Friedersdorf shows that neither of these responses will actually prevent sexual assaults—which is the goal everyone shares. His "third way" sounds like a better solution because it promises to focus everyone's energies on "what's really required to make college campuses safer for women" (p. 313). That makes sense. However, I wish that Friedersdorf would describe exactly what these required steps are. He criticizes the public's extreme reactions, but he does not outline how administrators can actually protect students from harm. He advocates "focusing on the core problem of rape" (p. 313), but what exactly does that mean? Without articulating a specific course of action, his argument leaves the reader hanging. He is guilty of leaving holes in other pockets of his argument as well. For instance, he asserts that Sharon Grigsby's response is way out of proportion. Grigsby, according to Friedersdorf, states that "anyone who believes that [the fraternity members were joking] is part of the problem" (p. 266). From Friedersdorf's perspective, that response is hyperbolic. He writes, "In fact, believing that they made a tasteless joke rather than an apology for rape culture does not make someone 'part of the problem' of sexual assault" (p. 266). However, Friedersdorf does not explain why he thinks this way. He makes this claim but does not explain or defend it. Although I find myself agreeing with Friedersdorf, I would be more fully persuaded if he elaborated and explained why Grigsby is off base. While I appreciate his tight, concise argument, claims like these leave me with questions. Overall, I would be more persuaded if he had developed some of these points more fully and specifically.

Work Cited

Friedersdorf, Conor. "Crass Frat Boys at Old Dominion." *The Atlantic* 25 Aug. 2015. Web. Rpt. in *So What? The Writer's Argument*. 2nd ed. Kurt Schick and Laura Schubert. New York: Oxford UP, 2017. 307–13. Print.

Note to Peer Reviewer

Dear [peer reviewer],
I'm worried that my focus is too broad and not sufficiently supported. Can you point out places that seem unfocused or unclear? Also, I don't know if I've organized the essay well, so I'd like some feedback on that. Finally, I'd like some general feedback about your reading experience: Does the essay make sense? What's most interesting? What am I missing?

Peer Review Comments

Dear [writer],
Good job on this assignment so far! You've included some good analysis and supports from the article. A few bigger questions and comments:

Focus & content: You cover lots of rhetorical elements, like context, style, organization, and reasoning. Why did you choose these elements to focus on? Are there others that are as or more important to discuss? (For example, I notice that you don't talk about the controversy categories.) As a reader, I'd like to hear more about the audience and the author's purpose for writing the article. That seems like a key element for answering whether this argument was effective.

Organization: Some paragraphs seem really long, and sometimes there seems to be more than one idea in a paragraph – or maybe I just can't figure out what your main idea really is. I would suggest trying to reverse outline this draft and then consider adding some clear topic sentences for your paragraphs.

So what? You seem to be heading toward a conclusion (thesis) along the lines of "This article was mostly effective but also had some weaknesses." Is there something more about this argument that you find compelling or significant? Does the author make any argumentative "moves" that really stand out? (I thought the last idea in the third paragraph was really interesting. Maybe run with that?)

index